THE HALLELUJAH EFFECT

The Hallelujah Effect
Philosophical Reflections on Music, Performance
Practice, and Technology

BABETTE BABICH
Fordham University, USA

ASHGATE

Published by
Ashgate Publishing Limited
Wey Court East
Union Road
Farnham
Surrey, GU9 7PT
England

Ashgate Publishing Company
110 Cherry Street
Suite 3-1
Burlington, VT 05401-3818
USA

www.ashgate.com

British Library Cataloguing in Publication Data
Babich, Babette E., 1956-
    The hallelujah effect : philosophical reflections on music,
    performance practice, and technology. – (Ashgate popular
    and folk music series)
    1. Cohen, Leonard, 1934- Hallelujah. 2. Music–Philosophy
    and aesthetics. 3. Songs–Social aspects. 4. Social
    networks–Social aspects. 5. Music–Performance.
    I. Title II. Series
    782.4'2164-dc23

The Library of Congress has cataloged the printed edition as follows:
Babich, Babette E., 1956-
    The Hallelujah effect : philosophical reflections on music, performance practice, and
technology / by Babette Babich.
        pages cm. – (Ashgate popular and folk music series)
    Includes bibliographical references and index.
    ISBN 978-1-4094-4960-7 (hardcover) – ISBN 978-1-4094-4961-4 (ebook) –
ISBN 978-1-4094-7310-7 (epub) 1. Cohen, Leonard, 1934- Hallelujah. I. Title.
    ML410.C734B33 2013
    782.42164–dc23
                                                                2012043465

ISBN 9781409449607 (hbk)
ISBN 9781409449614 (ebk – PDF)
ISBN 9781409473107 (ebk – EPUB)

MIX
Paper from
responsible sources
FSC® C018575

Printed and bound in Great Britain
by MPG PRINTGROUP

Contents

General Editor's Preface

The upheaval that occurred in musicology during the last two decades of the twentieth century has created a new urgency for the study of popular music alongside the development of new critical and theoretical models. A relativistic outlook has replaced the universal perspective of modernism (the international ambitions of the 12-note style); the grand narrative of the evolution and dissolution of tonality has been challenged, and emphasis has shifted to cultural context, reception and subject position. Together, these have conspired to eat away at the status of canonical composers and categories of high and low in music. A need has arisen, also, to recognize and address the emergence of crossovers, mixed and new genres, to engage in debates concerning the vexed problem of what constitutes authenticity in music and to offer a critique of musical practice as the product of free, individual expression.

Popular musicology is now a vital and exciting area of scholarship, and the *Ashgate Popular and Folk Music Series* presents some of the best research in the field. Authors are concerned with locating musical practices, values and meanings in cultural context, and draw upon methodologies and theories developed in cultural studies, semiotics, poststructuralism, psychology and sociology. The series focuses on popular musics of the twentieth and twenty-first centuries. It is designed to embrace the world's popular musics from Acid Jazz to Zydeco, whether high tech or low tech, commercial or non-commercial, contemporary or traditional.

Professor Derek B. Scott
Professor of Critical Musicology
University of Leeds

List of Illustrations

List of Abbreviations

BGE   Nietzsche, *Beyond Good and Evil: Prelude to a Philosophy of the Future*
BT   Nietzsche, *The Birth of Tragedy out of the Spirit of Music*
EH   Nietzsche, *Ecce Homo: How One Becomes What One Is*
GM   Nietzche, *On the Geneology of Morals*
GS   Nietzsche, *The Gay Science*
HH   Nietzsche, *Human, All-too-Human*
KSA   Nietzsche, *Kritische Studienausgabe*
KSB   Nietzsche, *Samtliche Briefe. Kritische Studienausgabe*
KGW   Nietzsche, *Kritische Gesamtausgabe*
Rep. Plato, *Republic*
TI   Nietzche, *Twilight of the Idols*
Z   Nietzsche, *Thus Spoke Zarathustra*

Citations from Nietzsche are from the German and follow the author's own translations. English titles are provided for convenience and the author has adjusted her translations to accord with conventional renderings where that is possible.

Acknowledgements

The first words to be said on the Hallelujah effect are those of thanks, words that usually go without saying, words that never say enough.

This, when it comes to music, is as it should be, for without music, so Nietzsche contended, life itself would be a mistake, as music transfigures so much of life and to comprehend this is such a challenge for philosophy. The theme in its many modulations is one I have been thinking about for many years, back to the 1970s and 1980s, and maybe all my life; yet despite this personal preoccupation, this book is one that could never have been written alone, in particular not without the electric and personal dynamism that may be traced back to an important catena of emails between myself and Ernest McClain at the end of April and early May 2011. Where other scholars dismiss and sometimes denounce alternate approaches as ones "they do not understand," McClain "transgressed" this common academic habitus, and this venture and the resultant adventure of this encounter continues to draw my admiration and respect. I could not begin to thank the great musicians, Leonard Cohen, John Cale, k.d. lang, Jane Siberry, Joan Baez—just to name some of the living voices I draw upon here. What is significant, and this is where Adorno's study of what he called the "current of music" comes in, is that this living power continues in sound and image, on YouTube, as k.d. lang's powerful performances make very clear, and as one can also see and hear in musicians lost to us, such as Nina Simone, whose performances I also discuss. I am grateful to the filmmaker Percy Adlon for conversation on k.d. lang, to Robert Kory for his kind and very human email correspondence with regard to Leonard Cohen, and I thank Joshua Grange (not only for retweets).

In addition, I gratefully acknowledge Jason Gross's kind permission to reprint parts of my original essay, "The Birth of k.d. lang's *Hallelujah* out of the Spirit of Music,"[1] which appeared in the fall of 2011 in *Perfect Sound Forever*. I note that *Perfect Sound Forever* differs from most journals as it also includes a very performative subtitle: *Perfect Sound Forever: on line music magazine presents* ... This journal is also itself an exemplar, or phenomenological illumination, of the value of an online publication which one might otherwise take for granted as a simple replication or virtual version of text or print. Bloomsbury Books also granted permission to reprint parts of my "*Mousiké techné*: The Philosophical Praxis of Music in Plato, Nietzsche, Heidegger," which had originally been invited for a Continuum collection edited by Robert

---

[1]   See, as this is part of the point of this acknowledgment: <http://www.furious.com/perfect/kdlang.html>.

Burch (to whom personally I also owe special thanks for inspiration and the graciousness of our correspondence) together with Massimo Verdicchio, *Gesture and Word: Thinking Between Philosophy and Poetry*. I am thankful to Ralf Kläs for permission to use his photography, as I am also indebted to Alois Steiner. I am very grateful to Janet Morgan for permission to use her mother Barbara Morgan's astonishing photography; I thank Ursula Zollna, Peter Zollna's widow, for permission to reprint his photograph of Theodor Adorno; and I am grateful to Michael Schwarz for his help. I thank Bettina Erlenkamp of the Staats- und Universitätsbibliothek Dresden for her help. I also thank Katharina Siegmann of the Schirn Kunsthalle in Frankfurt and I acknowledge the kind offices of the Villa Stuck for permission to use Franz von Stuck's Orpheus on the cover of this book. I am grateful to Joan Baez for permission to cite *Diamonds and Rust* and I thank Jane Siberry for her permission to quote from her song, *Love is Everything*. In addition, I acknowledge Sony/ATV and Random House for permission to cite Leonard Cohen's *Hallelujah* here. But above all, I thank the artist, I thank the poet Leonard Cohen for his song.

A version of this essay may be heard and seen, which synaesthetic combination is the heart of media today, in the form of a video lecture, available on YouTube[2] and, in a correspondingly higher quality, in a video stream on the Fordham University Library video on demand website.[3] I am grateful to the Director of the Fordham Library, James McCabe, and to Michael Considine, Director of Information Technology Services at the Fordham University Library, for making the production and hosting of this video a possibility. I thank the musicologist and television and video expert (and ice climber) Dr Mat Schottenfeld of Fordham University for his assistance, kindness, and productive expertise. I also thank Kate Motush for her help, indirectly, in matters concerning video.

I am grateful to Derek B. Scott as editor of the Folk and Popular Music Series at Ashgate. As an admirer of his work, I am grateful for his input which made a great difference to me. I also thank Heidi Bishop, Publisher, Laura Macy, Senior Commissioning Editor, Music Studies, as well as Pam Bertram, Senior Editor at Ashgate, in addition to expressing my special gratitude to Patrick Cole for his careful and invaluable help in copyediting.

I also thank, for their responses to my inquiries on this theme, and for kind words on this project, Geraldine Finn, Robert Fink, Lori Burns, Ruth A. Solie, and Rose Rosengarde Subotnik. I am also grateful to Lydia Goehr who gave me the opportunity to present a twitter-length version of the final chapter in the aesthetics seminar that she hosts at Columbia University in the fall of 2012. I also thank Fawzia Mustafa of Fordham University for the invitation to talk about this at Women's Studies Workshop at the same time. I also thank in advance, because of all his inspiration and kindness past, Gary Shapiro for organizing a philosophy

---

    ² See: <http://www.youtube.com/watch?v=CiqokYFnZec&noredirect=1>.
    ³ See: <http://digital.library.fordham.edu/cdm4/item_viewer.php?CISOROOT=/VIDEO&CISOPTR=214>.

panel on Leonard Cohen at the 2013 World Conference of Philosophy in Athens and for asking me to take part.

My friends and colleagues are named in part either in the text or the notes to the text, but I wish to express my gratitude to Eileen Sweeney who was very helpful to me on these themes, to Debra Bergoffen, to Nicole Fermon, to Frank Boyle, and to Fred Harris and Matthew McGuire. For friendship and for musical resonances, I thank Susan Nitzberg, Hans-Gerald Hödl, George Leiner and Bettina Bergo, as well as Nanette Nielsen and Tomas McAuley. In addition to my gratitude to Claire Katz, I also thank Andrew Benjamin for reporting to me that, in the course of one of his lecture tours, a student announced to him that he was "famous" *because* he was mentioned on YouTube in my lecture on k.d. lang. This is, of course, not true, but it is a charming notion all the same. I thank my husband Tracy Strong for his love and conversation, intellectual and musical. I also thank Richard Cobb-Stevens for his positive response (he is a k.d. lang fan), as well as Patrick Heelan, S.J. for his amused enthusiasm, and William J. Richardson, S.J. In addition, I am thankful to twitter colleagues for kind words, particularly Terence Blake, but also @synaesthete99, @dance_historian, @pettrust and Mark Carrigan and, just for fun, Tristan Burke—@svejky. For his help, long ago now, for his bravery in publishing an essay on the Sokal hoax, and all the complexities of hermeneutics that go along with that, I thank, just gratuitously, in the spirit of Hallelujah, Jeffrey Perl, editor of *Common Knowledge*; and another editor whom I admire for similar graciousness, William MacAllister, editor of *International Studies in the Philosophy of Science*. In the musical arena, where friendship crosses, I am grateful to my friends Annette Hornbacher and Jochen Schönleber for their responses to this work, important because for many years they have been involved in music together, performative on every level, Jochen as ongoing artistic producer and Annette as past stage director of *Rossini in Wildbad*. In addition, I am enthusiastically grateful to Alexander Nehamas and David Allison (I love them both), as well as to Alphonso Lingis and Stanley Aronowitz. I also thank my students, especially Michael Fabano and Thomas Beddoe. Craig Konnoth and Carrie Gillespie have my gratitude, as well as Jeff Bussolini who now teaches at CUNY in New York City, and I have to say, all my students as well.

I thank Holger Schmid for conversation and for the extraordinary friendship we have shared for more than two decades. And here too, and finally, I thank Bill Strongin, who taught me about David—and his songs.

Weimar, 12 June 2012

Well, I've heard there was a secret chord
That David played, and it pleased the Lord
But you don't really care for music, do you?
It goes like this
The fourth, the fifth
The minor fall, the major lift
The baffled king composing Hallelujah

Hallelujah, Hallelujah
Hallelujah, Hallelujah

Leonard Cohen, *Hallelujah*, 1984

Prelude:
The Hallelujah Effect on the Internet

This is a book about Leonard Cohen's *Hallelujah* and in particular it is about k.d. lang's several covers of that song, as well as about other songs that she sings, especially in their video presentations. It is also about the relevance of John Cale's cover of Leonard Cohen's *Hallelujah* for k.d. lang's cover, as this is relevant, although rarely noted, for everyone else who covers, however they vary it, Cohen's song. In particular, this is a book about music on Facebook and YouTube, thus it is about the phenomenon of pop popularity, such as that of the singers who have covered Cohen's *Hallelujah*, some of whom, like Rufus Wainwright and Jeff Buckley, get most of the attention, but also about the others without that much coverage, singers like Nina Simone (including her transcendent cover of Cohen's *Suzanne*, a song made famous by Judy Collins).

The "Hallelujah effect" here refers to the mediation of music in the age of digital, broadcast, technical reproduction in recordings of all kinds, broadcasts of all kinds, on radio, television, the internet, especially YouTube, especially Facebook and Twitter. But this book is also about Hallelujah as such—per se—both the "holy" Hallelujah that Cohen distinguishes from the "broken" Hallelujah, as it is about King David's own Hallel psalms, Handel's *Hallelujah Chorus*, and a certain American hobo song, *Hallelujah, I'm a Bum*.

Effects, Mediations, and Primes

And all of this and more will be needed to come to terms with the various versions of Cohen's *Hallelujah* and the Hallelujah effect that is the *Hallelujah* song on the internet—not at all unlike the ads that seek to illustrate, in a sometimes unintentionally humorous fashion: *this is your brain on drugs*. To this extent, the Hallelujah effect as a phenomenon is all about entrainment and addiction. Like drugs, the joke can be varied: *this is your brain on YouTube, Facebook, Twitter*. The 1998 movie, *You've Got Mail*, written by Nora Ephron, starring Tom Hanks, and documenting the erotic subversion of the then AOL experience, testifies in the interim to fair irrelevance by contrast with the larger phenomenon (and profit margin) of internet pornography, or the even more comprehensive phenomenon of sexting, but also online dating, from hook-ups to marriage. Thus, although it might have done so, Ephron's film centered upon, but was at the same time oblivious to, the stimulus effect of AOL's famous acoustic notification for the dynamic of the love story itself.

One waits for the stimulus: *you've got mail*. Today, with or without AOL, one's phone signals a tweet "connection." One looks for—one checks, as one says—one's email, Facebook account, blog, and so on. Anticipation *and* satisfaction are the same. The checking activity itself reinforces the activity *because* this mini-event, this little tone or buzz, is all the reward we get and, so advertisers have learned to their profit, as Twitter also knows: this is all we need.

Slavoj Žižek invokes this phenomenon in Lacanian terms, giving the example of the French minitel, a physically dedicated, chunkily retro-techno little screen and keyboard version of what would come to be translated into the intensified virtual encounters of AOL's and other online chatrooms.[1] Indeed, I remember using the minitel, both in terms of its *frisson* and the plastic insignificance or flatness of the same, in Paris in the mid 1980s. And as Žižek writes, "enjoyment is primarily enjoyment in the signifier."[2] Žižek's point recollects or sharpens Jacques Lacan's discussion of *jouissance*, that is to say: enjoyment *as* enjoyment, most especially erotic enjoyment. By its nature, desire is elusive, which is also why it is able to serve an ethical function, qua imperative, for Lacan.

In his own reminiscence, Žižek's analysis takes this apart in rather more fundamentally Hegelian terms:

> ... the idea of minitel is "sex is an Other." You type in your password but you do not communicate with a paid prostitute, you communicate with hundreds of people doing the same thing you are doing. So you pick up one of the messages and you do it: you send in your own message to him or to her—you don't know to whom, that is the charm. You only have the family name: it may be a man or a woman. You send your message to someone you don't know, you exchange dirty messages: "I will do this to you, you will do that to me." The point is that people became obsessed by this. Lacan says—he even uses vulgar terms—that if I'm speaking now about fucking it's the same as if I'm fucking. This is literally realized now in France; sex can be purely the matter of a signifier of exchanging dirt.[3]

---

[1] See Jaron Lanier for his reminiscence of the "Well" experience that he himself co-founded, and thus for a kind of virtual media archaeology in the mode of nostalgia in his Lanier, *You Are Not a Gadget: A Manifesto* (New York: Vintage, 2011)—and it is worth adding that this nostalgia has been a while brooding as he began this reminiscence in an online version, "One Half of a Manifesto," in 2000. And see also Lee Siegel's *Against the Machine: How the Web Is Reshaping Culture and Commerce – and Why It Matters* (New York: Spiegel & Grau, 1996), as well as, if in general, Patrice Flichy, *The Internet Imaginaire* (Cambridge, MA: MIT Press, 2007), especially 101f.

[2] Slavoj Žižek, *Enjoy Your Symptom! Jacques Lacan in Hollywood and Out* (London: Routledge, 1992), 27.

[3] Slavoj Žižek, *Flash Art* Interview with Josefina Ayerza (1992): <http://www.lacan.com/perfume/zizek.htm>. For a specifically political discussion of the French minitel qua telephone-based electronic information technology, as distinct from the internet, see

Here one can refer to the studies beloved of cognitive science enthusiasts—and this is standard (and standardizing) behaviourism all the way down to the advertising executives on Madison Avenue and all the way up to the campaign managers at the White House—and one can see the results of this standardizing in oneself, in one's own actions and responses. Of course it is sometimes still easier to see these responses, above all qua non-responsiveness, in the actions of others. Thus my students, most of them in their late teens and early twenties, can interrupt their own multitasking texting activity (in class) to condemn the behavior of their nearest cohort of still-younger youth, their younger siblings, friends or relatives; how old, I ask? Oh, eight, ten, they say, with hesitation, twelve, but these eight and ten or twelve year olds are, they assure me with the confident conservatism of the young, *so much worse than they are*. The younger youth, thus viewed from the perspective of the older youth, is said to text constantly, *no one can tell when* they are doing it and, what is worse (this is the autism factor), *they pay no attention* to those around them.[4] So the young observe of the yet younger and one has to suppose, as teachers can be neutral interlocutors (the university is the imaginary), that their parents are as clueless as they appear to be in television and Hollywood representations of "parents."

In the interim, AOL's stimulus signature announcement, like the popularity of MySpace, has peaked and diminished with the proliferation of other stimuli and other platforms for email, for texting, for personal web announcements and the commercial web advertising that is so ubiquitous that no one attends to the amount of attention they dedicate to it, given Google and given the expanding, more accurately said, *shifting* range of today's social networking (from Facebook to Twitter, from Tumblr to Pinterest to Instagram, and so on). Thus this book also reflects the growing enthusism among academics (the author is one of those) for what is rather haltingly called "digital humanities."[5] Digital scholarship as

---

Heather L. Moulaison, "The Minitel and France's Legacy of Democratic Information Access," *Government Information Quarterly* 21 (2004): 99–107.

[4]   It is the characteristic of the young to make precisions of this kind with an acuity that diminishes as hearing and eyesight soften. I recall having had no trouble conflating a man in his fifties, who asked me how old I thought he was, with a man in his eighties (which was my reply): both ages were equally old. Thus when I met Gadamer in 1980, I calculated his age, in an effort to process it, at 80; that means, I thought, that 20 years ago he would have been 60: that means still "old." Simultaneously, I knew, as my students, as everybody's students, still know, the exact difference between my age and my then husband's age, younger as he was than I was by three months but which counted as a year, crossing as it did from mid-November to early February.

[5]   There are a lot of studies of this and (often under different rubrics) these studies go back some time to 1940s' and 1950s' research on cybernetics and related reflective components. One can argue that Vannevar Bush offers one of the most popular, because calculatedly public, contributions (the editor glosses these as concerning "pacific instruments … which, if properly developed, will give man access to and command over the inherited knowledge of the ages." See Bush, "As We May Think," *Atlantic Monthly*,

such is an enterprise which studies and is in many ways indistinguishable from electronic, "digital" stimulus-driven solicitation and other demands for attention in an increasingly scattered world, more adumbrated by one's cell phone than by a computer, or even an iPad or tablet connection.[6] It is thus often observed that people are connected to one another online and that that connection increasingly trumps the so-called "real world," which "real world"—and just as the phenomenological critical theorist Günther Anders had already analyzed in his 1956 and earlier studies of radio, this is his point about the spectral qualities or spookiness of the radio experience—is increasingly "mediated."[7] Nor do we mind, manifestly enough, the diffusion implicit in the notion of mediation of this kind and on this level. And why would we? We are so very "primed," just to use the language of cognitive psychology, that we do not, that we cannot, notice the priming.[8]

---

published in July 1945, and republished more concisely, after the August 1945 punctuation of the atomic bombs dropped on Hiroshima and Nagasaki, in September 1945. See, for an early but perfectly, consummately, media archaeological analysis, David S. Bertolotti, "The Atomic Bombing of Hiroshima," in his, as far as I can see, utterly overlooked and thus undiscussed, *Culture and Technology* (Bowling Green: Bowling Green State University Popular Press, 1984), 81–112. For contemporary accounts of media archaeology, see the various contributions to the collection edited by Erkki Huhtamo and Jussi Parikka, *Media Archaeology: Approaches, Applications, and Implications* (Berkeley: University of California Press, 2011), and Parikka, *What is Media Archaeology* (Cambridge: Polity, 2012).

[6]   Media archaeology and other efforts should begin to pay attention to this, but as Nietzsche always reflected, it is hard to reflect on oneself.

[7]   See Günter Anders, published under his original name, Günter Stern, "Spuk und Radio," *Anbruch* 12/2 (February 1930): 65–6. And we should pay attention to the word media, although academic parsings of what "media studies" studies varies widely. Here, in addition to Anders who remains little discussed and even less understood, of course, Theodor W. Adorno, who is at the heart of this book, as well as Jean Baudrillard, Jacques Ellul, and Paul Virilio, in addition to and in spite of his datedness and sometimes his insularity, Ivan Illich, as well as the for some reason difficult to integrate Michel de Certeau who continues, not always to advantage for an understanding of his work, to be read together with, as he himself read with profit, Foucault and Bourdieu. And there are many, many others one can name in addition to the well-known Marshall McLuhan, Neil Postman, Jerry Mander, especially his *Four Arguments for the Elimination of Television* (New York: William Morrow, 1978) and so on. In addition to the work of Wolfgang Ernst, I shall also note the late Friedrich Kittler, and the more recent studies already mentioned by Lanier, Siegel, and Parikka, but also more politically, Evgeny Morozov, whom I cite below, and so on.

[8]   See, for a retrospective, John Bargh, "What Have We Been Priming All These Years? On the Development, Mechanisms, and Ecology of Nonconscious Social Behavior," *European Journal of Social Psychology* 36 (2006): 147–68, in addition to his many other studies, as well as, for example, Ap Dijksterhuis, Henk Aarts, and Pamela K. Smith, "The Power of the Subliminal: On Subliminal Persuasion and Other Potential Applications," in *The New Unconscious*, ed. Ran R. Hassin, James S. Uleman, and John A Bargh (Oxford:

The term "priming" is a technical one in behavioural and cognitive studies in psychology, but also marketing or advertising research. It applies to what Adorno characterizes as the "ubiquity" standard as the standardizing impetus for conditioning of all kinds, especially qua "covert priming." For its part, covert priming corresponds to what Vance Packard triumphantly reported as having made the front page of the *London Sunday Times* in 1956: "certain United States advertisers were experimenting with 'sub-threshold effects' in seeking to insinuate messages to people past their conscious guard."[9] To this day we speak of prime time, just as we speak of radio and television programming. And we think nothing of it. As the cognitive psychologist John Bargh would argue some 40 years later, priming *works* manifestly, obviously so.[10] When it comes to marketing, the term priming itself seems to illuminate the interest in such studies, ongoing now for more than a century.[11] And just as one "primes" the pump, one primes the consumer.

Oxford University Press, 2005), 77–106. See also, as its topic bears on the theme of this book, Shahira Famhy and Wayne Wanta, "Testing Priming Effects: Differences Between Print and Broadcast Messages," *Studies in Media & Information Literacy Education* 2 (May 2005): 1–12, along with Katharina Sophia Goerlich et al., "The Nature of Affective Priming in Music and Speech," *Journal of Cognitive Neuroscience*, MIT, posted online 23 February 2012. In addition, although somewhat abstruse, see Tor Nørretranders, *The User Illusion: Cutting Consciousness Down to Size* (New York: Viking, 1998), in addition to the more classic philosophical authors, Theodor W. Adorno, Günther Anders, Jacques Ellul (especially his informative *Propaganda: The Formation of Men's Attitudes*, trans Konrad Kellen and Jean Lerner [New York: Knopf, 1973]), Jean Baudrillard, and others discussed below. Ellul offers a critical reflection on the social, economic, and political implications of Edward L. Bernays's *Propaganda* (New York: Liveright, 1928), ultimately developed under the rubric of "consent," in deference to public abhorrence of the term propaganda as *The Engineering of Consent* (Norman, OK: University of Oklahoma Press, 1955).

[9] Vance Packard, *The Hidden Persuaders* [1956] (New York: Pocket/Simon & Schuster, 2007), 62.

[10] John A. Bargh, "The Most Powerful Manipulative Messages Are Hiding in Plain Sight," *Chronicle of Higher Education* 45/21 (1999): B6.

[11] Dating back, arguably, to Plato's *Republic*, the contemporary style of theorizing specific strategies for the manipulation of a target audience dates back to the early decades of the twentieth century. See Sigmund Freud's nephew, Bernays's 1923 study, *Crystallizing Public Opinion* (New York: Liveright, 1961). The Austrian advertising consultant, or "motivational researcher," Ernst Dichter was one of the first to advance the case for Bernays's "crystallization" in advertising practice; see Dichter, *The Strategy of Desire* (New York: Doubleday, 1960). For an account, see Stefan Schwarzkopf and Rainer Gries, eds, *Ernest Dichter and Motivation Research: New Perspectives on the Making of Post-war Consumer Culture* (London: Palgrave Macmillan, 2010), as well as Franz Kreuzer, Gerd Prechtl, and Christoph Steiner, *A Tiger in the Tank: Ernest Dichter: An Austrian Advertising Guru* [2002], trans. Lars Hennig (Riverside: Ariadne, 2007), and more recently still, "Sex and Advertising: Retail Therapy. How Ernest Dichter, An Acolyte of Sigmund Freud, Revolutionised Marketing," *The Economist*, 17 December 2011.

At the same time, social science scholars seem to fall over themselves to argue or, better said, to insist that there is no such priming effect, or else that such an effect is very general or very minimal, seemingly to reassure confidence in consumer choice and free will: it is not for nothing that a leading research trend in the social sciences is called *rational choice*. Thus an abundance of studies (particularly in disciplines *not* contributing to marketing research) insist upon the inefficacy of priming, not unlike US academic confidence in the non-existence of propaganda in the United States. Yet at the end of the day, empirical research repeatedly confirms that "priming" (that would be what the popular press calls "subliminal persuasion") does indeed work, down indeed to the brand itself— given to be sure that the subject or target is in the mood for what is primed. This efficacy is not unlike the similarly physiological efficacy of Viagra. *Drink Coke* does indeed lead to consumers buying the advertised soft drink, provided (pesky animals that we are) that the consumer is thirsty to begin with. The advertisers can wait: if we are not thirsty now, we will be.

The Sound of Music

With regard to the seduction of digital media and our experience of it, this study explores what may be called the "natural sound" of music, as Robert Hullot-Kentor attempts to characterize Theodor Adorno's own effort to express this in the introduction that Hullot-Kentor writes to his translation of Adorno's *Current of Music*.[12] For Hullot-Kentor, at least as specific to Adorno's era, Adorno's specifically technological investigation into the "natural sound" of music illustrates "the depredations that music undergoes when it is subjected to" radio production, depredations that, as we shall see further below, have only intensified since Adorno's day: "when broadcast artifice endeavors to appear as pristine nature, when sonic copy lays claim to origin, when music on the air acts as the reproduction of an original."[13] For Hullot-Kentor, Adorno's investigations

---

[12]   See Robert Hullot-Kentor, "Vorwort des Herausgebers," editor's foreword to Theodor W. Adorno, *Current of Music: Elements of a Radio Theory* (Frankfurt am Main: Suhrkamp, 2006), 7–69. In English as "Second Salvage: Prolegomenon to a Reconstruction of Current of Music," in Hullot-Kentor, *Things Beyond Resemblance: Collected Essays on Theodor W. Adorno* (New York: Columbia University Press, 2006), 94–124. Cited here and below from the English version.

[13]   Hullot-Kentor, "Second Salvage," 112. See, further, Arved Ashby, *Absolute Music: Mechanical Reproduction* (Berkeley: University of California Press, 2010), as well as Alf Björnberg, "Learning to Listen to Perfect Sound: Hi-Fi Culture and Changes in Modes of Listening, 1950–1980," in *The Ashgate Research Companion to Popular Musicology*, ed. Derek B. Scott (Farnham: Ashgate, 2009), 105–30. Björnberg extends Mark Katz's *Capturing Sound: How Technology Has Changed Music* [2004] (Berkeley: University of California Press, 2010), to which Greg Milner's *Perfecting Sound Forever: An Aural History of Recorded Music* (New York: Faber and Faber, 2009) is also indebted, as is Peter

depend upon a very specific historical and material basis: "[v]irtually all radio music presented performances of live vocal and instrumental music ... [r]adio, in other words, consistently claimed to reproduce live music as natural sound, every bit as live in the home and with the intention at least of a transparency of transmission, as if the radio itself played no part."[14] Of course, this no longer holds, and what we mostly hear on the radio are themselves recordings. Thus we listen to reproductions of "recorded sound" in the case of popular music that is itself, as Hullot-Kentor points out, "predominantly electronically sampled to begin with,"[15] and as we shall see, this recorded sound increasingly characterizes so-called "live" concerts as well. And such reproductive recording distinctions make Adorno's observations more and not less salient.

Thus this study raises the question of the difference made by the variety of technological means of what Adorno named and theorized as musical reproduction in terms of the mechanical recording process as this continues, digital or not, to make a difference in radio, as well as to social media, Facebook, Twitter, and YouTube, and other still changing internet involvements. In this sense, and in addition to being a book about music, specifically about Leonard Cohen's and k.d. lang's *Hallelujah*, this is also a book on Adorno and the musical sociologist H. Stith Bennett, as well as Günther Anders. Anders, a phenomenological theorist of music and technologized humanity, diagnosed our "obsolescence," as he named it, well in advance of the singularity, or the transhuman, or humanity 2.0, or what have you. It is also about some important others in passing, such as Siegmund Levarie who, as mathematical and musicological schematist, wrote on "sound," along with a study of tone and another book on harmony and musical acoustics with Stanley Levy,[16] and it is more centrally indebted to Levarie's disciple and colleague, my own email correspondent in the first phases of writing this book,

---

Wicke's reading of "The Art of Phonography: Sound, Technology, and Music," in Scott's edited collection, *The Ashgate Research Companion to Popular Musicology*, 147–68. See, also, Michael Chanan, *Repeated Takes: A Short History of Recording and its Effects on Music* (London: Verso, 1995). More theoretically, and especially with reference to Adorno, see for both rigor and admirable insights, Rose Rosengard Subotnik, *Developing Variations: Style and Ideology in Western Music* (Minneapolis: University of Minnesota Press, 1991), and her *Deconstructive Variations: Music and Reason in Western Society* (Minneapolis: University of Minnesota Press, 1996).

[14] Hullot-Kentor, "Second Salvage," 113.

[15] Ibid., 112.

[16] Siegmund Levarie and Ernst Levy, *Tone: A Study in Musical Acoustics* (Kent, OH: Kent State University Press, 1968), and their *Musical Morphology: A Discourse and a Dictionary* (Kent, OH: Kent State University Press, 1983), as well as Levy's book (as edited, but in this case, this is a close collaboration, by Levarie), *A Theory of Harmony* (Albany: State University of New York Press, 1985). See, also, Levarie's own *Fundamentals of Harmony* (Westport, CT: Greenwood Publishing Group, 1984), as well as Josef Mertin and Siegmund Levarie, *Early Music: Approaches to Performance Practice* (New York: Da Capo Press, 1986).

Ernest McClain who, having been born in 1918, not incidentally also remembered knowing, and not merely from Adorno's own acknowledgment of him, but as a colleague, George Simpson, the Queens College adjunct geographer engaged to help Adorno with some of his writing in English when he was in New York.

But, perhaps above all, if it is also true that this book can only be an introduction to this theme, this is a book on music and philosophy, including the *mousiké techné* of antiquity, as exemplified in a reflection on Nietzsche and Beethoven in the context of Nietzsche's *The Birth of Tragedy out of the Spirit of Music*. This last connection with Beethoven is also articulated, in the context of the German language, together with Nietzsche's related investigations into "Music and Word" and the sounding, the pitching, the tonality of ancient Greek, and in consequence of the Greek music drama, the musical art work that was tragedy.[17]

But we begin not in antiquity but in our own day.

The Hallelujah effect thus raises the question of the way music is mediated electrically,[18] and thus electronically, digitally, increasingly and almost exclusively so and together with its wireless and wired expressions, "online," on social networking sites and YouTube. It is with reference to music as this is increasingly heard on YouTube[19] that I explore k.d. lang's interpretation of Leonard Cohen's *Hallelujah*, together with the resonances of Cohen's own various recorded *Hallelujahs* with its own musical world of antecedent Hallelujahs. And if my engagement with Adorno's theoretical reflections on radio, music, and consumer culture may in this context seem to go without saying, it should still be underscored that everything I do in this book is for the sake of articulating what Nietzsche called the "becoming-human of dissonance."

All that said, the point of departure is neither Adorno nor Nietzsche nor indeed Leonard Cohen himself, although much of the discussion centers on his work. Instead, as I began above by noting, the initial focus is a particular "cover" of Leonard Cohen's *Hallelujah* by k.d. lang, a song which has to be sure seemingly been covered by nearly everyone: from Bob Dylan to the popular American opera star, Renée Fleming, not to forget the long-time singing phenomenon, Susan Boyle, who managed to accommodate a television interviewer's seemingly Skyped request to sing an *a capella* version of Cohen's *Hallelujah*. Boyle's achievement was both her goodwill in attempting the song, as few singers would attempt this

---

[17]   For a preliminary discussion of this complicated point, see Babette Babich, "The Science of Words or Philology: Music in *The Birth of Tragedy* and The Alchemy of Love in *The Gay Science*," in, *Revista di estetica*, n.s. 28, XLV, ed. Tiziana Andina (Turin: Rosenberg & Sellier, 2005), 47–78, and further references below.

[18]   Or as Hullot-Kentor expresses this characteristic with reference to Adorno's radio theory, "[t]he current of *Current of Music* is electricity." Hullot-Kentor, "Second Salvage," 98.

[19]   Listening to music on YouTube should be a disaster, musically speaking, but what is significant, as we shall explore further, is that even audiophiles seem to take this in their stride.

particular song without accompaniment—significantly, Cohen himself always requires back-up singers and the minimum for Jeff Buckley was a guitar, or indeed a piano for John Cale—*and* that Boyle was able to find her way to the music as she did without the support of the same.

"On the Radio"

I heard Leonard Cohen's *Hallelujah* for the first time as sung by Cohen himself. Naturally enough and to be precise, I should say that I didn't actually "hear" Cohen at all or in a "real" sense, because I was not in his physical presence. Of course not. And the point here is that the claim that one has "heard" a singer, any singer, is almost never meant as the report of an immediate or direct experience. This is different in practice from the classical enthusiast who usually means that he or she has heard Alfred Brendel or this or that other performer in concert, but even there, familiarity with a recorded performance can also be what is meant. In general, we take technical reproduction or mediation for granted, and we pay no particular mind to the where or the how of it. Thus, unless otherwise specified, to say that one has heard a singer or a particular song does not mean that one heard the song "live," as we do say to specify the distinctive or unusual circumstance of being physically present, in the presence of a singer singing his or her song, in real life, as it were, but rather that we have heard some recording, somehow.

The point of reproduction is important as one also need not even have access to a given physical recording "itself" in order to hear a recording: a recording is always virtual, reproducible. Thus until recently, I never had access to Cohen's original album, *Various Positions*, on which the song is listed as the center and which appeared in December of the Orwellian year, 1984, and again in February of 1985, part of which years I spent abroad, and I would be lying if I said that I remembered where I heard it, in New York, or (as I was) in Berlin, Paris or Brussels.

Yet, and like almost everyone else who knows this song, I heard the song as I heard it because I heard it "on the radio."

It matters in what follows that songs broadcast on the radio have a quality all their own, even if we scarcely attend to this quality today. Nor do we have trouble recalling the particular acoustic quality of radio: we know the sound radio makes and we can notice the quality of radio transmission as such and very specifically, say, to use Adorno's own example in his *Current of Music*, if we are tuning a radio set. But if new technology *can* (and it is important to note that it does not always) make this a less common experience—even satellite radio drifts, and the internet has a rather famous instability from time to time—we nonetheless notice the "sound" or the fact of radio transmission when the weather changes or else when we are moving about or driving, due to the call letters constantly announced, but especially because of the character of broadcast sound. As in the case of cellphones, this fading quality of wireless broadcasting is one of the things that has not changed since the beginning of publically accessible radio broadcasting in 1922 (which public broadcasting should thus be distinguished from Nikola Tesla's invention of the technology needed for radio broadcast or Guglielmo Marconi's first transmission in 1895).[20]

To be sure, there are other details characteristic of radio sound which we tend to notice even less. But later we shall see that it is worth talking about what Adorno calls the "radio voice" (even where many of us no longer listen to the radio per se), because it frames the way we hear music today, even, as I argue, so-called "live" music.

Thus, although my focus is on k.d. lang in addition to Leonard Cohen and others, and includes a discussion of gender and performance practice, I also discuss Adorno's radio theory and even his writings on music in general, including those on jazz (and I say this with some trepidation because few scholars care to discuss Adorno on jazz unless it is to attack him, more rather than less formulaically, for what he writes about it).

And again, all of this is needed to make possible an exploration of Nietzsche's notion of the "becoming-human of dissonance,"[21] a dynamic question that Nietzsche poses in his attempt to resolve his study of the "birth" which always also means his exploration of the *death* of the tragic musical work of art. It is Nietzsche's grasp of antiquity and his understanding of composition theory that will rejoin our initial discussion of k.d. lang's performance practice with Adorno's reflections on radio and jazz.

As a "closeted" musician, as considered from the perspective of music scholars, Nietzsche conceived the Greek notion of diaphony as *Dissonanz* (which in the nineteenth century was translated into English as "discord") as a *musical* term, diaphony, corresponding to his dynamic account of the "science of

---

[20]   Indeed, it is fairly difficult to talk about the "first" radio broadcast as this is a highly *national* (and not accidentally politically charged) concept, but also because it is essential to define what one means by such a first event: broadcast radio or wireless transmission requires the technology, this is the reason one needs to acknowledge Tesla's contributions, and in practice it also requires both a broadcast source and a receiver tuned at the right time. A lot of things have to come together to ensure that this works as it should and to this day, radio broadcasts cannot dispense with studio engineers. See, for a literary study, John Mowitt, *Radio: Essays in Bad Reception* (Berkeley: University of California Press, 2011); and for a political study of commercial radio in today's world, see Timothy D. Taylor, *The Sounds of Capitalism: Advertising, Music, and the Conquest of Culture* (Chicago: University of Chicago Press, 2012); and for a strikingly edgy discussion, see Steve Goodman, *Sonic Warfare: Sound, Affect, and the Ecology of Fear* (Cambridge, MA: MIT Press, 2010), including sonic branding, but extending the technology of radio beyond propaganda to its deliberately military deployment, both against political enemies as well as against other species such as birds, fish, cetaceans, pinnipeds, and so on.

[21]   Friedrich Nietzsche, *Kritische Studienausgabe* (Berlin: de Grutyer, 1980), *Die Geburt der Tragödie*, §1. Cited here and throughout with the initials of the English title, BT by section number.

aesthetics."[22] Thus the subtitle to his first book, *The Birth of Tragedy*, foregrounds this "aesthetic" science methodologically—and literally as we shall see—*out of the Spirit of Music*.

As an "out" classicist (not indeed that today's university classicists are inclined to acknowledge his contributions even where these same discoveries happen to have become standard in his field),[23] Nietzsche also used the term dissonance musico-philologically with reference to Pythagoras, Aristoxenos, and of course Heraclitus and Empedocles. As we shall see, this same "dissonance," both classically musical and classically philological, is the key to his still too little understood exploration of the specifically or literally musical origination of the ancient tragic artwork.

Theodor Adorno's filigree-feel for the physicality of things, which he recounts in overt coordination with Günther Stern's[24] own musicological research concerns with radio, corresponds to what Adorno means by the language of radio "physiognomy."[25] In passing, it should be said that this coordination is how one gets to command the full resources of "phenomenology" without paying the usual licensing obeisance to either Husserl or Heidegger (the last certainly not happening for Adorno), all for the sake of a theoretical analysis of radio.[26]

Indeed Adorno explicitly explains his method as phenomenological, and the explanation is a direct response to the routine publisher's query, *Who is your audience?*—as we know that Adorno sought an American publisher for *Current*

----

[22]   Nietzsche, BT §1.

[23]   See Babette Babich, "The Birth of Tragedy: Lyric Poetry and the Music of Words," in *Words in Blood, Like Flowers: Philosophy and Poetry, Music and Eros in Hölderlin, Nietzsche, and Heidegger* (Albany: State University of New York Press, 2006), 37f, as well as Babich, "The Science of Words or Philology."

[24]   Günther Stern, who tends to be better known indirectly for his relation to famous other names, was Walter Benjamin's cousin and also Hannah Arendt's first husband, and he was a student of Husserl and Heidegger. Stern would later change his name for journalistic but ultimately fateful reasons to Günther Anders; that is, something "other," "different," or "otherwise." On his writing on music and in addition to Adorno's reception of his work, see Reinhard Ellensohn, *Der andere Anders: Gunther Anders als Musikphilosoph* (Bern: Peter Lang, 2008).

[25]   See Adorno. *Current of Music*, and, again, Hullot-Kentor's translator's foreword.

[26]   But see, very patently, Adorno's later *Zur Metakritik der Erkenntnistheorie. Studien über Husserl und die phänomenologischen Antinomien* (Stuttgart: Kohlhammer, 1956); in English, and losing the Kantian and Hegelian reference to phenomenological antinomies, as: *Against Epistemology: A Metacritique*, trans. Willis Domingo (Cambridge: MIT Press, 1983). I recommend that one reads this together with or alongside Derrida's introduction to and translation of Edmund Husserl's *L'origine de la géométrie* (Paris: PUF, 1962), in English as Jacques Derrida, *Edmund Husserl's "Origin of Geometry": An Introduction*, trans. John P. Leavey Jr (Lincoln: University of Nebraska Press, 1989). See, for a discussion of Adorno and Husserl in the context of Sartrean phenomenology, David Sherman, *Sartre and Adorno: The Dialectics of Subjectivity* (Albany: State University of New York Press, 2007), 59ff.

of Music from the outset. Analyzed as a concept, the question could not but strike Adorno as amusing in the context of a sociological study of the *radio* audience per se. Thus Adorno highlights his own response to the question of the book's target audience, justifying the use of the word itself along with the methodological technique of *phenomenology*:

> The question of why we follow this descriptive or "phenomenological" method can easily be answered. We are dwelling on the phenomenon ["of music pouring out of the loudspeaker"] because it is actually the phenomenon which determines the reaction of the listeners, and it is our ultimate aim to study the listeners.[27]

It is worth noting in a preliminary fashion that the language of phenomenology illuminates the terminology of "physiognomy," as both physiognomy and phenomenology were deployed in Adorno's mid-century theory of the experience of radio. Indeed Adorno writes that his concern is with "the characteristics of the radio phenomenon as such, devoid of any particular content or material,"[28] and in this we recognize the Husserlian *epoché*. In this fairly classical phenomenological fashion, Adorno considers "the way any voice or any instrumental sound is presented over the radio," including the clarifying observation, here expressly reminiscent of Husserl's "to the things themselves," that "it will be very difficult to abstract this expression of the 'radio itself' from the expression of what is actually broadcast, and we shall see later that these two layers of expression influence each other."[29] Thus Adorno gives his own distinguishing resumé:

> Physiognomics intends only to define more correctly the inherent features of radio phenomena and to elaborate within these features certain relations ... we may confess here that the axiom which governs all these attempts is our conviction that the unity of the radio phenomenon, in itself, as far as it really has the structure of a unit, is simply the unity of society which determines all the individual and apparently accidental features.[30]

In Adorno's case, as we shall see, he takes the example of the symphony as one might hear it on the radio and for Adorno, as he theorizes the symphony, this means as one might hear it *in time*. In Adorno's era, and still in some cases, the reference to the symphony would be a live broadcast, specifically structured to the particularities of radio, as radio orchestras had to be structured for the sake of radio, that is, for the sake of the mechanical constraints of the recording studio as such. Above all, Adorno is particularly interested in the space of sound.

---

[27]   Adorno, *Current of Music*, 107. Italics in original. I am grateful to Holger Schmid for conversation on just this theme.

[28]   Ibid., 77.

[29]   Ibid., 77–8.

[30]   Ibid., 118–19.

Thus his physiognomic discussion includes space itself, and in this physico-phenomenological sense, that includes the room itself qua sounding board (as all rooms, not just concert halls or recording studios, happen to be sounding boards), and it is also about loudspeakers, and so on. For today's listeners, a corollary might be found in one's choice of earphones, and below it will be noted that a distinction between Adorno's "radio loudspeaker" and today's earphone experience makes a great difference for the sound engineering that must be considered, although it is usually taken for granted in the very technical business that is the "perfection"[31] of recorded sound today. These issues relate not only to the terms of production as such, whether in recording practice (as the esoteric centrality of mixes and soundchecks also makes clear), but also to music heard "on the radio" and even, albeit counter-intuitively, to live performance.[32]

Today, access to music is often all about having some kind of iPod (that is, for those who have an iPod or whatever one has when one does not have an iPod) or, increasingly more commonly these days, to any so-named "smart" phone, and so on, all the way up to the name-brand gadget or flat screen display/speaker array as set up for video and music streaming, be it genuinely high end (thus soon to be outdated) or increasingly commonly, be it a compromise between the cut-rate and the high end, all corresponding to the kind of stereo receiver one might yet and still have in one's living room.

As a philosopher and thinker, in addition to my interests in technology and performance practice, in questions of the subject and of desire (including some radical reflections on gender and feminism), I am also interested in fairly recondite or esoteric questions. Reflecting on the meaning of music between antiquity and the present day, Nietzsche's reflections on the birth and the perishing of tragedy (Why did the Greeks have tragedy? Why did they enjoy it? Why would anyone? What happened to it?) are for me relevant to the related question of the role of Nietzsche's own comments on Beethoven (rather than Wagner) in his book on tragedy. Why the focus on Beethoven? And some might wonder at this constellation of questions. For, so it may be asked, don't we already know all the answers to such questions? Wasn't Nietzsche smitten with Wagner? Or alternately, or ultimately, with Bizet?[33]

---

[31] This same notion of "perfect" sound inspires the title of the online music journal, *Perfect Sound Forever*. See, again, Katz's *Capturing Sound*, as well as Björnberg, "Learning to Listen to Perfect Sound," and Milner's *Perfecting Sound Forever*.

[32] I discuss this below, but this is one of the central and very practical themes of H. Stith Bennett's *On Becoming a Rock Musician* (Amherst: University of Massachusetts Press, 1980).

[33] Defenses of this favoring, for which Nietzsche provides straightforward evidence, goes back some time. See, for example, and the arguments have not varied, John W. Klein, "Nietzsche and Bizet," *The Musical Quarterly* 11/4 (October 1925): 482–505. Lydia Goehr adds a refined consideration of Rossini to the mix here in her discussion which centers rather more on Hegel and Schelling, Schopenhauer and Wagner, than Nietzsche, in her

I argue that, despite the scholarly tendency to read Nietzsche in connection with Wagner, indeed even as a pale shadow of Wagner as many do (Wagnerians excel at such readings, by no means limited to Nietzsche alone)—Nietzsche does invoke Wagner in this context, reminding us at the same time that Wagner is indebted too for his own part to Schopenhauer and that both Wagner and Schopenhauer have recourse to the Greeks with regard to aesthetics, which last theme constituted Nietzsche's particular thematic in his first book. But what captivates Nietzsche in *The Birth of Tragedy*, with particular reference to what he fairly literally in this case, as in many others, understands as a "birth"[34] *out of the Spirit of Music*, is less a focus on Wagner, as we might very justifiably, given the scholarly advance judgment on the matter, have expected, but overwhelmingly on Beethoven, and nothing less iconically "Beethoven," if one may put it this way, than the choral fourth movement of Beethoven's Ninth Symphony.[35] I will argue that we ought to raise this question together with or in the context of Nietzsche's earlier discovery

---

Elective Affinities: Musical Essays on the History of Aesthetic Theory (New York: Columbia University Press, 2008), Chapter 2, 45.

[34]   Thus the Nietzsche of genealogical thinking, as he is, repeats this notion of birth and distinguishes it in his "On Music and Words." It is no accident that Carl Dahlhaus, who is one of the few scholars to reflect on the influence of Beethoven in Nietzsche, also reproduces this text in his *Between Romanticism and Modernism: Four Studies in the Music of the Later Nineteenth Century* [1974], trans. Mary Whittall (Berkeley: University of California Press, 1980), 103–20.

[35]   At this point, as at any other, Wagnerians, enthusiasts, and scholars will point out that Wagner wrote on Beethoven even before Nietzsche was born. Which is quite correct and which I scarcely mean to gainsay here. To the contrary. Here I call attention to what the focus on Wagner's Beethoven has brushed aside and that is Nietzsche's Beethoven, and also, but I only raise this as a theme for possible research, the relevance of Nietzsche's own influence on Wagner, as this might perhaps begin to be seen in Wagner's *Beethoven* (Leipzig: E.W. Fritzsch, 1870). Nietzsche would, to be sure, publish his own text with the same publisher, and include a dedication to Wagner as "*Vorkämpfer*," a word choice and constellation to which Tracy B. Strong has called some attention. See, for example, Strong, "Philosophy and the Politics of Cultural Revolution," *Philosophical Topics* 33/2 (Fall 2005): 227–47. For me, the issue has to do with the conversations between Nietzsche and Wagner, beginning in 1869, and the possibility which I think worth considering that their influence was more mutual than one-sided. See, however, Dieter Jähnig who argues that priority must be given to Feuerbach for the duality of the Apollonian and the Dionysian specifically as unified in "dramatic festival" in his 1833 *Der vatikanische Apoll*. See Jähnig, "Emancipating the Knowledge of Art from Metaphysics in *The Birth of Tragedy*," trans. Babette Babich and Holger Schmid, *New Nietzsche Studies* 4/1 & 2 (Summer/Fall 2000): 77–121, here especially Jähnig's page 94; and see, also, Anselm Feuerbach, *Der vatikanische Apoll. Eine Reihe archäologisch-ästhetischer Betrachtungen* [1833], 2nd edn (Stuttgart, Augsburg: Cotta, 1855). To me, the relevance of Feuerbach for Nietzsche suggests the influence of Otto Jahn more than Ritschl, as Jähnig contends. Cf. the very Wagnerian but no less useful discussion by Martin Vogel, *Apollinisch und Dionysisch. Geschichte eines genialen Irrtums* (Regensburg: Gustav Bosse Verlag, 1966).

of the role of ictus in ancient Greek as the standard for pronunciation already mentioned in connection with musical phrasing, and just this constellation is rarely considered—even by musicological experts and even with reference to the same Hugo Riemann on phrasing in music, and about whom Nietzsche writes, rather insistently, in his correspondence with the musician Carl Fuchs towards the end of the 1880s, which was at the same time the end of Nietzsche's relatively short creative or productive life.[36]

My concern, then, is to raise the larger question of what Nietzsche *meant* by dissonance as such (Adorno's reflections on dissonance in his Beethoven book, as well as in his *Aesthetic Theory*, may help us here, but they are not directly related to Nietzsche) and in particular what Nietzsche meant by the elusive formula that he deploys at the conclusion of *The Birth of Tragedy*, the "becoming-human of dissonance."[37] I argue that we must at least initially understand dissonance in Nietzsche's historical context, not in terms of modern music of the kind we know and indeed of the kind that Adorno knew better than most, but and much rather as the traditionally, theoretically musical notion of dissonance as (together with consonance) a component of harmony as it functions in Nietzsche's text and as he understood it, together with his investigations into Greek rhythm and meter. All this is for the sake, once again, of his very gnomic notion of the "*Menschwerdung der Dissonanz*," that is to say, the "becoming-human of dissonance" as this ought perhaps to be phrased in a single word.

Readers whose interests do not run to Nietzsche's musings about the archaic "spirit of music" (and its relation to the tragic work of art, ancient and modern) may and will certainly leave off reading[38] in advance of the movement of this book to its third division.[39]

---

[36] Nietzsche, letter to Carl Fuchs, 26 August 1888, *Samtliche Briefe Kritische Studienausgabe: In 8 Banden*, ed. Giorgio Colli and Mazzino Montinari (Berlin: de Gruyter, 2003), vol. 8, 399ff, and see also 403ff. See, for a brief discussion, the conclusion of Alexander Rehding's *Hugo Riemann and the Birth of Modern Musical Thought* (Cambridge: Cambridge University Press, 2003), 180ff. Leslie David Blasius also addresses this in his "Nietzsche, Riemann, Wagner: When Music Lies," in *Music Theory and Natural Order: From the Renaissance to the Early Twentieth Century*, ed. Suzannah Clark and Alexander Rehding (Cambridge: Cambridge University Press, 2001), 93–107.

[37] Nietzsche, BT §24.

[38] This prediction, and this is the beauty of a book, takes care of itself. Thus I began above by pointing to the range of topics to be discussed, including Adorno's analyses, and I will add a discussion of Bennett's recording consciousness to this. But one need not attend to these later topics in order to find topics covered earlier of interest, and this book can also be read as the reader likes, chapter by chapter, and readers can pick and choose the themes they find interesting. The book was written as a whole, but the different chapters may be read independently.

[39] Phenomenologically, this works best with a physical book: chapters at the start can be set off from the others, sectioned off from later sections, and one can thus distinguish one section from others. One can do this with a digital or ebook, or a pdf of a text, in a variety

Thus I seek here, as I have elsewhere sought, to raise the question of "the artist," explicitly or focally by means of Leonard Cohen and k.d. lang, as well as theoretically, and as Nietzsche also posed this specific question of the artist or indeed as he also spoke of the actor, we may say the performer, a question which was always problematic for him, given the centrality of effect attributed to the magic of the genius or the charisma of the star in his day, a centrality which has not abated in our time. And from this, I turn to Nietzsche's concern with the problem of the artist in antiquity, but above all to the birth of the tragic art form out of music, and to Nietzsche's concern with Beethoven in this context.

Note that even if one does not follow this book to its conclusion,[40] one should at least keep in mind from the start that it is Nietzsche's extraordinary and complex conception of the becoming-human of dissonance that drives this exploration of the Hallelujah effect. Hence Nietzsche's conception of the becoming-human of dissonance is present from the start, at least conceptually, as it must be in a text that begins with a study of Leonard Cohen's *Hallelujah* sung by k.d. lang, together with an analysis of its dissemination on YouTube, Facebook and Twitter.

Thus, if the concern at the outset appears to be an analysis of a single song, and indeed an analysis of a single, albeit singular and singularizing, video performance of that song, the Hallelujah effect as I discuss it throughout sheds light on much of our network culture in all its media-mindedness. And of course, it should go without saying that for an understanding of this effect, we need more than a single book is able to summon, even one with as many footnoted under- and overtones as I have taken care to include here.

---

of ways, but the point is that one need not even be aware of it in the case of a book; one's fingers do this, the hand itself does this before one begins to think about it. In this sense, the book is more efficient than its digital counterpart.

[40]   Of course, the reader who is only interested in k.d. lang can easily skip to those sections, if it is also true that it is not always wise, theoretically speaking, to follow such advice, but I offer it in a spirit of practical sympathy. Indeed, I may be guilty of a kind of interpretive undercutting, as Hans Gerald Hödl sagely pointed out in his kind and no less insightful review of my own first book on *Nietzsche's Philosophy of Science*, and one should thus perhaps take this advice only in this sense. See Hödl, "Rezension: Babich, *Nietzsche's Philosophy of Science*," *Nietzsche-Studien* 26 (1997): 583–8.

Chapter 1
The Hallelujah Effect, Cohen's Secret Song, and the Music Industry

Money Makes the Music

The first recording of *Hallelujah* by Leonard Cohen was not a hit, as more than a few commentators have noted, some expressing surprise, others more diffidently.

It has been argued that the basic reason for this initial "non-hit" status was publicity or the lack thereof. Everyone seems to be well aware of the fact that it is less a singer's genius or the sterling qualities of a song than it is media coverage or exposure that makes the difference in the short and the long run. Adorno had already argued the same when it comes to musical programming on the radio, as this is very literally a "programming."

Adorno explains the virtue of social critique, contra the prima facie plausible impression that "radio, by a kind of Darwinian process of selection, actually plays most frequently those songs that are best liked by the people and is, therefore, fulfilling their demands."[1] In fact radio "works" on an altogether opposed basis. Radio programming "programs" (to use the cognitive science language mentioned above, it "primes") its listeners:

> the "plugging" of songs does not follow the response they elicit but the vested interests of song publishers. The identification of the successful with the most frequently played is thus an illusion, an illusion, to be sure, that may become an operating social force and in turn make the much-played a success because through such an identification the listeners follow what they believe to be the crowd and thus come to constitute one.[2]

This "programming" is of course the product of what Adorno calls the culture industry. Yet as Adorno himself immediately remarks precisely with regard to "popular music" and with seeming prescience when it comes to the montononic Facebook "like" button, this only "shows how problematic the notions of like and

---

[1] Theodor Adorno, *Current of Music: Elements of a Radio Theory*, ed. Robert Hullot-Kentor (Frankfurt am Main: Suhrkamp, 2006), 213–14. The study in question refers to Duncan MacDougald, "The Popular Music Industry," in *Radio Research 1941*, ed. Paul Lazarsfeld and Frank Stanton (New York: Duell, Sloan and Pearce, 1941), 65–109.

[2] Adorno, *Current of Music*, 213–14.

dislike are."[3] To this day, only what is promoted is popular—not the other way around. And a music-loving public consumes, to use Adorno's culinary language, what it is offered.

For this reason, it has been argued that because *Hallelujah* was included on a record that happened not to have been released in the United States, namely the album *Various Positions*, Cohen's song failed to gain hit status.[4] Other things, too, are at stake. For if the "culture industry" is adumbrated by way of the recording industry, on every level and in every way, the arcane perversity of the record industry as such ought not to pass without mention: and I have observed this from only the simplest, most vulgar or venal of encounters, that is to say, as this bears on the condition for publication per se of the current book, and in my efforts to secure permission to cite Leonard Cohen's lyrics to his *Hallelujah*, an undertaking that took months, delaying publication. Attempting to deal with or to interact in any way with record companies (or singers, for that matter) is like dealing with a classical moloch or behemoth. However often one approaches, whatever tack one uses, the response is no response, either literally or effectively.[5] This is the same non-response that, as Adorno analyzes, and Jacques Lacan takes up in another context, also happens to be the discourse modality of fascism. For Lacan, this is the discourse of the master.[6] This discourse strategy ensures that

---

[3]   Ibid., 214.

[4]   See, for a representative discussion of this point, Tim Footman, *Leonard Cohen, Hallelujah: A New Biography* (New Malden, Surrey: Chrome Dreams, 2009).

[5]   Thus when I inquired of Cohen's current manager, Robert Kory Esq., for advice about gaining permission to use some of Cohen's albums in this book, he directed me to SONY, but his gloss (which I read as akin to the device inscribed over Dante's Hell) left little hope: "You need to contact the copyright department at SONY Music in Manhattan. Find a law student at Fordham law school to help you. It will be a worthwhile challenge." Email to the author: Tuesday 19 July 2011, 08:27pm. I finally did get permission, hence this book, but the 500 pounds sterling that SONY required went directly to them and to them alone, paid directly from me, as author, to SONY—for all the difference that makes to Cohen's fragile fortunes as a singer. When people denounce music piracy with the claim that it injures the artists, be aware that for the most part it injures corporate interests. In fact, such piracy accrues to an author's account in the invaluable form of fame. In the interim, I was also able to obtain, again thanks to Kory's suggestion, duplicate permission from Random House to cite from Cohen's *Stranger Music: Selected Poems and Songs*. That cost the author $45.

[6]   See on the theme of this mastery (minus the reference to Lacan), again, Footman, *Leonard Cohen, Hallelujah*, 121 and so on. For an introductory discussion of Lacan and popular culture, see Slavoj Žižek, *Looking Awry: An Introduction to Jacques Lacan through Popular Culture* (Cambridge, MA: MIT Press, 1991). For a discussion of Lacan and mastery in a context connected to Nietzsche, see Babette Babich, "On the Order of the Real: Nietzsche and Lacan," in *Disseminating Lacan*, ed. David Pettigrew and François Raffoul (Albany: State University of New York Press, 1996), 48–63.

when the inquiry finally gets a response, the questioner recognizes—deferral thus forces deference—that the record company has all the power.[7]

To turn from the problems of getting to print this study of Cohen's *Hallelujah* to the story of Cohen's *Hallelujah*, Cohen's song itself came and went, as popular songs do, and then Cohen's *Hallelujah* caught John Cale's fancy. And just like that, as sung by John Cale, Cohen's *Hallelujah* went from its non-hit status to extraordinary success, both in Cohen's own work and especially, and therein lies this tale, as mediated by other performers who "covered" it, including, and in this instance prior to Cale, performers of mythic resonance such as Bob Dylan. It is Cale's recording that is decisive, as the great majority of subsequent covers do not follow Cohen's initial recording or indeed Cohen's concert performances (and there may be a lesson for performers here), but grow instead out of the haunting lyricism of Cale's cover.

Cale's recording fascinated, and rightly, a long list of singers, and it also got coverage, by no means incidentally, in two film soundtracks: it is of the nature of film music to stay with us, subliminally, whether we know it or not. This is the way commercials also work on us, the acoustic equivalent of Proust's madeleines. By the same token, and probably owing to the same Proustian dynamic, a certain invisibility or confusion goes along with this, and this invisibility proves relevant for both Cohen and Cale.

Many listeners today who know and enthuse about the *Hallelujah* song in whatever cover they take to be canonic have no idea that the song happens to have been Leonard Cohen's to begin with. Nor do they know that it was John Cale who gave it its most influential interpretation. Indeed, in spite of the popularity of the movie, and this will matter more for the great majority of fans, most will not even be aware that it was Cale's version that was originally featured in the *Shrek* movie.[8]

---

[7] Thus, despite the above mentioned £500, not one of my specific author's questions to SONY received an answer from SONY of any kind at any time, in spite of the fact that I managed to have a kind of email correspondence that led to a permissions licence.

[8] There are more than a few accounts of the trajectory of Cohen's *Hallelujah*. See the last chapter in Footman's *Leonard Cohen, Hallelujah* for an extended account, in part derived from Michael Barthel's analysis (which Footman duly acknowledges), which was presented at the 2007 Pop Conference at Experience Music Project and was subsequently published and modified in blog form, online. See: <http://www.scribd.com/doc/37784045/It-Doesn-t-Matter-Which-You-Heard-The-Curious-Cultural-Journey-of-Leonard-Cohen-s-Hallelujah>. Barthel's lecture is unpublished but "preserved" as a pdf for archival purposes (according to the title on the page still posted on the internet). In fact, the link can be tough to track as Barthel has gone on to doctoral studies at the University of Washington and the original locus of the archive pdf has shifted. If this is a topic of further research interest, I would urge the reader to download from Scribd.com because this discussion of *Hallelujah* is decidedly "broken," not only metaphorically (in the sense of links) but in the sense of the author's own self-distancing. Maybe this is fallout from the Strunk & White style police or just a case of changing enthusiasms.

The shadow side of the phenomenon of Cohen's success with this particular song is thus that his own name is not always associated with his own song, and the reasons for this are worth reflection. In part, as I have already suggested, and as the singer himself is fond of emphasizing, this may have to do with the limitations of his voice. But in part this is also because Cohen's song, as he wrote it and as he sung it, is in a sense designed for, or shall we say doomed to, being taken up and thus taken over—for better or for worse—by the one who sings it.

Voice matters, and it makes a difference whether Cohen's *Hallelujah* is sung by Dylan or by Cohen himself or by Rufus Wainwright or by Jeff Buckley, and so on. And, of course, when it comes to Cohen's own recent performance, we also hear not only his voice, such as it is, but also his age.[9] Below we will return to this notion of "voice" and the aging and maturation of a singer in the case of Cohen and of k.d. lang.[10]

In addition, I have also mentioned the nature of the song itself, as Cohen initially wrote it. Here there is also the sheer variety of lyric content, as Cohen seems to have written both a *holy* and, so some contend—but this is the stuff of apocrypha, if the facts of the original version support this claim—a separately *broken*, which is code for a more erotic and sensual, that is to say, more bodily, *Hallelujah*. We shall see that this interpretation of two distinctive *Hallelujah* songs is itself mixed, although it has the support of appearance on its side, and borrows a bit from Cohen's reputation as what one calls a ladies' man (that weirdly rude term used to characterize men who make a habit of treating women badly until these same men get too old to continue to do so, whereupon the last "lady" they are with is praised for having somehow mellowed them). The question of the ladies, and the question of woman and of Eros, matters from the start and, as we shall see, all this makes a difference when it comes to k.d. lang's performance.

The dual reading of the holy and broken *Hallelujah* appeals to certain articulations of the sacred and the profane, even as it turns out to be no more than illusion: superficial as appearances always are, as Nietzsche reminds us, where

---

[9]   One reviewer whom we cite below has been particularly unforgiving in Cohen's regard, although, and to be fair, Cohen's own visceral and bodily emphases over the years have also invited this to a great extent. There is also a certain amount of heterosexual macho enthusiasm, that is, a celebration of love and above all of lust, evident in Cohen's fans. And this may mean, though one cannot be sure, that such a critique expresses the reviewer's own anxieties.

[10]   I mean by this what is often used by writers such as Stanley Cavell and others, to a great extent in the wake of Roland Barthes. See, for a specific discussion of voice in terms of expression relevant to the current context, Lori Burns, "Vocal Authority and Listener Engagement: Musical and Narrative Expressive Strategies in Alternative Female Rock Artists (1993–95)," in *Sounding Out Rock*, ed. John Covach and Mark Spicer (Ann Arbor: University of Michigan Press, 2010).

both religious and erotic dimensions happen to be present from the start, unfolding as they do with what may therefore be counted as the song's *incipit* or first verse, beginning "Well I heard ..." as Cohen tells us, "there was a secret chord ..."

"... it doesn't matter which you heard ..."

Changed as Cohen's *Hallelujah* is across different instaurations and in so many differing performances, the song sung is not quite Cohen's own.[11] This takes none of the credit away from Cohen's original composition, nor, indeed, from Cale's determinative version of that composition, although, and to be sure, this is not the same as the question of royalties for Cohen himself or for Cale, who is an insider if anyone is, or for the music industry in general.

And this too is due to the Hallelujah effect: as this is the working efficacy of media access.

Thus, and in connection with Cohen's financial woes, money is always a prime motivation in the music industry, as it is a direct sign of success. And it is always a mistake to assume that art is for its own sake: this was never true in the past, and it is not true today. Cohen's biographer, Tim Footman, offers this useful summary of the industry consequences of this same phenomenon of instant access, noting that:

> The decades old financial model by which an act would record an album, then play live gigs (often barely breaking even) to raise its profile had been shot to pieces. Major stars such as Madonna and Paul McCartney were signing innovative contracts, which meant they derived a far higher percentage of their incomes from touring, with the album now more an advertisement for the gigs, rather than the other ways around.[12]

In an important fashion, one Adorno had already predicted, this is due to the phenomenon of repetition, and a kind of seemingly eternal repetition of the same old, same old is what is on offer, always more literally than not, always more so than one can imagine, and this is so even where there is no whiff of the supposed "inauthenticity" of lip-synching (though what a band, especially one that sings back-up, and they all do, *does* for a singer is manifestly not irrelevant here, a musically resonant point that never goes unmissed in Cohen's case, and his recordings of his *Hallelujah* depend on back-up singers and not less on collaborations—once again: as all musicians do—with other musicians).

One can vary versions or interpretative performances as much as one likes. What matters is the take that "takes." This is also where the issue of performance

---

[11]   The occasional claim that has Cohen calling for a moratorium on new covers witnesses to this sense: the song is now so omnipresent that listeners take performances by Wainwright or Buckley as the "original."

[12]   Footman, *Leonard Cohen, Hallelujah*, 161.

practice becomes relevant in the same protracted influence of Cohen's *Hallelujah* on so many musical artists (and featured as it has been in numerous sound tracks for film and television and what have you).

I found myself inspired to write this book although I am arguably less a pop music fan than many others.[13] This is relevant to say here because it is only the fan who has access to, because it is only the fan who *notices*, what one might call the musical "history of influence" of Cohen's *Hallelujah* on other musical artists of pop culture in general (that would be its *Wirkungsgeschichte*, to use Gadamer's term in this context).[14] This means that, in spite of my previous familiarity with Cohen's singing of his own *Hallelujah*, I myself qua non-fan—fandom or fanhood is a particular ontological category that cannot be explored here—had no, or, perhaps better said, *little*, knowledge of the range of covers of that same song. Certainly I had not seen *Shrek* (a blockbuster "spectacular," as they say, of Hollywood animation) and to this extent I was as unaware of the many versions of the *Hallelujah* song as many readers reading now might similarly suppose themselves to be. What is at stake here is that this effective ignorance (be it a matter of genuine non-knowledge or non-attention, and these are different things) is also part of the exemplary and popular commonality of the Hallelujah effect. It doesn't matter, as Cohen would add in a later verse, which you heard, and it tends to be the case that, no matter what one thinks, one has heard some version of it, whether one knows it or not.

As Bryan Appleyard emphasizes with regards to this point, you *do* know the song, whether you happen to recognize your own familiarity with the song or not:

> Even if you think you haven't heard it, I can guarantee you have. It has been covered by, among many others, Allison Crowe, k.d. lang, Damien Rice, Bono, Sheryl Crow and Kathryn Williams. Bob Dylan has sung it live in a performance that has, apparently, been bootlegged. It has been used endlessly in films and on TV. Rufus Wainwright sang it on the sound-track of *Shrek*, Jeff Buckley's version was used on *The West Wing* and *The OC*, John Cale sang it on *Scrubs* and so on.[15]

---

[13]   Although pop music is called pop music because it is popularly known, some of us know more of it than others. I am on the low end of the scale and, in writing this book, I have come to regret this deficit.

[14]   No less than Adorno, Gadamer too found himself drawn to reflect on concert programming and uses the example of a "religion of culture" in his introduction to *The Relevance of the Beautiful and Other Essays*, trans. Nicholas Walker (Cambridge: Cambridge University Press, 1986), p. 7.

[15]   Bryan Appleyard, "Hallelujah! On Leonard Cohen's Ubersong," *The Sunday Times*, 9 June 2005. This is, indeed, among other things, part of Steven Lloyd Wilson's "The Minor Fall, The Major Lift," along with a useful discussion of rhythm, illustrated in his own text with paratactical interpellations. See: <http://www.pajiba.com/miscellaneous/the-minor-fall-the-major-lift.php>.

Appleyard is not the only commentator to emphasize Cohen's *it doesn't matter which you heard*, and thus he characterizes our collective musical consciousness as, at least partly, unconscious. Here I am talking about the first time I noted what I heard long before all the fuss (this is one of the advantages of having been listening to music in the 1970s and 1980s), which, given my musical listening habits, mostly classical, new music, experimental and so on, I suspect to be accurate enough. At the same time, my brief in what follows does not challenge Appleyard's reading. To the contrary.

Thus at the beginning of my own experience with the Hallelujah effect, and not being too, too much of a fan, be it of Cohen or anybody in the pop music world, I "liked"—this is the Facebook-speak that has made "liking" more charged as conventional affect than it should be, and this remains true whether one substitutes a google+1 or a heart or a thumbs up avatar or what have you—Cohen's *Hallelujah*. Perhaps this was due to Cohen's rhythmic delivery—I confess to a special weakness for his *Who by Fire*—perhaps this is just because I am fond of words, be it plainchant, spoken music, spoken poetry, word jazz, and so on.

But at the same time as I "liked" Cohen's song, it was also true that it was not my thing. I could, as we say, take it or leave it.

That was that, until what I call dueling video-posts on Facebook.

Now the thing about Facebook is the chance to pretend to be in contact with people with whom one is (in truth) no longer in actual contact (friends from one's youth, colleagues from various past acquaintances, and, in what is perhaps the largest category of Facebook, "friends": that would also be people one has never met but whom one supposes one ought to have met or whom one would like to meet or *just because*—this would be the California or "whatever" kind of friend—as well as family members and such). Facebook achieves this, as its name suggests, by including pictures of the same, along with the aforementioned video-posts, most of which are borrowed from YouTube, and, because this is a virtual rather than a real "book," also by a "wall," like nothing so much as a public bathroom wall: one is often alone when writing on said wall, on one's own wall or those of others, and one writes precisely with the expectation that others simply passing through or vaguely loitering—and the increasing wasting of time and energy in social networking gives a new meaning to that phrase—will chance to read it, and, like such scribblings, Facebook posts often have a kind of high or distant humor: provocative or conceived just to get a rise out of people: it is not for nothing that Facebook has an odd category of the "poke," which I have never used but propose to understand as of a piece with this character of provocative instigation. And this matters for the video-post.

Facebook denizens craft their posts to ensure a response, and even if they do not admit this, it is clear that they are frustrated if this is not successful.[16] The

---

[16]   See, for a sophisticated and productive discussion focusing on adolescents, to the discomfit of the youth culture of online and network life, Sherry Turkle, *Alone Together: Why We Expect More from Technology and Less from Each Other* (New York: Basic

addictive effect of simply getting a response is perhaps the most important aspect of the subjective experience of computer culture, qua computer culture, which I had observed already as a student working with computers in college in the mid- to late 1970s and early 1980s in grad school. I recall my surprise (and disappointment) at realizing that *the* reason that my peers at MIT (I preferred to use the MIT gym when I was working on a PhD at Boston College) were so very fascinated by their computers was that literally everything they did was reinforced, instantly and unconditionally. Touch a key and the response is an immediate, psychologically supportive, direct echo: no countering word, no dissonance, no unpredictability.[17]

For my own part, I post mostly informative, that is to say, didactic posts—and "friends," so I believe, counter or filter these by simply tuning them out[18]—there are a number of ways to do this, although much of this filtering is in turn similarly (and far more insidiously) filtered by Facebook.[19] Filtered *and* filtering, the experience

---

Books, 2011); and see too her earlier *Life on the Screen: Identity in the Age of the Internet* (New York: Simon and Schuster, 1995; Touchstone Paper, 1997); and *Simulation and Its Discontents* (Cambridge, MA: MIT Press, 2009).

[17]   The then popular Eliza program was only a variant on the same and so it continues to this day, and here it is significant to add that the new sexbots simply continue the Eliza vein for (pornographic) fun and, of course, profit—there is nothing more profitable than pornography for the new media, and nothing more dreary than staffing interactive sites. The sex industry is as if made to order for a bot—the prostitute is, after all, only a living robot: the idea is that she does what the client wishes, as if she herself desires just what the client desires.

[18]   Joseph Kugelmass analyzes this as a key part of the reason for his own decision to—as the TSA says before they either radiate or lay hands upon your person—"opt out" of Facebook, at least temporarily. Kugelmass, who has since finished a PhD at the University of California at Irvine, is a relative of the late Dr Isaac Newton Kugelmass, who was my pediatrician when I was a child. This personal connection is my reason for having taken notice of his blog, but anyone with an interest in popular culture will find the well-written *Kugelmass Episodes* worthwhile. See his blog: <http://kugelmass.wordpress. com/2012/04/08/why-i-am-leaving-facebook/>.

[19]   See, for a start, the popular writer, Eli Pariser, *The Filter Bubble* (Hassocks: Penguin Press, 2011). Parsing the significance of this "filtering" mechanism turns out to be the challenge for commentators, and yet one can also recall Jean Baudrillard's thesis concerning virtual reality in *The Intelligence of Evil or The Lucidity Pact*, trans. C. Turner (Oxford: Berg, 2005), that is, the idea that the only real is what is promulgated via the media, television, internet, what have you, an idea confounded by the sheer fact, common to much reflective writing, that it is confounding. Or if one wishes, one might, one certainly ought, also go back (again) to Jacques Ellul's *Propaganda: The Formation of Men's Attitudes*, trans. Konrad Kellen and Jean Lerner (New York: Knopf, 1973), or indeed Ellul's *The Technological Society*, trans. John Wilkinson (New York: Vintage Books, 1965). For a recent reading, see Karim Haiderali Karim, "Cyber Utopia and the Myth of Paradise: Using Jacques Ellul's Work on Propaganda to Analyse Information Society Rhetoric," *Information, Communication & Society* 4/1 (2001): 113–34; or Ivan Illich's *Deschooling Society* (New York: Harper & Row, 1971); or else, and perhaps most saliently because

of Facebook thus tends to be more, rather than less, autistic and, in a wired age, this autism may be its most subversive quality. Nevertheless, and within the safe space of friendly faces and sympathetic voices, and modulated in accord with what Derrida once called a higher tone, that is, language elevated to a public level, by way of a lighter, more gracious, and occasionally ironic tone, there are also inspiring occasions.

Thus when Claire Katz, my friend and philosophical colleague at Texas A&M, posted the *Shrek Hallelujah*, expressing enthusiasm for the same, I was moved to a bit of what I call YouTube poker, an exchange very common on Facebook. Thus I saw her Rufus Wainwright post and raised it by a k.d. lang.

Not just any k.d. version either, but her live 2005 Juno version, which I found among many other singers and several other versions. And Andrew Benjamin (it mattered to me that this came from Australia) returned with an absolute hands down yea-saying. Now, and this is also a peculiar advantage of Facebook, it is significant that Andrew is a *practical* aesthetics person: architectural theory, philosophy, and so on, are his thing. Thus, sheerly theoretically, Andrew's comment brought me to think on what had moved me to join the poker game in the first place and indeed to what that seemingly idle gesture had brought me.

Now this may sound as if I am cooler than your average professor or Nietzsche scholar, as if I—like Andrew—know my k.d. lang, but this would be a lie: looking for Leonard Cohen, which is to say (and this is what I mean about didacticism), looking as I was for the "original" (conventionally understood), I found k.d. lang's version instead and instantly and spontaneously added a link. That's what my internet activity would show.

In real life: I fell off the floor, as I say, in response to the song I heard, which was indeed the song, the YouTube post, I saw.[20] The piano, almost enough for the absolutist (musically speaking) in me, had taken me from the start, but k.d. lang's poise was also a living embodiment of the song as well. Indeed, everything was dynamic poise, possession, lived expression. Now the engineering of the visuals of the video itself, lights, camera, design—here I include stage, setting, lighting— as well as the camera crew who filmed the live Juno 2005 performance, had a lot to do with its effect.[21]

---

coined in San Diego's consumerist Californian light, Herbert Marcuse, *One-Dimensional Man: Studies in the Ideology of Advanced Industrial Society* (Boston: Beacon Press, 1964).

[20]   This is a personal idiom but I claim it as native to my New York, although I do not personally know anyone else who says this. "Falling off the floor" is *not* a possibility. Hence the phrase functions as a superlative.

[21]   Nor is this a new claim, as Andrew Goodwin has observed: "pop has always stressed the visual as a necessary part of its apparatus," in *Dancing in the Distraction Factory: Music Television and Popular Culture* (Minneapolis: University of Minnesota Press, 1992), 8. See, too, Marsha Kinder, "Music Video and the Spectator: Television, Ideology and Dream," *Film Quarterly* 38/1 (1984): 2–15, as well as, two decades later, Carol Vernallis, *Experiencing Music Video: Aesthetics and Cultural Context* (New York:

This is the smoke and mirrors part of a stage show, the movie magic of *L'année dernière à Marienbad* or k.d. lang's own music video for her *Constant Craving*, and this points to the centrality of television for music and still more so for YouTube today, and it exemplifies the genre of the music video.[22]

Thus, although one ought to emphasize the difference that it makes to be physically really, really present in performance, in person, really there, just and in order to speak about music at all and to begin with,[23] there can be no doubt that most of us experience music today in the hard or non-wired way, often with earbuds, such that the music is in our skull, meaning that we hear (Adorno's notion of listening would not quite be correct here) recorded, usually digital, music with no resonant dimensionality at all, save from that engineered into the music as such.[24] This is cooked sound, digitally so, and what is at stake here will be all about space, time, and life.

Columbia University Press, 2004). See, for a useful analysis of consumerism and the social networking efficacy of music videos, Patricia Aufderheide, "Music Videos: The Look of the Sound," *Journal of Communication* 36/1 (1986): 57–8. Aufderheide's interest has, not surprisingly, given the thicket of licenses and permissions involved with music video and music in general, turned to issues of copyright and fair use. See, for one example that bears on the current study, Aufderheide's article, co-authored with Peter Jaszi and Renee Hobbs, "Media Literacy Educators Need Clarity About Copyright and Fair Use," *The Journal of Media Literacy* 54/2–3 (Winter 2008): 41–4; and Aufderheide's *The Daily Planet: A Critic on the Capitalist Culture Beat* (Minneapolis, MN: University of Minnesota Press, 2000), in addition to James Boyle, *The Public Domain: Enclosing the Commons of the Mind* (New Haven: Yale University Press, 2008). For a discussion of the distinction between music television and music video, see Blaine Allan, "Music Television," in *Television: Critical Methods and Applications*, ed. Jeremy G. Butler (Mahwah, NJ: Erlbaum, 2007), 287–324; see, on music video, 300ff, lighting, 309, and so on.

22   See, again, the authors cited above.

23   For another illustration of this point from a different theoretical perspective, see Babette Babich, *Words in Blood, Like Flowers: Philosophy and Poetry, Music and Eros in Hölderlin, Nietzsche, and Heidegger* (Albany: State University of New York Press, 2006); as well as my "Postmodern Musicology," in *Routledge Encyclopedia of Postmodernism*, ed. Victor E. Taylor and Charles Winquist (London: Routledge, 2001), 2nd edn, 153–9; and more obliquely in my "*Ex aliquo nihil*: Nietzsche on Science and Modern Nihilism," *American Catholic Philosophical Quarterly* 84/2 (Spring 2010): 231–56; and my "Adorno on Science and Nihilism, Animals, and Jews," *Symposium: Canadian Journal of Continental Philosophy/Revue canadienne de philosophie continentale* 14/1 (2011): 1–36.

24   Again, Adorno's *Current of Music* is hard to better. But see, too, Michael Chanan, *Musica Practica: The Social Conventions of Western Music from Gregorian Chant to Postmodernism* (London: Verso, 1994), along with his *From Handel to Hendrix: The Composer in the Public Sphere* (London: Verso, 1999); and, for an analysis of the "engineered" conventions of the same, see Frances Dyson, "When Is the Ear Pierced?" in *Immersed in Technology*, ed. Mary Anne Moser and Douglas MacLeod (Bloomington: Indiana University Press, 1999), 73–101. See too Mark Katz, *Capturing Sound: How Technology Has Changed Music* [2004] (Berkeley: University of California Press, 2010),

By direct extension, we have been talking about popular music as it is routinely so transmitted, not via radio, but by way of recordings, records, mp3s, and now, and more face-to-face than ever, YouTube videos. Indeed, part of my effort in what follows will be to underline that there is a world to unpack in the digital character of today's music—if it is also and only one part of the issue at stake. And then, and quite apart from this, there is the whole package of the YouTube experience which, like the closed world of Facebook, is intriguingly another thing altogether, although it also, and this is part of its success, blends seamlessly with Facebook as well.

In the case of the YouTube offerings, it is the full production, theatrical light set of the 2005 Juno performance that turns out to be important, if and initially, subliminally so. For k.d. lang's performance is set against the crucial backdrop of a light show: a shifting and subtle series of slides, blue light cut-outs in religious frames, stained glass, including a blue rose window, crosses and high gothic rectangles of light. And as she sings, imperceptibly, the framed illuminations change with the music: piano, contrabass, single guitar, thus comprising what one might call an orchestra band: all cellos and strings, including a conductor, the setting clearly delineated from verse to verse, chorus to chorus, shifting from religious forms to a blue starry-night expanse at the climax.

Nor does it turn out to be any kind of accident that lang speaks of the "cinematic" quality of Cohen's *Hallelujah* as making the song, for her—she is always careful to qualify this—an easy one.[25] Then, too, we might add in a consideration of the age-old question of content and musical style important for Nietzsche, who always wondered about the fate of music where the words themselves demanded to be understood (this is, of course, with reference to music and word in antiquity and in

---

along with Arved Ashby, *Absolute Music: Mechanical Reproduction* (Berkeley: University of California Press, 2010), as well as Alf Björnberg, "Learning to Listen to Perfect Sound: Hi-Fi Culture and Changes in Modes of Listening, 1950–1980," in *The Ashgate Research Companion to Popular Musicology*, ed. Derek B. Scott (Farnham: Ashgate, 2009), 105–30, and Milner's *Perfecting Sound Forever: An Aural History of Recorded Music* (New York: Faber and Faber, 2009), and so on.

[25]   Thus in an interview, k.d. lang says that "Leonard Cohen is probably the greatest prophet of human desire—'your love was strong but you needed proof / You saw her bathing on the roof / Her beauty in the moonlight overthrew ya' ... in fact all the verses from *Hallellujah*. It's amazingly simple yet it gets across the real complexity of human emotion. Leonard Cohen gives you a lot to chew over as a singer, and it never loses its flavour, something to bite on everytime. When a lyric has a deep metaphor, you can jump off at every point. His lyrics are very easy to sing." k.d. lang, "Interview," *Word* (January 2005). Of course, it may be argued that Rufus Wainwright could make the same claim, and of course, and unlike, say, the *Star Spangled Banner*, a song that inspires this many interpretations would not be likely to be intrinsically difficult. At the same time, as we shall see, that same ease points out a certain threnody, a dirge-like element that is hard to eliminate, even in Cale's faster version. Here it can be instructive to recall that musicological analyses are sometimes fond of comparing the speed (tempo) of music from era to era.

the then current context of European opera), while at the same time emphasizing when it came to antiquity that the ancient Greeks went to the theater to hear beautiful speech, that is, the beauty of the spoken word, where, as Nietzsche recalls for us, there would be no difference between speech and song.

It is for Nietzsche's reasons that I found myself led to pose the question of k.d. lang's performance practice seeking thereby a better understanding of what Nietzsche called "the spirit of music." That spirit is very literally, very exactly sounded in the case of the Greeks' own voicing of their own language, especially in lyric poetry, as Nietzsche foregrounds this analysis in his book on tragedy, because as he had discovered, one could not articulate or pronounce ancient Greek tragedies without singing them, and not because he argued for missing musical scores, and not because of the lyre or cithara accompaniment, but because, and again, for the Greek, to speak was to sing.[26]

To get to a discussion of the ancient Greek work of music drama for Nietzsche, that is tragedy and lyric, is elusive because, and through nothing more conspiratorial than the passage of time and the stone fact of the death of a cultural way of life, it has been eternally silenced.[27] The same applies or holds, as Adorno reminds us, even for Beethoven, even when it comes to the notes that he wrote.[28] And Nietzsche's Beethoven, especially in the context of his book on tragedy, is even more elusive. I find that Adorno helps, and in order to get to Adorno without losing Nietzsche's life practice, I turn here to look at popular music on the radio and as we now experience it on YouTube, and that means that I look at what k.d. lang does with Leonard Cohen's *Hallelujah*.

To do this, we also need to look a little more closely at the context of Cohen's *Hallelujah*.

---

[26]   Babette Babich, "The Science of Words or Philology: Music in *The Birth of Tragedy* and The Alchemy of Love in *The Gay Science*," in *Revista di estetica*, n.s. 28, XLV, ed. Tiziana Andina (Turin: Rosenberg & Sellier, 2005), 47–78.

[27]   This is one of Nietzsche's recurrent emphases and I detail this point, with further references in my discussion cited in the note above.

[28]   Adorno thus writes that "musical works exist only as mediated through writing, because interpretation does not have the direct sound to go on, only its notated form …" in his *Towards a Theory of Musical Reproduction: Notes, a Draft, and Two Schemata*, trans. Wieland Hoban (London: Polity, 2006), 179 and ff. See also 186 and 189.

Chapter 2
Leonard Cohen's *Hallelujah* and Other Hallelujahs: From Handel's *Hallelujah Chorus* to the Hallel Psalms

Nietzsche, Adorno, and Cohen's Holy Hallelujah

The Hallelujah effect goes beyond Leonard Cohen's *Hallelujah*, and not just because Cohen's *Hallelujah* has been rather well documented as a musical phenomenon that has taken on a life of its own. Rather than looking at this phenomenon as is generally done, either by focusing on Cohen himself or else on John Cale or Jeff Buckley or Rufus Wainwright, or indeed many, many, many others, k.d. lang's[1] several interpretations, particularly her 2005 Juno performance, exemplify what I am here calling the "Hallelujah effect" in a way that also permits us to see something about music and desire, but also something about men and women, and even, if I am correct, something about the particular qualities of today's recording consciousness, and ultimately about Nietzsche's notion of the "becoming-human of dissonance." It will take a bit to get us there.

I focus on k.d. lang for many reasons, not least because k.d. lang's interpretations are iconic enough for the icons themselves, and when Judy Collins was invited to sing Cohen's *Suzanne* at the 2006 induction of Leonard Cohen into the Canadian Songwriters Hall of Fame, k.d. lang was invited on the same occasion to sing Cohen's *Hallelujah*. The same vision of k.d. lang's qualities also held to extraordinary effect at the 2010 Winter Olympics in Vancouver. Indeed, one can argue, with a certain risk of bathos, that this iconic persuasion has moved to the dance itself with an Alberta ballet company's plans to produce *Balletlujah*: giving us the Hallelujah effect on (quite possibly literally) steroids.[2]

---

[1]   Here one is a bit tempted to write "k.d. lang©" inasmuch as the artist specifies her own name precisely as a brand of the sort that might appear on a high-end kitchen stove or a pair of jeans. And although it is commonly claimed that the stage name k.d. lang was chosen in the spirit of e.e. cummings, it is just as patent that women (and some men)—think, in the current instance, of P.M.S. Hacker—choose a public presentation of their names with initials alone. In what follows, I refer to k.d. lang in lower case in deference to the artist's own preference.

[2]   I refer here to k.d. lang's currently planned dance collaboration with Jean Grand-Maitre, the director of the Alberta Ballet, on a project called *Balletlujah!*—including the exclamation point.

All kidding aside: if what you want is someone to take the house down with *Hallelujah*, what you want is k.d. lang.

I seek now to explore the reasons why this should be so and it is to raise this question that I have recourse to a seemingly unrelated number of themes, bearing on men and women and being a sex object, Facebook and YouTube, in addition to the separate chapters on Adorno and Nietzsche.

Inevitably, given my own scholarly formation, I write and cannot help but write from a philosophical perspective, rather than from either a musicological, sociological or ethnological perspective (although my research has drawn upon all these disciplines and more). In part this breadth is needed because the overall concern of this study is inherently complicated. It is because of this complexity all around that I pursue a hermeneutic and phenomenological[3] study of what Nietzsche called "the spirit of music" by way of k.d. lang's *Hallelujah* rather than the tragic musical texts of antiquity, though I will turn to these too in a later chapter.[4] And this turns out to be of benefit for the present theme, because in addition to the high and the low of music and of mood, of love and life, it is indispensable for a reflection upon what Nietzsche named the complicatedly erotic "problem" of the artist.[5]

I have already referred to Adorno's analysis of the "radio voice," which he first articulated some 70 years ago. I consider this below, along with a reference to H. Stith Bennett's musicological reflections on pop music and including Bennett's reflections on what he called "recording consciousness" as I apply it to Facebook

---

[3]   There are instantiations of such phenomenological studies, and I mention them here although I am not following directly in this tradition, not because I am disinclined to do so but because I wish to bring Nietzsche into the mix. Thus in addition to Weber and Halm and Adorno himself, see F. Joseph Smith, *The Experiencing of Musical Sound: Prelude to a Phenomenology of Music* (New York: Gordon and Breach, 1979), which examines, as its title suggests, music experience, which one might, as Adorno himself describes it, equate with music appreciation but indeed goes much further, as Adorno's own engagement with Stern also illustrates in *Current of Music: Elements of a Radio Theory*, ed. Robert Hullot-Kentor (Frankfurt am Main: Suhrkamp, 2006). I am seeking a very different engagement to the extent that I am attempting to unpack what Nietzsche means by the spirit of music, as I have already noted this as inherent in his notion of the "becoming-human-of-dissonance."

[4]   There are several translations of Friedrich Nietzsche, *The Birth of Tragedy out of the Spirit of Music*, but it is worth looking at the German original as it is included at the start of the paperback edition of his collected works, *Studienausgabe* (Berlin: de Gruyter, 1980), vol. 1. See, for a discussion, the first chapters of Babette Babich, *Words in Blood, Like Flowers: Philosophy and Poetry, Music and Eros in Hölderlin, Nietzsche, and Heidegger* (Albany: State University of New York Press, 2006), as well as Babich, "The Science of Words or Philology: Music in *The Birth of Tragedy* and The Alchemy of Love in *The Gay Science*," in *Revista di estetica*, n.s. 28, XLV, ed. Tiziana Andina (Turin: Rosenberg & Sellier, 2005).

[5]   Notably, Nietzsche himself connected the "problem" of the artist with that of the actor, woman, and Jew. See Babette Babich, "Nietzsche's Erotic Artist as Actor/Jew/Woman" in *Words in Blood, Like Flowers*, 147f.

and other quasi-social interactions, but also and more generally to music. Indeed, its application is much wider if Jean Baudrillard is correct, as I believe that he is, to thematize not entertainment expressly advertised as such, but news in general, especially as we get (or do not get) our news reports today, and also as mediated by digital media and networking, on Twitter, Facebook, multiply posted blogs, especially in the form of videos on YouTube, all of it as experienced online and on cell phones, iPads, what have you.

I am hardly claiming that Nietzsche anticipated today's "recording consciousness." However, the efforts of Ivan Illich, Walter Ong, and again Jacques Ellul, even—if less directly, but vastly more influentially for the fields of media studies and communications and media archaeology—Neil Postman and Friedrich Kittler and others, all in differently important ways advance the work of Milman Parry and Albert Lord in attesting to just such a consciousness and the conditions for the possibility of the "recorded" transmission of song. Even Nietzsche matters here, as I have sought to show, for the sake of a certain "recording consciousness," as this turns out to correspond to the acoustic "recording" that is the text itself in the case of ancient Greek, as written Greek required nothing less than a speaker and, indeed, an entire cultural world in order to give it voice.[6] Reading aloud breathes breath into letters, calls the music of the poet's voice to life once again. This is the spirit in the letter, as Nietzsche spoke of the spirit of music.

Despite this understanding of the word as music, as Nietzsche understood ancient Greek lyric poetry and tragedy, whereby the text is itself an acoustic record, for our analysis, for our contemporary sensibilities, it is above all the age of mechanical, technological, digital reproduction that matters here.

As Benjamin observed, in an observation that was immediately taken up and transposed by Adorno into the time-space of music, to be modern is to be involved in a relation to the world in terms of the signal character of modernity: that is mechanical reproduction. This technological involvement changes the conditions of the possibility of art, as such and henceforth, insuperably. For Benjamin, this was the case for all sight, but it was notably so or especially the case when it came to the produced as such, the specifically engendered *work* of art, a rubric that also includes the *working* of art.

As Adorno argues: "The authenticity which Benjamin attributes in the visual arts to the original must be attributed to live reproduction in music. This live

---

[6] I foreground Nietzsche's discovery as such in my "The Science of Words or Philology," and I take this up again in this book. See, for Illich's analyis, his *In the Vineyard of the Text: A Commentary to Hugh's Didascalicon* (Chicago: University of Chicago Press, 1996), in addition to his book written with Barry Sanders, *ABC: The Alphabetization of the Popular Mind* (San Francisco: North Point Press, 1988); and see, too, Eric A. Havelock, *The Muse Learns to Write: Reflections on Orality and Literacy from Antiquity to the Present* (New Haven: Yale University Press, 1988); and Walter Ong, S.J., *Orality and Literacy: The Technologizing of the Word* (New York: Routledge, 2002).

reproduction has its 'here'—either the concert room or the opera—and its 'now'—the very moment it is executed."[7] To the extent that studio recordings not only drive but inform live performances, an attention to media and recording practice is as important as an attention to what is traditionally named performance practice. As we shall see, it is this practice that makes all the difference for k.d. lang.

As noted to begin with, Cohen first recorded *Hallelujah* in 1984, and went on subsequently to perform and modify and to re-record the song in the decades to come.[8] After John Cale's 1991 cover, the Hallelujah effect for other artists would begin and Cohen's song would go on to be recorded by numerous artists, counted in the hundreds; adding YouTube performances, that number grows to thousands of "maybe" or "wannabe" renderings.

Key for this particular reading of Cohen's *Hallelujah*, k.d. lang would record her own interpretation—called a "cover" by a music business (we shall return to this business aspect) hell-bent on keeping clear records of royalties—20 years after Cohen's original 1984 recording, on her religiously attuned, religiously titled, 2004 album, *Hymns of the 49th Parallel*. The white font color change of "hymns" on her own album cover makes that clear, but she also underlines this same religious and spiritual dimension herself, claiming as she does in an early interview that *everything* she does should be seen as religious or spiritual.[9]

Although I focus here on Cohen's *Hallelujah* and k.d. lang's several interpretations of the song, the Hallelujah effect corresponds, as already suggested, to the breadth of influence of Cohen's *Hallelujah* overall, an influence that works both forwards and backwards as well (those who are feeling nostalgic for what used to be called the postmodern may call this the postmodern part).

In this way, Cohen's *Hallelujah* sings the song of a song that has, so to speak, "been around," beginning with its biblical origins and a staple of hymns and spirituals, in masses and oratorios, and continuing in popular music on every level. Although I will attempt to trace a more detailed account of the historical horizon of influence of Cohen's *Hallelujah* below, and although I suspect that a complete outline may well be impossible, Cohen's song took off only following the first and also paradigmatic interpretation on Cale's 1991 album (which he enthusiastically dedicated to Cohen), *I'm Your Fan*. It is essential, once again, to note that it is Cale's version that "makes" or sets the *Hallelujah* we now know as Cohen's *Hallelujah*,

---

[7]   Adorno, *Current of Music*, 141.

[8]   *Hallelujah* is the center track on Leonard Cohen's album, *Various Positions*, released at the end of 1984 and again in early 1985.

[9]   Thus lang emphasizes, and we shall see that this particular kind of both/and inclination is important to her, that she is "partially a Buddhist, and partially a Christian," adding: "But I couldn't stress enough how much of *me* is rooted in religion, well, religion is in lack of a better term: *in spirituality*, everything I do, every song I sing is strictly for the better of us, as a human race, spirituality is *what* I am." 1986 TV interview with the late Peter Gzowski, *Our Stories*, on the Canadian Biography Channel. None too surprisingly, the producers let this stand as the last word of the interview.

that is, in the form that inspires so many covers in so many different venues. After Cale, too, there would be the dissemination that makes all the difference in our age of visually adumbrated media by way, yet once again, of the movie *Shrek*. For films, and film music has everything to do with this, have a way of rendering the singers of songs more invisible than ever,[10] and although I emphasized above that Cale's initial "cover" version served as the *Shrek* soundtrack in 2001, the subsequent DVD version of the movie soundtrack does not feature Cale but Rufus Wainwright, who nevertheless follows or at least acoustically "covers" Cale's paradigmatic setting of the song, as does indeed the smash cover version sung by Jeff Buckley (1966–1997), and so on and on.

Hallelujah, as we cited Appleyard as underscoring its subliminal omnipresence, is also featured in numerous other films, along with many television shows, series, and variety shows alike. In addition, Cohen's *Hallelujah* appears in a variety of "background music" options, from athletic performances, including, as already mentioned, the Olympic Games, but also, in the ordinary or quotidian instauration of the Hallelujah effect, in kitchen and living room and garage performances, some of which variety can be seen on YouTube. And this goes along with its scheduling as music for various ceremonies, such as marriages and funerals.

Hallulujah for marriage? Why not? A bit ironic, a bit postmodern, and it could well add a perhaps not entirely useless elegiac note to the event, which would be part of the erotic ambivalence of the song. On the same continuum, *Hallelujah* is also appropriate for a funeral. This versatility is unsurprising if it is also necessary to disentangle it from the point that the musicological sociologist H. Stith Bennett makes in another connection, when he reminds us that we live and breathe a certain disconnect when it comes to popular music. An element of academic *ressentiment* (although the Nietzschean in me does need to recall that this cuts both ways) goes with the territory in pop musicology (as in gender musicology, and so on), but is always par for the course when it comes to pop music and the dismissal that is built into flip terminology (and pop is about as flip as it gets). To quote Bennett here: "Popular music, like all manifestations of popular culture, lives on in spite of recurring criticisms that cast it as somehow inauthentic."[11]

Today, few would find popular music a questionable choice for a funeral service, and thus at the 2012 New York City performance of k.d. lang and her band, the Siss Boom Bang, I found myself sitting next to a woman who turned to me spontaneously in order to explain that she was there for the sake of her plan to ask k.d. lang to sing "live" at her funeral.

Her confidence that the singer herself, just barely older than she was, might be counted upon to be able to fulfill the request, even if she accepted it, gave me

---

[10]   Studio engineers tend to be more invisible, with some major names commanding attention from the cognoscenti, but even the most major of these names are relatively recondite.

[11]   H. Stith Bennett, "Notation and Identity in Contemporary Popular Music," *Popular Music* 3 (1983): 215–34, here 215.

pause. It is more significant to note that such enthusiasm can turn ugly, and fans commonly punish a singer for aging, taking this as a personal attack, a betrayal of the memories of youth. This habit, always real, is perhaps still more dangerous in the age of recorded music video, so that the k.d. lang of living life will always be required to match, à la Nelson's melancholy *Garden Party*, the images concurrently available of the "youthful" k.d. lang, the "middle" k.d. lang, and so on. Here, a reference to the trailblazing efforts of Chavela Vargas are well in order,[12] as indeed might be a remark about the fate of Madonna and Lady Gaga. By contrast, one can argue (I would) that age is more than accepted in Johnny Cash's 2003 video recording of Trent Reznor's *Hurt*, itself a transcendent cover of the song beyond any predictability.[13]

The question of age is one that we will come back to in discussing sexuality and the now routine convention in feminist writing suggesting that sexualization in the case of a woman is a matter of "power." But we do well to ask whose power?[14] And as the above remarks suggest, we do well to ask to what end that power and how long? Hence, when the musicologist Susan McClary turns to a discussion of Madonna—a pop icon who is, like Britney Spears or these days like Lady Gaga, vastly more popular than k.d. lang (a popularity fact not lost on lang when it comes to what matters most in the rightly named pop music industry)—she quotes Madonna's own assertion that it is she herself rather than her managers who control her sexualized appearance, noting indeed that "a puppet she's not."[15] McClary is well aware that she is abandoning the role of the critic as she takes Madonna at her word here, but she reflects that she does so "because there is such a powerful tendency for her agency to be

[12]   See my blog here: <http://bataillessurnietzsche.blogspot.de/2011/08/in-bataille-as-in-sade-as-in-lacan-what.html>.

[13]   Reznor is cited as having misgivings regarding the cover, misgivings that evaporate when he sees the video: "I pop the video in, and wow ... Tears welling, silence, goose-bumps ... Wow. I just lost my girlfriend, because that song isn't mine anymore ... It really made me think about how powerful music is as a medium and art form. I wrote some words and music in my bedroom as a way of staying sane, about a bleak and desperate place I was in, totally isolated and alone that winds up reinterpreted by a music legend from a radically different era/genre and still retains sincerity and meaning—different, but every bit as pure." Trent Reznor, of Nine Inch Nails, in an interview with Thursday's Geoff Rickly in *AP Altpress* 194 (September 2004).

[14]   This is the thesis of Catherine Hakim's *Erotic Capital: The Power of Attraction in the Boardroom and the Bedroom* (New York: Basic Books, 2011), but it develops a Foucauldian claim and has been around for a while in studies of prostitution. See, too, Samantha Holland, *Pole Dancing, Empowerment and Embodiment* (New York: Palgrave Macmillan, 2010), as well as, among other such studies, the collection edited by Jill Nagle, *Whores and Other Feminists* (New York: Routledge, 1997).

[15]   Susan McClary, "Living to Tell: Madonna's Resurrection of the Fleshly," in *Feminine Endings: Music, Gender, and Sexuality* (Minneapolis: University of Minnesota Press, 1991/2002), 148–66, here 149.

cancelled altogether."[16] In her subsequent reflections, McClary qualifies her own concession of authority somewhat further if she leaves it within the sphere of social construction, rather than what Adorno and the Frankfurt School and related Marxist cohort would analyze in terms of the commodity, or what we tend today to speak of as the market. But McClary's point is a critical one in another sense, for music is part of a larger schema in which "mind is defined as masculine and body as feminine in Western culture."[17] In this binary, the "danger" for music, and for musicology in particular, is that music might come to be "perceived as a feminine (or effeminate) enterprise altogether."[18] We will take up this point later, but for now the issue depends on the role of the declaration of love, masculine, feminine in Leonard Cohen's *Hallelujah*.

How one sings Cohen's *Hallelujah*, and indeed the question of *who* sings Cohen's *Hallelujah*, will, as we shall see, make all the difference here. Cohen himself, who writes with some distaste about permanence when it comes to holding or declaring love on the model of a public protest—*I've seen your flag on the marble arch / but love is not a victory march*—would seem to be writing a song about a very finite, that is, a cold and very broken, *Hallelujah*, as he himself adds in his later renderings of his own *Hallelujah*, itself dangerously bordering on a dirge.[19]

Analysts have, of course, already attested here and there to this dirge-like character, and this was also my friend and Fordham colleague Nicole Fermon's response when I wrote to her about this song. In fact, her only response was to condemn the song for its dreariness, recommending other tunes instead. Nicole herself did not quite allude to A.E. Houseman's *Shropshire Lad*, with its "Come, pipe a tune to dance to lads" tonality, but it is obvious that she had a point.

Where some will always choose Bach's cello suites or Beethoven's string quartets for family memorial services, no one less spiritually discerning than the French Jesuit psychoanalyst and anthropologist of everydayness, Michel de

---

[16]   Ibid. This uncritical reception of the authority of the pop musician on matters pop musicological continues when Susan McClary quotes David Lee Roth, whom she characterizes as "macho" and one "rarely accused of being an ardent feminist" (ibid., 150), in his analysis of the reasons for the paucity of female rock stars, noting parental opposition, as if that settled it and as if parents never opposed their sons' choices to do the same. In fairness, as H. Stith Bennett notes, it is indeed very usually parents or relatives who support the initial investment of money, time, and space that are the prerequisites for becoming, in Roth's words here, a "rock star" (ibid., 151) and thus it is a key part of Bennett's *On Becoming a Rock Musician* (Amherst: University of Massachusetts Press, 1980).

[17]   McClary, "Living to Tell," 151.

[18]   Ibid.

[19]   When I wrote to the musicologist Robert Fink, to whose insightful discussion of McClary I will return later, he noted that one of the problems of analyzing Cohen's song, speaking as a musicologist, was its strophic character; thus he—very crucially—noted the difficulty of finding or fixing upon an original beginning. Email to the author, August 2011.

Certeau (1925–86)[20] could opt for Edith Piaf's *Non, je ne regrette rien* at his own memorial service in Paris.[21] Cohen's *Hallelujah*, as sung by Cohen or anyone, could serve, one would suppose, in the same way and for another sensibility.

And many people, in many ways, do seem to regard Cohen's *Hallelujah* as a kind of all-purpose life soundtrack.[22]

Indeed, and this has been more than well analyzed in the literature, by adding Rufus Wainwright's and k.d. lang's versions, one can also lay claim to have a tracked version for a gay lifestyle as well. Although the present work is peripheral to readings of this last kind, I have taken them into account in a related chapter below.

To explore the Hallelujah effect, here I am especially interested in what musicologists could (though it is to the point of some of the disputes and divisions within the discipline of musicology, popular and not) name k.d. lang's *performance practice*, just to the extent that musicologists would speak of it as such (and it has to be noted, especially with reference to k.d. lang's iconic and icon-shattering "performance art" cover of Joanie Sommers's *Johnny Get Angry*,[23] that this has its own and inevitable limitations given 'the genre specificity of musicology, and more due to established and received musicology, even in its newer academic investitures, than it is due to k.d. lang per se).[24] Yet performance practice is not the

---

[20]   Michel de Certeau, *L'Invention du Quotidien. Vol. 1, Arts de Faire* (Paris: Union générale d'éditions 10-18, 1980). In English as *The Practice of Everyday Life*, trans. Steven Rendall (Berkeley: University of California Press, 1984).

[21]   For an account of de Certeau, see François Dosse, *Michel de Certeau: Le marcheur blessé* (Paris: La Découverte, 2002).

[22]   See, again, Bryan Appleyard, "Hallelujah! On Leonard Cohen's Ubersong," *The Sunday Times*, 9 June 2005.

[23]   For a very classical, indeed Schenkerian, analysis, *bien entendu*, to the express discomfort which is always expressed as a censoring move of other scholarly tendencies in pop musicology, see Lori Burns, "'Joanie' Get Angry: k.d. lang's Feminist Revisions," in *Understanding Rock: Essays in Musical Analysis*, ed. John Covach and Graeme M. Boone (New York: Oxford University Press, 1997). See, by contrast, Guy Capuzzo, "Neo-Riemannian Theory and the Analysis of Pop-Rock Music," *Music Theory Spectrum* 26/2 (2004): 177–99; Martha Mockus, "Queer Thoughts on Country Music and k.d. lang," in *Queering the Pitch: The New Gay and Lesbian Musicology*, ed. Philip Brett and Elizabeth Wood (New York: Routledge, 2006); Judith Halberstam, *Female Masculinity* (Durham, NC: Duke University Press, 1998); John M. Sloop, *Disciplining Gender: Rhetorics of Sex Identity in Contemporary US Culture* (Amherst: University of Massachusetts Press, 2005); as well as Keith Negus, *Popular Music in Theory: An Introduction* (Cambridge: Polity Press, 1996), and so on; but see, too, Stella Bruzzi, "Mannish Girl: k.d. lang from Cowpunk to Androgyny," in *Sexing the Groove: Popular Music and Gender*, ed. Sheila Whiteley (London: Routledge, 1997), 191–206.

[24]   Musicology tends to be focused either on classical music or the departure from the same, including new music, a kind of misnomer as new music has more than a century behind it, without for that having become anything like a mainstream affair. For one recent discussion of the American new music scene dating from the second half of the last

same as (although it is surely related to) performance art, a point that should be made in the case of k.d. lang, who originally emphasized precisely performance art at the start of her career, an emphasis that framed her style as a musical artist.[25] This confluence matters: it has been observed that art and pop music belong together, and as the authors of one book on the subject observe, empirically enough, at least with reference to England, "a significant number of British pop musicians from the 1960s to the present were educated and first started performing in art school."[26] For the point here, and it almost goes without saying, is that this same empirical observation applies in k.d. lang's case, as in, ceteris paribus, John Cale's case, and even, still further things being equal, Leonard Cohen. Frith and Horne, the authors of *Art into Pop*, are to be sure not writing about either Cohen or Cale or k.d. lang, but they explain that the reason their theoretical inquiry matters is because art schools as such cross the high culture/mass culture divide, which antagonism they usefully define in terms of the vaunted autonomy of true art. Hence "while high art meaning is derived from the artists themselves—from their intentions, experience and genius—mass cultural meaning lies in its function (to make money/to reproduce the social order)."[27] And considering the difference between the US and the UK, they reflect that it "is certainly arguable that high culture is itself simply now a mass cultural myth, a category created by specific state and market forces, specific middle-brow mass media …"[28]

---

century, see John Adam's retrospective account, which is, in the current context, rather conveniently titled *Hallelujah Junction: Composing an American Life* (New York: Picador, 2009). Contemporary musicology has responded to the broadening context of critiques of Eurocentric focus by turning, while retaining a largely Eurocentric lens, to what it calls (thus the Eurocentric perspective) "ethnomusicology." For a discussion of musicology from a postmodern perspective (invited for an encyclopedia dedicated to the same), along with further references to alternative approaches, see Babette Babich, "Postmodern Musicology," in *Routledge Encyclopedia of Postmodernism*, ed. Victor E. Taylor and Charles Winquist (London: Routledge, 2001), 2nd edn, 153–9. See, too, for a more established account and more generally, and in addition to Rosen's aptly titled classical account, Joseph Kerman, *Musicology* (London: Fontana, 1985); Nicholas Cook, *Music: A Very Short Introduction* (Oxford: Oxford University Press, 1998). In the current context, but also relevant to any discussion of musicology, see Susan McClary, *Feminine Endings*, as well as McClary and Robert Walser's "Start Making Sense! Musicology Wrestles with Rock," included in the outstanding collection *On Record: Rock, Pop and the Written Word*, ed. Simon Frith and Andrew Goodwin (London: Routledge, 1990), 277–92.

[25] However, Bennett, in his *On Becoming a Rock Musician*, also emphasizes the point here in a term that he coins as "recording consciousness," of the importance of the intersection of practice and performance practice, that has become influential as it is included in his contribution, "The Realities of Practice," in Frith and Goodwin, eds, *On Record*, 185–200.

[26] Simon Frith and Howard Horne, *Art into Pop* (New York: Methuen, 1987), 1.

[27] Ibid., 2.

[28] Ibid., 3.

For her part, k.d. lang continues to exemplify performance art, even to the extent that some critics argue that her own music video for her singular hit, *Constant Craving*, almost undoes its own hit status: prison-stripe pajamas and all. This self-undoing, to the extent that this is the case (and take this with a grain of salt as we are talking about a "hit" in any case) is no doubt as a direct result of staging a backstage, indeed a back-country, and not merely summer-stock, but Indian summer-stock, touring show *and* postmodern rendering of Samuel Beckett's *Waiting for Godot*, all of it uncannily framed, and shot to boot in black and white. Of course.[29] And whether one prefers the style or setting of one music video or another, what is essential to note is that the role of practice, together with the repetition of a fixed or iconic recording, informs what the same Bennett we have already cited calls "recording consciousness," and which "recording consciousness" once again should be heard in terms of Adorno's analysis of the culture industry in general and the physiognomy of radio in particular.[30]

Bennett goes beyond both Simmel and Adorno to argue that such "consciousness" as it applies to both producers and consumers—or "reproducers," to use Adorno's prescient terminology—is an inevitable concomitant of "a society which is literally wired for sound."[31] Here, an important but difficult corollary remains to be drawn between Bennett and Adorno, and Jaron Lanier's critique of the technological determinism built into MIDI standards.[32] Significantly, Lanier's

---

[29]   For an esoteric illumination of this point, see Theodore W. Adorno et al., "'Optimistisch zu denken ist kriminell'. Eine Fernsehdiskussion über Samuel Beckett," in *Frankfurter Adorno Blätter*, vol. III, *Theodor W. Adorno Archiv* (Munich: edition text + kritik, 1994), 78–122. For a discussion of the *Constant Craving* video and k.d. lang's interest in performance art, see almost any biography of k.d. lang, especially early ones (and most of them are early), for example, Victoria Starr, *K.D. Lang: All You Get Is Me* (New York: St. Martin's Press, 1994).

[30]   See Theodor Adorno, *The Culture Industry: Selected Essays on Mass Culture* (London: Routledge, 1991), as well as his *Current of Music*. On Adorno and music, see, again, Rose Rosengard Subotnik, *Developing Variations: Style and Ideology in Western Music* (Minneapolis: University of Minnesota Press, 1991), and her *Deconstructive Variations: Music and Reason in Western Society*. Minneapolis: University of Minnesota Press, 1996.

[31]   Bennett, *On Becoming a Rock Musician*, 114.

[32]   See Jaron Lanier, *You are Not a Gadget: A Manifesto* (New York: Vintage, 2011), 7ff. Cf. Geert Lovink's interviews with a certain range of the media/cultural theorists, technicians, and digital artists, in his *Uncanny Networks: Dialogues with the Virtual Intelligentsia* (Cambridge, MA: MIT Press, 2002). Here beyond questions of technological evolution, often overstated, there are the issues of the sound of sound, as well as the challenges already from Adorno's perspective, argued as having been overwhelming, even by the 1940s, of hearing this sound at all. This is the meaning of mediation. Thus, although on an utterly different theme concerning Wilhelm von Humboldt on language (not music), Holger Schmid's *Kunst des Hörens* (Cologne: Böhlau, 1999) invokes media in the very first sentence of the book. That this is a complicated issue for Adorno is clear inasmuch as

reminders of the determinist elements that ineluctably follow from original design decisions on music (and thus regarding what we hear and do not hear) have elicited a considerable amount of annoyance on the part of some of his reviewers.

I note here that, although this cannot be my own task in this book, Leonard Cohen's own performance style or practice ought to be reviewed, together with other performers, rather and metonymically speaking, say in the way that Cohen is usually compared with Dylan, but also in terms of the background singers with whom he always worked—Cohen, too, is always part of a band, even if that band is not foregrounded (and in part k.d. lang's recent band, The Siss Boom Bang, like her earlier band The Reclines, is evidence of that, as is her overt effort to include them in what she does)—but also the musical working efficacy of the French singer Serge Gainsbourg, all along the way to raising the more elusive issue of performance practice per se (elusive because we lack any kind of evidence whatever, apart of course from hearsay) regarding Friedrich Nietzsche's own performance practice as a pianist, together with the further question of the significance of nineteenth-century musical culture for that practice (improvisation) and for his own judgment of the musical culture and language of ancient Greece.

I have noted that the mode of my own exploration is philosophical, inevitably so, not musicological, and the technical terminology for my approach is the same terminology that Adorno found himself compelled to use, namely phenomenology, including its application by means of philological, hermeneutical, and historical reflections, in addition to more properly critical and cultural theoretical concerns.

On this same aesthetic path, however, more informal personal musings on music and practice, including reflections on recorded music and live performance, are essential to the extent that this mode of analysis is explicitly hermeneutic and phenomenological. Thus when Susan McClary draws upon her own scholarly background in musicology, and when Lori Burns brings in nothing less than Schenkerian analysis,[33] both are deploying the framework and methods of their own musicological training. As a philosopher, I draw upon my own formation and it can also seem as if I am writing about my own impressions (a truism for all authors, even if one takes steps to pretend otherwise). For my part, I call upon the reader to include his or her own experience as the vehicle through which, and in terms of which, we know the things of this world and indeed the things with which we have to do in this analysis. Thus wherever I say "I," the reader will both know that I am speaking only from one point of view, and that I mean this—this is the

---

writing is already mediation: "… musical works exist only as mediated through writing." Theodor Adorno, *Towards a Theory of Musical Reproduction: Notes, a Draft, and Two Schemata*, trans. Wieland Hoban (London: Polity, 2006), 179.

[33] See, for an overview, Adam Krims, "What Does it Mean to Analyse Popular Music," *Music Analysis* 22/i and ii (2003): 181–209. Other musicologists, such as Robert Walser, have expressed qualified reservations.

phenomenological move—as a viewpoint which very explicitly invites readers to confirm their own perspective, be it shared *or* opposed.[34]

Here, the reader has a good deal of his or her own experience to draw upon, and hence I discuss social networking as it has come to inform contemporary musical experience. I offer an exploration of the effects of virtual connectivity, focusing in particular on Facebook, but controversially including the author's own observations regarding society's generic objectification of women by contrast, but of course, regarding men, as men are those members of society who usually do the objectifying. And to this end, I have already invoked Adorno among other theorists of music and media per se, including the question of the role of technology.

On the *Hallelujah Chorus* as Analytic Philosophy Sings it to the Sciences (or From the Secret Chord to the Death of Philosophy)

There are numerous additional instantiations of what I am here calling the Hallelujah effect, and not just in the Bible and the hymns inspired by the Hallel psalms, but and most particularly, at least for this author, the Handel chorus of the same name in the *Messiah* oratorio. I recall bugging close acquaintances and most of my siblings over the years (I note that annoyances of this kind tend to take up residence in one's brain, which is why, so I think, they annoy), by singing Handel's *Hallelujah Chorus* which, in order to express a certain underwhelming sentiment, I was fond of varying both verbally and on a downbeat as: *"How exciting"*—a transposition which works, as one can hear for oneself (though I am not recommending this practice) by substituting a chorus of *How exciting* just where Handel has *Hallelujah* ...[35] On the other hand, it is to the point that one can always do this with Western music, but not so with the music of ancient Greece. This last is Nietzsche's elusive point concerning the ictus (pitch and *not* stress), as he rightly regarded this as his discovery of the spirit of music in the text itself.[36] In other words, in Western musical convention and practice, different words can be set to the same musical setting: thus, for instance, the American informal anthem, *My Country 'Tis of Thee*, the English *God Save the Queen*, and *Rufst Du mein Vaterland*, that is, the former Swiss national anthem (also sung in French as *O monts indépendants*, as well as Italian and, of course, because this is Switzerland, Romansch) are instantiations of just this kind of lyric variability.

---

[34]   Thus it is useful to recall that Nietzsche reverses the strategy, writing that anywhere he reads the name Wagner, the reader should substitute Nietzsche's own name: "in all decidedly psychological passages of this book the reader may simply read my name, or the name 'Zarathustra' wherever the text contains the name 'Wagner'" (EH, *Wagner in Bayreuth*).

[35]   In German, though this only works with a certain levity, one can convey the same understatement (more explicitly because that is how that works in German) with *wie entsetzlich* ...

[36]   This is the point of the previous range of footnotes above.

The classical "Hallelujah" is also a referent for the philosopher P.M.S. Hacker, who invokes it to make a point with which I myself have a great deal of sympathy (I make a similar point more critically and generically with regard to *analytic* philosophy as such).[37]

At the same time, Hacker is himself an analytic philosopher and there are many other differences, beyond our common fondness for taking Handel's *Hallelujah* illustratively[38] and a shared sense of the philosophical importance of critique, qua rigorously conceived.[39]

Nevertheless, Hacker argues that there "are far too many philosophers who take their task to be to sing the *Hallelujah Chorus* to the sciences. It seems to me we should be serious, and one hopes helpful, conceptual critics of the sciences."[40]

Hacker's reference to mainstream, that is, "analytic," philosophers singing "Handel's *Hallelujah Chorus* to the sciences" underscores the affirmative, uncritical tonality of analytic philosophy vis-à-vis the sciences, and this tonality continues even when analytic philosophers distinguish their adulation from what they call scientism.[41] By contrast, Cohen's *Hallelujah* is anything but uncritical,

---

[37] Here, and when used to characterize philosophy, the term "analytic" refers to a *style* of philosophizing where the alternative genre of philosophy, namely "continental philosophy," similarly refers not to a locus but and only to a specific style or, better said, to a disparate array of styles of "doing" philosophy. Where my own philosophic position is uncompromising, I have argued that it is essential to take a critical perspective on science precisely or for the sake of a philosophy of science worthy of the name. See Babette Babich, "Towards a Critical Philosophy of Science: Continental Beginnings and Bugbears, Whigs and Waterbears," *International Journal of the Philosophy of Science* 24/4 (December 2010): 343–91.

[38] Perhaps Hacker's referent is not Handel, although I do assume that it is, and there are other possibilities, such as, for instance, though this is culturally unlikely, *The Battle Hymn of the Republic*, and so on. But Handel's chorus is likely what is meant. This is why it works as the soundtrack for the fertilization of an egg in the fertility clinic in the animated video short, with a few nods to Michelangelo and the odd Flemish master, by Nina Paley, *Fertco*, 2001.

[39] In addition to writing on Wittgenstein, Hacker has also co-authored a book (or two) on the topic of analytic philosophy and cognitive science (and the advantages and limitations of that same conjunction). See M.R. Bennett and P.M.S. Hacker, *Philosophical Foundations of Neuroscience* (Oxford: Wiley-Blackwell, 2003), as well as M.R. Bennett and P.M.S. Hacker, *History of Cognitive Neuroscience* (Oxford: Wiley-Blackwell, 2008).

[40] P.M.S. Hacker, "Hacker's Challenge," Interview with James Garvey, *TPM, The Philosopher's Magazine* 51 (25 October 2010).

[41] See, for a discussion of this tendency, some of my discussions of the infamous Sokal hoax, which succeeded on Sokal's part precisely owing to this mainstream adulation, and which hoax was never seriously engaged, again owing to the same adulation. Most discussions of Sokal's hoax simply attack the humanities—rather as Sokal had done. And the discipline of science studies, in history and sociology, which had until then had some critical elements, very quickly jettisoned those components in the wake of the media efficacy of the hoax. To my knowledge, my own discussion is the only one to call attention

and critics, especially younger ones, are fond of using the word irony to describe it. Indeed, Cohen's *Hallelujah* sings the highest word of praise that also happens to seem to take itself back in the process, but which also ultimately withholds nothing at all. Thus any reproach directed at Cohen only recedes as Cohen's broken *Hallelujah* recedes into impotence—and blessing.

This is what Nietzsche called *amor fati*, and it is an unconditional affirmation. Such an affirmation *only* matters in hard times, in tribulation, challenge, as illuminated classically by the Book of Job. The shattered Hallelujah, like it or not, approbative of the divine or not, is the only proof of faith, and it only works for those whose faith begins where it ends.

It is the Hallelujah that moves into one's head and stays there for the duration, and that will be, and this is significant, for high and dark times alike, and Cohen himself is careful to emphasize the dark times. Following the email correspondence with Ernest McClain that inspired this book,[42] McClain himself was moved in his subsequent email, sent in another context, to recall that a particular way to express one's own limitations *and* achievements was already at work in the old hobo song, *Hallelujah, I'm a Bum.*

Like Julia Wad Howe's 1861 *Battle Hymn of the Republic* (with its connection to the abolitionists' song, *John Brown's Body*), *Hallelujah, I'm a Bum* is a traditional song with murky roots. It seems to have its earliest publication in association with

---

to these issues. Without exception, and this is rare in the academy, other discussions tend to lionize Sokal. An editorially censored version of my essay (which I recall as having been obscenely difficult to get published in the first place—even Robert Scharff, editor of the then-titled *Man and World*, refused it, as did Robert Crease, although I originally presented it at his invitation at a 1996 conference on hermeneutics and the history of science at SUNY Stony Brook), appears as "Physics vs. *Social Text*: The Anatomy of a Hoax," *Telos* 107 (Spring 1996): 45–61, and again, and thanks to the graciousness of the editor, Jeffrey Perl, with its original points intact, as "The Hermeneutics of a Hoax: On the Mismatch of Physics and Cultural Criticism," *Common Knowledge* 6/2 (September 1997): 23–33. And see too, again, "Towards a Critical Philosophy of Science."

[42]   Ernest McClain is a musicologist with a fair range of esoteric interests and an extraordinary technical competence, both arithmetically and musically. McClain's own interests focus on numerical, numerological analyses of the Bible, musically and algebraically conceived. He has also written two books on the topic with respect to Plato and Indian philosophy, *The Pythagorean Plato: Prelude to the Song Itself* (York Beach, ME: Nicolas Hays, 1978), along with his *The Myth of Invariance: The Origin of the Gods, Mathematics and Music from the Rg Veda to Plato* (York Beach, ME: Nicolas Hays, 1976). The points that he pursues there have recently been "independently" (and of course vastly more "narrowly," which is probably not unrelated to their new palatability) rediscovered by Manchester, UK-based American scholar, Jay Kennedy, who expectedly enough has managed to "overlook" McClain's—and not only McClain's—precedent, a tendency Nietzsche would have characterized as "a lack of philology," scholarship-deficient-scholarship that does not mind reinventing the wheel just where the reinvention permits a new and "approved" cast of characters. See below for further references.

the Industrial Workers of the World, *IWW Industrial Union Bulletin* on 4 April 1908. Importantly for the current context, it also serves as the title of Al Jolson's 1933 movie, *Hallelujah I'm a Bum*, originating in a classically American fashion as a parody of the Salvation Army song, "Revive Us Again."

The song's words bear upon both Cohen's *Hallelujah* and the reading to follow, but the lyrics remain as relevant to the real circumstance of the currently growing army of the unemployed as ever they were:

> O, why don't you work
> Like other men do?
> How in hell can I work
> When there's no work to do?
> *Hallelujah, I'm a bum,*
> *Hallelujah, bum again,*
> *Hallelujah, give us a handout—*
> *To revive us again.*

The next verse includes a response to the still common advice proferred by popular economists, from Suze Orman to the self-help gurus who recommend strategies for "retiring wealthy." The get-rich stratagem for the acquiring of wealth amounts, none-too-mysteriously and seemingly without exception (this is the current political point of what is called "austerity"), to the recommendation that, rather than "using" one's money to live on, one "save" one's money instead. Such recommendations assume that one has money to save. Instead, why not pretend that one has money and why not pretend that one chooses to save it rather than spend it? If money is never to be spent, the outcome would be the same. An imaginary hundred thalers in the bank that one is never spending, to vary Kant's famous example, is no less a sum than a hundred real thalers in the bank that one is never spending. The sum—and note that this permits us to equate the imaginary and the real—is the same. In the case of the bum's lament, one explicitly defers the question of the precise mechanism that such pundits have in mind both for acquiring as well as for *not* spending what resources one has (so as to save it):

> O, why don't you save
> All the money you earn?
> If I did not eat
> I'd have money to burn.
> *Hallelujah ...*

The paradoxes of capital and the integration of capital (that is, the capitalists or the owners) into society are part of the same reflections. Rather than a society of enemies, as Plato analyzed it long ago, one supposes oneself on friendly social terms with the individuals who, inevitably, are one's oppressors. The bosses, that includes those who live from dividends, those who have no idea what things cost because they have "people" to buy things for them, take themselves—these would be politicians, then as now—to speak in the name of the people. The paradox is that the worker, even the out-of-work worker, does not see through the illusion but repeats it, as the song teases here:

> O, I like my boss—
> He's a good friend of mine;
> That's why I'm starving
> Out in the bread-line.
> *Hallelujah* ...

The solutions that we take today, namely what we neutrally and euphemistically name "job creation," or focusing on strategies to reduce unemployment (similarly generically defined), or recommending that one pursue additional or further and higher education to the same end, despite the egregious and increasing costs of the last, are thus uncannily analyzed or countered (already a century ago—assuming we don't choose to go back to Plato for this) in the next verse:

> I can't buy a job,
> For I ain't got the dough,
> So I ride a box-car
> For I'm a hobo.
> *Hallelujah* ...

And the final verse requires a good bit of dialectical and indeed Marxist savvy to unpick, but it is striking for its concision in just this context, just because it underscores both the necessity for alienated labor and the source of capital's profit:

> Whenever I get
> All the money I earn,
> The boss will be broke
> And to work he must turn.
> *Hallelujah* ...

From the Holy Hallelujah to Adorno's Jazz and Cohen's Poems

If Cohen's *Hallelujah* inspires an array of interpretations, the song is itself a result of the Hallelujah effect preceding it, inasmuch as it is indebted to a longer and older religious tradition, the same tradition that inspired both Handel's Hallelujah and the hobo's revivalist Hallelujah, itself in the lineage of *The Battle Hymn of the Republic* which was a songwriter's "cover" or revision of the lyrics (while saving the *Glory Hallelujah* chorus) of the *John Brown Song*. This same religious origination is also patent for Cohen as he emphasizes the difference between the "holy" and the "broken" Hallelujah.

The Hallel psalms, or *Tehillim*, are songs of praise. And we can read the first word of the first of these for which these psalms are named: Hallelujah!

הַלְלוּ-יָהּ :יְשַׁפֵּן יְלָלָה, תָּא-הָוהִי. Hallelujah! Haleli nafshi et YHVH.
Hallelujah! O my soul, praise the Lord.

And as it ends:

הַלְלוּ-יָהּ. Hallelu-jah! Praise you the Lord

The psalm is a comparison, so it goes with psalms and parables, much like the contrastive scheme and cosmological electronic conceit of Terrence Malick's 2011 *Tree of Life*, and like the angrier tension of Archibald MacLeish's 1950s verse-theater, *J.B.* (it is purely coincidence that Malick's film is set in the fantasy time world of the 1950s-cum-1960s, or whatever available props permit in a specific dreamscape, and Malick's film draws as much from St Augustine's "late have I loved thee" as from Hildegard of Bingen as it retells Job). The psalm intones a parallel, the same parallel that Nietzsche later identifies as the heart of a slavely moral faith in his own analyses of slave morality, beginning in *Beyond Good and Evil*, which carried the musical subtitle *Prelude to a Philosophy of the Future*.[43]

> While I live will I praise the LORD: I will sing praises unto my God while I have any being.
> Put not your trust in princes, [nor] in the son of man, in whom [there is] no help.
> His breath goeth forth, he returneth to his earth; in that very day his thoughts perish.
> Happy [is he] that [hath] the God of Jacob for his help, whose hope [is] in the LORD his God:
> Which made heaven, and earth, the sea, and all that therein [is]: which keepeth truth for ever:
> Which executeth judgment for the oppressed: which giveth food to the hungry. The LORD looseth the prisoners (Psalm 146:1–7).

---

[43]   Nietzsche, inaccurately as it turned out, supposed that the text would be understood, but when a readerly public failed to take his point, he simply reprised the same "prelude" in his *On the Genealogy of Morals: A Polemic*. It is regrettable but not surprising, given Nietzsche's luck with his lifelong project of "being understood," as he put it, that despite a perfect and even embarrassing abundance of recent studies dedicated to Nietzsche's *On the Genealogy of Morals*, virtually none of these take up the question of the relationship between this book and its antecedent. It is to his credit that, rather than simply adding *Beyond Good and Evil* to his own study, *Reading the New Nietzsche* (Lexington: Rowman and Littlefield, 2001), David Allison simply left it out, and to date there is no comprehensive study of *Beyond Good and Evil* (this does not mean that there are no books on the topic). I refer to some of the difficulty involved in Babette Babich, "Artisten Metaphysik und Welt-Spiel in Fink and Nietzsche," in *Welt denken. Annäherung an die Kosmologie Eugen Finks*, ed. Cathrin Nielsen and Hans Rainer Sepp (Freiburg im Briesgau: Alber, 2011), 57–88.

The word of praise that is Hallelujah is an affirmation, and affirmation to be affirmation has to be, and must be, *unconditional*, even as it outlines its conditions—this is the emphasis upon the cold and the broken—so the "loosened" prisoner speaks. "Happy [is he] that [hath] the God of Jacob for his help, whose hope [is] in the LORD his God."

Nietzsche's analysis of *ressentiment* is relevant where, as Adorno writes in his stunningly unkind analysis of jazz (and there is almost no critic, no thinker, no philosopher, no musicologist today who has forgiven him for this, whether they have read his essay or not, and most have not),[44] the "subject of weakness integrates itself precisely through its weakness—as if it were actually being rewarded for it—into the collective [here the deity] that made it so weak in the first place."[45]

And in the Oxford additions of the following year, Adorno quotes Walter Benjamin to make his point for him: "in jazz one sees the gestures of people who might appear in a pogrom: clumsy people who are forced to be skillful."[46] Adorno goes on to analyze what the "impotence" of *ressentiment*, that is to say, "the prematurity of weakness," entails: it is that "the subject flees from the system into the system."[47] Uncompromising as Adorno is, his point remains as accurate to the facts as ever, and not less precise when it comes to the music.

Here it should be noted in advance, and as I commit the cardinal sin of quoting Adorno on jazz at all, that the implications of his analysis leave no room for his readers—and these have been mostly men—to tolerate the claims that he makes as these inevitably implicate them. But the point is needed nonetheless, and Adorno observes that jazz syncopations "are not expressions of an accumulated subjective force directing itself against the given until it produces the new law from within itself. They are aimless; they lead nowhere and are arbitrarily revoked by an undialectical, mathematical resolution within the main beats."[48]

In just this way, Adorno goes on to explicate popular music as it is popularly supposed to have every subversive element under the sun, a presupposition that continues in contemporary analysis, and in a manner that could only be alienating to his Anglophone readers (as to his readers in Nazi Germany), and just because his is a point that cuts too close.

Adorno uses the gendered language of musicology to be sure not as is currently done, but in his case with reference to sexuality to make his point, contending here that the jazz syncopations he speaks of "are simply instances of coming too

---

[44]   See, for an almost defense, the reflections on jazz, and especially artistic engagements with jazz in the context of Adorno's putative elitism, in György Markus, "Adorno and Mass Culture: Autonomous Art Against the Culture Industry," *Thesis Eleven* 86 (August 2006): 67–89, esp. 69–72.

[45]   Theodor Adorno, "On Jazz" [1936], in *Night Music: Essays on Music 1928–1962*, trans. Wieland Hoban (Chicago: Seagull Books, 2009), 159.

[46]   Adorno, "On Jazz: Oxford Additions" [1937], in *Night Music*, 165.

[47]   Ibid., 167.

[48]   Ibid., 158.

early, just as fear leads to premature orgasm and impotence expresses itself in early and incomplete orgasm."[49] In other words, invoking the parodic conventions of jazz and "American film grotesques, such as Harold Lloyd or sometimes even Chaplin," Adorno argues, to quote this again, here in context, that the:

> decisive interventional tendency of jazz lies in the fact that this subject of weakness integrates itself precisely through its weakness—as it were actually being rewarded for it—into the collective that made it so weak in the first place, and whose standard it cannot meet in its weakness. Psychologically speaking, jazz squares the circle.[50]

Thus this works on the level of impotence and just because the subject of impotence, the non-subject, cannot set terms. As Adorno explains: "In coming to fear the society's authority and to experience it as the threat of castration ... the fear of impotence—it identifies with the very authority that it should fear, but now suddenly belongs to it too, and is allowed to join in the dance."[51]

It is Adorno's similarly unflinching insistence on the role of music as commodity that makes reading him a necessity, especially where many authors, even those who write on music and consumption, emphasizing as they do the "consuming" or consumer element, often leave out the business of business, the crass fact of commodification. Indeed, this "fact of life," as we often regard this capitalist construct, for it is itself part of the system of exploitation and "production," and the absurdity of excess value as Marx analyzes this,[52] is part of Leonard Cohen's own return to the stage to sing his own songs (in a different sense than Nietzsche intended when he writes in his *Ecce Homo* about a hail of inspiration, corporeal compulsion, that he had no choice).

The meaning of success for an artist is always about popular success, that is to say, financial, commercial success, and artists have always sought this kind of success, even when, perhaps most often when, they seek it on their own terms. Thus k.d. lang always urged and continues to urge her fans to encourage radio stations to play her songs—because all the conventions for success tied to airplay, remain tied to airplay. Increasingly, in fact, her songs are played, but, and this is a corollary of success, and even as her Twitter fans tease her that her songs are on their way to elevator music status, k.d. lang still contends that they are not.

---

[49]   Ibid., 158–9.

[50]   Ibid., 159.

[51]   Ibid., 159–60. As Adorno continues: "The sex appeal of jazz is a command: parry and you can take part too, and the dream thought, as full of contradictions as the reality in which it is dreamed, is: I can only be potent if I allow myself to be emasculated." Ibid., 160.

[52]   For a useful reading, see, again, Michael Chanan's *Musica Practica: The Social Conventions of Western Music from Gregorian Chant to Postmodernism* (London: Verso, 1994).

This is not unique to k.d. lang. The artist, as an artist, has a certain ethos. And part of that ethos is the conviction of misrecognition, a conviction that endures long after this has ceased to be the case. Here, too, we also understand Cohen's enthusiasm for the idea of the poet as such, as he reflected on the idealism of his youthful days at McGill:

> We really wanted to be good writers, good poets, great poets. We really took seriously Shelley when he said that poets are the unacknowledged legislators of the world. An incredibly naïve description of oneself, but we certainly fell for that. We thought it was terribly important, what we were doing. Maybe it was. Who knows?[53]

What Hölderlin says about the role of the poet, what Nietzsche says about the role of the philosopher, hearkens back to the archaic role of song, and so, if the singer claims the same for himself or for herself, poet and writer and songwriter, they are not wrong, even if they may be embarrassed by having to make such a claim. Nietzsche himself famously took the point to the wall in his understanding of its implications. The point is not to influence a group of fans, although that is probably the greatest interest from the point of view of today's singer. And so thinketh SONY or Nonesuch. But the point for the archaic singer—who always gives the laws, as Lycurgus does, as Solon does—is, as Nietzsche also emphasized it in his own oblique late work, to "rule the world." Where Nietzsche's focus was on culture, the music industry has no such limited concern. It's all about money, as we shall see again, and on every level, when we get to Adorno.

---

[53] Leonard Cohen, in *I'm Your Man*, cited in Tim Footman, *Leonard Cohen, Hallelujah: A New Biography* (New Malden, Surrey: Chrome Dreams, 2009), 21.

Chapter 3

On Male Desire and Music: Misogyny, Love, and the Beauty of Men

"becoming a subject"

One cannot talk about Cohen's *Hallelujah* (or indeed many of his other songs) without offering a discussion of sex. Such a discussion includes reflections on love and Eros, but it also includes a particular sensibility with respect to love which is seemingly endemic to popular music, as a reflection of popular culture.

In his biography of Leonard Cohen, which—a nice consonance in the current context—coincidentally enough happens to be subtitled *Hallelujah*, Tim Footman defends Cohen's casual misogyny as auto-affection, self-absorption, auto-reference, and Footman gets this right, although it should also be said that this kind of absorption characterizes many men: "There is also a deep thread of solipsism in his love-lyrics, in that, instead of focusing on the woman he loves, his attention is on the love itself, the transaction with himself as protagonist. It's all about Leonard."[1] Thus it is also all about every Tom, Dick, or Harry (or Tim). In this way, Footman can write off feminist concerns, which he dismisses by using the gendered word "complain" (that is, rather than "critique"), that Cohen "objectifies women"[2] by insisting on Cohen's auto-focus: "To Cohen, the most exciting thing—perhaps even the sexiest thing—about the woman is what she reveals about him, he's the one who's been illuminated."[3]

And indeed, after emphasizing, as Footman does, that Cohen, in effect, backs into poetry as a seductive strategy, these would be so many pick-up lines on Canadian beatnik steroids. Footman cites Cohen's later reminiscences, all canny diffidence, when Cohen later reflects: "I wrote notes to women so as to have them. They began to show them around and soon people started calling it poetry. When it didn't work with women, I appealed to God."[4]

Cohen was born in 1935, like my own father (this helps me locate the date), and thus I can point out that Cohen, in truth, would have been too young to have been a proper part of the beatnik era and so it goes when one misses one generation— he was also a little too old (in fact) for the hippy generation that he nevertheless

---

[1]   Tim Footman, *Leonard Cohen, Hallelujah: A New Biography* (New Malden, Surrey: Chrome Dreams, 2009), 184.

[2]   Ibid.

[3]   Ibid.

[4]   Leonard Cohen, quoted in ibid., 19.

joined on the folk music side. Too old to be "trusted," as one said at the time, Cohen was 33 in 1968.

Nevertheless, let's not forget John Donne's timelessly appealing erotic poetry—writing poetry to pursue women is neither new nor rare. One comes on to the ladies, one seduces them, perhaps one even marries one, but one continues to come on to other women, rinse and repeat, again and again, with the kind of justification that depends upon the absence of any real recognition, any real *relation* to women as such, apart from the collectivity that *women* are from the point of view of many men. At his best, and he seems to have been good at this, Leonard Cohen related to women as sex objects, and that also means that he related to his wife when he married as do most men (and not only Emmanuel Levinas or Martin Heidegger), that is to say, not at all directly but obliquely via his children, and eventually, so it goes with wives and first loves, forgetting them altogether as he moved on.

Thus Footman, in spite of his enthusiasm for what he early on calls Cohen's "testosterone"-induced creativity, expresses some doubts about the autobiographical character of Cohen's *Is This What You Wanted?* as containing "a couplet ('You got old and wrinkled / I stayed seventeen') that is so phenomenally impolite that one presumes it must be ironic; although Cohen's selfish philandering throughout his time with Suzanne suggests he might be playing the lack of gallantry straight."[5] This too is consistent with Cohen's "love" of women as a word for his misogyny, as a word for self-absorption. And for the most part, this kind of fond interest is undone by its own almost immediate and constant distraction (dalliances/dissipation), but this too is only because such an interest in the other sex is only a cover for an interest in oneself. Note that Footman's point is made in Cohen's defence: Cohen is not as misogynistic as one might think because, so goes the argument, it is all only about Cohen himself.

This is not dissimilar to Nietzsche's reflections on women that so inspired Derrida that he turned it over and over again in his *Spurs*. To imagine—that is to say, to pretend—that women constitute the fairer, higher sex is only a way of dis-imagining their humanity (a point that Nietzsche catches very well indeed when it comes to his analysis of Goethe's *Faust*). One projects oneself upon "women" as one's better or higher self, as Nietzsche put it. Cohen reflects upon this very fantastic or imaginary projection:

> I thought that all women were poets. I thought that all women inhabited this highly charged landscape that poetry seemed to arise from. It seemed to be the

---

[5]   Ibid., 96. As Footman goes on to note: "Cohen rarely allowed his relationships to interfere with his pursuit of other women, neither was he averse to commemorating those encounters in his verse: 'I could grow to love / the fucking in New York' he crows in 'Far From the Soil.'" Ibid., 88. Footman does not denounce Cohen, but explains that he was a child of his era, noting that Cohen was nearly 40 in the 1970s and so on. See, further, 186ff.

natural language of women and it seemed to me that if you wanted to address women … you had to do it with this highly charged language.[6]

The distance is the one that Nietzsche emphasizes and the distance covers a certain alienation, fascination, an ambivalence which runs throughout Cohen's *Suzanne* and which, together with high religious tonality, also forms the heart of Cohen's *Hallelujah*.

Here, formally speaking, it is relevant to note that the referent for the second person singular pronoun *you* varies as it functions in these two songs. Thus the *you* that speaks in *Suzanne* is the singer's own self, sung between the singer and the selves of his compatriot listeners who know what he means, *you* meaning you the (male) listener and the singer, you who are and have been subjects of desire, subjects of salvation: thus the you that sings and the you that hears *you have no love to give her* is also the one that Suzanne gets *on her wavelength*, not through what she says, she doesn't really speak, *half crazy* as she is, which is also the reason the you that is Cohen, or the listeners who identify with him, are able to *spend the night beside her*. Cohen's listeners have been there and understand; they also understand how—at least for the space of the moment (but this is how we have Eros in the first place, this is how Penia seduces Poros)—it is already a given *that*, as the song continues, *you've always been her lover*.

And male and female, we all listen with men's ears.

Cohen's *you* in *Suzanne*, as this refers to the singer, himself, taking the perspective of Jesus's touch, of Suzanne's touch, is not the same *you* invoked when we get to his *Hallelujah*: *You don't really care for music, do ya?*

This *you* stings with reproach, this *you* is a target, it is the object. This *you* is not the singer, not the listener; this is an other, one who later undergoes unwanted changes from the *time you let me know*, to the time, now, when, *you never show it to me, do you?* This *you* flies a flag on a marble arch, or wants to, wears its heart on its sleeve, telling others too much, especially when one is already thinking of other conquests. *Love is not a victory march.* This you is female, generically, ineluctably so. This is both the woman who (only) speaks poetry and the woman who "gets old and wrinkled" while Cohen stays "seventeen," and I shall argue that singing the song as a woman, as k.d. lang sings it, as, arguably, only k.d. lang can sing it, makes all the difference for the song. For it is important to add that most of the women who "cover" Cohen's song do not in fact do this: they take the male voice or point of view without taking it for their own; they sing the lines, they do not mean them. But k.d. lang can and, this is her mode, does mean them, as she is singing the song. Every word. By contrast, as I have noted that it matters that k.d. lang can sing Cohen's song, it is significant that when Renée Fleming sings it, she cuts his song down to its barest essentials so that there is almost nothing to mean, keeping the chorus as the key, a literally bitesize, and not incidentally patentable, version

---

[6] Cohen, quoted in ibid., 184.

of a popular song, perfectly timed for short, walk-on song-bites on television shows and YouTube.

The contrast invoked between Fleming's and lang's covers of Cohen's *Hallelujah* is matched, transcendentally so, by Nina Simone's performance of Cohen's *Suzanne* in 1969 as we can hear it and see it. Simone's performance controverts most accounts on every level, testifying to what she does as music as *Gesammtkunstwerk*, as well as to her range as a classically trained performer on the highest level and then some. Simone plays the piano (and how—consummate, easy grace without fanfare, this was *her* instrument) and she dances the center of the music, and she can dance, as by contrast, and quite mysteriously, k.d. lang cannot. The same distinction as Michael Chanan observes below can apply to Maria Callas, as an opera singer one might distinguish from Renée Fleming (Chanan's reference is Dame Joan Sutherland).[7] A queen—as Nina Simone calls herself in another performance sung to the singers Janis Joplin, Billie Holiday, and others—Simone enacts what she sings and thus she transmutes everything about Cohen's song as she sings it.[8] Just as John Cale's classical formation made all the difference with his canonic setting of Cohen's *Hallelujah*, it is not hard to recognize the importance of her very classical formation in what made Nina Simone the extraordinary musician/performer that she was. But as she writes of herself, recalling her experience tutoring and making her living accompanying students, the same experience also engendered a certain conflict and resentment that she unpacks with refreshing honesty. Working as an accompanist, as she put it—and this goes hand in glove with popular songs and taste—seemed to her distinct from "music" per se:

> it was just a job. Because I spent so long accompanying untalented students I came to despise popular songs and I never played them for my own amusement. Why should I when I could be playing Bach or Czerny or Liszt? That was real music and in it I found a happiness I didn't have to share with anybody.[9]

Nina Simone foregrounds the high art, high music tension that Hullot-Kentor emphasizes in his discussion of Adorno as increasingly eclipsed today, yet it is this that made all the difference for her. By no means an accidental bleeding over from her background formation into her performative art, what Nina Simone accomplishes cannot thus be discovered or teased out via an external musicological analysis, here or elsewhere. This is an eternal trajectory to be experienced both for

---

[7]   See the more extended discussion of Nina Simone below.

[8]   See, for a discussion of Simone's own background in historical context, Russell A. Berman, "Sounds Familiar? Nina Simone's Performances of Brecht/Weill Songs," in *Sound Matters: Essays on the Acoustics of German Culture*, ed. Nora M. Alter (Oxford: Berghahn, 2004), 171–82, here 178.

[9]   Nina Simone with Stephen Cleary, *I Put a Spell On You: The Autobiography of Nina Simone* (New York: da capo, 1993), 51; cf., too, 33–4.

the performer in practice and for the audience, that is to say, it is an emergent phenomena, assuming that it comes to presence at all. Thus Simone reflects:

> the only way I could stand playing in the Midtown was make my set as close to classical music as possible without getting fired. This meant I had to include some popular music and I had to sing, which I had never thought of doing. The strange thing was that when I started to do it, to bring the two halves together, I found a pleasure in it almost as deep as the pleasure I got from classical music.[10]

When it comes to her 1969 performance of Cohen's *Suzanne*,[11] Simone does this to the primal beat of a pair of conga and bongo drums, not unlike what Susan McClary characterizes as a "phallic backbeat"[12] in her discussion of Madonna. In this performance, there is a small life-beat; Simone gets inside of the song, turning it and the listener inside out. In this way, "getting"—to use the term Bennett uses—what Bennett also calls with a determinative particle, "the music,"[13] Simone also seems to use all the resources of grace, and spirituality, even, 1950s, 1960s tongue in cheek, the glamor of hypnotism.

Hearing k.d. lang sing *Hallelujah* when I first heard it, looking, as I have freely conceded above, not for k.d. lang herself but for "the" authentic or original version, the one sung by Cohen himself, and thus for the sake of what I supposed to be the song as such or in itself, what I heard in k.d. lang was more than I had imagined I was looking for: it was the song, it was the lyric, the music of Cohen's *Hallelujah*.

What is important to note here, hence the focus on "the secret chord," is that Cohen's *Hallelujah* is a song about its own progression, and as a song about itself, it diagrams the architecture of its music from the start, in the words themselves as a song. It is worth noting that this particular point about music and words in Cohen's singing *would* be remarkable if it were not implausible from the start. It is because Leonard Cohen doesn't quite "sing," as critics like to say, that in fact it is not difficult to understand the words that he sings: his is not that kind of music. At the same time and for the same reason, the chord can go missing. With k.d. lang singing, the words themselves, the song itself, began to make all the difference.

Listening to Cohen himself, it is not difficult to see "through" the song, its artifice (or call it artfulness). Nor are his words advanced by a calculatedly vulgar,

---

[10]   Ibid., 51.

[11]   Ibid., 92.

[12]   Susan McClary, "Living to Tell: Madonna's Resurrection of the Fleshly," in *Feminine Endings: Music, Gender, and Sexuality* (Minneapolis: University of Minnesota Press, 1991/2002), 148–66.

[13]   H. Stith Bennett, *On Becoming a Rock Musician* (Amherst: University of Massachusetts Press, 1980).

overtly and self-consciously masculine tonality (did it matter that Cohen's Toronto compositions would be written in the wake of the contagious success of Serge Gainsbourg's *je vais et je viens*, in the song he sings with Jane Birkin, *Je t'aime, moi non plus*; that is, this is self-indulgence qua religious eroticism.

This did not mean that I would not acknowledge that just this confession would for many be the theological heart of the song itself. It would seem that there is nothing like mentioning the holy dove where the church itself has banned talk of the ghost in favor of the spirit, and doing so in the same context that inspired Gainsbourg.

Voice: k.d. lang, Laurie Anderson, and Madonna

> It amounts to this: just as for the ancients there was an absolute vertical with reference to which the oblique was defined, so there is an absolute human type, the masculine. (Simone de Beauvoir)[14]

k.d. lang's version of Cohen's *Hallelujah* offers an entire world, "cinematic," as she herself says, but one that, as she walks into that world, opens the meaning of the song, the verses, each word. If this surely points to the influence of her work with the German LA-based filmmaker, Percy Adlon, both in his *Salmonberries* and in his direction (in the same year) of lang's music video of Cole Porter's *So in Love*,[15] it is also clear that the video performance that I am talking about in 2005 is just not that kind of filmic video. Nor indeed is her performance of Cohen's *Hallelujah* in any of her live concerts any kind of cinema. Nevertheless, as I am told that Katharine Hepburn says to Humphrey Bogart in *The African Queen*, "nevertheless," k.d. lang *tells*, she *lives*, a story in the song she sings in what she does on stage, and manifestly, this is a filmic consciousness either won from or convergent with the experience of her youthful work with Adlon, as Adlon himself attests. At the same time, this consciousness is also something that belongs to the singer's art and we are back to the extraordinary coherence or integration of the pop culture industry, as Horkheimer and Adorno had emphasized for us at the start.

Hence the experience that k.d. lang had as a young actor with a travelling company in Canada (including pretty much the same critical reservations as followed her performance in *Salmonberries*) also led her to display an extraordinary aptitude for following direction when it came to conviction and

---

[14]   Simone de Beauvoir, *The Second Sex*, trans. H.M. Parshley (New York: Vintage, 1989), xxi.

[15]   For a discussion of this video, particularly attuned to the social context of AIDS, see Lori Burns, "Genre, Gender, and Convention Revisited: k.d. lang's cover of Cole Porter's 'So in Love'," *Repercussions* (Spring/Fall 1999/2000): 299–325.

belief.[16] If she is anything, as Percy Adlon underscored, k.d. lang is a quick study.[17] Thus Eileen Sweeney, a philosophical friend and colleague who specializes in the hermeneutics of medieval philosophy, with a new book on Anselm and another study of Boethius, Abelard, and Alain of Lille,[18] and who also happens to perform regularly in Boston choral groups, responding to a query of mine with regard to k.d. lang's 2005 Juno video, recalled her own memory of being part of a chorus where the music director insisted that they sing it "like they believed it." Her point to me, as I understood her, was that this did make a difference and that, as far she could tell, she had never seen anyone who did that quite to the extent that k.d. lang does.[19] Eileen Sweeney's observation corroborates the analysis on offer below: every word is enunciated, every word comes to life in k.d. lang's performance. And note that I say "performance" here, just because what k.d. lang is doing goes beyond singing, although it is fair to say that one cannot begin to go beyond singing unless one's singing is, as k.d. lang's singing is indeed—and this is the first and last thing critics say about her—in consummate voice.

Where k.d. lang goes in her performance practice is to a veritable embodiment, incorporation, that is, a physical and even physiological *inhabiting* of Cohen's song. Although this is hardly his reference, this is the point that Chanan makes when he contrasts the singer's technique, here as instrument, as this makes the difference for *bel canto*, and the difference again between a singer like the late Dame Joan Sutherland and Maria Callas:

> As a simple description the term *bel canto* is next to useless. Nowadays it is sometimes employed to distinguish a certain style of singing—the pure pitches and nightingale trills of Joan Sutherland, say—and a certain repertoire— Donizetti and Bellini rather than Moussorgsky and Wagner. In this sense, Rossini lamented the loss of *bel canto* as long as the 1850s when ornamented coloratura

---

[16]   Victoria Starr makes this point in her early k.d. lang biography, *K.D. Lang: All You Get Is Me* (New York: St. Martin's Press, 1994).

[17]   Percy Adlon, telephone conversation with the author (Summer, 2011).

[18]   Eileen Sweeney's work thus bears on the present theme. See her *Logic, Theology, and Poetry in Boethius, Abelard, and Alan of Lille: Words in the Absence of Things* (London: Palgrave Macmillan, 2006), as well as her *Anselm of Canterbury and the Desire for the Word* (Washington, DC: Catholic University of America Press, 2012). On Boethius and education, with resonant, musical echoes in Ivan Illich's *In the Vineyard of the Text: A Commentary to Hugh's Didascalicon* (Chicago: University of Chicago Press, 1996), see, too, Anja Heilmann, *Boethius' Musiktheorie und das Quadrivium* (Göttingen: Vandenhoeck & Ruprecht, 2007).

[19]   Referring to the YouTube recording here in question, Professor Eileen Sweeney writes: "I do remember a choral director once telling us as we sang 'I don't believe you' and somehow we all knew what he meant and then we sang like we believed it and it was hugely but somehow inexplicably better. I'm not sure I've ever seen a singer 'believe' it more than KD Lang in that song." Email to the author, Wednesday 8 June 2011, 09:27pm.

began to give way to a more dramatic style of expression in middle-period Verdi. But in the next breath Joan Sutherland is compared to Maria Callas, the first modern singer to revive the classic *bel canto* … It is not just that Callas knew how to act and Sutherland didn't, but that Callas could act with her voice, and *that* is *bel canto*.[20]

Chanan here goes on to analyze both the history of *bel canto* and its revival, but he points to the anatomy of the voice beyond the throat to the body itself and indeed to a particular awareness—and k.d. lang has this awareness—of the microphone, which Chanan expresses in terms of its contradiction from exoteric point of view.[21] Here we can take that further to k.d. lang, and, including the *parlando* describing for Chanan, among others, Nina Simone, as already discussed above, as well as Billie Holiday, Elvis Presley, and Edith Piaf, Chanan writes that this vocal achievement "is unimaginable without the microphone, to which the closest thing without it is singing quietly to oneself."[22]

This same kind of "microphone consciousness," although a full discussion must wait for the chapter on Adorno, if it will be engaged using other terminology, entails that Chanan's point about "singing quietly to oneself" is actually a *practically* musical point in every technical sense. This is what carries the sound in the case of popular music of the kind we hear on the radio, the kind we play in the recording chamber-like sound box that is the automobile when driving (much more than the shower: people sing in the car as musicians sing in the studio, with back-up in their ears, in the sounding space that is the car with one's windows rolled up—with windows rolled down, the point will be to share whatever is playing on the radio, ideally with a custom sound system to match, in order, seemingly, to include as much of the neighborhood airspace as possible). Recording and microphone (and loudspeaker) technology makes all the difference for the kind of vocal music that can be produced and that one can, impossibly in some cases, seek to replicate, and karaoke proves part of this.[23] In his analysis, Chanan moves on to Barthes

---

[20]   Michael Chanan, *Musica Practica: The Social Conventions of Western Music from Gregorian Chant to Postmodernism* (London: Verso, 1994), 190.

[21]   "A whole tradition of popular singing, from crooning to bossa nova," Chanan, *Musica Practica*, 16.

[22]   Ibid., 193. This is related to, is the same, as the now increasingly digital manipulation of voice. A nice testimony to this can be seen in a Berlin newspaper discussion of the Canadian singer, Grimes (Claire Boucher), who is thus characterized as a "genuine 'singer-trackwriter.'" Martin Böttcher, "Wir sind die Roboter. Wie in der Popmusik mit der Stimme experimentiert wird," *Tagesspiegel* (22 May 2012): 21.

[23]   See, on this topic that deserves more than a few books of its own, among other studies, Allan F. Moore, beginning with his "Analizzare il rock: strumenti e finalità," *Musica realtà* 62 (July 2000): 95–118, as well as his *Rock: The Primary Text* (Aldershot: Ashgate, 2001), chapter 2 and part of chapter 4, and his *Song Means: Analysing and Interpreting Recorded Song* (Aldershot: Ashgate, 2012), especially chapters 2–4. See, too, Moore's "U2

and the complex tissue of associations that Barthes brings to bear on his reflection on voice, where Chanan adds significantly in this context that "our relation to a favorite voice is virtually erotic."[24]

Virtually, indeed, when k.d. lang sings *Hallelujah* and drops the note in the middle of the last *Hallelujah* in the first chorus, to the delighted squeals of the audience, and again at the third, you get some of that visceral rush: and this is quite independent of whether one is "attracted" to k.d. lang or not (and judging from dissonant comments on her video on YouTube, the only objections would appear to be from those who find her appearance off-putting, while her fans to be sure blissfully assert the contrary). For her part, to sing the song, especially as it continues, lang goes far beyond the erotic, getting under the listener's skin in the low note that draws one to hear the tones of time, timeless time, almost under the breath of what Matthew Arnold once described as "the eternal note of sadness" in his 1867 *Dover Beach*. With this range, k.d. lang is well able to go further than many singers, especially female singers, and her singing *is* embodiment.[25]

And when it is a matter of the body for k.d. lang, who began, as we have already emphasized, with experimental and performance art, we can recall that she early on describes a picture-book perfect demonstration of "pomo" (N.B. not postmodern) performance art in her 1986 interview with Peter Gzowsky, that had her placing a tambura (nothing less timely an instrument for musical performance at the time) on stage and crawling, as she emphasizes, "very, very, very" slowly— and anyone who has seen k.d. lang's early performances of *Johnny Get Angry*,[26] including her extended collapse at the end, knows already, then, that she would

---

and the Myth of Authenticity in Rock," *Popular Musicology* 3 (1998): 4–24, along with his "Authenticity as Authentication," *Popular Music* 21/2 (May 2002): 209–23.

[24]   Chanan, *Musica Practica*, 193.

[25]   Here, it is worth noting McClain's characterization of k.d. lang's range, despite reservations regarding the complexities of his qualifications: "Lang's great skill is with a wholly ambiguous sexuality and vocal sound that is neither beautiful nor ugly but proves immensely 'serviceable' under her easy, smooth transitions across an abnormally wide range. She is a professional indeed, and I think also the composer is in his own way (he bluntly advertises his technology). Aristotle would have been immensely gratified by this example of the NEED to address the public in its OWN terms. Chromatic interest is nil; the materials are almost exclusively diatonic. The Greek strophe is present (to me) in the singer's effort (4 times over) to create the selfish life yearned for by the soul, answered SOLO four times by the self in its retreat and frustration playing knowingly on public experience of our private failures (experienced singly but wholly banal). The whole song, like the occasions for which it is written, is 'ironic put-on' fake at every moment, yet none-the-less 'universal' for being so. You are dealing with a total public success of this moment and we intellectuals (if we really deserve that title) are helpless in the face of it." McClain, email to the author, Saturday 30 April 2011, 07:02am.

[26]   See, for example, k.d. lang's Much Music Big Ticket Special, 1985: <http://www.youtube.com/watch?v=-D9-61oUaM8>, and her 1990 performance recorded for Channel Four in the UK: <http://www.youtube.com/watch?v=p8OyRj1NkJw&feature=related>.

have been well past, well post-Cage, musically speaking, in a performance that takes "slow" to the limit of nearly everyone else's tolerance, as she also uses utter stops, more silent than John Cage's own, in her popular songs (if only because with digital recordings one can have what amounts to total silence), like the stop or caesura in *Sexuality*.[27] Intriguingly, McClary offers a wonderful analysis of silence, highlighting the extraordinary confluence of performance art with the musical dimension of Laurie Anderson's genuinely epochal, and just as genuinely insufficiently celebrated, 1981 "hit single,"[28] *O Superman*. Yet, despite McClary's astuteness in noting Laurie Anderson, and where McClary does indeed take care to highlight the musical adumbration of Madonna's "sinking" to the stage in her 1986 performance of Patrick Leonard's film or soundtrack composition, *Live To Tell* (the official music video is dedicated to cuts between a very subdued Madonna and scenes from Sean Penn's film, *At Close Range*, and it is significant that McClary does not analyze this last video), McClary does not refer, although she might well have done, to k.d. lang's 1984 *Johnny Get Angry*. A theorist can hardly engage everything, but in this case this omission is conspicuous, and not just given McClary's own emphasis on "subversion." Instead, McClary's point highlights and, as she says, seeks to put in question "the assumptions that guarantee the tonal narratives of the masculine canon since the seventeenth century."[29] Part of the way that McClary does this is to analyze the counterpoint between harmonic key and resolution, the lyrics themselves, and Madonna's singing of the same: "As she sings, her voice repeatedly falls lethargically back to the void of the C-pedal, as though she cannot overcome the gravitational pull it and the meter exert."[30] Again—and shades of the official music video qua Sean Penn vehicle—McClary

---

[27]   "I don't have to say that but this was before garbage bags were in … not for garbage but for clothes. But any way, I've dressed up in garbage bags, and I have this tambura," here lang describes the width of the instrument with her arms raised and outstretched, "which is like the sitar but it's the drone instrument in eastern music," and here lang describes a small circle with her left hand, and, with this pause, continues "and I set it halfway across the stage, and entered from this side of the stage and I literally crawled, like *really slow*, like *pulling* myself across the floor, *like that*," here, with her arms crossed, resting on a grand piano as if it were a college desk, lang mimes the action of pulling herself across the floor, with a certain intensity, "and I crawled across the stage and my friends in the audience and I had, we had pre-determined this, that they would start doing something, I left that up to them, I thought they'd have alarm clocks but they started this primal rhythmatic thing … and I crawled very, very, very slowly across the stage, and I crawled basically past the tambura, and I reached back and I touched it and I crawled off the stage and that was the end of the performance." "Umhmm," said Peter Gzowski, the interviewer. "Umhmm," answered k.d. lang. *Our Stories*, 1986 interview with the late Peter Gzowski on the Canadian Biography Channel.

[28]   See Susan McClary, "This is not a Story My People Tell: Musical Time and Space According to Laurie Anderson," in *Feminine Endings*, 132–47, here 141ff.

[29]   McClary, "Living to Tell," 155.

[30]   Ibid., 159.

observes that: "after this escape-recontainment process has occurred a couple of times, the bottom suddenly drops out. It sounds as though the piece has ended in the foreordained defeat of the victim—she who is offered only the second-position slot in the narrative schema."[31]

The point for McClary is Madonna's subversion of the same "tonal narratives of the masculine canon" already adverted to above, thus McClary observes that: "In her live performance, at this point Madonna sinks to the floor and lies motionless for what seems an interminable length of time."[32] In the live video versions available (from Nice, Turin, and Tokyo), Madonna does not actually fall, but she does sink down or simply walk slowly through what McClary describes as "silence except for the low, lifeless synthesizer drone on D."[33] McClary's analysis makes this work: Madonna's tale is not about a triumph but "tells" what amounts to ambiguity, whereby such subversion looks like defeat but is the ultimate accomplishment of the survivor, in order to be able to tell the tale that, in truth, Madonna never tells, while—thus the achievement—managing nonetheless to have a tale to tell. For McClary, this works in and through the music:

> As she sings "If I ran away, I'd never have the strength," she sings over a bass that moves up and down indecisively between D and A (mediant of F, but dominant of D), suggesting a blurred region in which both keys cohabit. When the opening dilemma returns, she prevents the recontainment gesture of the fifths by anticipating their rhythmic moment of reentry and jumping in to interpose the F-major refrain instead. So long as she manages thus to switch back and forth, she can determine the musical discourse. To settle for an option—either option— is to accept a lie, for it is flexibility in identity rather than unitary definition that permits her to "live to tell." The piece ends not with definitive closure but with a fade. As long as we can hear her, she continues to fluctuate.[34]

It may be because of the sexual, gendered violence or indeed it may be because of the ultimately rather different point that k.d. lang makes, as contrasted with the point that McClary means to make, that McClary can argue that Madonna controls what she does precisely in this song, with its illumination of the conflicts of her relationship with Sean Penn that brought her, indeed, to feel compelled to sing the same song crowned with thorns, on a cross, and after descending from that cross, not by falling to the stage but, head dropped to her breast like a late-Renaissance Christ figure, framed in fire (evoking nothing less than Johnny Cash's paean to the power of erotic lust, *Ring of Fire*) in her 2006 video performance of it. One could argue that the ambiguity was more painful than a subversion for inhabiting both masculine and feminine subjectivities;

---

[31] Ibid., 159.

[32] Ibid., 159–60.

[33] Ibid., 160.

[34] Ibid., 160.

tonally speaking, as McClary argues, Madonna thus again very dialectically "inhabits" or takes up musical residence in "both and thus refuses closure."[35] Once again, just to the extent that McClary rightly contends that it may be argued, without assuming explicit theoretical deliberation on the level of critical or musicological theory on Madonna's part, that "Madonna is as much an expert in the arena of musical signification as de Lauretis is in theoretical discourse. It seems clear that she has grasped the assumptions embedded within these basic musical mechanisms and is audaciously redirecting them."[36]

But just to the extent that this is correct, the orchestration of Madonna's 2006 performance suggests the contrary and takes the song back, as decisively as possible, removing it from its association with Sean Penn, all the way to charges of blasphemy. It is for this reason that I have suggested a contrast with k.d. lang's 1984 *Johnny Get Angry*. Joanie Sommers's song does not tell us that she has "a tale to tell;" much rather she tells it: she tells us, she tells Johnny, and above all, she tells herself: *makes me wish I were dead*. As Lori Burns analyzes it, picking up on McClary, lang plays both male and female roles in the song, noting that in this parodic fashion, lang is able to act as "interpreter throughout her performance by playing both the role of Johnny's girlfriend and the role of Johnny."[37] Burns gives a textual, performative, and musicological interpretation, noting that lang uses syncopation and the out of sync, stops in sum, in order to indicate the shifts in what she does.

Thus lang's performance mimes being struck: she begins one taped performance by thumping herself in the forehead to the music, and again in the course of the song, so that her collapse, and I follow Burns's analysis here, suggests that she has been knocked out by the "anger" that she has at the same time, if one listens to the lyrics, very literally, very explicitly, seemingly been calling for.[38]

A child is being beaten. Ask and you shall receive. Which convention is, of course, almost the script for any scene of domestic violence, including rape. She asked for it. This is and has been implicit in the song itself, beginning with Joanie Sommers's original 1962 recording of Hal David's song.[39]

---

[35]   Ibid., 161.

[36]   Ibid., 161.

[37]   See Lori Burns, "'Joanie' Get Angry: k.d. lang's Feminist Revisions," in *Understanding Rock: Essays in Musical Analysis*, ed. John Covach and Graeme M. Boone (New York: Oxford University Press, 1997), 97.

[38]   Ibid.

[39]   The Joanie in the title of Lori Burns's essay alludes to Joanie Sommers, but also plays on k.d. lang's, at the time fairly marked, androgyny as she performed this piece with her then band, The Reclines. A representative video can be seen in her 1990 performance, again for UK's Channel Four, and her 2 December 1989 *Saturday Night Live* performance, introduced by John Goodman. Note that, as with Madonna, the silent intervals are truncated for the television version.

k.d. lang and the Beauty of Men

If Leonard Cohen is a poet,[40] to emphasize the performance qualities of k.d. lang's rendering means that lang enacts or realizes his song as a singer, she brings his words to life, conducting herself as an instrument: she is the embodiment of the song as he, when he sings, is not. My point here is that the only way that she can do this as a female singer is because by 2005 she is also singing as a lesbian singer. And I say this noting her initial personal resistance to coloring her work by means of underscoring her sexual preference.

To be sure, rather as I appear to be doing now, musical journalists like to characterize her as a lesbian, just as they are also fond of calling her, in what would ordinarily be a sexist characterization, a "chanteuse." But surely this is no more than an ordinary journalistic sobriquet, one might be inclined to reply; surely this merely works by riffing the alliterative play of "Canadian chanteuse" and the bilingual character of Canada to boot, and what else do we hear with Anglophone ears in *Miss Chatelaine*? Yet, and in spite of my personal appreciation for this idea, I cannot concur. Just try to get the same assonance or camp kick by calling lang's fellow Canadian, the singer Celine Dion, a "chanteuse." In the same vein, and this is quite predictably the subject of a good deal of transgender challenge-discourse, critical authors in the tradition of queering theory observe, as does Erik Steinskog, that Jeff Buckley had the seemingly genial prescience to have described "himself as a chanteuse or, even better, 'a male chanteuse with a penis.'"[41] Precisely so, my point here has to do with the great enthusiasm that theorists retain for just this consummate challenge to ordinarily gendered voice assumptions in Buckley's case, a challenge which, despite the existence of good theory, for some time seems not to involve a discussion of k.d. lang. If we want our genders challenged, we seem to prefer to have a male do it for us. That is why the counterpoint for Steinskog's argument as he refers to her is Martha Wainwright, a conspicuously odd choice, although of course tied to the stars of the 2005 music film, *Leonard Cohen: I'm Your Man*, while k.d. lang makes her usual bit appearance only in a footnote; odd, at least, given the title of Steinkog's essay: "Queering Cohen."[42] And this anticipates Frith and Horne's claim, cited and to be further discussed below, that a man can dress as a woman, but a woman cannot quite dress *as* a man. And the reason has everything to do with the supposed and very gendered, queer or not, difference in their sexualities between k.d. lang and Jeff Buckley.

---

[40] This is the point of Steven Lloyd Wilson's paean to Cohen's *Hallelujah*, "The Minor Fall, The Major Lift": <http://www.pajiba.com/miscellaneous/the-minor-fall-the-major-lift.php>.

[41] Erik Steinskog, "Queering Cohen: Cover Versions as Subversions of Identity," in *Play It Again: Cover Songs in Popular Music*, ed. George Plasketes (Farnham, Surrey: Ashgate, 2010), 139–52, here 143.

[42] The locus here would be ibid., 140, note 5.

Lang is able to sing Cohen's *Hallelujah* as she does because, in a very important way, as I argue, she is able to take over *his* voice, his poet's voice, Cohen's voice *as* singer. And that also means that she takes Cohen's part as subject. Where Cohen sings of his desire, he sings as a male with a particular history of desire, a history quite coincidentally not unlike King David's own personal history, including a tale of calamities incurred thereby and through his agency on the part of others, calamities that David's own subjective persona never once takes into account.

And that inattentiveness is the male subject's trick. It is the only trick men need.

I do not see it that way, replies the subject in response to a "complaint," hearing nothing of what the other says, content–wise, but hearing only agita, tone, mood.[43] We are back to feminist readings of *Johnny Get Angry* when it comes to communication between men and women.[44] Affectively speaking, that is. Thus *Johnny Get Angry* tells a woman's story and the convolutions that follow from adopting, as she adopts, a male point of view: "one beats the dog one likes best," as Nietzsche characterizes the self-justification of slave consciousness,[45] or indeed as he originally put the point more directly in his earlier *Beyond Good and Evil*, quoting here as he does "From old Florentine novels—moreover, from life: *Buona femmina e mala femmina vuol bastone.*—Sacchetti, Nov. 86."[46]

We reject the claim that both good and bad women *need* beating, and perhaps we had better do so as so many feminist readings have had so much trouble already with the Zarathustra quote: "You go to women, don't forget the whip!" as it is (the majority reading has decided, as Footman argues away Cohen's misogyny, that it is really only about Cohen, as if that were not the misogynistic point to begin with). But Nietzsche's insight turns on his consequent observation in the next aphorism, as he reflects: "To seduce one's neighbor to a favourable belief, and afterwards to believe implicitly in this same neighborly conviction—who can perform this magician's trick as well as women can?"[47]

Only the male *subject*'s consciousness matters to the subject and not the other, save that the other's consciousness coincides with one's own consciousness, which means of course that one desires the consciousness of the other as the reflected or amplified consciousness of one's own desire. It is, as a generation of French Hegelians could have and indeed have already told us, *mirrors* all the way down. Thus the point of desire is the desire of the consciousness of the other in accord with, attuned to, that is, matching and not other than, the consciousness of the subject.

---

[43]   The writers of *The Rules* emphasize that one can counter this by suppressing any tendency in this direction. Harmony in the family is the result, the cost, as ever, borne by the female psyche. Repress, repress, repress.

[44]   The best of these, as already cited above, is again Burns, "'Joanie' Get Angry."

[45]   Nietzsche, *On the Genealogy of Morals* GM I: 14; Nietzsche, KSA, vol. 5.

[46]   Nietzsche, BGE, §147; Nietzsche, KSA, vol. 5.

[47]   Nietzsche, BGE, §148; Nietzsche, KSA, vol. 5.

As Cohen desires women and also, and this is part of this, as Cohen rebukes the object of desire for any resistance to the trajectory or destining of what he calls love (not only *but you don't really care for music do ya*, but *love is not a victory march*), so too k.d. lang. And beyond the complex question of k.d. lang's subjectivity, it should be noted that most women have no problem at all assuming the male point of view, both in themselves and others. One judges as men do, one sees oneself just as men and as other women do. And this male point of view is the view for which one dresses, even where, as Simone de Beauvoir notes, only women tend to notice fashion matters, sometimes quite cruelly—think of fashion magazine critics; think, as k.d. lang certainly has thought, of Joan Rivers's critical Hollywood eye.

And women do see women as attractive, admiring them, emulating them. What else is depicted on the cover and what else is on the pages of *Vanity Fair*, or even Oprah Winfrey's magazine *O*? Women (in Oprah's case, Oprah) are the focus of women's magazines—think of *Elle* and *Vogue*, but also *Redbook* and so on. For me, here, as an author (and phenomenologically it is important to admit this), I presuppose something in this analysis that I myself do not because I cannot fully embrace in my own person. What I can observe, however, and I have analyzed this elsewhere, is that, by contrast, most women very manifestly can.[48] Thus I am stretching things as an author, but I think it important to emphasize that most women admire women, bodily, physically, and they say that they do, and I am not speaking of women as role models or sex objects explicitly, but certainly aesthetically, certainly as objects of attraction. Most women have a version of Cohen's idealized ideal of women, not as "poets," but certainly as the beautiful sex. In the same way, speaking in terms of the object of desire, whatever her original claims to androgyny, k.d. lang identifies herself these days and for some time now as lesbian.

It is not uncommon to find that women do not think much of men's appearance, in both senses of not "thinking much of" or about. This is a matter of valorization, whereas women are instead very concerned about their own looks and about the looks of other women. Hence, without pausing to inspect their male partner, to note his appeal or to ask themselves whether he looks attractive or whether a certain pair of trousers makes him look fat, women ask their partner to adopt the position of the universal subject, to speak for everyone in giving his judgment qua subject on their own looks. Does this dress, these jeans—so goes the joke that is, of course, vis-à-vis woman, no joke at all—"make" me look fat?

This inattention to their own looks is to the decided advantage of men qua subject and thus not as object for woman (that is, not there for women's desire). Not being the focus of female desire allows one to be desired in fact, in essence, *just* as one is, and thus we have the new canon of the male movie star, featuring the kind of nebbish look that always was (think of Adorno's examples of Harold Lloyd and Charlie Chaplin, and we can go ahead and add all the Marx brothers to

---

[48] See Babette Babich, "Great Men, Little Black Dresses, and the Virtues of Keeping One's Feet on the Ground," *MP: An Online Feminist Journal* 3/1 (August 2010): 57–78.

the mix), but is today still more, dominant in film (especially Woody Allen, but also Adam Sandler, Chris Black, and a spate of new geeks whose names I do not wish to remember). In other words: geek- and nerd-dom is ok, provided you are male; not so much if you are not.

In this sense, pop culture has no problem with a series like the *L-Word*, just as men are perfectly happy to watch girl-on-girl porn; and supposedly heterosexual porn, by which I mean porn that is supposedly meant to appeal to women as well as men, tends, being as it is in truth mostly for men, to feature men who are often stunningly unattractive, a casting characteristic that does not describe pornography designed for male homosexual, that is, gay erotic, "consumption."

Thus, and sheerly contingently, I have a different sensibility. It is this sensibility with regard to men that brings me to raise different questions, although it also means that that neither the ethos nor the Eros of k.d. lang's sexuality turns out to be mine (and at the same time, I admire this life-choice and am convinced that it is by far the better course for women in the current world).

What I am thus noting here as a key difference vis-à-vis k.d. lang's performance practice, as an artist and singing Cohen's song as she does, is that she shares—she does not merely channel—Cohen's subjectivity when she sings *her beauty and the moonlight*.

There is a personal point here for me as, throughout my erotic life, I have been one of those rare (they really are rare) women who objectively likes men *erotically* as objects—which is not at all to say *personally*, that is, as men actually are, in fact and in the world, in their ways and in terms of their character, as this way of being is often not so very nice at all, especially when it comes to the way that they treat the women in their lives, from their mothers to the women they love, but much rather and very exactly in terms of their beauty, in terms of the male body as such.

I include here as an example that cannot really work as such an example, and not just because it is manifestly a gay icon, Jean Hyppolyte Flandrin's 1836 *Young Man Seated at the Sea's Edge*. Apart from the homoerotic aesthetic, the subject here is also very much as he is titled to be: seated in himself. He does not offer himself to the gaze; nothing sexual, nothing of erotic interest, is revealed: the pose is the quintessence of modesty. This self-seclusion does make of this gestalt a non-risqué image, and when Friedrich Nietzsche visits Messina, he writes of happiness as he does to his composer friend, Heinrich Köselitz (whom he calls Peter Gast), referring to "the divine beauties" that he sees there, beauties that to be sure also inspired, in Flandrin's mode, a certain style of homoerotica, namely Wilhelm van Gloeden's *Caino* series. Some scholars have taken this to be evidence of Nietzsche's homosexuality, if elsewhere I argue that such arguments are unpersuasive to the extent that Nietzsche still and always protests too much about women (and about their unfairness), and withal and just because of the excess of attention he pays women, tends to offer his misogynistic judgments in a rather more heterosexual than homosexual modality, although it is also true that misogyny tends to cross sexual preference all too smoothly.

Figure 3.1   Jean Hyppolyte Flandrin, *Jeune Homme Assis au Bord de la Mer,*
              1836. Photo: Erich Lessing/ArtResource, NY.

Male erotica, like all erotica, is for men: it involves a certain availability
to the viewer's gaze, and those of van Gloeden's images that happen not to be
modeled on Flandrin give one all the full frontal nudity one might wish, with
figures of naked young men that match similar erotic photographs of females
nudes of the time. The poses are no different because the viewers are the same,
male, in one case, with homoerotic interests or else, in the case of van Gloeden's
photographs—and he photographed both young men and young women—
heteroerotic interests.

Like the majority of van Gloeden's male nudes, his female nudes (and
everyone else's female nudes, all the way up to *Playboy* and any other magazine or
film featuring female nudity) turn to and literally "invite" the gaze of the viewer,
lacking both shame or sense of self. It is clear that these women "want" to be
seen, they are there to be seen, they exist for the viewer, for the observer, and this
observer is typically assumed to be male—Cindy Sherman's art has made much of
this as objectly as possible, as have other, more theoretical analyses.

In his beautiful *Only a Promise of Happiness: The Place of Beauty in a
World of Art*, Alexander Nehamas points to William Adolphe Bouguereau's
1884 *Seated Bather* as a conventional but far more sensual vision of woman, in

Figure 3.2   Wilhelm van Gloeden, *Caino*, 1902. Photo: Public domain

a picture that Nehamas clarifies, with a gentle apology, as "primarily a painting for men,"[49] explaining that the "open picture plane and spatial recession of Bouguereau's picture issue an invitation to the viewer and encourage him ... to enjoy the radiant sensuality of the young woman's flesh, soft and bright against the dark and craggy background."[50]

---

[49]   Alexander Nehamas, *Only a Promise of Happiness: The Place of Beauty in a World of Art* (Princeton: Princeton University Press, 2007), 25. I take this discussion somewhat further in Babette Babich, "The Aesthetics of the Between: Space and Beauty," in *Jeff Koons: The Painter and The Sculptor*, ed. Vinzenz Brinkmann, Matthias Ulrich, and Joachim Pissarro (Frankfurt: Schirn Kunsthalle Frankfurt, 2012), 58–69.

[50]   Nehamas, *Only a Promise of Happiness*, 25.

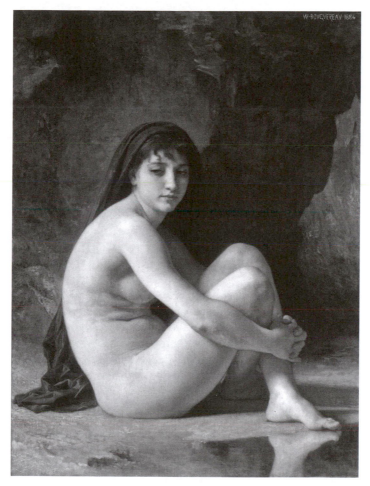

Figure 3.3   William Adolphe Bouguereau, *Baigneuse Accroupie*, 1884. Sterling and Francine Clark Art Institute.

And just to speak personally here, and because such things are matters of exactly personal inclination, I like men fairly in the way, as I would suppose—and there are obvious limitations to this claim, and so offended are we at the idea of women's desire with men as object that some will immediately declare that such talk can only *prove* the conflicts of my sexual orientation—that a homosexual man might say that he likes men, *aesthetically-erotically* speaking. Certainly, it is for the sake of the latter (almost in every case as an ideal rather than a reality) that for most of my life, I have put up with the men that I have loved. I mourn the loss of the first boy I ever loved all because of his lost beauty. He died young, everything inconsummate, pure potential, unsullied and unsulliable perfection: all John Keats's destiny and undying power for my soul.

Conversely, as noted above, I think that it is important to qualify what I write here to the extent that, rather than female beauty—as both men and women and k.d. lang love female beauty—I am myself an enthusiast of male beauty. I like male beauty—face, body, every erotic aspect.[51] And this is not exactly the usual conventionality, although men can certainly—this is Foucault's point about the ancients in his *History of Sexuality*—find both beautiful women and pretty boys attractive. Hence, Sheila Whitely begins her discussion of "the dynamics of desire" in popular music by quoting the Christian Slater character in the 1993 film *True Romance*: "Man, Elvis looked good. Yeah, I ain't no fag, but Elvis, he was prettier than most women, most women."[52] Women, by contrast, are usually not able to claim this versatility and it is certainly not conceded. Hence, as already pointed out above, Frith and Horne are able to argue that the image of Patti Smith in the *Horses* album, produced by John Cale, cannot escape the male gaze, and exactly not the way a man can dress up as a woman and "create a thrill of unease from the obvious misconnection but the question will still be asked: what is his sexual taste *really*?"[53] Thus they are able to contend that in fact "women can't dress up as men, only wear men's clothing; the *Horses* sleeve tells us nothing about Patti Smith, its messages concern her clothes, the imagery itself."[54] Here there is an obvious parallel to the cover (and the sensibility) of k.d. lang's album *Drag*, in which she borrows both Tony Bennett-style pinstripes and the smolder of Elvis's gaze, an Elvis "look" that she had, when younger, spent some time making her own. What is significant is that exactly this claim may not be made for her video *Sexuality*, with its light art schematism and not less with its parodic images in contrast with its tone.

In making such claims about gender, I am not using the canon of established gender theorists such as Judith Butler and others, useful as these readings are.

---

[51]   My colleague, the New York actor, playwright, and director, Matthew Maguire, saw an early video lecture of mine on this topic and wrote to me of my "bravery" in speaking so frankly: <http://digital.library.fordham.edu/cdm4/item_viewer.php?CISOROOT=/VIDEO&CISOPTR=214&CISOBOX=1&REC=1>. Sherry Turkle recommended that I suppress the personal, though she surely meant this more broadly, perhaps because this book does not follow the social science standard of interview excerpts. And this too is part of the point. Women are not to speak from their own point of view unless they speak as convention would have them speak. I cite Elfriede Jelinek on just this point (just because she has already taken quite a bit of heat for it) in my essay, "Great Men, Little Black Dresses, and the Virtues of Keeping One's Feet on the Ground."

[52]   Sheila Whitely, "Popular Music and the Dynamics of Desire," in *Queering the Popular Pitch*, ed. Sheila Whitely and Jennifer Rycenga (New York: Routledge, 2006), 249–62, here 249.

[53]   Simon Frith and Howard Horne, *Art into Pop* (New York: Methuen, 1987), 155.

[54]   Frith and Horne, *Art into Pop*, 155. Whitely challenges this on the surface, while ultimately conceding the point that Frith and Home make, at least when it comes to ambiguity, when characterizing Smith "as lesbian, androgyne, martyr, priestess, and female God," Whitely, "Popular Music and the Dynamics of Desire," 257.

Thus, although I make a contribution here to gender theory, as I have sought to do without much resonance in the literature for many years, I am also attempting to say something other than what is conventionally argued (and this is doubtless the reason for that lack of resonance). Thus as a long-time academic, and one who also thinks about the particular politics of academic writing and citation,[55] I know that the gender theorists themselves will have reservations, if they are even able to read this without insisting on their own terms and indeed on their own conclusions. But this is endemic to any paradigm. Nor am I saying that their conclusions are not valuable, not at all, but I am trying to add just another perspective to the canon.

It is relevant to this point, and to the androgyny or ambivalence that k.d. lang's youthful persona sought to cultivate, a certain androgynous or masculine aesthetic, a boyish beauty, and she did so quite explicitly, to the extent of mixing cowboy shirts with cowgirl skirts, and however much that confounded her broader musical audience, k.d. lang has also and to this day never made a secret of the fact that she is sexually attracted to men. Indeed, k.d. lang *still* says so, but what is at issue in every case is and remains her own looks, never her subjectivity, never her desire, never what she says, and she is aware of this. Hence, in an interview given in 2008, she notes in a matter-of-fact fashion what is also in evidence and not always kindly in the comments made on her 2005 video performance on YouTube: "I am mistaken for a man every day of my life." That this has to be said is important because androgyny seems to follow a Foucault script: a beautiful boy—so the above-mentioned Christian Slater film character muses vis-à-vis Elvis—or—so the enthusiasm for the androgyne goes—a boyish girl, but not a woman regularly mistaken for a man. And of course, inasmuch as k.d. lang has indeed been compared to Elvis throughout her life, we should certainly consider the ambiguity relevant.

That k.d. lang's audience, her press, indeed academics writing about her in gender and queer studies, overlook her statements in this regard, desiring women and desiring men, is part of the point here.[56] But it is not the whole of it, for what I am suggesting is that the difficulty with being attracted to men sexually is that that attraction can only find a fulfillment, apart from being ignored or violently turned around (and this is not the same thing as a consummation) or undercut (as it is consistently ignored or simply smiled at in the case of k.d. lang's sexuality), on terms other than those of the female subject (desiring the male as object of desire).

The subject in question is, however, labile enough, provided one (male or female) takes the male point of view, and this is at work in the repeatedly quoted

---

[55] See, for one statement here, my interview published as "An Impoverishment of Philosophy," *Purlieu* 1/3, special edition: *Philosophy and the University*, ed. Dennis Erwin and Matt Story (2011): 37–71.

[56] Armchair psychoanalysis, like any psychoanalysis, is precisely about ignoring what is said to project one's own better-knowing interpretation instead. All the better if it comes from the mouth—this is the proof of a successful analysis, according to the terms of the profession, of the subject of analysis.

retort attributed to lang in reply to a reporter's question regarding the Herb Ritts photograph of her in pinstriped vest and trousers, lathered for a shave, with Cindy Crawford in a swimsuit, for the August 1993 cover of *Vanity Fair*. As Fiona Sturges reminds us in a recent interview, when "asked by a male journalist what was going through her mind at the time, lang replied: 'Pretty much what would have been going through yours in the same circumstance, I imagine.'"[57]

k.d. lang tells us that she *relates* to Crawford erotically—and we have already seen that there is plenty of room for such a relation of desire in our culture. Lesbian desire is exactly non-subversive to the extent that the erotic object is the same as it is in the dominant heterosexual culture, and that is female. What is genuinely subversive is for a woman to relate to a man in *this* fashion, as erotic object. That is taboo, really taboo in our culture, meaning that transgression is impossible for us: it is not done. To echo Jacques Lacan: it is *impossible*.

To say that it is impossible in Lacan's sense does not mean that it never finds expression; we already saw that in McClary's analysis of Madonna's *Live to Tell*. This point may be made even stronger if coupled with an analysis that McClary does not offer us of the music video of the same tale, foregrounding the young Sean Penn. Thus one can reflect ruefully, as Madonna seemingly does, on being given over to male desire, use, abuse, and so on, learning one's *lesson well*, as she writes, or else as Joan Baez does when she recollects in her *Diamonds and Rust*:

And there you stayed,
Temporarily lost at sea
The Madonna was yours for free;
Yes, the girl on the half-shell would keep you unharmed

Thus in Baez's *Diamonds and Rust*, as in Madonna's *Live to Tell*, the singer recalls her life as if in a dream; one sees the scene. But if one dares to speak as a woman desiring men—and it is clear that Baez writes of her desire, noting his eyes *bluer than robin's eggs* and at the same time his hygiene, which she withstood, and that, we know, means that she accepted Dylan as *the unwashed phenomenon*—that is, to lay claim to the right to be able to say this,[58] to speak this desire as a woman with respect to men, as a desire for men, is only to underscore this with reference again to Lacan, that *there is no sexual relation there*, none at all, no possibility, not a chance. To say that *there is no sexual relation there* is not to say that for women desiring men, there is no sex. To the contrary, there is/can be tons of it, all you want and all you do not want. Thus it would be false and silly to say that it is difficult to find an opportunity to sleep with men. The only point to be made is that men are not about being desired for their beauty as such, for their bodies as such,

---

[57]   There are many citations of this quote, but for one recent instantiation, see k.d. lang's interview with Fiona Sturges in *The Independent*, Friday 17 June 2011.

[58]   And I have already noted that traditional theory does not permit this.

and if it comes to light that they are so desired, it unmans them, literally so. And there is nothing erotic in that.

As the ruling gender (and just guess which "gender," despite all the gender theorists' claims of ambiguity, has an utterly unambiguous hegemony in this imaginary, symbolic, and real world?), men are, when it comes to erotic encounters, exceedingly advanced at having those encounters only and precisely on the very specific terms that they themselves set. Hence, there is an erotic object in every heterosexual erotic encounter, and the guys themselves are *not* that object.

Of course, I am not saying, although I imagine that some will take it so, that women do not in general enjoy the beauty of their lovers' bodies, in all possible ways, and I am also sure that this varies from person to person. What I am saying is that women *are* inevitably limited in expressing, articulating, bringing this out in any but the most oblique ways.

And I realize that men reading this and women reading this will protest that this does not apply to them: a fair enough claim. But I beg to differ. Nor am I sure that I can do much beyond such a petition: it is hard to argue a case that is prima facie refused, and this is the case of women's subjective repression. It is for this reason that de Beauvoir begins her reflections on *The Second Sex* as a kind of dialectical surprise, a quandary, a paradox: "What is woman?"[59] she asks, and then goes on to reflect on the range of replies that can be given to this seemingly obvious question, in a passage inflected with references to Nietzsche:

> "*Tota mulier in utero*," says one, "woman is a womb." But in speaking of certain women, connoisseurs declare that they are not women, although they are equipped with a uterus like the rest. The biological and social sciences no longer admit the existence of unchangeably fixed entities that determine given characteristics, such as those ascribed to woman, the Jew, or the Negro.[60]

Here de Beauvoir makes the point that makes her study rather less an account of women per se, although woman is certainly her object, to paraphrase Derrida, paraphrasing Nietzsche as he was, the existentialist text *par excellence*:

> yet we are told that femininity is in danger; we are exhorted to be women, remain women, become women. It would appear, then, that every female human being is not necessarily a woman; to be so considered she must share in that mysterious and threatened reality known as femininity.[61]

---

[59] Simone de Beauvoir, *The Second Sex*, trans. H.M. Parshley (London: David Campbell [Everyman's Library], 1993), xix.

[60] Ibid., xix. See here, in this context, Deborah Bergoffen, *The Philosophy of Simone de Beauvoir: Gendered Phenomenologies, Erotic Generosities* (Albany: State University of New York Press, 1996).

[61] De Beauvoir, *The Second Sex*, xix.

Not only existentialism, but the greater part of cultural analyses of the masculinity of k.d. lang and gender studies in general, depend on this precision. "If today femininity no longer exists, then it never existed." For de Beauvoir, philosophically speaking, our troubles only begin with this, for if "her functioning as a female is not enough to define woman, if we decline also to explain her through 'the eternal feminine', and if nevertheless we admit, provisionally, that women do exist, then we must face the question 'what is a woman'." And this is the point and the heart of the problem:

> To state the question is, to me, to suggest, at once, a preliminary answer. The fact that I ask it is in itself significant. A man would never set out to write a book on the peculiar situation of the human male … In actuality the relation of the two sexes is not quite like that of two electrical poles, for man represents both the positive and the neutral, as is indicated by the common use of *man* to designate human beings in general; whereas woman represents only the negative, defined by limiting criteria, without reciprocity.[62]

De Beauvoir's question develops the radicality of this distinction as it means, as she develops the point that woman is an other other, an utterly unique other. Thus if no group defines itself as "the one" or as "the" people without setting up a counterpart, an other, Hegel finds "in consciousness itself a fundamental hostility towards every other consciousness."[63] The point here, the dialectical point in question, is that, centrally, "the other consciousness, the other ego, sets up a reciprocal claim."[64]

Indeed—and this is the ethnographer's insight, hence de Beauvoir's reference to Lévi-Strauss as she might well have referred to the pre-Socratic Xenophon—such an absolute instauration inevitably gives way to relativism, once one takes a broader view. But, she asks, why, in this more cosmopolitan, traveled, sophisticated, and enlightened sense, has an analogous reciprocity "*not* been recognised between the sexes, that one of the contrasting terms is set up as the sole essential, denying

---

[62]   Ibid., xxi. De Beauvoir cites Julien Benda at length, as it is important for her further reading: "And Benda is most positive in his *Rapport d'Uriel*: 'The body of man makes sense in itself quite apart from that of woman, whereas the latter seems wanting in significance by itself … Man can think of himself without woman. She cannot think of herself without man.' And she is simply what man decrees; thus she is called 'the sex', by which is meant that she appears essentially to the male as a sexual being. For him she is sex—absolute sex, no less. She is defined and differentiated with reference to man and not he with reference to her; she is the incidental, the inessential as opposed to the essential. He is the Subject, he is the Absolute—she is the Other." Ibid., xxii.

[63]   In other words, as de Beauvoir glosses Hegel, "the subject can be posed only in being opposed—he sets himself up as the essential, as opposed to the other, the inessential, the object." Ibid., xxiii.

[64]   Ibid.

any relativity in regard to its correlative and defining the latter as pure otherness? *Why is it that women do not dispute male sovereignty?*"[65]

With women, it seems, things are different. And de Beauvoir is as unflinching as Adorno (who is, despite his own sexism, surprisingly alive to this question, just to the extent that woman in a capitalist economy, and there is no other, is a market commodity) in drawing the consequences of this "difference":

> If woman seems to be the inessential which never becomes the essential, it is because she herself fails to bring about this change. Proletarians say "We"; Negroes also. Regarding themselves as subjects, they transform the bourgeois, the whites, into "others." But women do not say "We," except at some congress of feminists or similar formal demonstration; men say "women," and women use the same word in referring to themselves. They do not authentically assume a subjective attitude. The proletarians have accomplished the revolution in Russia, the Negroes in Haiti, the Indo-Chinese are battling for it in Indo-China; but the women's effort has never been anything more than a symbolic agitation. They have gained only what men have been willing to grant; they have taken nothing, they have only received.[66]

This is the great issue, and much of the Foucault-spiced claims that women gain "power" by their collaboration, collusion, submission is already put in question, some might say refuted in advance, in de Beauvoir's analysis. "In truth woman has not been socially emancipated through man's need—sexual desire and the desire for offspring—which makes the male dependent for satisfaction upon the female."[67] And in part the reason is economic, as most things are (back to Adorno and capitalism), which means that is again also a matter of power: "Even if the need is at bottom equally urgent for both, it always works in favour of the oppressor and against the oppressed. That is why the liberation of the working class, for example, has been slow."[68] We note that this halting process corresponds to the relatively meager gains of the so-called "women's movement," that would-be feminism which passed almost immediately into self-evidence and consequent irrelevance as sexism and the corollaries thereof continue apace, as expressed in a growing range of studies focusing on the (lack of) advancement and (limited) presence of women scientists in the academy,[69] and recently in studies of the surprising durability of the chilly unfriendliness or

---

[65] Ibid., xxiv. My emphasis.

[66] Ibid., xxv.

[67] Ibid., xxvi.

[68] Ibid.

[69] Virginia Valian, *Why So Slow? The Advancement of Women* (Cambridge: MIT Press, 1998); and, more recently, Kristen Monroea, Saba Ozyurta, Ted Wrigley, and Amy Alexander, "Gender Equality in Academia: Bad News from the Trenches, and Some Possible Solutions," *Perspectives on Politics* 6 (2008): 215–33.

even hostility of the climate of academic philosophy to women.[70] Not to mention the new rage, now recurrent through more than one season, for frilly feminine fashion, inconvenient footwear, and so on.

Again, and very like Nietzsche, though to be sure taking a critical vantage, de Beauvoir analyzes the heart of what she later thematizes as "complicity":

> to decline to be the Other, to refuse to be a party to the deal—this would be for women to renounce all the advantages conferred upon them by their alliance with the superior caste. Man-the-sovereign will provide woman-the-liege with material protection and will undertake the moral justification of her existence; thus she can evade at once both economic risk and the metaphysical risk of a liberty in which ends and aims must be contrived without assistance. Indeed, along with the ethical urge of each individual to affirm his subjective existence, there is also the temptation to forgo liberty and become a thing ... Thus, woman may fail to lay claim to the status of subject because she lacks definite resources, because she feels the necessary bond that ties her to man regardless of reciprocity, and because she is often very well pleased with her role as the Other.[71]

Many suppose that de Beauvoir's readings are done deals, long since incorporated into a range of second, third, and however many waves of feminism. But on closer examination, this is not the case, and with rare exceptions, most readings of de Beauvoir suppose that she can be dispensed with and that one can move on. This moving on is the very point of the "wave" discourse. Thus one supposes that de Beauvoir's analyses are incorporated and, this is the contradiction, already superceded, usually by way of the efforts of the commentator in question, such that one need not take account of her critical arguments. And indeed, many who consider themselves specialists in feminist theory disagree with her (some even take this disagreement as inspiration for what they do), and of these, many do not

---

[70]   See Louise Morley, *Quality and Power in Higher Education* (Maidenhead: Society for Research into Higher Education and McGraw Hill, 2003); and see, in the case of linguistics in terms of the "status dilemma," Senta Troemel-Ploetz, "Selling the Apolitical," *Discourse Society* 2/4 (1991): 489–502. In the case of philosophy and for a mainstream example, see Sally Haslanger, "Changing the Ideology and Culture of Philosophy: Not by Reason (Alone)," *Hypatia* 23/2 (2008): 210–23. In addition, see Julie Van Camp, "Tenured/Tenure-Track Faculty Women at 98 US Doctoral Programs in Philosophy": <http://www.csulb.edu/~jvancamp/doctoral_2004.html>, updated 14 April 2008, accessed 9:34 PM, 23 February 2010, New York City; as well as Miriam Solomon and John Clarke, "The CSW Jobs for Philosophers Employment Study," *APA Newsletter: Feminism and Philosophy* 8/2 (Spring 2009): 3–6. For further references to Haslanger and beyond, including a discussion of "guerilla phenomenology," see Babich, "Great Men, Little Black Dresses, and the Virtues of Keeping One's Feet on the Ground."

[71]   De Beauvoir, *The Second Sex*, xxvii.

even write on her at all. At best, her work is quoted in passing, often out of context, and often without hermeneutic generosity.[72]

Becoming a Subject

François Poulain de la Barre is argued, as de Beauvoir cites her, to have been the first to deflect masculinist critique and then to advance her own project:

> Very well, but just how shall we pose the question? And, to begin with, who are we to propound it at all? Man is at once judge and party to the case; but so is woman. What we need is an angel—neither man nor woman—but where shall we find one? Still, the angel would be poorly qualified to speak, for an angel is ignorant of all the basic facts involved in the problem.[73]

Looking for an angel (de Beauvoir assumes that we have read our Augustine), most commentators have in the interim had recourse to a kind of god trick. Rather than the hermaphrodite (this is de Beauvoir's further choice and it echoes the classic recourse to Tiresias to settle such questions), or the fourth or seventh sex, we can "queer" the question, and for this we have gender studies and for this we

---

[72] Thus Peg Simons's edited collection, *The Philosophy of Simone de Beauvoir: Critical Essays* (Bloomington: Indiana University Press, 2006) is representative of this trend, as would be a good many of the essays on de Beauvoir that appear in the feminist philosophical journal, *Hypatia*. A notable exception, that is, however, not ultimately a complete exception, may be found in the work of Luce Irigaray. See too, again, Bergoffen, *The Philosophy of Simone de Beauvoir*. Note that Penelope Deutscher's insightful *The Philosophy of Simone de Beauvoir: Ambiguity, Conversion, Resistance* (Cambridge: Cambridge University Press, 2008) also coins the notion of auto-resistance to explain dissonances (that would be claims with which today's feminist scholar would be inclined to disagree) as so many inconsistencies, that is to say, self-contradictions on de Beauvoir's part. Psychoanalytically speaking, the tradition of resisting de Beauvoir might be similarly so accounted.

[73] De Beauvoir, *The Second Sex*, xxxiii. De Beauvoir's angel corresponds to the angelic nature detailed by Augustine and St Thomas himself. It is de Beauvoir's rigorous clarity that matters here, and this also accounts for the extraordinary force of the claim to brotherhood (*fraternité*) as de Beauvoir, in a Schillerian voice that also happens to be utterly Cartesian and utterly French, concludes her study: "by and through their natural differentiation, men and woman unequivocally affirm their brotherhood" (732). The "sisterhood," for all its charm, has nothing on this. This assessment informs the title of the English translation of François Poulain de la Barre, *Three Cartesian Feminist Treatises*, trans. Vivien Bosley (Chicago: University of Chicago Press, 2002). For a discussion of François Poulain de la Barre, see Siep Stuurman, *François Poulain de la Barre and the Invention of Modern Equality* (Cambridge: Harvard University Press, 2004), and directly antecedent to this, Elsa Dorlin, *L'Évidence de l'égalité des sexes. Une philosophie oubliée du XVIIe* (Paris: L'Harmattan, 2001).

have the lesbian subject. But is this so? Does queering solve the problem? In fact, it solves it for some, if it is true, as it always is in these cases, that queering might also replicate (this is the point that the philosopher Penelope Deutscher makes with her analysis of auto-resistance)[74] or duplicate some of the same problems on another level. And to the extent that the problem of woman as subject is also the problem of desire, it is to this question I will turn. And I note in advance that I am aware that there are many who have raised just this question from the perspective of gender or queer studies, often further specified as lesbian theory.

Note that I am not saying that I disagree with such approaches as such. Rather my project is different and what I attempt to do here is to raise a *complementary* set of related questions that, at least as I see it, happen to go back not only to Adorno and Nietzsche (neither one of whom can be counted as having been overly friendly to feminist interests, just as most "ladies men," like Leonard Cohen, tend to be antagonistic to women, an antagonism that is noted as misogyny in the title of the current chapter).

And to be sure, rather as de Beauvoir unkindly but insightfully reminds us:

> men profit in many more subtle ways from the otherness, the alterity of woman. Here is a miraculous balm for those afflicted with an inferiority complex, and indeed no one is more arrogant towards women, more aggressive or scornful, than the man who is anxious about his virility.[75]

De Beauvoir's work deserves attention and not least because, having become a cliché—this is the paradox of success—it has become the functional equivalent of the many texts that are not read. Thus we have already had cause to note that her work suffers from a lack of attention and not a little bit because scholars these days tend to focus on Judith Butler or Michel Foucault or more recherché names that change from moment to moment. (We are, in the academy, in constant fear of not being up-to-date). These tensions notwithstanding, I suggest that reading de Beauvoir comes before a similarly needful and similarly valid reading of Irigaray,[76] even of Irigaray on de Beauvoir,[77] and so on and so on.

It is women who are the objects of desire (for *heterosexual* men, but not less for women, as argued, both heterosexual and homosexual), such that—save in the

---

[74]   See, again, the reference to Deutscher, *The Philosophy of Simone de Beauvoir*, in note 72 above.

[75]   De Beauvoir; *The Second Sex*, xxxi. As she argues, to make a related point in her conclusion, men also find in women more complicity than the oppressor usually finds in the oppressed. And in bad faith they take authorization from this to declare that she has *desired* the destiny that they have imposed on her (721).

[76]   See, for example, Luce Irigaray's "The Question of the Other," trans. Noah Guyum, *Yale French Studies* 87 (1995): 7–19.

[77]   See, for an illustration here, Margaret Whitford, ed., *An Irigaray Reader* (Oxford: Blackwell, 1991).

case of lesbian desire, which is why both men and women find it so fascinating—the desire of the heterosexual woman *is*, as Nietzsche put it, rather more flatly than Hegel, *to be desired*—and not to desire.[78] By contrast with the desire to be desired, men are subjects all the way down. It is not that they do not desire to be desired, it is, as already noted, that they take that desire and desirability as a given and thus need not and do not "desire" it. This is what it means in truth to be a subject of desire. One is, qua subject, the one who desires, the one for whom the object is an object of desire. There are biblical ways to put this, but I will do no more than note it at this juncture, as also indeed that Nietzsche himself made this an extended focus of his reflections.[79]

It is significant that even the word "beauty" as applied to men already bothers them and just because it objectifies them.[80] I am excluding homosexual men for convenience, and even the so-called metrosexual trend works to the extent that it embraces a certain ideal of masculine "beauty" and only because it bounces off, glances off, men dressing not for women but *for men*. And not only homosexual but also heterosexual men dress for men, GQ, corporate style, the sky's the limit, provided we note that men do this themselves as subjects for subjects, and thus *for* one another. So it goes at Savile Row. Thus the mystique of Hong Kong tailoring, and so on. But so too, and this is the capitalist point, corporate style, corporate convention: what jackets are worn, what length the jacket, what shoes to wear. The same rules hold on the golf course.

That men dress for men as the subject of conventional approbation, that women dress for men (or what is the same dress for women who dress for men) is relevant to the current analysis to the extent that neither k.d. lang nor indeed any other lesbian takes issue with the ruling identification of *the* erotic object of any interest as women. And to this extent, and this is my point, there is no difference between a homosexual woman and the heterosexual woman who also sees herself (and other women) as men do. This is de Beauvoir's point, which she takes as her point of

---

[78] To be sure, Nietzsche for his part uses the language of *will* or *command*. See my discussion, as noted below.

[79] I have several reflections on this theme: see Babette Babich, "The Logic of Woman in Nietzsche: The Dogmatist's Story," *New Political Science: A Journal of Politics and Culture* 36 (1996): 7–17; and Babich, "Nietzsche's Erotic Artist as Actor/Jew/Woman," in *Words in Blood, Like Flowers: Philosophy and Poetry, Music and Eros in Hölderlin, Nietzsche, and Heidegger* (Albany: State University of New York Press, 2006), 147ff.

[80] They prefer, indeed, as k.d. lang herself prefers, to be called "handsome" as opposed to "pretty," and we have already mentioned the limitations that come with speaking of the "looks" of male philosophers in cases where one is not, say, Socrates. And it is just to the point that I have been making that, not unlike Woody Allen, Socrates's personal lack of objective erotic appeal becomes, qua master subject, exactly appealing. Thus Nietzsche reminds us that Socrates, knowing this and knowing it backwards and forwards, was in the end and even consummately—philosophy is named for this—a great erotic. It would take Lacan to rediscover this without in the process meaning to make Nietzsche's point. Nor was Lacan one to give anything away.

departure in her introduction, as cited above, and which she develops at length in the latter sections of *The Second Sex*, to the great annoyance, as already observed, of the greater majority of feminist scholars who take her to be anti-woman in this regard. But this, too, is the point of de Beauvoir's thesis that "one is not born, one becomes a woman" [*On ne naît pas femme, on le devient*].[81]

Thus an established k.d. lang—as she has indeed been established for some time and this in spite of her insistence on outsider status—can tease her audience by describing her banjo magnetism, saying, as her fans quote her as saying in Carmel, Indiana (and I note that she said something fairly identical to this at a concert I attended at the Beacon Theater in New York City in June 2011, which only means that, like her interviews, her stage commentary tends to be more stock or standard than not): "all you females in the audience may begin to experience a pull toward the stage—this is normal!!"[82]

And to be sure, there is a tradition of scholarship analyzing this very phenomenon,[83] important in the present context, where the issue of musical consumers cuts to the heart of the technologically mediated and thereby ineluctably transformed relationship to music. I note here that a reflection on the significance of that metaphor is already, if perhaps indeliberately, at work in k.d. lang's *All You Can Eat*. There are also specific analyses of k.d. lang and musical "consumption"[84] which, so far from examining the commodification of music from a critical theoretical perspective, look at it from the side of enjoyment. One speaks, indeed, as one finds this again and again, of so many "consuming passions."This is Adorno's culinary turn.

---

[81]   De Beauvoir, *The Second Sex*, 267.

[82]   TAnnie, at 25 June 2011, 16:05:19: kennedyflairs kd lang Site > Talk and Twang > k.d. & Indy—a match made during "Heaven", post # 22.

[83]   See Louise Allen, *The Lesbian Idol: Martina, kd and the Consumption of Lesbian Masculinity* (London: Cassell, 1997).

[84]   See, most notably, Gill Valentine, "Creating Transgressive Space: The Music of k.d. lang," *Transactions of the Institute of British Geographers* ns. 20/4 (1995): 474–85.

Chapter 4
"Covering" Leonard Cohen's
Hallelujah: Music Makes the Song from
John Cale to k.d. lang

John Cale and the Genesis of Cohen's *Hallelujah*

Leonard Cohen himself tells us that he took some two years or so (and, rather like the total number of verses, the interval in question has become an inevitable subject for embroidery) in order to write *Hallelujah*.

In addition, and we have already begun to explore this above, noting several accounts of the genesis of Cohen's *Hallelujah*, the song proceeds via several covers—and it is important to note that the terminology of the "cover" is derived from a music business hell-bent on keeping clear records of royalties—canonically to John Cale, and to a good deal of success as a result with other recording artists who cover Cohen/Cale, especially Jeff Buckley and Rufus Wainwright. The great bulk of commentary on Cohen's *Hallelujah* that has been published, be it in print or on the web, centers on Buckley and Wainwright,[1] when it does not dwell on ideal alternates; this would be the melancholy wishing for more or for different kinds of covers, say, from Bob Dylan.[2]

A live recording of what Cohen himself characterizes as the "broken" Hallelujah was performed in Montreux in 1985 which, like many of Cohen's performances,

---

[1]   See, specifically on this, Erik Steinskog, "Queering Cohen: Cover Versions as Subversions of Identity," in *Play it Again: Cover Songs in Popular Music*, ed. George Plasketes (Farnham, Surrey: Ashgate, 2010), 139–52. As we noted above, and in spite of Steinskog's declaration of the dependency of his reading on Judy Butler, he does not indeed consider any but the usual suspects, Buckley and Wainwright. See, too, and more importantly, as it frames Steinskog's reading, Robert Fink, *Repeating Ourselves: American Minimal Music as Cultural Practice* (Berkeley: University of California Press, 2005). Importantly, Alan Light's *The Holy or the Broken: Leonard Cohen, Jeff Buckley, and the Unlikely Ascent of "Hallelujah"* (New York: Atria Books, 2012) does not depart from this focus as it foregrounds Cohen and Buckley.

[2]   In fact, we are told that Dylan was one of the first to sing Cohen's song in a concert. If Cale's or Buckley's *Hallelujah* tends to appear in film, there is also George Down's cover for the soundtrack of the Canadian film, *Saint Ralph*, a kind of coming of age *Chariots of Fire*, with all the homoeroticism related to the genre (also to be seen in *Going My Way*), while restoring some of the beauty of Cohen's cadences as well.

can be heard on YouTube.[3] Central to our analysis of the iconic birth of Cohen's *Hallelujah* with Cale's 1991 recording are two verses included in Cohen's 1985 performance which do not appear in subsequent covers (including k.d. lang's *Hallelujah*). This is Cohen as priest, this is his confession:

> You say that I took the name in vain
> but I don't even know the name,
> But if I did, well really, what's it to ya?
> There's a blaze of light in every word,
> it doesn't matter which ya heard,
> the holy or the broken Hallelujah
>
> I did my best, it wasn't much,
> I couldn't feel, so I tried to touch,
> I told the truth, I did not come to fool ya,
> And even though it all went wrong,
> I'll stand before the Lord of song,
> with nothing on my tongue but Hallelujah

Cohen recorded another version, with some differences, in 1988. At about the same time, and this is no accident as this is all about marketing, Cohen gave an interview with Vera Kvaa on Danish television where he is asked about the religious dimension but refuses to comment (and indeed about his political engagements, about which he is more forthcoming). Instructively, one can see an erotically charged clip from Cohen's performance in Oslo in May 1988, just as musically keyed as anyone might wish.[4]

Though it is not included in his 1990 *The Best of Leonard Cohen*, *Hallelujah* features again at the heart of a compilation issued in 1994, along with many other hits, including the virtually perfect song, *Who by Fire*, and the enormously popular, thanks to Judy Collins, *Suzanne* (which was discussed above with reference to Nina Simone's own cover of it) in the reprisal album, *Cohen Live, Leonard Cohen in Concert*.

The Canonization of Cohen's *Hallelujah*

There are any number of accounts, and this will be just another story of how it was that Cohen came to write his *Hallelujah* song.[5] As Greg Kot writes:

---

[3]   <http://www.youtube.com/watch?v=S6KLK_8Tg6Y&feature=related>.

[4]   <http://www.youtube.com/watch?v=zcbnQeRT65M>.

[5]   See, for a recent and comprehensive account, the appendix to Tim Footman, *Leonard Cohen, Hallelujah: A New Biography* (New Malden, Surrey: Chrome Dreams, 2009), 198ff.

Cohen labored over the song for years before recording it. And he has performed different versions of the song in concert ever since the initial studio recording, indicating that he has never quite felt the song to be fully "finished." If anything, Cohen's restlessness has only added to the song's allure, its seemingly bottomless mystery.[6]

If Cohen's song also works on several levels, finished and unfinished, which is the great advantage of championing the "broken" *Hallelujah*, what Kot calls the "finishing" process depended upon Cale's transcription of it for his own 1991 version, which cover is to be heard in Cale's 1992 performance, which can today be seen on YouTube.[7] As Bryan Appleyard puts it, Cale's version is "pure, cold and scarcely inflected at all—it sends shivers down the spine."[8] Nor is this trajectory at all surprising for a song inspiring nearly 100 artists to "cover" it, that is, to re-interpret and record it. The literal Hallelujah effect, as engendered by Cale's cover, exemplifies Hillel Schartz's notion, as Robert Fink's also appropriates this for musicology, as Steinskog also quotes Fink of the "culture of the copy,"[9] of American culture. Cohen's *Hallelujah* inspires nothing if not imitation, which is not to say, with the possible exception of Bob Dylan's early cover, that most artists attempt—or could attempt—to sing it as Cohen does, but as Cale does.

Cale's musical formation ranged from Berg to Schoenberg, as well as John Cage and La Monte Young, and also included a marathon performance of Erik Satie, some 18 hours of Satie to be precise, as well as Brian Eno, and for many readers, none of this matters apart from the detail that, together with Lou Reed, Cale founded the Velvet Underground, which was in turn associated with everything that was music and art, performance and otherwise, in New York in the 1960s and 1970s.

Cale's *Hallelujah* was recorded for his Cohen dedicated album, *I'm Your Fan*,[10] and as noted, this is its definitive version: Cale's version determines *all* the covers we know. Thus we may add the genesis of Cale's *Hallelujah* to our list, as this too makes a difference. For when Cale asked Cohen for the song in order to record it, we are told that Cohen faxed him 15 pages—and one may argue that this is the numerological or quasi-kabbalistic source of the apocryphal account that it took Cohen fifteen *years* to write the song, an account that has in the interim become true in any case, inasmuch as every performance changes the song. What

---

[6]   Greg Kot, "Turn it Up: Why Leonard Cohen's Hallelujah Endures," *Chicago Tribune*, 30 April 2009.

[7]   See, for a biography of Cale's musically and personally complex life, Tim Mitchell, *Sedition and Alchemy: A Biography of John Cale* (London: Peter Owen Publishers, 2003).

[8]   Bryan Appleyard, "Hallelujah! On Leonard Cohen's Ubersong," *The Sunday Times*, 9 June 2005.

[9]   Hillel Schwartz; *The Culture of the Copy: Striking Likenesses, Unreasonable Facsimilies* (Cambridge, MA: MIT Press, 1996). I cite Fink as well as Steinskog above.

[10]   Obviously, the title *I'm Your Fan* echoes Cohen's earlier album, *I'm Your Man*.

is certain, as we have already emphasized, is that Cale knows his way around a song, and what is also certain is that Cale can sing. My point with respect to k.d. lang above, and in what follows, is that it is the singing (and the singer) that makes all the difference.

Indeed, we may count Cohen himself among the ranks of his own interpreters, as he changes, very significantly, his own lyrics, at least his rendering of them, although this may also be a Canadian homage to the British in his London performance, that is, to the English of English, which in some astonishing way always comes down to how one articulates an affirmative, or one's pronouns, that would be the second person, singular. Thus my admired friend and colleague, the philosopher Debra Bergoffen, chided, as she thought, albeit erroneously, that k.d. lang had changed the articulative form of the pronoun *You don't really care for music, do ya* to "you," as in: *You don't really care for music, do you.*[11] But Bergoffen's point, apart from the contingent detail here, is spot on: interpreters tend to change the words, and k.d. herself, as we will have occasion to note, changes her breathing from rough to smooth, Christianizing David's *hallelujah* to a more well-known *alleluia*.

In fact, k.d. lang does not touch the pronoun, although Cohen himself does do so, at his own liberty, and with every justification, as the author of the song itself, and again when he tours England and Ireland in 2008, perhaps inspired by a certain North American sensibility or deference to the precisions of Irish and English articulation.

What k.d. lang does, as we explore at greater length below, is to pronounce, to enunciate, and thus to sing the song itself—here I invoke Ernest McClain's esoteric language of the "song itself." Cohen, for his own part, enunciates his own rendering and this is striking. The song works backwards on the singer.

Thus Footman reports John Lissauer as characterizing Cohen's *Various Positions* as having what Footman calls a "secret status," that is, in Lissauer's words "'one of the great undiscovered, should-have-been-a-hit-records,'"[12] contributing to the labile qualities of the song. And in a sense Lissauer's reflections have to be true, to quote Footman's summary account: "Because Cohen's original version remained obscure, there was no fixed idea of how it should sound … Cohen taped it first, but it's not really 'his'. You don't have a Cohen song, you have a song."[13]

Erotic Sophistications

Tim Footman did not write what he calls a "new biography" of Leonard Cohen subtitled *Hallelujah* in order to give the store away. Thus he reminds us that the song

---

[11]   In email correspondence with the author.

[12]   Footman, *Leonard Cohen, Hallelujah*, 200.

[13]   Ibid.

evolves, such that as Cohen performs it in Austin on Halloween in 1988, "much of the religious imagery had been replaced by the secular and the sensuous."[14]

I would argue with the notion of "replacement," as I read the evolution of *Hallelujah* as just that, namely an engendering evolution as opposed to a substitution, revision, or replacement. That said, Footman's account is useful if it is also true that there is always an enlightenment streak in popular biographies that seeks to vacate the religious, an enlightenment streak that corresponds to the tendency to denounce academic studies as "too highbrow," and Footman shares this, quoting an early review of Cohen's poetry by fellow Toronto resident, Northrop Frye, only to denounce it for being shortsighted enough to criticize Cohen's erotic poetry when Frye writes, as Footman cites him, that "the erotic poems follow the usual convention of stacking up thighs like a Rockette chorus line."[15] Although given over to Frye's particular sense of humor, and not less given the subsequent trajectory of Cohen's erotic explorations, the comment would seem to have been more a matter of social commendation and prescience than it was an expression of any kind of unease[16]—Frye himself was, after all, an extraordinarily learned scholar of satire, and traditionally, historically, satire is not for the faint of erotic heart.[17] Indeed, Footman's detailing of Frye's point (and there is rather a lot of this on offer in theoretic studies of popular music, rock and otherwise) corresponds to Footman's idea of what "older academic" types are likely to like and to dislike, framed here more for rhetorical convenience than accuracy. And how better for Footman to come to the end of his second chapter than to get to conclude by writing "Unfortunately for the fragile sensibilities of Frye, Donaldson and their like … things were going to get rather sexier and considerably more violent."[18]

The "we-have-a-patent-on-sex" confidence of those who write on pop music is thus mollified when speaking, by contrast, of more "with it" academics who just happen to be macho enough to get the point that Frye is supposed to have missed. Thus Footman endorses Paul Monk's non-criticism: "Erotically, Cohen makes Keats seem as though he had freeze-dried testicles and Byron as though he had no heart …"[19] This contravenes Cohen's own absorption in poetry; reflecting

---

[14]   Ibid., 201.

[15]   Ibid., 25, citing Northrop Frye, "Review of Leonard Cohen," *University of Toronto Quarterly*, April 1957.

[16]   Thus Footman's journalistic point compels him to highlight what he presumes to be Frye's discomfort with the "disturbing aspects of life." Footman, *Leonard Cohen, Hallelujah*.

[17]   I mention Northrop Frye in this cynico-satirical context, with further references, including Jonathan Swift, in Babette Babich, "Le Zarathoustra de Nietzsche et le style parodique. A propos de l'hyperanthropos de Lucien et du surhomme de Nietzsche," *Diogène. Revue internationale des sciences humaines* 232 (October 2010): 70–93.

[18]   Footman, *Leonard Cohen, Hallelujah*, 26.

[19]   Ibid., 130.

on his own youthful idealism, as we have already quoted above, and here again worth repeating:

> We really wanted to be good writers, good poets, great poets. We really took seriously Shelley when he said that poets are the unacknowledged legislators of the world. An incredibly naïve description of oneself but we certainly fell for that. We thought it was terribly important what we were doing. Maybe it was. Who knows?[20]

What is true enough is that the *Hallelujah* that Footman goes on to characterize as "King David the psalmist—the implied model for Cohen's writing in *Book of Mercy*—meets King David the Sex Pest" seems to him to approximate "a case of an artist unable to live up to the elevated aspirations of his own work."[21] But here the point may have gone begging, the point may be the one that Greg Kot underscores, as cited above, if he also undermines it by solving it on a note of hopefulness, male optimism:

> The narrative explores how the erotic becomes political, how relationships are defined not by trust but by conquest, and how lovers become trophies to be discarded. And, somehow, the survivors hope it will be different next time. The broken Hallelujah is life itself.[22]

The unspoken point is that it will not be different next time.

For Cohen, to highlight the broken *Hallelujah* (this is what makes this preternaturally male), the cold *Hallelujah*, is for him to say that this is all we have.

But given the range of interpretations and given the dominion of the song's influence, what kind of song do we have here? What kind of *Hallelujah* are we on about? In Appleyard's demystifying formulation: "Either this was a wistful, ultimately feel-good song or it was an icy bitter commentary on the futility of human relations."[23] And for Appleyard, everything turns on the songwriter because, as he argues, Cohen does not write the first kind of feel-good song, even if it can seem that he does on first glance. Much rather what Cohen "most commonly does is pour highly concentrated acid into very sweet and lyrical containers. Never in his entire career has he done this as well as he did in the second version of 'Hallelujah.'"[24]

But as Nietzsche mused with regard to Wagner, we need to worry just a bit whenever it comes to the artistry of the artist. As Appleyard reminds us, here,

---

[20]   Cohen, cited in ibid., 21.

[21]   Ibid., 121.

[22]   Kot, "Why Leonard Cohen's Hallelujah Endures."

[23]   Appleyard, "Hallelujah."

[24]   Ibid.

very like Ernest McClain in his analysis below, we are dealing with a ruse, an aesthetic ruse to be sure, but a ruse nonetheless. And it matters, to catch the point of Appleyard's reflection, that ruses are dangerous and that is the point:

> The aesthetic trick at the heart of this is the undermining of the word Hallelujah. It means praise to the Lord but it is, basically, just a musical sound, like *la la la* or *yeah, yeah, yeah.* Describing the chord structure in those three lines in the first verse makes the words, sort of literally, into the music. Similarly, the chorus, which consists simply of the repetition of the word, is pure song in which the words and music are inseparable. And it is a pure pop song or contemporary hymn—a catchy uplifting tune and a comforting word. It has almost a sing-along quality. The words become the happy tune, the tune gets into your head and, once there, reveals itself as a serpent. For what you will actually be singing along to is arid sex, destroyed imagination, misogyny and emotional violence.[25]

Appleyard began his own analysis by reminding us that "Leonard Cohen's 'Hallelujah' has been papped, drivelled, exploited and massacred."[26] Indeed, as we have already noted above, Appleyard warns his Sunday newspaper readers, "Even if you think you haven't heard it, I can guarantee you have."[27] And this goes to the heart of the "aesthetic trick" in question. And later we shall see that this is also Adorno's point if, in its technical development (as Adorno stands at the beginning of such reflections along with Rudolf Arnheim and Günther Anders), it also points to what H. Stith Bennett analyzes as "recording consciousness."[28]

Indeed, Michael Barthel begins his lecture, "It Doesn't Matter Which You Heard," by taking us "back," as he suggests, a useful move if only because it reminds the reader that temporal sense is itself always related to and relevant to one's age (recalling both Henri Bergson and Eugen Fink who have analyzed this existential, temporal trajectory, if more scholarly attention has been paid to Bergson than to Fink), beginning with a certain *Hallelujah* cover-cum-mashup, and I note here that Barthel includes his own mash-up/cover at a safe distance towards the end of his online-posted talk:

> Let me take you back to the long-ago time of mid-February, 2007. Popular emo band Fall Out Boy had the number one album in the country and, being a responsible music critic, I of course illegally downloaded it. As my train crossed

---

[25]   Ibid.

[26]   Ibid.

[27]   Ibid.

[28]   H. Stith Bennett, *On Becoming a Rock Musician* (Amherst: University of Massachusetts Press, 1980), 126 ff. I discuss Adorno in a chapter below and see, further, the section in Bennett's book, "Mastering the Technological Component," 99ff.

the Manhattan Bridge, I reached track five on the album. And I heard this: Fall
Out Boy = Hum Hallelujah.[29]

Footman cites Barthel's analysis in the recent biography that we have been
discussing and he borrows from it a bit, as we see when we turn to it ourselves.
And it is worth turning to both because it offers a nice discussion of Cohen's
Hallelujah as television series soundtrack music (as opposed to film music,
though Barthel does note that Cale's 1991 cover appears in the 1996 film
Basquiat, well before *Shrek*), and because of its guileless self-confidence: it is
written from the perspective of a then rather more youthful Barthel, and youth,
whether it is the young k.d. lang or the young(er) Michael Barthel or even the
once-upon-a-time younger Leonard Cohen, tends to be characterized by a clarity
that is as pretentious as it is insightful; age teaches one understatement, and that
plays to the crowd.

Thus Barthel states his project and explains the clip from Fall Out Boy.

> What they're singing there, aside from what I believe professionals call
> "twaddle," is the chorus of a Leonard Cohen song. This is mildly incredible.
> Twenty-five years ago, a character on the TV show *The Young Ones* named
> Neal—the hippie—said, "I'm beginning to feel like a Leonard Cohen record,
> cause nobody ever listens to me." Today, in contrast, one particular Leonard
> Cohen song is featured prominently in no less than three separate episodes
> of teen uberdrama *The OC*, and can be heard in at least twenty-four separate
> movies and TV episodes, almost always as the soundtrack to a montage of
> people being sad.[30]

Twenty-four, let us say: and counting.

Barthel explains why this "incredible" transformation counts as such by
looking at the history of it:

> What's now considered the definitive version of this song is by dreamy, dead
> troubadour Jeff Buckley. (Some people are even under the impression that
> Buckley's cover is the original version.) [Jeff Buckley, *Hallelujah* (clip)]

---

[29]   See, here, Michael Barthel, "'It Doesn't Matter Which You Heard': The Curious
Cultural Journey of Leonard Cohen's 'Hallelujah'": <http://www.scribd.com/doc/37784045/
It-Doesn-t-Matter-Which-You-Heard-The-Curious-Cultural-Journey-of-Leonard-Cohen-s-
Hallelujah>. Footman quotes from this essay, footnoted with a now-nonfunctional link, by
noting it as presented in 2007 at the Experience Music Project in Seattle. Ergo Barthel's
beginning reference; and thus the frame of influence or *Wirkungsgeschichte* that he traces
reduces to mere *months*. And there is no one reading this, at any age, who does not know
how that cadence of time can be further compacted.

[30]   Barthel, "'It Doesn't Matter Which You Heard'."

It's an almost unbearably sad song in this incarnation—slow, keening, and heartbroken. But originally it was something different. [Leonard Cohen, *Hallelujah* (original) (clip)]

It is Barthel's parrhesic take on Cohen's original that is worth noting: "This is more like your uncle's band playing in a warehouse, assuming your uncle was weird and labored under the impression that he was a crooner."[31]

I have already noted that what is of greatest interest to Barthel is the history of the *Hallelujah* song on television in general, and for him, its history on *The OC* is particularly significant, arguing that, although "the gradual revision of the song" might have contributed to its appeal:

> … as a soundtrack device, it's also possible that when directors saw that the song was so potent, it could impart gravitas on a cartoon Ogre voiced by Mike Myers, it could make even the shallowest character seem tragic.

> After these two uses of Cale in movies, the song, almost always Buckley's version, begins to pop up on television shows. *The West Wing* is the only usage in 2002, but in 2003 it was everywhere.

> "Hallelujah" appeared in the fourth episode of Zach Braff's medical dramedy *Scrubs*, and twice in the first season of teen drama *The OC*, including an extremely prominent use in the finale.[32]

The reading here is, and can only be—and that alone is instructive—*postmodern*. Just as Bennett emphasizes recording consciousness, so one can speak of a "TV consciousness"; earlier that might have meant an "Ed Sullivan consciousness" or an "MTV consciousness," but increasingly that means, today, the soundtracks of movies and especially of popular programs, cartoons for children (even more than the public programming of *Sesame Street* so beloved of today's academics,[33] who, obviously, grew up with it), and above all popular American television series. That would be *Scrubs*, that would be *The OC*, at the moment that would be *Glee*, and, for those with cable or pay subscriptions, that would be *True Blood* (but, and this is instructive, that would not be *Game of Thrones* nor yet the *Borgias*, and I want to say it would be *Nurse Jackie*, but I'm not buying it).

---

[31]   Ibid. And as Barthel continues to say: "It passed into the public realm almost unnoticed, and remained that way for some time; in the major Cohen biography, published in 1996, there's no entry for the song in the index, despite the fact that the book's name is the same as the album on which 'Hallelujah' originally appears."

[32]   Ibid.

[33]   A not at all unrequited love, as attested by *The Muppets*, a recent and middling-terrible American movie.

For Barthel, however, the point is not that *Hallelujah* appears rather as what Adorno called a "ubiquity standard," but rather that "it's used in the exact same way every time" and this conventionality flies in the face of the usually labile quality of music, especially as background or soundtrack music, which "can be used sincerely, ironically, as background shading, as subtle comment, as product placement."[34] The difference here is the cliché qua cliché, and this parodic point, here more Linda Hutcheon than Adorno,[35] is what makes all the difference for Barthel, who observes that:

> "Hallelujah" always appears as people are being sad, quietly sitting and staring into space or ostentatiously crying, and always as a way of tying together the sadness of different characters in different places. In short, it's always used as part of a "sad montage."[36]

Well, so much for using *Hallelujah* as a wedding song or victory motif, except that, of course, Barthel pays too much attention to music to imagine that the song, any song, can be done to death, and he offers one of the more charming variations of Lawrence Lessig, also to be seen in cartoonist and creative commons activist Nina Paley's own reprise of the economic counter, but yet utter conventionality concerning creative property and appropriation:[37]

> This is the beauty of the pop song: it's an artistic hooker with a heart of gold, always willing to be used. It can become a tool, but a song isn't a Matisse—if it's used as a washcloth, just wring it out and it's good as new.[38]

So how shall we take it here? And why is it that none of the above interpreters, including Barthel, pay much attention to k.d. lang, and why is it that they all (including Barthel) attend, some more, some less, mostly to the men?

---

[34] Barthel, "'It Doesn't Matter Which You Heard'."

[35] See Linda Hutcheon, *A Theory of Parody: The Teachings of Twentieth-Century Art Forms* (Champaign, IL: University of Illinois Press, 2000). There is, of course, also Northrop Frye, as already mentioned above.

[36] Barthel, "'It Doesn't Matter Which You Heard'."

[37] Nina Paley recounts some of the difficulties encountered in making her 2008 film, *Sita Sings the Blues*, an animated film re-telling of the Indian epic, the *Ramayana*, and particularly the galvanizing travail of obtaining the licensing rights to use Annette Henshaw's 1929 *Mean To Me* in her film. When an artist tries to gain the rights to use another artist's material, what comes into view, often for the first time, is that these rights are not the creator's but the publishing company's. The record companies rule. See, further, Cameron Parkins's interview with Paley on the CreativeCommons blog, 3 June 2009 <http://creativecommons.org/weblog/entry/14760>.

[38] Barthel, "'It Doesn't Matter Which You Heard'."

Barthel emphasizes Buckley and suggests that it's all about the aura, and if Bryan Appleyard hears it, as we quoted him above, in Cale's version, Barthel suggests, with no small ironic distance, that the same aura can come through Buckley, and if so, it is because, "well, he's this beautiful dead boy with an apparently 'ethereal' voice, and he's singing this song that sounds like a long-ago thing."[39] For those who like Cohen's version, Barthel credits them, with the nice condescension of the young (and it was already noted that Barthel is no longer as young as he was, just because that's the way that goes), with responding to a kind of Yoda-like effect.

So we respond not to Cohen but, as Barthel puts it to begin with, to "dreamy, dead troubadour Jeff Buckley,"[40] and to Wainwright, and indeed, and to his credit in the case of Appleyard, who hears him as Barthel does not, to Cale.[41]

And, of course, as always, as we mentioned, there are the mourning allusions to the myth that is Dylan, and so on.

For all the considerable literature on covers of Cohen's *Hallelujah*, there is not much on k.d. lang, save as a "mention," that is to say, in passing. Why the central focus on Buckley or Wainwright as opposed to John Cale (I have said that I find Cale transcendent), or even, if only for authenticity's sake, Cohen himself? Why not k.d. lang?

"I'll be your daddy"

I ask why not k.d. lang because the question is rarely asked and it is well worth asking. For however good k.d. lang is, however omnipresent her performances are, her name—and we can call this the "woman effect," as women continue to be discounted, however astonishing some women may find this empirical fact—and her covers seem not to command attention. If one writes, as Appleyard, Barthel, and others write, about Cohen's *Hallelujah*, they'll be damned, this is homophobia, but it is also more generically female-phobic, if they write about k.d. lang. Alexandra Burke, well sure, a little, but not k.d. lang.

I delay a fuller analysis of this phenomenon here, though I have of course been talking about it and around it from the start. Here it will have to do to note that k.d. lang's version is everywhere, that she outsings (without outsinging, but that of course is the point of outsinging) Wainwright and most other interpreters, making it clear that if it were to come to outsinging, she *will be*, and this *is* her new word, the listener's/singer's "daddy."[42]

---

[39]   Ibid.

[40]   Ibid.

[41]   Barthel concedes this point completely: "And so when Jeff Buckley decided to cover 'Hallelujah,' he didn't really cover Cohen, he covered Cale." Ibid.

[42]   I would dearly like to be able to exclude the opera singer, Renée Fleming, from this comparative estimate, as I already mentioned her popular cover above, but even with this comparison, k.d. lang owns the song.

Exactly this claim is made by the Nashville and music industry enthusiasms of her new group, with whom she recorded her 2011 album, *kd lang and the Siss Boom Bang*, where her band members have begun to call her K-Daddy, an appellation drawn from the leading song, *I Confess*, written by k.d. lang and Joe Pisapia. When asked what it means for her to sing the words, "I'll be your daddy," lang replies by deflecting the question back to the questioner, something she has apparently learned to do with such questions: "it's pretty self-evident, don't you think?"

Here it is worth reflecting on the pop industry that is behind the Daddy allusion, rap, money, control, and not just Nashville. At the same time, one also notes that k.d. lang, although she has always been surrounded by men on stage, now undertakes quite specifically to draw attention to that fact. Thus she suggests that, emphasizing her age as she does so, she finds it useful to surround herself with an array of "boyfriends"—in New York, and I am sure, as noted above, at every other stopping point on the *Siss Boom Bang* tour circuit—she joked, while introducing her band as her "boyfriends," that she simply had to have five rather than one, an ambiguous comment on a number of levels. And as observed above, lang has always noted that she is attracted to men and that she is interested in being attractive to them. Thus she points out, as she understands it, that everyone is, at some level, *bisexual*. None of this matters because scholars *and* fans alike focusing on her lesbianism simply ignore this.

The assumption is that one is gay or one is not gay, and thus one comes out, revealing the "truth" about one's sexuality, and that is then that. In the process, and this is the point for cultivating a fan base, one eliminates complexity and that targeting simplification simplifies consumption.

It's all about the brand.

Nevertheless, this issue goes beyond marketing but has everything to do with our current reading of homosexuality, a reading which runs through philosophy, sociology, musicology, and so on. And that is an all-or-nothing understanding. Better said, more precisely said, that is an understanding of homosexuality as if it were the same as voting Republican or not, being Jewish or not (and this question, among others, haunted Leonard Cohen, only switching in later years, of all the times to change focus, but that was our point, to the question of his own sexuality).[43] But this all-or-nothing sexuality is a conviction that is fairly recent. Arguably, even so famous a homosexual as Oscar Wilde found no special exclusion of the opposite sex necessary for his own attraction to those of his own sex. And it perhaps goes along with the celebration of homosexuality as a preferred or ideal lifestyle choice (I certainly myself hold it in this esteem). Yet it can get in the way of our understanding, not only of the complexities of everyday sexuality and everyday life (which also includes, and this will come

---

[43]   Thus Tim Footman quotes Cohen's bemusedly tolerant response to the question, ending with the world-wise but very coy reflection that it might now be too late for him to find out for sure: "Perhaps I won't find anyone." Footman, *Leonard Cohen, Hallelujah*.

as no surprise to women, a-sexuality as well), but of theoretical entanglements associated therewith. Hence, we have trouble understanding the way that the ancients related to their own erotics, their own sexual relationships. So, we ask if, or better said we *assume that*, Socrates was gay, and it may be thought that this is a fair assumption, given his relationship to Plato and others like Phaedrus, and others, even more famously, like Alcibiades, but it is also an assumption that happens to make the other allusions also present in the same text harder to parse, be this in Plato's *Republic* or still more so with his discussion of beauty, or indeed of love, in *The Symposium*,[44] but also with reference to Aristotle's discussion of friendship in the *Nicomachean Ethics*.

In any case, today's mainstream tendency is one I find that my students reflect, not always to their advantage when it comes to reading the above dialogues, readings that suffer from today's exclusivist definitions of sexuality, such that if one appreciates the beauty of boys, as Socrates does, this also entails, as one assumes, that Socrates prefers men to women. This can make the understanding of the focus on youth harder than it need be to grasp, and I recommend reading Davidson's *Courtesans and Fishcakes*—and here I do need the full subtitle: *The Consuming Passions of Classical Athens*[45]—for a good many reasons, but not least for its illumination of a point that Foucault, himself very respectably and very exclusively homosexual, details with care as the point of departure for his analysis of erotics in his *The Use of Pleasure*.[46] And for much the same reason, that is, for its depth, I recommend the Canadian poet Anne Carson's *Eros the Bittersweet*,[47] and along the lines, between the lines of the same theme, now more with reference to beauty, the reader might also read, once again, Alexander Nehamas's *Only a Promise of Happiness: The Place of Beauty in a World of Art*.[48]

---

[44]   Again, for further discussion of this point, see Babette Babich, "The Aesthetics of the Between: Space and Beauty," in *Jeff Koons: The Painter and The Sculptor*, ed. Vinzenz Brinkmann, Matthias Ulrich, and Joachim Pissarro (Frankfurt: Schirn Kunsthalle Frankfurt, 2012), 58–69.

[45]   James Davidson, *Courtesans and Fishcakes: The Consuming Passions of Classical Athens* (New York: Harper, 1999 [1997]); and see also Davidson's "Dover, Foucault and Greek Homosexuality: Penetration and the Truth of Sex," *Past and Present* 170 (2001): 3–51; as well as his *The Greeks and Greek Love: A Radical Reappraisal of Homosexuality in Ancient Greece* (London: Weidenfeld and Nicolson, 2007). Much, though hardly all, of Davidson's reading follows Dover's structuralist account in his *Greek Homosexuality* (Cambridge, MA: Harvard University Press, 1978). For another reading that is in greater accord with the now-mainstream, anti-Dover account, see William Percy, *Pederasty and Pedagogy in Archaic Greece* (Champaign/Urbana: University of Illinois Press, 1996).

[46]   Michel Foucault, *The Use of Pleasure* (New York: Pantheon Books, 1985).

[47]   Anne Carson, *Eros the Bittersweet* (Normal, IL: Dalkey Archive Press, 1998 [1986]).

[48]   Alexander Nehamas, *Only a Promise of Happiness: The Place of Beauty in a World of Art* (Princeton: Princeton University Press, 2007).

I could also say that k.d. lang is preternaturally aware of this, as she seems to be of most things, although by saying this I do not mean to say that she would either be cognizant of the same,[49] or indeed that she would concur with its significations as I take these to be significant here.

---

[49]   As k.d. lang herself tells us, and I have no reason to think that she is being disingenuous, she does not read books, although she did mention in a radio interview that she had heard that "someone in New York" (Alan Light) was writing a (trade) book on *Hallelujah*. Light's book, as already cited above, features Leonard Cohen in his own youth and Jeff Buckley in all the beauty that he would never outlive, framed against the center circle and vinyl grooves of a 45 record.

Chapter 5
"You don't really care for music, do ya?"

Baby, I've been here before

I have elsewhere had good occasion[1] for arguing that during the heyday of the sexual revolution, which also for good measure included women's 'liberation' (if we may speak of that failed undertaking in that way),[2] when it was popularly protested that women ought not perhaps be regarded as sex objects, men were fond of countering with the assertion that they would *love* to be sex objects. And they claimed this then, as they would like as not repeat the claim, not because it was "true," but because they were keen on what they called "free love," sex without strings (and sex with strings of the S&M variety was not, until k.d. lang's singing of Cohen's *Hallelujah*, any part of Cohen's reference to the real anxiety, the unmanning threat consequent to being tied to a kitchen chair, as in the circumstance that that was for Samson himself).

In fact, that is, in practice or real life, men do not "like," or would not know what to do with (and this is the same thing, in effect, as not liking) women who come on to them (ladies at the bar, please take note).[3] Women know this and this is why heterosexual women have to dress, and act, and walk the way they do. But

---

[1] Better said, I happened to have supposed I had such an occasion, invited as I had been in April of 2009 to address the theme of the "Status of Women in Philosophy" at the New School for Social Research in New York. This was not accurate, as I learned in retrospect: the lecture series title was called *The Status of Women in Philosophy* and merely represented a dedicated effort to feature women speakers in the department lecture series.

[2] See, for a text based on part of this lecture, Babette Babich, "Can't You Smile? Women and Status in Philosophy," *Radical Philosophy* 160 (March/April 2010): 36–8 (the title was added by the editors—my preference, such are my tastes, was for my original title, "Philosophy, Power and the Socialization of Men"). It is worth adding that I had submitted my New School lecture to *Hypatia*, hoping to publish it there, as it was there that I supposed—in my innocence—it to belong. The essay has since appeared as "Great Men, Little Black Dresses, and the Virtues of Keeping One's Feet on the Ground," but it does not appear in *Hypatia*, as the greater portion of that text pleased the late-wave feminist editors very little indeed, such that, even after massive cuts (and an astonishingly painful process of revision through several sets of editors), they wanted only that small portion of the text that was also desired by *Radical Philosophy*. Chalk it up to the allure of Alexander Nehamas's shoes.

[3] See the popular best-seller, now re-issued in an edition marketed under a related title, to take texting into account, *The Rules*. The two authors are modern Machiavellis, writing not for the eponymous prince but for women intending to subvert (or coopt, or

even suborned as objects to the one subject who gets to desire in the first place, women do not get close to loving men for their beauty, unless, to be sure, this desire is arranged in such a way that men do not notice it. At best, one might adjust a tie, choose a shirt, mend a shaving scar, and so on. Woman, as such, continues to remain the sexual, the erotic object for both heterosexual men and for *both* heterosexual *and* lesbian women, though one can take a shot a changing that if one wishes to stage some kind of performance-inspired drama, not a full-on erotic encounter.

Not really.

Although it is the erotic encounter that matters here for Cohen, it is *music* that is in question in Cohen's song: *You don't really care for music, do ya?* Set up by the inside talk of *a secret chord, that David played and it pleased the Lord*, it was, I have said, k.d. lang's rendering of Cohen's exposed illustration of the verse: *it goes like this: the fourth, the fifth, the minor fall, the major lift*, that caught me, utterly. The point bears on the 2005 Juno performance in question, that is, on the video of that performance as it can be seen on YouTube. Seeing this video makes all the difference for the effect I am talking about as this bears on the greater phenomenon of the hallelujah effect overall. Not only acoustic, but visual, not only visual, but dramatic, and add to that the resonance with life, the body, God, and time, the intellect, and sex: and it turns out that what we have on our hands is an internet-mediated riff on the nineteenth-century ideal of the *Gesammtkunstwerk*.

This is true of nearly all versions in some way. Is k.d. lang's version different from other covers? How so? How does she do what she does? Indeed, how does she manage to do it again and again—though professional singers do this all the time: *c'est son métier, quand même*, but many do not, and this is also why pop singers lip-synch their songs from time to time, singing back up, as it were, with recorded versions of themselves.[4] Got to preserve the exact sound. Perfect sound, as the online music magazine of the name repeats it, *forever*.[5]

---

whatever it takes) men into marriage. I doubt that they have read their Lacan, but their recommendations are in due Hegelian accord.

[4] See on this, again, Robert Fink's musicological study, *Repeating Ourselves: American Minimal Music as Cultural Practice* (Berkeley: University of California Press, 2005).

[5] *Perfect Sound Forever* is the online music magazine founded in 1993 by Jason Gross. See the current issue here: <http://www.furious.com/perfect/>. My original essay, "The Birth of kd lang's *Hallelujah* out of the 'Spirit of Music': Performing Desire and 'Recording Consciousness' on Facebook and YouTube," *Perfect Sound Forever* online music magazine (October/November 2011), out of which this book was developed, was initially published here: <http://www.furious.com/perfect/kdlang.html>, and it offers a combination of text, video, and sound that, in the case of this discussion, makes all the difference. *Perfecting Sound Forever* is also the title of Greg Milner's study of recorded music, cited above, and *Perfect Sound Forever* is the name of a music album by the group Pavement, released in 1991, and explicitly drawn from SONY's own 1982 advertising campaign. Milner's book traces this locution further.

Gender Crossing and the Erotic *Hallelujah*

I have already noted that part of k.d. lang's appeal for her following apparently derives from what some call her cross-dressing.[6] For my part, I find her clothes unremarkable,[7] but then I myself admit to never having quite understood why only a man might be permitted to wear a comfortable jacket, covering most of his body with decent tailoring (ah bespoke!), and be thought to look well-dressed, but women were seemingly required to uncover theirs.

This exactly double standard holds when it comes to song and dance shows—think Ginger Rogers and Fred Astaire—and only Gene Kelly or more recently Patrick Swayze (and both had good, muscular reasons to do so) opt for form-fitting dance clothes; I will not mention Dean Martin or k.d. lang's Tony Bennett because they, of course, exemplify the evening jacket point I am making.

The form-fitting clothes rule is hard on middle-aged women singers—even if they are, as k.d. lang is, in fact, in good shape (but, some will sigh, she has turned from 49 to 51 in my writing of this book). And these days, and for a while now, Madonna has struggled to match the bodies of her more youthful competitors; and then, too, there is the always debated issue of damaging one's voice by starving oneself. And so on.

k.d. lang's own sexuality made the difference here, perhaps it made all the difference.

And this takes us back to Debra Bergoffen's cautionary word about changing Cohen's language.

For it surely matters, as pointed out in the previous chapter, though this emphasis does not concern us here, that lang does change Cohen's lyric in a minor way, in certain versions (and even then only from time to time) by shifting the breathing, rendering as she does Cohen's "Hallelujah" as "Alleluia" in her first recording of it. Here the point is that breath, rough or smooth, is a small thing, a subjective thing, perhaps inevitably a question one can lay claim to (or refuse).

Leaving out or including verses is something else again.

Which of Cohen's many verses will one set to song in one's own claim to the song; this is the point of a cover after all; which verses will one cut or leave out? If the full length of Cohen's canonic *Hallelujah* seems by most accounts to include some eight verses (there are nicely exaggerated claims of 80 verses and this may be true, or it may be a sheerly metonymic expansion of eight—and what's a zero

---

[6]   There is a massive literature on this topic, and for that reason I do not need to begin to cite it here.

[7]   I will say, however, that I am quite keen on the very idea of performing in bare feet, but perhaps because I notice shoes (usually men's shoes) and find women's shoes, especially heels, both unattractive and uncomfortable. See, for a discussion of Alexander Nehamas's shoes in particular, Babich, "Can't You Smile? Women and Status in Philosophy."

between friends?),[8] the original recording featured only four verses, including several that k.d. lang does not sing.

I cited one of these above:

> You say I took the name in vain
> I don't even know the name
> But if I did, well really, what's it to you?
> There's a blaze of light in every word
> It doesn't matter which you heard
> The holy or the broken Hallelujah[9]

She also leaves off the final verse, a verse which, as we shall see, matters to Cohen as an Omega word, recessional, as this also matters for a song written by one conscious of the meaning of his own name and his priestly calling as a singer:

> I did my best, it wasn't much
> I couldn't feel, so I tried to touch
> I've told the truth, I didn't come to fool you
> And even though it all went wrong
> I'll stand before the Lord of Song
> With nothing on my tongue but Hallelujah.[10]

Once again, the 1988 version counts eight verses, with a crucially erotic addendum as Cale consecrates it in the center or third verse:

> There was a time you let me know
> What's really going on below
> Ah but now you never show it to me, do you?
> Yeah but I remember, yeah when I moved in you
> And the holy dove, she was moving too
> Yes every single breath that we drew was Hallelujah.[11]

It is this verse that made the song, as it were, in its paradigmatic form for John Cale. And here the question of the singer's sexuality makes all the difference. This

---

[8]   I have already cited Robert Fink's email remark above that it matters precisely that this is a strophic song, and his point about finding the start would apply if the total count were eight or 80. For my part, I take it that the song begins where Cohen's first (and indeed most recent) recording of it begins.

[9]   Cited from the Leonard Cohen files: <http://leonardcohenfiles.com/album8.html#61>.

[10]   Ibid.

[11]   See, for the 1988 version, the Leonard Cohen files: <http://leonardcohenfiles.com/album11.html##G>.

is the verse that makes this a song about sex and not merely about temptation ("her beauty and the moonlight"), as it also makes it about love, reproach, memory, as we have earlier cited Bryan Appleyard's ascerbic reflections.

If the venue (or if their label) permitted other singers who have "covered" Cohen's song to take the risk of offending so-called family values (though one wonders how families innocent of sex became families in the first place, just to echo Nietzsche's complaint about Wagner's *Parsifal*),[12] these same other (male) singers did not fail to repeat Cohen's weaker Gainsbourg lyrics (though Gainsbourg himself could not have been more heterosexually overt); Cohen's central erotic verse is also the one that male singers cannot wait to get to, perhaps because men tend to blame their partners for what changes in love between them, perhaps because it is the most explicit.

> And remember when I moved in you
> The holy dove was moving too
> And every breath we drew was Hallelujah.

Lang cuts this utterly, but what is astonishing is that, at the same time, she also manages to keep every bit of erotic tension on hand and from the start with Cohen's reference to David and Bathsheba (2 Samuel 11), *You saw her bathing on the roof / her beauty and the moonlight overthrew ya*, which some male singers, like Buckley, to continue the above subject's point of view, opt to sing as "her beauty *in* the moonlight."

Lang keeps the conjunction clear and her phrasing separates it: this is the whole of Eros, already in place. Overcome, overwhelmed: we are talking about the way that Eros works on us, from without, ready or not, it comes upon us, and this is the working force of desire.[13] By keeping this on the level of desire, we are also able—this is the mystery that is also already present from the start—to discover that we are talking about God, and lang does this without Cohen's *But now you never show it to me, do you? / And remember when I moved in you / The holy dove was moving too.*

Thus in the middle of another YouTube post including a number of other songs, k.d. lang, preternaturally conscious (this makes her both a very good and a very

---

[12] See the third essay in Nietzsche's *On the Genealogy of Morals*, and for Nietzsche and sex and sexuality, see Babette Babich, "Nietzsche und Wagner: Sexualität," trans. Martin Suhr, in *Wagner und Nietzsche. Kultur—Werk—Wirkung. Ein Handbuch*, ed. H.J. Brix, N. Knoepffler, and S.L. Sorgner (Reinbek b. Hamburg: Rowohlt, 2008), 323–41, of which an English translation is due to appear next year with Cambridge University Press, On women in Nietzsche, see my "Nietzsche and Eros Between the Devil and God's Deep Blue Sea: The Erotic Valence of Art and the Artist as Actor—Jew—Woman," *Continental Philosophy Review* 33 (2000): 159–88, as well as my "Reading Lou's Triangles," *New Nietzsche Studies* 8/3 & 4 (2011 / 2012): 82-114.

[13] See, on this, Anne Carson on language, consonants and the edge, edges, edginess of desire in *Eros the Bittersweet* (Normal, IL: Dalkey Archive Press, 1998 [1986]).

bad subject for television interviews), says "Welcome to church," a double joke at a concert in a church, to introduce a rendition of *Hallelujah*.

As a songwriter, Cohen's own words work as poetry and it matters in this that Cohen gives us rhymes to hear. The incipit—*I heard there was a secret chord*, and the second line *that David played and it pleased the Lord*—takes us in, the rhyme between *heard/chord/Lord* secured with an echoing assonance between *heard there.*

These are the mystery cults—the rites, the esoteric circles of both religion and music—*and it pleased the Lord.* This chord, this *secret* accords with those same rites: this chord pleases, which should very well entail that this chord would—ah, if one only knew it, ah, but it is a secret—work for us too: if only we might learn it.

We are taken in, we are captivated, and it would seem that this is precisely what the songwriter wishes of us, as he promotes himself, not hesitating "to advertise his technique"—I borrow the words from Ernest McClain, a musicological friend, who emphasizes that the proclamation is direct enough.[14]

Indeed, to draw upon McClain's musicological analysis, just as he offered it informally, just in personal correspondence,[15] only confirms what Cohen says when he tells us (this telling us so would be the postmodern move) that he is telling us what he is doing: *it goes like this: the fourth, the fifth, the minor fall, the major lift*—and it is exactly here, and just in the way that Nietzsche wrote of Beethoven, that his music is "music *about* music,"[16] that I am undone. This author, this voice. And *this* is also the way lang sings it, acts it, lives it, is it. This song is the song of itself, and this singing is the secret to the power of k.d. lang's interpretation, and this is the Hallelujah effect.

Now one might be inclined to say that, sure, everyone sings it this way; Cohen "sings" it this way, Wainwright and Buckley and any number of singers sing it this way, four Norwegian tenors sing it this way, in a round, trading verses. Yes, and again, no. *Everyone* does not sing it this way because k.d. lang sings the song

---

[14]   Email from Ernest McClain to the author: Friday 29 April 2011, 02:31pm and Saturday 30 April 2011, 07:02am. This would be almost like the immensely popular 1955 song by Alex North, with lyrics by Hy Zaret, *Unchained Melody*, composed (and who else pays for compositions?) for film in the version sung by Bobby Hatfield, recorded by the Righteous Brothers (as a B-side) in 1965. Note that the "unchained" in the title does not refer to the melody, although there are commonalities in what can be done with the song. As songwriter, as both musician and lyricist, Cohen is able to do things with his music and his words. This is his "cleverness" as McClain puts it: "sticking to basics in a genre that invites performers to vary his melody at their pleasure, shifting to higher tones in the same harmony, singing the text either with or AGAINST the background of the accompaniment, as if the musical discipline is as relaxed as the morals." Ibid.

[15]   Other musicological analyses are not in conflict with McClain's reading, but it remains a question whether what is to be analyzed is the score, and this is what McClain focuses upon, or the video of the performance, as I offer this here for my own part.

[16]   Friedrich Nietzsche, *The Wanderer and his Shadow*, Part Two, Section Two of *Human, All-too-Human*, Part Two, §152.

itself and her gestures are crucial. She builds and moves into the song. Thus in the YouTube video of the live performance that I am talking about here (a performance which qua YouTube video is not live, which is why we can analyze it), it is as if she were directing herself, directing the song itself, directing her own verse, her own chorus. Thus she plays with open fingers, *the fourth, the fifth*, and with a downturned hand smoothly traces *the minor fall*,[17] recovering with an upturned hand, *the major lift*, and, powerfully, *the baffled king composing Hallelujah*.[18]

Because then there is the walking. Beginning by standing by the piano, in contemplative reflection, poised in time, that is the time of the singer's musical silence, the time of the piano introduction, k.d. lang begins by singing and walks into and through the song, and it seems as if the song takes her through the whole of time and space. Musical time, musical space. This is the time/space, as we shall see below, that matters for Adorno in his physiognomic analysis of the face of, not Facebook, not YouTube, but radio when it came to listening, to hearing music.

Well, your faith was strong but you needed proof—and here it helps to be either Leonard Cohen singing of David and Bathsheba or k.d. lang singing exactly the same lines, with the same sympathy: *You saw her bathing on the roof, her beauty and the moonlight overthrew ya.*

Again, as lang sings it, every word, every sentiment comes clear.

Dissonance follows, mixing David and Samson and every manchild: *Well she tied you to a kitchen chair, she broke your throne, and cut your hair.* The whole of trauma is here, this is what shatters a lifetime, it is this—pent up and waiting—that brings down a temple.

It will be lang's gestures, it will be her eyes, the turn of her head to speak of the moonlight and its rapture, winding the cord of her microphone to illustrate being tied to the kitchen chair, but also looking straight at the audience as she does so, that make it plain that this is a sexual come on, *she*, of course it was she who did this, *broke your throne and*, cutting with her fingers to illustrate, *cut your hair*.

---

[17]   This is almost "textbook," as are many things in this song. See, for example, Alexander Rehding's glossary of Riemann's notion of "harmonic dualism," as "the major consonance (from the principle tone downwards) and the minor consonance (from the principle tone upwards)," in *Hugo Riemann and the Birth of Modern Musical Thought* (Cambridge: Cambridge University Press, 2003), 188. To say that this is textbook is not to say that musicologists concur with this reading (and many do not, the balance of tone accounts having shifted to Helmholtz and still further to contemporary neuropsychology); it is only to say that the schema as such is not a new one.

[18]   Robert Fink, to my mind, insightfully highlights just this phrase as he picks up on McClain's correspondence with me, which I sent to him, as published in Babich, "The Birth of kd lang's *Hallelujah* out of the 'Spirit of Music'": where Fink writes "McClain hits it pretty well on the head—his larger analytical point about how the song's chord cycle peaks deceptively at the first 'Hallelujah' and then kind of runs down into energy-discharging repetitions is very apt. I have to say that I love how the 'baffled king composing' line lines up with the most 'tricky' moment in the song's tonal arc." Email to the author: Thursday 11 August 2011, 05:46pm.

Here, after all this, is nothing more than the space of the musical phrase and the listener knows, this gets under your skin, that the one addressed is you yourself. This is a different you, some other you, son of man: *and from your lips, she drew*, and here there are disputes between the need to add an article, Wainwright and most men, including Cohen himself, name it determinate—*"the" Hallelujah.*

What is it, what would it be, as Nietzsche says, to praise the demon who speaks thus? What kind of belief do you have to have, what kind of abased, abashedly awful love do you have to have, to still say, as Abraham, Job, David did—*Your faith was strong, but you needed proof*—Hallelujah? Anyone who has felt at all knows that it is all about—what? What is the reference here? It is you, centrally, as subject, as the one who desires, and it underscores sensuality. *Her beauty in the moonlight.*

On the matter of affirmation, Nietzsche reflects that if there is just one thing to which you would say "Yes," then you also and inevitably affirm every other thing, because everything is inextricably intertwined, interknotted. This is also the point that Erwin Schrödinger draws out from the Vedanta and that Georges Bataille takes from Christian mysticism, divinity of self and world. Tied, broken, cut—*and from your lips she drew*, what? A groan? Of ecstasy? Suffering? *Hallelujah.*

The four hallelujahs that follow are small miracles of understatement and perfectly articulated power, one after another.

If the composer's confidence is that he can tell us what he is doing with his chord, the composer/singer brings it home, and brings us back to the present as s/he does so, referring to the song itself, sung as the singer sings it: *Baby, I've been here before / I've seen this room, I've walked this floor*, eroticized, consummately so in the Juno performance where k.d. cocks her head and puts her hand on her hip, the classic instantiation of Eros, I need you, I don't need you: *I used to live alone before I knew ya.* Doing this, exerting distance, one is brought to the extraordinary pathos of Cohen's song: *But I've seen your flag on the marble arch*, and this is k.d., this pathos she takes home, this point of desolation, abasement, sorrow, wounding reproof: *our love is not a victory march, it's a cold and it's a broken hallelujah.* This is all we are given, all we have, this is all there is. This is a deity whose only redemption, whose only blessing for us, whose only grace is emptiness, indigence, frailty.

This is also what Nietzsche named the "becoming-human of dissonance," this is what I once named elsewhere, in a reflection on Eros, love "coolly and mightily wrong,"[19] not the redemption of love, not the saving love, the kind that works out

---

[19]   Babich, "Nietzsche and Eros Between the Devil and God's Deep Blue Sea." Bryan Appleyard makes a similar point when he observes that "the *Hallelujah* that adorns the flaccid sexual crises in *The OC* and adds soul to the babbling shenanigans of *The West Wing* is a brilliant fake. It sounds like a pop song, but it isn't. Like the Velvet Underground's 'Heroin,' Bob Dylan's 'Leopard Skin Pillbox Hat,' John Phillips's 'Let it Bleed, Genevieve' or even Frank Sinatra's 'I Get Along Without You Very Well,' it is a tuneful but ironic mask worn to conceal bitter atonal failure." Bryan Appleyard, "Hallelujah! On Leonard Cohen's Ubersong," *The Sunday Times*, 9 June 2005.

in the end, the love that ends well, finding glory and secured joy, but a shattered love, wrong from the start, all the way down, *a cold and broken hallelujah.*

Cascade, crescendo, hallelujahs in chorus, ascending again and again.

Maybe there's a god above. Maybe indeed. But this god is already close enough to the Jewish and close enough to the Christian that Cohen, like Nietzsche, turns to reflect on what it might mean to be a god at all, *and* to be implicated in love.[20] A line from the 2004 Canadian film, *Saint Ralph*, sets this into a younger priest's mouth, calling an older priest on his hypocrisy: "*Oh, and about anarchists, Nietzsche had nothing on Christ.*"[21]

Here, and this we may call the *Liberty Valance* moment, as k.d. plays it perfectly, all mimesis, given away: *All I've ever learned from love*, she confesses, *is how to shoot somebody who outdrew ya.* Shaking her head, we know that this is no achievement, that this shows nothing but the abjection, the inadequacy of love: what we are moved to do, and what we ultimately do do, anyway. And this is brought all the way to the top, to what it is to love God, to praise God, pleasing/ displeasing and the vast distance between what that is and what we commonly take it to be. *It's not a cry you hear at night, it's not someone who's seen the light: it's a cold and it's a broken hallelujah.* And it is what lang does with the hallelujahs to follow, punctuated and powerfully sung, and in contrast with the visceral as she crouches into the pain of these hallelujahs, finally unutterably, impossibly sustained, eyes closed, an extraordinary peace out from the center of being, her being, to open and raise her eyes and our thoughts.

The song affects everyone who hears it,[22] perhaps because k.d. lang's great secret is that she listens to the space around her, even to the extent of feeling it bodily[23]—she even does this in 2010 at her live performance at the Olympic Winter Games in Vancouver. This listening also means that she is affected as well, and in 2005, the smile that she gives the audience in response to their response after the song ends is a striking contrast to the composed professionalism of the song in its pace and delivery. Indeed, when k.d. lang sings this to Leonard Cohen's own approbation on the occasion of his 2006 induction into the Canadian Songwriters Hall of Fame, she knows at every instant exactly where she is and in

---

[20]   See, again, my reflection in the prior note, as well as my reflection on friendship and education in "Become the One You Are: On Commandments and Praise—Among Friends," in *Nietzsche, Culture, and Education*, ed. Thomas Hart (London: Ashgate, 2009), 13–38.

[21]   Written and directed by Michael McGowan.

[22]   As one YouTube comment, responding to k.d. lang's 2006 performance for Cohen's Songwriters Hall of Fame induction, puts it: "If you told me that God brought the universe into existence 15 billion years ago because he wanted to hear K.D. Lang sing Hallelujah, I just might believe you ..." Waltham1892 1 year ago 29.

[23]   H. Stith Bennett, who repays reading and re-reading of his *On Becoming a Rock Musician* (Amherst: University of Massachusetts Press, 1980), attests to the complex and elusive thing that it is to do this. This same acoustic spatiality is also key to Adorno's reflections on Bekker and the symphony to which we turn in Chapter 7 below.

whose presence she sings. And she also knows whose song it is, giving utter and moving homage to Cohen: running down from the stage to greet him as suppliant, touching her head to his solar plexus, all deference, concession, gratitude.

Chapter 6
Performance Practice and the Hallelujah Effect

Technique and the Art of the Standing Ovation—*da capo*

Pop performance, to be popular, is deliberate: controlled, contrived, packaged. To say this is to say that every bit of it is as advertised: it is always a performance and a good deal is involved: what is seen, what is heard, but also what we do not see and do not hear. Thus a good part of this takes place behind the scenes, beforehand. This is the work done by the performers and the production teams that support them, and this is also the work done by the listeners themselves, as Adorno stresses, as Anders argues, and as Bennett, Baudrillard, and others also argue. To say this takes no part of the achievement away from either k.d. lang or Leonard Cohen. We are always watching a consummate artist at work. And as Nietzsche said, speaking of Wagner, we might do well, for aesthetics sake, for the sake of the artwork itself, to ignore all issues of technique, along with all questions concerning or considerations of the conditions/motivations/practices of the artist where, as Nietzsche supposed, what matters is the work, the *working* of the work of art, as music. And Nietzsche also distinguished art before witnesses, art for the sake of spectators, for the sake of an audience, from what he called the creator's art, the artist's art, which was also what he called monological art of the non-histrionic variety, which he also spoke of in terms of the "music for forgetting"[1] the self, forgetting oneself.[2]

At the same time that Nietzsche raises the question of the artist as the "problem" of the artist and the "problem" of the actor, he also sets the problem of the artist into a cadential array: actor—Jew—woman, thereby delineating the classic constellation of anxiety and suspicion. Much of Nietzsche's resentment of women is also to be found here, and at the same time as we recall that Nietzsche characterizes himself as the supreme diagnostician of *ressentiment*, he also suggests a certain ironic tone in his reflections entitled "Why I am a decadent"—with all its resonances with Cohen's *Beautiful Losers*, with all the implications for k.d. lang's fans, especially as she addresses them.[3] I say this

---

[1] Nietzsche, GS, §367.

[2] See, for references and discussion, Babette Babich, "Nietzsche and Eros Between the Devil and God's Deep Blue Sea: The Erotic Valence of Art and the Artist as Actor—Jew—Woman," *Continental Philosophy Review* 33 (2000): 159–88.

[3] And not only k.d. lang's fans, but indeed any member of the well-heeled "middle class," as many so insist on naming themselves, despite an absurdity undermined by the

in the context of Facebook and its geek founders and today's celebration of the anti-mystique of the same in a consummation that transfigures spectator and artist alike.

Any mainstream contender to center stage may also fit Nietzsche's description of the slavely moral, while at the same time, Nietzsche also offers us an analysis of the outsider/insider aesthetic in what he speaks of as a certain "enlightenment about *ressentiment*."[4] I read this self-enlightenment into his own analysis of his unteachable "stupidity," a stupidity, that is to say, that goes all the way down, "down deep," to use his own words about his own reflections concerning women. And Nietzsche teaches us that, by announcing one's idiocy, one can often feel oneself entitled to it. Certainly one supposes that one thereby gets away with it.

Thus one calls oneself a geek or a nerd (or a freak) to celebrate oneself in the process, without having to be anything more than one is. Leave the bed unmade.

Nietzsche's relationship to women is, of course, worth a study all its own, and there are many such on offer, if most of them suffer from some of the same weaknesses that Nietzsche analyzes, and if few of them begin from Simone de Beauvoir's analyses, as I submit one ought to begin, rather than on the basis of a review of Nietzsche's nineteenth-century vision of femininity, or indeed on the whiggish, that is to say, presentist basis of assuming that today's view, that *our* view, of women applies to him in the first place. And which view of ours will that be? Will that be Leonard Cohen's view? k.d. lang's view? Judy Butler's view? Or, and rather more esoterically still, Luce Irigaray's view? Or shall we continue to count in public intellectuals such as the insister-on-the-status-of-the-same Camille Paglia, or will it be, rather more soberly, Naomi Wolf, or shall we stick to the older fantasy of Susan Sonntag who remains, as she should be and even now and even as dead as she is, the intellectual's pin-up imago of woman?[5]

What is plain is that Nietzsche makes the question of woman, as we already cited Derrida as explicating, his own question. As he tells us in a brief against the "'Emancipation of women'" in his auto-bibliography—his self-composed

---

current economy of the same unemployment and upside down mortgages, and devalued pensions, which, according to Adorno, at least, the culture industry as a whole is designed to keep one from noticing. And it works. Instead, we ourselves name ourselves "freaks," just as k.d. lang, in what vaudeville comedians used, once upon a time, to call a schtick, invites her audience to do.

[4]   Nietzsche, EH, *Why I am so Wise*, §6, KSA, vol. 6.

[5]   If you are German, you might opt to substitute the poet Ingeborg Bachman; for another generation it might have been Alma Mahler, or Lou von Salomé. For a discussion of the latter, see my reading of Nietzsche and Lou von Salomé, including a discussion of the triangulation of their relationship with Paul Rée, in Babich, "Nietzsche, Lou, Art and Eros: The 'Exquisite Dream' of Sacro Monte," in *Lou Andreas-Salomé, muse et apôtre*, ed. Pascale Hummel (Paris: Philologicum, 2011), 174–230. And for an excellent study, *inter linea*, see Geraldine Finn, *Why Althusser Killed his Wife* (Amherst, NY: Humanity Books, 1996). *Nota bene*, the point I seek to make above, although consonant with Finn's reading, is not her major point, which renders her reading all the more insightful.

catalogue of his own books, *Ecce Homo*, which we should read as a kind of Nietzsche retrospective, rather exactly as a recording artist down on his funds, or noticing a lack of attention, might throw such a retrospective together (and some artists do these again and again)—"I *know* women ... I am the first psychologist of the eternally feminine."[6] Ambivalent to the core, Nietzsche excludes "abortive females, the 'emancipated' who lack the stuff for children."[7] And for Nietzsche— this will be the nineteenth century in him, indeed every other century including the present one—what women are for is exactly children, and thus he writes in utter resonance with this view that a women needs a man (and this is the same remedy that he prescribes for the "problem of woman" in general) in order to "give her a child."[8] Nor have we changed: the fundamental legacy of women's liberation in our age has been the introduction of child-friendly rules for the workplace. Not equal rights, not equal pay. Heavens, no. What else do women need? Child-friendly legislation ought to do it. Rather than Take Back the Night, rather than Off Our Backs, younger feminists recommend Slut Walks, arguing that exuding sex appeal, lipstick, high heels and all, is just "power."

And this is good feminist thinking, then as now. As Nietzsche observes (and I would suggest that in this context we might recall k.d. lang's performative interpretation of *Johnny Get Angry*):

> Woman, the more she is a woman, resists rights in general hand and foot: after all, the state of nature, the eternal war between the sexes, gives her by far first rank ... [the abortive woman wants by contrast] to lower the level of the general rank of woman; and there is no surer means for that than higher education, slacks, and political voting-cattle rights.[9]

As already noted, we do not need to go too far to find this argument among the great majority of feminist thinkers. Subvert away. It goes without saying that male fundamentalists (garden variety conservatives) all-too-naturally concur. Add more subversion and stir.

But Nietzsche also meant this in a musical sense. And in the same locus, in his same self-composed catalogue of his works, he writes: "I shall say another word for the most select ears: what I really want from music."[10] To parse this here, I have emphasized that it makes all the difference that Nietzsche's reference is indeed music, even if it is the case that—and this very likely has more to do with Aristotle (one should always be on guard against personalizing even a personal biography, as Nietzsche warned us)—it does not offer us special or private access

---

[6] Nietzsche, EH, *Why I Write Such Good Books*, §5.

[7] Ibid.

[8] Ibid.

[9] Ibid.

[10] Nietzsche, EH, *Why I am so Clever*, §7.

to Nietzsche's personal erotic tastes per se.[11] Thus qualified, we note that Nietzsche speaks of music by means of the same metaphor that he uses for truth as for life and for eternity: namely "woman." Thus music, as he lists his desiderata, should "be cheerful and profound like an afternoon in October. That it be individual, frolicsome, tender, a sweet small woman full of beastliness and charm."[12] What seems clear is that this is an aesthetic that at least seems opposed to any but a certain traditionally masculine sense of woman (this will be the antithesis of k.d. lang's *Big Boned Gal*).[13] If Nietzsche goes on here to explain what he understands as "his own south in music,"[14] he tells us what he means: "When I seek another word for music, I always find only the word Venice."

Thus we have what I regard as Nietzsche's most beautiful poem, a poem which also happens, as I argue elsewhere, to be itself a tone-poem, composed in Hölderlin's tones, to be sure,[15] tones recalled, called forth in the physical proximity of, in the city that could not but in this context remind Nietzsche of Wagner's death. Thus we hear what makes some commentators regard Leonard Cohen as an existentialist, as it is the same thing that induces some readers to read Nietzsche as an existentialist (and where Cohen might have because he *could have* been, Nietzsche was not), where

---

[11]   Perhaps we do better to trust Nietzsche's negative animadversions contra Lou Salomé as a "scrawny, dirty, bad-smelling monkey with her false breasts" (Nietzsche in Sils Maria to Georg Rée in Stibbe, mid July 1883, in Nietzsche, *Sämtliche Briefe, Kritische Studienausgabe*, vol 6 [Berlin: de Gruyter, 1986], 402), as the late Rudy Binion rather psychoanalytically insisted. See Rudolph Binion, *Frau Lou: Nietzsche's Wayward Disciple* (Princeton: Princeton University Press, 1968). Certainly, Binion's analysis takes us further than assuming that Lou was Nietzsche's erotic ideal or, indeed, that she was the love of his life. See, for further discussion and references, Babich, "Nietzsche, Lou, Art and Eros." I am grateful to Binion for having responded, as he did, at what proved to be the end of his life, to the essay I originally sent him, an essay reminding him of the lasting influence and value of his work for future scholarship. I develop some of this in Babette Babich, "Philosophische Figuren, Frauen und Liebe: Zu Nietzsche und Lou," in *Nietzsche-Forschung*, ed. Renate Reschke (Berlin: Akademie Verlag, 2012), 113–39.

[12]   Nietzsche, EH, *Why I am so Clever*, §7. And maybe that is Lou, or maybe Nietzsche is talking about the ladies of Naples—or the boys; who, at this distance, can tell?

[13]   See, here, Sheila Whitely, "Who Are You: Research Strategies of the Unruly Feminine," in *The Ashgate Research Companion to Popular Musicology*, ed. Derek B. Scott (Farnham, Surrey: Ashgate, 2009), 205–20. Alas, and disappointingly, Whitely refers to neither Burns, "'Joanie' Get Angry" or Stella Bruzzi, "Mannish Girl," although citing McClary's *Feminine Endings* and Mockus, "Queer Thoughts on Country Music and k.d. lang." Whitely, to be sure, is not focusing on lang, but has a very complicated theme which she follows, after her citation of Judith Butler's reflection that "'for a woman to identify as a woman is a culturally enforced effect'," (205) to Jung and archetypes/symbols including Rosicrucian constructions for a reading of Tori Amos's *The Beekeeper*.

[14]   Nietzsche, EH, *Why I am so Clever*, §7.

[15]   See Babette Babich, "Between Hölderlin and Heidegger: Nietzsche's Transfiguration of Philosophy," *Nietzsche-Studien* 29 (2000): 267–301.

Nietzsche writes a beautiful prose line to frame a comparably beautiful song sung in tones of inimitable poetry, sung to the city of songs, to Venice itself: "I do not know how to distinguish between tears and music—I do not know how to think of happiness, of the south, without shudders of timidity."[16]

We may, if we are inclined, call this Nietzsche's own *Hallelujah*; it is certainly a word of praise, affirmation that speaks to what is blessed and what is failed, weak, painful, tragic. This is the broken *Hallelujah* that resounds in Cohen's song. This is life not only in its good aspects, but also including, as life includes, as life *is*, suffering, ageing, and death. Nietzsche called it his Yay saying or affirmation (*Bejahung*), his *amor fati*, and he linked this to his teaching of eternal recurrence, the eternal return of the self-same. Thus we read here the epigraph to *Ecce Homo*:

> On this perfect day, when everything is ripening and not only the grape turns brown, the eye of the sun just fell upon my life: I looked back, I looked forward, and never saw so many and such good things at once. It was not for nothing that I buried my forty-fourth year today: I had the right to bury it; whatever was life in it has been saved, is immortal ... How could I fail to be grateful to my whole life?

In a way, Nietzsche's own poem to Venice and to music also serves to echo this epigraph, now heard as prelude:

> At the bridge I stood
> lately in the brown night.
> From afar came a song:
> as a golden drop it welled
> over the quivering surface.
> Gondolas, lights, and music—
> drunken it swam out into the twilight.
> My soul, a stringed instrument,
> sang to itself, invisibly touched,
> a secret gondola song,
> quivering with iridescent happiness.
> —Did anyone hear it?[17]

In the section to follow, Nietzsche emphasizes what is required for the sake of the exercise itself, that is, to emphasize the subtitle of the book, *Ecce Homo*, "*how one becomes what one is*"[18] And everything here bears as much upon Nietzsche

---

[16]   Nietzsche, EH, *Why I am so Clever*, §7.

[17]   Ibid., §7. I discuss this poem-song and its relation to Wagner and Hölderlin in Babich, "Between Hölderlin and Heidegger," as well as in "Songs of the Sun," in Babich, *Words in Blood, Like Flowers: Philosophy and Poetry, Music and Eros in Hölderlin, Nietzsche, and Heidegger* (Albany: State University of New York Press, 2006).

[18]   Nietzsche, EH, *Why I am so Clever*, §8.

the thinker as upon the artist, and the keynote to this is "selfishness."[19] This is the heart of what makes the artist an artist, the thinker a thinker, the philosopher a philosopher, in every earnest sense. And this also and at the same time requires an absolute self-innocence, oblivion. Assuming, as Aristotle would say, that one is truly worthy of great things, given, indeed to begin with, that one possesses greatness:

> For let us assume that the task, the destiny, the fate of the task transcends the average very significantly: in that case, nothing could be more dangerous than catching sight of oneself *with* this task. To become what one is, one must not have the faintest notion of *what* one is. From this point of view even the blunders of life have their own meaning and value … where *nosce te ipsum* would be a recipe for ruin, forgetting oneself, *misunderstanding* oneself, making oneself smaller, narrower, mediocre, become reason itself.[20]

Music and the "Problem" of the Artist-Actor

To return to k.d. lang (and then to Cohen), in all this we add, on another note, Nietzsche's suggestion that he would be both drawn in by and made anxious at the same time by what he, in *The Gay Science*, described as *Women who Master the Masters*. As Nietzsche reflects, and his observation touches on the voice quite apart from gender, even apart from music, if not apart from the stage:

> A deep and powerful alto voice of the kind one sometimes hears in the theater can suddenly raise the curtain upon possibilities in which we usually do not believe. All at once we believe that somewhere in the world there could be women with lofty, heroic, and royal souls, capable of and ready for rule over men because in them the best elements of man apart from his sex have become an incarnate ideal.[21]

The problem for Nietzsche is that this ideality is usually then read back into men and that the entire project nevertheless still falls short of what real human beings do, or better said, what they do not do. If Nietzsche had learned one thing from his reading of Goethe's *Faust*, it was to see through love and its vanities.

Nietzsche challenged that the theatrical bet placed on the efficacy of such voices tended not to succeed, that is, qua female (or, as he pointed out, mostly

---

[19]   Ibid.

[20]   Ibid.

[21]   Nietzsche, GS, §70. This point is one that Erik Steinskog disattends to, by focusing on Martha Wainwright's covers of Cohen rather than k.d. lang's, in his "Queering Cohen: Cover Versions as Subversions of Identity," in *Play It Again: Cover Songs in Popular Music*, ed. George Plasketes (Farnham, Surrey: Ashgate, 2010), 139–52.

male, as in "the ideal male lover such as Romeo,"[22] and here, to move beyond Nietzsche to later and even more recent popular culture, we can add the literary Heathcliff's moody distance, or the cross-dressing aesthetic that is the vampire in the daylight in Stephenie Meyer's vampire series, *Twilight*, and the more conventionally hysterical vampires of the evening in the *True Blood* series on HBO cable television today). And this may be behind the suspicion sometimes placed on an extraordinary vocal range.[23] And Nietzsche's point also cuts to the

---

[22] Nietzsche, GS, §70.

[23] It is this range that Ernest McClain invokes in k.d. lang's case as he writes of what he characterizes as an "abnormally wide range." For McClain, "Lang's great skill is with a wholly ambiguous sexuality and vocal sound that is neither beautiful nor ugly but proves immensely 'serviceable' under her easy, smooth transitions across an abnormally wide range. She is a professional indeed, and I think also the composer is in his own way (he bluntly advertises his technology)." Email to the author, Saturday 30 April 2011, 07:02am. Here, and despite its length, it is worth contextualizing this point, as McClain prefaces his remarks by emphasizing that they are as much about Cohen's song as about k.d. lang's cover: "I say the song is a perfect 'embodiment' of its own text. That it indeed 'tells all' at the start. I propose to comment 'as if' in the key of C. You sent me copies in 3 keys, remarkably different. These are efforts to 'universalize' profitably at EVERY level of sophistication. This song is a 'piece of music' that is 'going nowhere.' Four verses telling the same failed effort. And the melody fails in every verse. 'As if' four times we start out on life, defeated each time. Your Greek strophe's take over and complete each verse with its failed Hallelujah's as 'Chorus commentary.' The singer can sing all, as Lang does, or let the chorus enter them. Every effort 'breaks down,' into hysterical catharsis, freely expressed. But what a 'cosmic theme' this is. This is brilliantly subversive public 'entertainment,' inviting empathy and winning storms of applause. The main oscillations are around a hopeful major third of C:E common to the major triad C:E:G with its own relative minor triad a third below as A:C:E (with the minor third alternating 'weakly'. This 'weak' progression is merely a bland harmonic oscillation. This is a very 'weak' 'Non-progression,' merely a slight 'oscillation' of chord color blending with the innocuous triplet rhythm. Another paired group concerns the 'dominant' triad G:B:D with its major third below 'oscillating' weakly with its OWN relative minor, E:G:B. Actual harmonic Progressions by a fifth (strong, 'normatively') Upward injects energy F to C and/ or C to G and Downward retracts it C to F and/or G to C happens seldom but strategically. Change by a wholetone F:G in roots is VERY strong Upward and VERY recessive Downward (and happens VERY little, perhaps once in each verse). I am analyzing with the language of my theorist friend Ernst Levy and will explain and illustrate in the key of C to make it easier for readers schematically. The slow triplet pulse is almost entirely unbroken oscillation in duple groupings from beginning to end, but the melody occasionally bravely asserts a duple movement against the triplet underlay, and the melody also advantageously interjects counter rhythmic accents of its own (syncopations) that register 'resolute independence' but end hysterically." As McClain concludes this point, after his reflections on k.d. lang's extraordinary voice/range: "Aristotle would have been immensely gratified by this example of the NEED to address the public in its OWN terms. Chromatic interest is nil; the matrials are almost exclusively diatonic. The Greek strophe is present (to me) in the singer's effort (4 times over) to create the selfish life yearned for by the soul, answered SOLO four times by the self in its retreat and frustration playing knowingly on public experience of our private

heart of what we above considered as Leonard Cohen's idealization of woman, however intrinsically misogynist (idealizations, when one has power, are always a way to take revenge on the object of one's supposed ideal).[24]

For, as Cohen's many commentators have also noted, McClain's musicological reading reminds us, both as cited above and in the notes to this text, that Cohen's achievement is a real, *working* achievement. And as I have been noting throughout, what Cohen effects—and this by the same token constitutes the difference that makes all the difference in k.d. lang's interpretations of Cohen's *Hallelujah*—is effected in practice. That is why I have been emphasizing here the unfortunately literal terminus "performance practice" to the degree that such practice is not about the score, the written text, but a practiced consummation—this would be improvisation for Nietzsche, given what we know about his musical gifts and in his nineteenth-century context—attuned to musical efficacy, as this efficacy *works* on us, today, and below I shall have to return to Adorno, just in order to be able to explore this point further. Here the point can be made without the radicality and complexity of Adorno's reading of musical culture (and it is to the point that musicologists of popular music, even those who can otherwise bear to read Adorno, always find it necessary to distance their own reading from Adorno, in order not to be saddled with Adorno's criticisms, criticisms we have learned to overlook in our day, which means that, at times, we also have no idea what our simplifications cost us).

Here, in the context of the Hallelujah effect that is my larger concern, I initially wrote to McClain in order to ask him about the chord in question, just to be sure, as I am fond of checking and over-checking my own readings.[25] The extraordinary and extraordinarily genial thing about McClain is that he answered my question about what "secret" might be meant—not to solve it (this is not the problem, as the chord itself was never arcane). What is elusive is, as we have seen, the claim of the "secret," underscored as it is between the Lord and the David who sings and who pleases God with his song. And in this case we happen to be touching the very heart of what Nietzsche describes as the triumph of the slavely moral, that is, historio-biblically. Thus, with David, we are talking about a shepherd boy with a bent for real-world subversion, one who takes the clever, easy way out when it comes to a fight, but who also thereby always guarantees his own supremacy. *And everybody loves a winner.* When it comes to love, David does the same thing, that would be Bathsheba, one among his many lovers, whom (after seeing her bathing on the roof, meaning indeed that she was out of view of everyone's eyes,

---

failures (experienced singly but wholly banal). The whole song, like the occasions for which it is written, is 'ironic put-on' fake at every moment, yet none-the-less 'universal' for being so. You are dealing with a total public success of this moment ..." Email to the author.

[24]   The master, to which the whole of Lacan's irony attests, has ways to ensure his mastery, contra the alluring vision of Hegel's schema. Marx likewise. And this is empirical.

[25]   My footnotes are some of the evidence of this, and of course there is always more that could have been added to these.

everyone's but the king's) David was prepared to effect—this is sovereignty as Nietzsche also understands it, if it is not "noble" as Nietzsche would say—to do *whatever* it took, including, as David did, get rid of her husband, in order to have her. *And all's fair in love and war.* This David, this king, cheats in everything he does: he is nobody's saint, he is neither Abraham nor Job. Thus, as we have already seen, there is a great deal of literature on Cohen's chord that also raises the same question, only to answer it, disposing of it at once.

In an off-the-cuff analysis, at least, after I sent him the scores,[26] inasmuch as McClain is an old school musicologist, I myself meant the question not in terms of the song as Cohen (or indeed as k.d. lang) sings it, but rather as the referent, whatever that might be, and once again, I asked: what about *the chord itself.* And in once reading this—and this email exchange took place in real time, that is, the real time of an obsessive checking of one's email (substitute Twitter, if you prefer, it is all the same), an obsession of the kind that today's internet accessibility makes possible, for me with an internet connection and an iPhone during my travels between New York and Berlin, for the then-92 year old McClain in Washington— he immediately explained that there is no secret in the context of the chord, or none at all, everything is overt, announced.[27] The song elaborates what musicologists technically name a musical joke, let's call it a tease:

---

[26] I purchased several versions to facilitate this.

[27] Later on, as mentioned already, I corresponded with Robert Fink and others, including Rose Subotnik. Fink's immediate response was beautiful and confirmed McClain's reading, as Fink also noted an important practical detail: "as it happens I have been practicing that song in my guitar class (I am learning guitar after decades of being a keyboardist), and so I can recall the passage in question right away. The nice thing is that the song is self-reflexive at that point. That is, the musical accompaniment does, syntactically, exactly what the lyrics are describing, so that, in effect, the song 'analyzes itself.' The song is often played in the key of G. Here is a G-major scale, with the steps numbered as they are in music theory:

G   A   B   C   D   E   F#   G
1   2   3   4   5   6   7   8 (=1)

'the fourth' (is accompanied by a C-major chord, which is built on scale degree *four* of G)

'the fifth' (is accompanied by a D-major chord, which is built on scale degree *five* of G)

'the minor fall' (is accompanied by a deceptive E-*minor* chord, which is a '*fall*' down (6 instead of 8) from G major, the chord we expect)

'the major lift' (is accompanied by a C-*major* chord, which gives the feeling of a '*lift*' up again)

So 'the secret chord,' which, as Cohen writes, 'goes like this: the fourth, the fifth, the minor fall, the major lift,' is actually a *chord progression*, and it is hardly a secret one. It's a completely basic tonal progression (I-IV-V-vi-IV-I in music theory terms) which any musically trained person would already have heard a zillion times before. The first two chords you could decipher from the words alone; the second two are less precise (i.e.,

The jest in the words is exactly what they describe. He mainly oscillates on the mild colors of major tonic and relative minor, with two tones in common, as I described. His first "very strong" "progression" is a truncated cadence (*You don't [really] care for music, do ya?*) (meaning MOVEMENT, a whole tone upward from Subdominant to Dominant) but he is late getting to the latter and "throws it away" on the tonic "do ya."[28]

For McClain, all this is calculated artistry, not only brilliantly plain but consummately effective, and that is to say: on musical terms. Here McClain's further, and astonishingly fluent, "sight" musicological analysis of Cohen's music is worth citing:

> But the 16 measure traditional "bar-form" has a jest in the harmony for the king approaches his own Hallelujah by arcing over the upper octave and then veering off to a "deceptive cadence" (the G sharp seventh chord in measure 14 is the dominant of the tonic's relative minor, and the only "chromaticism" [repeated in each verse]). This harmonic "dislocation" motivates the string of muttered hallelujahs that follow as the tonic is recovered in time for the next verse.[29]

Of course, beyond sight is sound, and this is where k.d. lang's voice, its physicality, its depths and range, makes all the difference. Thus this is sight reading, in every sense.[30] In any case, in every case, it is Cohen's song that allows k.d. lang to do what she does. And this is also why it is quite believable, whether true or not (I do not know, how could I know this? How can anyone, including the author himself, at this late date, "know"), that Cohen wrote some 80 verses to it. Hence, I have already suggested, as do others, that this is apocrypha, while at the same time, I believe it.

What is certain—and I referred to this above in the conclusion of the previous chapter—is that when he accepted his induction to the Canadian Songwriters Hall of Fame in 2006, and after listening to k.d. lang's performance, Leonard Cohen

---

there is only one 'fourth' and one 'fifth' in any key, but there are a few different choices for 'minor falls' and 'major lifts' you could make). Fink, email to the author: Wednesday 10 August 2011, 06:44pm.

28   McClain, email to the author: Saturday 30 April 2011, 06:58pm.

29   McClain, email to the author: Sunday 1 May 2011, 06:41pm.

30   I noted above that McClain was a few months away from 93 (we've known each other much longer) when this correspondence first began. Thus his own hearing, and this is to say on his own account as he repeated again and again, was so diminished that he required the scores themselves to talk about the chord that I was asking about. Scores I purchased on his behalf, as he himself also did. Cf. here too, Adorno's repeated reflections on written music, symbols, writing, reading scores: "The study must offer a theory of sight-reading. In general, while looking over and absorbing the score, I can already assess a piece of music before I can imagine it precisely." Theodor Adorno, *Towards a Theory of Musical Reproduction: Notes, a Draft, and Two Schemata*, trans. Wieland Hoban (London: Polity, 2006), 69, and also 162.

himself was moved to reclaim his song, which he did by reciting—and for Cohen that is not very different from singing—just one more verse. And that was, of course, the original, priestly verse that Cale had clipped from his version.

Instructively, even the most apocryphal extension of the length of the song itself is already articulated in the structure of the song itself, and not just because, as McClain was cited in a note above: "This song is a 'piece of music' that is 'going nowhere.'"[31] As McClain analyzes it: "After the 3rd verse Cohen extends these responses by six measures, and after the last he writes an extended coda of 2 measures (longer than his song of only 26)."[32] In this way, as McClain argues, Cohen loses nothing by telling us what he does, in a never-mind, why-not-be-postmodern kind of way:

> The composer is whimsically describing his effort by "embodying it."—AND HE HASN'T ANYTHING MORE TO SAY! THE ALLELUJAH'S THAT FOLLOW ARE "ANYTHING BUT." It doesn't matter who says them, they are ironic nothings where you might expect a real answer from the chorus. This is a burst bubble. Subsequent verses introduce slight rhythmic variations that are not really motivic but inspired by his—which needs the words pronounced with proper stress. This man's (wo-man's) bubble bursts four times in a row (four strophic verses to the same melody and harmony), and all the halleluyahs are "sour grapes" (milking the audience for sympathy, that it gladly gives).[33]

Concinnity: k.d. lang and the Body

There is a lot that McClain says in this and if we bracket the breadth of the claims that he makes for the moment, it is worth noting his emphasis on the audience's sympathy here, and this is common for popular music, as a kind of "singing with" (this is McClain's reference to the audience and the "sympathy … it gladly gives"). This is what I have—and one might well suspect that it is this that drew me to this analysis in the first place—elsewhere called *concinnity*, as concinnity is also an interpretive "singing with" in the specific context of Nietzsche's philosophical style, and which I argued to have been specifically necessary with regard to his epistemology with reference to both science and art.[34]

Prescient and insightful as she was, Nina Simone also offers us a confirmation of McClain's conviction here. Recollecting her experience of the "power and

---

[31]   McClain, email to the author: Saturday 30 April 2011, 07:02am.

[32]   McClain, email to the author: Saturday 30 April 2011, 06:58pm.

[33]   Ibid.

[34]   See Babette Babich, "On Nietzsche's Concinnity: An Analysis of Style," *Nietzsche-Studien* 19 (1990): 59–80; and further Babich, *Nietzsche's Philosophy of Science: Reflecting Science on the Ground of Art and Life* (Albany: State University of New York Press, 1994), chapter 1.

spirituality" that she felt in connection with an audience, Simone writes of her experience in the mid-1960s: "I felt a kind of state of grace come upon me in those occasions when everything fell into place."[35] For Simone, "this was like electricity hanging in the air. I began to feel it happening, and it seemed to me like mass hypnosis—like I was hypnotizing an entire audience to feel a certain way."[36]

I quote Simone as this "hypnotic spell" speaks to the question of the efficacy of k.d. lang's *Hallelujah* and to what I have been calling the Hallelujah effect. If Cale's case is different, if Buckley's case is different, the question of the difference when it comes to k.d. lang is all about *how* she gets her audience to soar with her song? This is the effect, this effective or working power is what she does with Cohen's *Hallelujah*.

What has been said above goes some way to answer the question of how, and the rest would take us to an aspect that is, if anything, rather overexplored in the literature on k.d. lang's performance practice. That aspect is her sexuality, the fact that she sings—or better said, perhaps, as this is the effect of a calculated androgyny from the start, that she is "heard" as singing—as a lesbian, as someone who can voice the voice of desire as her own, because desire, as we have seen, is always *desire for a woman* (when it is not a man's desire, a male desire for a male). Whatever complex issues are involved in the matter of women's desire, where the overt desire for men is proscribed in different ways for both homosexual and heterosexual women, this would suggest that k.d. lang's desire is the only subversive move available. Another example might be in ballet and in Barbara Morgan's photographs, where Martha Graham claimed the choreographer's advantage for her own part, with her desire for Erick Hawkins, her younger lover, including a later marriage in 1948, which, predictably, as one might suppose, did not last.

With k.d. lang, we can think of her bemusedly camp but exactly intended *Sexuality* as a come-on: *Shed the skin that's held you in,*[37] a woman moves into the space of desire. And lang writes her single hit song (as she says, it is the only one she has had), *Constant Craving,*[38] to speak her own longing, her own subjectivity. Or, and this is still something, we remember what Plato tells us about artists and dissimulation, about appearances, and what Nietzsche tells us about art, and about truth and lies, and k.d. lang expresses this to an audience that thinks it can recognize desire when it hears it. Androgynous, they get that, which androgyny is only another word for and can only mean lesbian, and as k.d. lang hit 50 in 2011, an androgyny said with a certain smile: K-Daddy.

---

[35]   Nina Simone, with Stephen Cleary, *I Put a Spell on You: The Autobiography of Nina Simone* (New York: da capo, 1993), 92. Indeed, one can see some of this in the YouTube videos from this time.

[36]   Ibid., 92.

[37]   *Sexuality,* written by k.d.lang and Ben Mink, was released in 1995 on the album *All You Can Eat.*

[38]   *Constant Craving,* also written with Ben Mink, was included on the 1992 album *Ingenue.*

Figure 6.1   Barbara Morgan (1900–1992), *Martha Graham and Erick Hawkins (Kneeling)*, Bennington College, 1938. Gelatin silver print, 6 1/4 × 8 1/4 in, 15.9 × 21 cm. 2003.30.2 Gift of Lloyd and Janet Morgan. Collection of the Haggerty Museum of Art, Marquette University, Milwaukee. Permission of Janet Morgan.

And as we have already noted, lang decided long ago to be whatever the audience wants her to be. And her manager manages to keep this clear to her.

To be sure, k.d. lang articulates her singing of Cohen's song not as she sings Jane Siberry's *Love is Everything*, that is, as a song of desire condign, leaving, of push-me-pull-me, resignation, an achieved word of wisdom and regret, but in the only space that there is for this in Cohen's song. What is key is that lang is able to sing it in Cohen's voice, without the cracks of his age, his singer's limits, his grace, and allure, and I myself have already said that I love Cohen's voice.[39] And

---

[39]   I share (and that is despite the sense that he seems to have of our judgment on this) the view of Frank Boyle, a Swift scholar, in both senses of the word, and over all the years that we have been together at Fordham, the very best of my colleagues (that is so in spite of the rarity of contact, as I am in a philosophy department with no colleagues who do what I do or have interest in any of it, and he is in the more prestigious English department). As he writes: "I too marvel at kd lang's performance, but I find myself wanting to retire to a Buddhist monastery where I can just study Leonard Cohen's songs. And while I listen to all

his *Hallelujah* was the first I went looking for. And yet: k.d. lang's voice gives a gentler edge, a purer edge to the voice of longing, the longing for beauty, for love, for the lover. There is more forbearance in k.d. lang's interpretation than in the voice of nearly any other: no sardonicism, and at this point in the song, she believes *everything* that Cohen says.

There was only a need for proof; there was/is no question of faith: *her beauty and the moonlight*. Thus k.d. lang is not sagely, purely didactic as she is singing of love in its aftermath—where it is always the other's fault—as in her cover of Siberry's *Love is Everything*. As Lacan tells woman—he does not need to tell men—never give up on your desire. lang concedes, and her concession is a rebuke, the "you" here (as analyzed above) is the other, the beloved, the object, especially as the beloved moves from object in one sense to object in another.

Thus we hear Jane Siberry's warning crescendo, *But love forgot to make me too blind to see / You're chickening out, aren't you? / You're bangin' on the beach like an old tin drum / I can't wait for you to make the whole kingdom come / So I'm leaving*, or languorously reflective, as in singing *Hush Sweet Lover* or *Summerfling*, nor in this case does k.d. lang mock or ironize the sentiment as she does in her *Johnny Get Angry*;[40] this, again, is not the campy erotic seduction of her *Sexuality*'s drawn out and repeated come on's, which is how her song begins (and probably how a good many forbidden love affairs also begin). Instead, singing neither of abandonment nor the anxious prelude, don't leave me, here singing of beauty in Cohen's *Hallelujah*, k.d. lang sings the captivated side of seduction, in all demonstrative compulsion to be enraptured as it always is by beauty.

Like Nietzsche and Adorno, Stanley Cavell has also laid a claim to be one who has written about voice; Paul Feyerabend, too; Tracy Strong, and we can add a range of others: Attali, Derrida, Lacoue-Labarthe, Applebaum, and so on. In fact, this listing already betrays this point: "voice" has become an extraordinary fetish word in academic culture (I don't quite want to say theory here, because those who write about voice, although they often write in the name of theory, are short on theoretical or critical reflection). But, we ask here, what does it mean for a singer to lay claim to a voice? We know some of their names: let me start with Johnny Cash; I could add Elvis Presley who could, whatever one might wish to say about him, really, *really* sing. Who else? Lena Horne, Ella Fitzgerald, Billie Holiday, Edith Piaf, Yves Montand, as well. Who else? Joan Baez? Judy Collins? Of course. And who else then? Well, among others, Roy Orbison, in fact, and k.d. lang. And others, and others.

---

sort of covers—from the Wainwrights to Allison Crowe (I know, I know), I almost always prefer the master himself, whose voice channels mortality, even if I can understand the claim that it sounds like the voice of someone who died a while ago." Frank Boyle, email to the author, Wednesday 15 February 2012, 07:54am.

40   See, again, Lori Burns, "'Joanie' Get Angry: k.d. lang's Feminist Revisions," in *Understanding Rock: Essays in Musical Analysis*, ed. John Covach and Graeme M. Boone (New York: Oxford University Press, 1997).

And then in the current context, with reference to Cohen and his voice, I am once again reminded of the enormous power of Nina Simone, as we cited her own words above, who is also able to transfigure Leonard Cohen's *Suzanne* in her incomparable 1969 performance, which can be seen, and this is to the point here, reproduced on YouTube, conveying the one-time, for all time, experience at the Teatro Sistina in Rome, where Simone reconstitutes *Suzanne*, transforming it, making of it a song all her own.[41]

Who else?

Here—there is no help for it, for this is real music, "heard" music, music as it affects the body, as certain traditions say—the reader will have to chime in, adding each for his or her own part, the reader's particular experience and particular taste to the mix: for by claiming that a singer lays claim to a voice, one is saying a lot on their behalf. So we can add opera stars for those who listen to opera; thus we earlier mentioned Renée Fleming, and Michael Chanan spoke of Maria Callas, country music stars too, and popular singers like Susan Boyle, and so on.

Thus when it is repeated in popular reflections on k.d. lang that in the end, as she is said to have said, it all comes down to the music, we know that this will have to be true, and that it is also said by Bob Dylan and Cohen too, to name the singers who are perhaps most famous (but they are not the only ones) for not being quite able to sing (though to be sure they are professionals about not being able to sing—their voices, in the words of one analyst, are "golden").[42]

For k.d. lang, it is all about the way that she sings. This is what gets her listeners, and the marvel of it is not that it gets her fans every time, but that it gets everyone who hears her, fan or not, when what she sings is Leonard Cohen's *Hallelujah*.

---

[41]   I owe the reference to this performance to a tip from Ernest McClain, who transmitted an email reflection from a colleague. But YouTube also offers a video illustration of this performance beyond sound alone; the original report spoke of background music, in a French café, over dinner, and the initial confusion of familiarity and non-recognition and its convergence. Simone's live 1969 performance is nothing short of incandescent.

[42]   See Steinskog on Cohen's golden, "patriarchical or priestly" voice in "Queering Cohen," 142.

Interlude

We have looked at Cohen's *Hallelujah* and how he came to it, and we have looked at how it came to have the popularity that it enjoys. Along the way, particular care has been given to a study of one particular YouTube performance of Hallelujah by k.d. lang, illuminated with reference to some of her other performances of the same piece, together with a discussion of "performance practice," as one may speak of this both artistically and musically in k.d. lang's case, as in Leonard Cohen's case; and in all this we have sought to underscore the role of Bennett's "recording consciousness" and in what follows we highlight this consciousness in pragmatic, functional or performative terms.

Here, the focus turns to Theodor Adorno's analysis of the overarching profit motif of the music industry, which we already adverted to in terms of priming at the outset, and which Adorno also analyzes in social cultural terms as what he technically calls the regression of listening, that is, the "fetish character of music,"[1] which he also names "Commodity Music."[2]

---

[1]   Theodor Adorno, "On the Fetish Character of Music and the Regression of Listening," in Adorno, *The Culture Industry*, ed. J.M. Bernstein (New York: Routledge, 1991), 29–60.

[2]   Theodor Adorno, "Commodity Music Analysed," in *Quasi Una Fantasia: Essays on Modern Music*, trans. Rodney Livingstone (London: Verso, 1992 [1963]).

Chapter 7
Adorno's Phenomenology: Radio Physiognomy and Music

From Adorno's Radio Physiognomics to Günther Anders's Television and YouTube

Adorno is interested in the social power of dissemination, which he writes about quite technically as "reproduction,"[1] both of music, qua "the music," or as such as well as its reproduction on every level, especially with respect to the listener. As Susan McClary reminds us, as does Robert Hullot-Kentor with a different emphasis, Adorno remains "the only major cultural theorist of the century whose primary medium was music, as opposed to literature, film, or painting."[2] In musicology as in philosophy, and cultural theory in general, Adorno is a commonplace, and as is common enough with commonplaces, Adorno is more often reacted to than he is read, especially where, as noted, it tends to be assumed that when it came to popular music, he was "simply wrong,"[3] a claim that endures, despite decades of efforts at refutation.[4]

---

[1]   Theodor Adorno, *Towards a Theory of Musical Reproduction: Notes, a Draft, and Two Schemata*, trans. Wieland Hoban (London: Polity, 2006).

[2]   Susan McClary, *Feminine Endings: Music, Gender, and Sexuality* (Minneapolis: University of Minnesota Press, 1991/2002), 28.

[3]   This is what Lydia Goehr, for her own part, also alludes to as "the large literature on 'what's wrong with Adorno.'" See Goehr, *Elective Affinities: Musical Essays on the History of Aesthetic Theory* (New York: Columbia University Press, 2008), xiii.

[4]   Thus Thomas Y. Levin's 1990 report on the accomplishments of what he, at the time of his writing, dubbed "[f]resh scholarship" and its "displacement" of a "longstanding misreading of Adorno" now seems premature, and one can only hope that it will eventually prove prescient: Levin, "For the Record: Adorno on Music in the Age of Its Technological Reproducibility," *October* 55 (Winter 1990): 23–47. Levin himself pays a great deal of attention to the details, particularly, and literally, the soundstripe details in his own work, and if this were a still broader book, one could connect Levin's own reading of Chladni with Nietzsche's account. I discuss Nietzsche and Chladni in my "Nietzsche's 'Gay Science': Poetry and Love, Science and Music," in *Words in Blood, Like Flowers: Philosophy and Poetry, Music and Eros in Hölderlin, Nietzsche, and Heidegger* (Albany: State University of New York Press, 2006), and "The Science of Words or Philology: Music in *The Birth of Tragedy* and The Alchemy of Love in *The Gay Science*," in *Revista di estetica*, n.s. 28, XLV, ed. Tiziana Andina (Turin: Rosenberg & Sellier, 2005), 47–78; and Robert T. Beyer gives a physicist's account in his *Sounds of Our Times: Two Hundred Years of Acoustics*

In this insistent fashion, Adam Krims contends that Adorno's presence in popular music scholarship seems to be preserved "as something of a scene of trauma, infinitely relived and denied, while never losing its status as some sort of awful and exaggerated truth."[5] These sentiments can be repeated at will, as another reviewer summarily condemns Adorno in an essay on philosophical and musicological approaches to rock music:

> Adorno, convinced that any art that had mass appeal must have some sinister capitalist scheme directing it and therefore be non-art, never bothered to understand the language of popular music. This led him to misinterpretations of the popular music of his day, finding it weak as he examined it through the ornate frame of classical music.[6]

For my part, I remain persuaded that Adorno is far from understood and just as far from being passé.[7] Indeed, it is just because we do not understand Adorno that he can remain the one to whom, as Lydia Goehr writes elegantly but still apologetically, "even those most irritated turn when in search of something new or interesting to say."[8]

I have already had cause to refer to Adorno for the sake of his attention to the medium by which we encounter music, as this makes a good deal of difference, as I argue, indeed, both with respect to Cohen and to k.d. lang (and in order to get to Nietzsche), that this mediation makes all the difference. Adorno focused on the difference made by the medium of transmission, and he did this virtually from the start, speaking of recording and of musical transmission over the air, namely as he conjoined his studies of media with an analysis of the relevant engineering technology, speaking of the radio voice and its role in marketing (music or what have you), along with the predominance in our day of the totalizing supremacy of what H. Stith Bennett has quite phenomenologically described as our "recording

---

(Dordrecht: Kluwer, 1999). On the soundstripe, see Thomas Y. Levin, "Tones From Out of Nowhere," *Grey Room* 12 (Summer 2003): 33–79; and see, too, on the soundstripe, or the "hear-stripe," Veit Erlmann, *Reason and Resonance: A History of Modern Aurality* (Cambridge, MA: Zone Books, 2010), which Erlmann connects and contextualizes with Georg von Békésy's spatially distributive or locative theory (Erlmann's term is "'place' theory") of hearing (312ff).

[5]   Adam Krims, "What Does It Mean To Analyse Popular Music?", *Music Analysis* 22/i and ii (2003): 181–209, here 187.

[6]   Donald C. Meyer, "Review," *American Music* 16/4 (Winter 1998): 487–91, here 488.

[7]   See the beginning sections of Babette Babich, "Adorno on Science and Nihilism, Animals, and Jews," *Symposium: Canadian Journal of Continental Philosophy/Revue canadienne de philosophie continentale* 14/1 (2011): 1–36, and my note on Roger Scruton's lecture, "Is Adorno a Dead Duck?" in Chapter 10 below.

[8]   Goehr, *Elective Affinities*, xi.

Figure 7.1   Theodor Adorno, radio broadcast, mid-1960s. Photo: © Peter Zollna/
Theodor W. Adorno Archiv

consciousness," which same recording consciousness or *awareness* continues to
dominate musicians, as they increasingly record for sales and "conscientiously,"
as it were, perform or recreate those same "recordings" in concert.[9]

For Adorno, writing a series of essays resulting from his work on the Princeton
Radio Research Project,[10] the phenomenon of radio mediates culture on every level,

---

[9]   Adorno, himself an accomplished pianist, was also no stranger to the tradition of
spoken German expression (*Redekunst*) and was similarly accomplished in presenting radio
programs upon his return to Germany. See, for example, Michael Schwartz, "'Er redet
leicht, schreibt schwer'. Theodor W. Adorno am Mikrophon," *Zeithistorische Forschungen*
8/2 (2011): 286–94.

[10]   Theodore Adorno, *Current of Music: Elements of a Radio Theory*, ed. Robert
Hullot-Kentor (Frankfurt am Main: Suhrkamp, 2006). For a review of the Princeton Radio
Research Project more attuned to Lazarsfeld and that, regrettably, sheds little light on

as sheer "broadcasting" between, as Adorno put it, telephone and phonograph.[11] If today we can also add email and texting, Twitter, Facebook, and YouTube, and a variety of shifting claims to "social platforming" to this communicative array, it is worth reflecting that a century ago, Nietzsche had already characterized the arrival of a letter as an importunate, unexpected, and thus unannounced visitor, calling "the mailman the mediator of impolite incursions."[12] Nietzsche went on to propose, curmudgeon style, a kind of near Sabbath interval, including a minimalist rationing that seems both increasingly therapeutic *and* increasingly impossible: "One ought to have one hour in every eight days for receiving letters, and then take a bath."[13] Both letters and radio have the character of what we call "media," digital and otherwise, as this adumbrates nothing less politically and socially pernicious than what Adorno, along with Max Horkheimer, dubbed the "culture industry."[14]

For Horkheimer and Adorno, "Films, radio and magazines make up a system which is uniform as a whole and in every part. Even the aesthetic activities of political opposites are one in their enthusiastic obedience to the rhythm of the iron system."[15] This "iron system" is the cultural industry itself and the music industry works by way of this same industrial complex, mediating and so dominating/ adumbrating culture, society, political, philosophical, and sociological scholarship, human relations on every level and in every "sense." For Horkheimer and Adorno, what is at stake is nothing but the totalizing co-optation of capital, at every level:

> But any trace of spontaneity from the public in official broadcasting is controlled and absorbed by talent scouts, studio competitions and official programs of every kind selected by professionals. Talented performers belong to the industry long before it displays them; otherwise they would not be so eager to fit in. The attitude of the public, which ostensibly and actually favors the system of the culture industry, is a part of the system and not an excuse for it.[16]

Adorno but a bit more on the initial or empiricist context of sociological research in media studies, see Dustin W. Supa, "The Origins of Empirical Versus Critical Epistemology in American Communication," *American Communication Journal* 11/3 (Fall 2009). But see, too, David E. Morrison, "*Kultur* and Culture: The Case of Theodor W. Adorno and Paul Lazarsfeld," *Social Research* 44 (1978): 331–55.

[11]   Adorno, "Chapter V. Time Radio and Phonograph," in *Current of Music*, 120–28.

[12]   Friedrich Nietzsche, HH, *The Wanderer and his Shadow*, §261. KSA 2, 265.

[13]   Ibid.

[14]   Although it is important to refer to Adorno's *Culture Industry* in this context, it cannot be read apart from its original context in *The Dialectic of Enlightenment*, written with Max Horkheimer, or Adorno's *Minima Moralia*, or his *Beethoven*.

[15]   Max Horkheimer and Theodor Adorno, *The Dialectic of Enlightenment* (New York: Continuum, 1993), 120. See, also, their "Kulturindustrie: Aufklärung als Massenbetrug" [1944], in *Dialektik der Aufklärung. Philosophische Fragmente* (Frankfurt am Main: Suhrkamp, 1969), 128–76.

[16]   Horkheimer and Adorno, *The Dialectic of Enlightenment*, 122.

Little has changed, as shows like *Glee*, *American Idol*, and other sorts of stylized forms of "reality" TV make plain.

This is the ultimate meaning of what counts as democracy today, American style, and by its nature it excludes differing views by the simple expedient of denying them airtime, insisting that those excluded are no good.[17] So co-opted is this fact of cultural life (and it is not limited to entertainment) that it can be broadcast, as it has been for some time now in popular reality television series and contests.

Horkheimer and Adorno are unremitting in their emphasis that this is a top-down matter, writing in 1944 of the then already patent "agreement—or at least the determination—of all executive authorities not to produce or sanction anything that in any way differs from their own rules, their own ideas about consumers, or above all themselves."[18] Although this continues to be as true as ever, it was with respect to the news but more obviously with reference to music, and as Horkheimer and Adorno take this to the level of political marketing—and Günther Anders restates this for his own part in his own studies of the same phenomena—we turn to public media, particularly politically produced, that is to say, mass media and expect, as audience, as consumers, that some producers of the same will be trustworthy and others not. But what holds for music marketing holds perhaps even more for what is disseminated as news. And even here, so we might argue, Nietzsche already made the same case for what counted as journalism in his judgments of the same and the consumers of the same in his day.

Here what may be counted as personal taste or "choice" is anything but personal, but is instead thoroughly mediated, thoroughly dictated, as Horkheimer and Adorno continue their argument:

> The ruthless unity in the culture industry is evidence of what will happen in politics. Marked differentiations such as those of A and B films, or of stories in magazines in different price ranges, depend not so much on subject matter as on classifying, organizing, and labeling consumers. Something is provided for all so that none may escape; the distinctions are emphasized and extended. The public is catered for with a hierarchical range of mass-produced products of varying quality, thus advancing the rule of complete quantification. Everybody must behave (as if spontaneously) in accordance with his previously determined and indexed level, and choose the category of mass product turned out for his type. Consumers appear as statistics on research organization charts, and are divided by income groups into red, green, and blue areas; the technique is that used for any type of propaganda.[19]

---

[17]   YouTube stars, or those who aim to be, do their competitive best to gainsay this assertion.

[18]   Horkheimer and Adorno, *The Dialectic of Enlightenment*, 122.

[19]   Ibid., 123.

For the most part, and this is the way that this mechanism works, we read such things as this, even scholars read such remarks as these, without "believing" them for a moment.[20]

And when Herbert Marcuse repeats this analysis, in some cases almost verbatim, in his *One Dimensional Man*,[21] using examples far more attuned to standard American culture, we still do not believe it. Or if we do, we certainly do not take it as applying to us or to our listening (how could it? We listen all by ourselves, even in public places, with earphones in our ears, Odysseus's ears as Nietzsche spoke *ironically* of such), or indeed our comparably and, tendentially speaking, increasingly autistic viewing habits, that is, likewise increasingly personal. As Anders would say, *alienating* and *alienated*.

Arguing that the prime function of the culture industry was to engender or render the service of schematizing on behalf of the consumer, the consumer loses nothing but what Adorno here described as Kant's secret, that is, the "secret mechanism in the soul which prepared direct intuitions in such a way that they could be fitted into the system of pure reason."[22] The consumer's consciousness is thus the product of the culture industry and hence the point of this "prepared" consciousness—echoing Bennett's "recording consciousness"—entails that there is:

> nothing left for the consumer to classify. Producers have done it for him. Art for the masses has destroyed the dream but still conforms to the tenets of that dreaming idealism which critical idealism balked at. Everything derives from consciousness: for Malebranche and Berkeley, from the consciousness of God; in mass art, from the consciousness of the production team.[23]

Exceeding Husserl's now common phenomenological coin, "all consciousness is consciousness of something," Adorno goes beyond Husserl in a very Nietzschean, that is to say, critical fashion. In the case of the music industry, the product, of course, is music: and its genesis, its birth, comes to us as we hear music today *everywhere* we go: we take it with us, as programmed, reduced, rendered, reconstituted, reproduced, packaged, consumed. Under the rubric of "Space Ubiquity," Adorno has recourse to Walter Benjamin's cousin, Günther Anders (then still called Stern) to make this point.[24] And Benjamin, too, both in his elusive

---

[20]   I take up the question of this issue of propaganda and our disattention to it with reference to Jacques Ellul, Jean Baudrillard, Ivan Illich, as well as Adorno, in Babich, "Adorno on Science and Nihilism, Animals, and Jews."

[21]   Herbert Marcuse, *One-Dimensional Man: Studies in the Ideology of Advanced Industrial Society* (Boston: Beacon Press, 1964), 9, 12, and so on.

[22]   Horkheimer and Adorno, *The Dialectic of Enlightenment*, 124.

[23]   Ibid., 125.

[24]   Günter Stern [Günter Anders], "Spuk und Radio," *Anbruch* 12/2 (February 1930): 65–6, here 65. This should be linked to Saul Austerlitz's reading of the inveigling of image and sound exemplified in the title borrowed from the eponymous Dire Straits single, which

discussion of aura but especially in his discussion of Baudelaire, has recourse to ghostly metaphors, like Stern's ghosts, like Adorno's, where Benjamin writes about the "flâneur."[25]

Stern, as we have already noted, is known today as Günther Anders. Anders, who continues to be still too little discussed, had been Husserl's student, completing a doctoral dissertation under his supervision, as well as studying with Heidegger in a crucial integration with Hannah Arendt, whom Anders would later marry (a marriage that did not last, whereas, correspondingly, the affection between Heidegger and Arendt did endure),[26] and was just about to go on, as Anders had hoped, to complete a habilitation under Paul Tillich in Frankfurt when the reality of the National Socialists, that is, the Real by any measure, intruded. Adorno quotes Anders here, arguing in his essay on the ghostly character of radio broadcasts that: "Music is nowhere and everywhere it is heard. It transcends the 'here-itself' in spite of its 'thereness' and never finds its unity in a limitation of space."[27]

---

aired on MTV at its inception in 1987, proving rather more than McLuhan's point, the medium is the message/massage, but rather Marcuse's reflection that desublimation works more effectively than repression as alienation, and nothing hides anything from attention so well as plain sight, or, as in this case, repeating, as a commercial spot, which indeed it was in effect, "I Want My MTV," in *Money for Nothing: A History of the Music Video from the Beatles to the White Stripes* (London: Continuum, 2006). See, also, as counterpoint, Kembrew McLeod, "Making the Video: Constructing an Effective Counter-Hegemonic Message in Only Forty-Nine Minutes," *Journal of Popular Music Studies* 14 (2002): 79–88.

[25] I apply this notion, together with a reflection on gender, in Babette Babich, "The Aesthetics of the Between: Space and Beauty," in *Jeff Koons: The Painter and The Sculptor*, ed. Vinzenz Brinkmann, Matthias Ulrich, and Joachim Pissarro (Frankfurt: Schirn Kunsthalle Frankfurt, 2012), 58–69. See, for a discussion of the gender issues, although these turn out *not* to be discussions of female autonomy or subjectivity (the theme throughout is prostitution), Janet Wolff, "The Invisible Flâneuse: Women and the Literature of Modernity," *Theory Culture and Society, The Fate of Modernity*, 2/3 (1985): 37–46, as well as Susan Buck-Morss, "The Flâneur, the Sandwichman and the Whore: The Politics of Loitering," *New German Critique* 39, *Second Special Issue on Walter Benjamin* (Autumn 1986): 99–140, and Elizabeth Wilson, "The Invisible Flâneur," *New Left Review* I/191 (January–February 1992): 90–110. Buck-Morss also notes the "aural flanerie" in Adorno, without, regrettably, mentioning Benjamin's cousin, Günther Anders.

[26] I discuss some of this in my review of "Daniel Maier-Katkin, *Stranger from Abroad: Hannah Arendt, Martin Heidegger, Friendship and Forgiveness*. NY: Norton, 2010," *Shofar: An Interdisciplinary Journal of Jewish Studies* 29/4 (Summer 2011): 189–91. Cf. here Anders's own later reconstitution: Günther Anders, *Die Kirschenschlacht, Günther Anders und Hannah Arendt—eine Beziehungsskizze* (Munich: Beck, 2011).

[27] Cited in Adorno, *Current of Music*, 129; here I cite Adorno's translation of Stern's/ Anders's "Spuk und Radio." See, too, Anders's later essay, "Die Welt als Phantom und Matrize. Philosophische Betrachtungen über Rundfunk und Fernsehen" ["The World as Phantom and Matrix: Philosophical Observations on Radio and Television"], in *Die Antiquiertheit des Menschen, Bd. 1: Über die Seele im Zeitalter der zweiten industriellen Revolution* (München: Beck, 1987 [1956]). On Anders and music, which cannot, however

Adorno, being Adorno, appropriates Anders's point, while criticizing it nonetheless as too existentialist, meaning, in this case, "too" Heideggerian.[28] Like many scholars who have commented on Adorno and Anders, Veit Erlmann discounts Adorno's characterization of Anders as Heideggerian. But what is at stake concerns phenomenology, and in this regard one can link Anders with Heidegger, and Husserl, and likewise, as I argue below, Adorno himself. In *Being and Time*, Heidegger had written that "Dasein hears, because it understands,"[29] phenomenologically to tie this hermeneutic claim to what Heidegger named "hearkening" [*Horchen*], as distinguished from Helmholtzian "hearing," as Heidegger characterized the more basic physiological convention of "the sensing of tones and the perception of sounds."[30] What would be salient for Heidegger—and Adorno could not fail to recognize this emphasis in Anders—was "hearing which understands."[31] Contra "tone-data,"[32] and hence contra the reductive tendencies of analytic or, better said, logically empiricist philosophy and its (to this day) ongoing preoccupation with sense-data, Heidegger goes on to make one of the most dynamic phenomenological distinctions in *Being and Time*: "What we 'first' hear is never noises or complexes of sounds, but the creaking waggon, the motor-cycle. We hear the columns on the march, the north wind, the woodpecker tapping, the fire crackling."[33]

Heidegger thus helps to articulate, note that I am not saying that he anticipates,[34] the "silent effect" of John Cage's famous 1952 piano composition, *4'33"*—an ironic working effect which is, of course, about anything but silence. On the one hand, there is instrumental preparation, along with the performative composure, corresponding to the fetish notion of "prepared piano" (for instance, among other earlier pieces, Cage's 1951 *Concerto for Prepared Piano and Orchestra*, which also includes extended silent intervals) and its new music and minimalist compositional charms (Satie's influence and precedence is usually cited, as is Heitor Villa-Lobos), along with everything else done by a performer or a conductor

---

(and despite the author's title to the contrary), be understood apart from his techno-social thinking, see Reinhard Ellensohn, *Der andere Anders: Günther Anders als Musikphilosoph* (Bern: Peter Lang, 2008).

[28]   A reading that does refer to Heidegger (on the way to get Agamben) is useful here. See John Mowitt, *Radio: Essays in Bad Reception* (Berkeley: University of California Press, 2011).

[29]   Martin Heidegger, *Being and Time*, trans. John Macquarrie and Edward Robinson (New York: Harper & Row, 1962 [1927]), 1.5, §34, 206.

[30]   Ibid., 206.

[31]   Ibid.

[32]   Ibid.

[33]   Ibid., 207.

[34]   For Heidegger and Cage, and including useful references to Gerry Stahl, Michael Eldred, and Daniel Charles, as well as F. Joseph Smith, see Eduardo Marx, *Heidegger und der Ort der Musik* (Würzburg: Königshausen & Neumann, 1998).

"to prepare." But in addition to the prepared piano and performer, there is also the role played by the audience, and it makes some sense to speak of a "prepared audience," and accordingly it makes all the difference to hear Cage's *4'33"* "in concert," as it were. In her discussion of Cage and Adorno, and in keeping with her own overall thesis regarding the notion of the "work,"[35] Goehr reminds us that Cage himself dictates the "usually" concert hall venue and related practices engendering the musical or noise effect of supposed silence. As Goehr writes: "In ironic gesture, it is Cage who specifies that a pianist should sit at a piano to go through the motions of performance. The performer is applauded and the composer granted recognition for the 'work.'"[36]

Goehr is here concerned to make the slightly forced case for Cage's didacticism contra Adorno's cynical reading of Cage's commodification. And to be sure, and although this is not Goehr's example, it might be argued that performances of this piece over the years were what ultimately made it possible, in 2004, for the BBC to broadcast a first radio performance by the BBC Symphony Orchestra.[37] On the other hand, one can also contend that it was a somewhat inevitable prospect and Holger Schmid, a German friend and philosophical colleague, who was also a dedicated fan of radio (this did not mean that he paid his subscription fees), was in the habit of joking about a radio transmission of *4'33"* in the 1990s.[38]

The phenomenological issue for Adorno, reading Anders on what Adorno will coin, in a modification of this same point, "radio ubiquity," subjects both phenomenology *and* Anders's insight into music to such a hard critique that one can be persuaded that Adorno rejects both. Manifestly this, too, is a kind of negative dialectics, and one will need to look past it in order to recuperate the points that both Adorno and Anders have in common.

In the next section, Adorno's notion of ubiquity standardization recurs in connection with a review of Bennett's "recording consciousness," *consciousness* understood in this context in terms of our inculcated and hence automatic

---

[35] Lydia Goehr, *The Imaginary Museum of Musical Works: An Essay in the Philosophy of Music* (Oxford: Oxford University Press, 1992). To be clear here, Goehr's context has nothing to do with Heidegger, whom she mentions only in her introduction, and only in passing with regard to the notion of the "work" of art.

[36] Goehr, *The Imaginary Museum of Musical Works*, 264. This is exemplified by the copyright decision that the British composer Mike Batt very manifestly invited by co-signing his composition, *A One Minute Silence*, with the signature "Batt/Cage," on his classical rock album, *The Planets*. It goes without saying that the judgment could not but be decided in favor of Cage rather than Batt—which decision says a great deal about musical "plagiarism."

[37] The BBC needed to point out, and this is repeated twice in the *BBC News* article, that in "readiness for the performance, Radio 3 bosses switched off their emergency back-up system—designed to cut in when there is an unexpected silence on air." *BBC News*, Monday 19 January 2004, 14:29 GMT.

[38] In the course of long, late-night conversation, when we were solving, as friends do, all the problems of the universe.

sensibility to recording practice, *as well as* its material conditions, that is also to say, its limitations and its conventions, such that and to an invisible extent—and this will be the sociological point common to Adorno, to Anders, and to Bennett— we cannot think otherwise than by way of this consciousness, be it in terms of radio or recordings, that is, music or speech qua transmitted or mediated. Adorno's terms give us music as "reproduced," not by being performed, as music is always constituted anew in each playing, but much rather in the age of what Benjamin called *technical reproducibility*, as Robert Hullot-Kentor emphasizes this term with care, as what is usually rendered as *mechanical reproduction*.[39] Thus a recording sensibility schematizes or informs not only the way that we hear music, on the radio, on our iPods, i-Smartphones, iPads, or over the internet, but also, and this is the focus of Bennett's own analysis, the musicians, the artists themselves, even "live," that is, when we hear them in concert, in an interview, in person as we say, and just to the extent that the artists are those who become what they are by way of this same reflexive consciousness: simulacra of their studio productions, "covering," as it were, their own songs.

Adorno, k.d. lang, and H. Stith Bennett's *On Becoming a Rock Musician*

I have argued that there is no way to talk about what k.d. lang does with Cohen's *Hallelujah* without talking about Adorno's critical phenomenological analysis of music, although it would still be of use to reflect that the trajectory of k.d. lang's career, as career-wise as it "has always been," exemplifies almost every recommendation to be found in H. Stith Bennett's classic and classically influential *On Becoming a Rock Musician*,[40] especially where Bennett focuses with extraordinary and explicitly phenomenological acuity on what he calls, following Adorno, but not less in the wake of Simmel, "the *business* of sound."[41]

---

[39]   Robert Hullot-Kentor, *Things Beyond Resemblance: Collected Essays on Theodor W. Adorno* (New York: Columbia University Press, 2006), 139ff. Pointing out that, throughout "the essay each occurrence of mechanical can be replaced by technical," Hullot-Kentor's point is that the mechanism of the machine can capture our imagination, whereas what is at issue is the machinery, as it were, the mechanics, technical, digital, whatever, of reproduction.

[40]   This is not remarkable as it is a how-to book, like the *Meditations* of Marcus Aurelius, or perhaps better still, like Aristotle's *Nicomachean Ethics*.

[41]   H. Stith Bennett, *On Becoming a Rock Musician* (Amherst: University of Massachusetts Press, 1980). My emphasis. At the outset, we pointed out that we were interested in considering the Hallelujah effect in terms of what we described and have above analyzed as k.d. lang's "performance practice," at least in a preliminary fashion— and one hopes that others will take these first steps further, adding their own observations in the process.

At the same time and to the degree that any such reflection must draw upon traditional musicological language, even as qualified as I have conceded that this must be, traditional musicology itself has drawn its own set of lines in the sand contra such analyses.[42] This disciplinary tension, compounded by the author's own and insuperable outsider status, as the author is a philosopher of a continental kind (which means that this is the reading of an outlier in an outsider field), is not ameliorated by saying that traditional musicology does not matter here because, after all, the theme thus far is pop music, especially and to be sure, when written, as I happen to be writing, from an extra-disciplinary perspective, because it must be anticipated that this analysis might well appear to step (although it surely does not mean to do so) on pop musicological toes. And I say inevitably because there are trends in pop musicology and the most conspicuous of these is all about declaring that too much attention has been paid to Adorno (which is not to say that Adorno is not influential—he is—but much rather, as noted above, that a careful engagement with him is more simply taken for granted than it is taken up as a task). In fact, Adorno is often overtly excluded and with good conscience, for the same reasons likewise already noted above. Hence I would argue that begging off a consideration of Adorno covers a certain anxiety, given both his content and the complexity of reading him.[43]

Philip Tagg offers this summary of the defensive tack characteristic of pop music (Tagg's reading, although "influenced" by Adorno, does not engage Adorno here), and it is significant to cite this defensive outline at length because the points detailed are also those of contemporary media studies, especially of the digital kind, digital humanities and others to boot:

> The argument is that popular music cannot be analyzed using only the traditional tools of musicology. This is because popular music, unlike art music, is (1) conceived for mass distribution to a large and often socioculturally heterogeneous group of listeners, (2) stored and distributed in non-written form, (3) only possible in an industrial monetary economy where it becomes a commodity and (4) in capitalist societies, subject to the laws of "free" enterprise, according to which it should ideally sell as much as possible of as little as possible to as many as possible. Consideration of these distinguishing marks implies that it is impossible to "evaluate" popular music along some sort of Platonic ideal scale of aesthetic values …[44]

---

[42] See, for this, the beginning of most pop musicological readings, some of which seem enthusiastically reactive, so much so that this reactive character has itself become a theme for analysis. See, for instance, Philip Tagg, cited on just this issue below.

[43] Obviously, one person's too-much-Adorno may be another person's too-little-Adorno.

[44] Philip Tagg, "Analysing Popular Music: Theory, Method and Practice," *Popular Music* 2 (1982): 37–69, here 41. For Tagg's own efforts in this direction, see his *Fernando the Flute* (New York: Mass Media Music Scholars' Press, 2000 [1991]). For another reading,

By contrast with the analyses of music extant more than a century ago, assuming that one makes the appropriate transpositions, critics like Adorno (and others) contend that a lack of formal familiarity with music—meaning musical illiteracy, lacking musical competence, most particularly the ability to read music, meaning the ability to sight read and in this way conversant with musical composition, to play a musical instrument, and consequently a lack of the actant familiarity that Adorno takes to be essential for a truly encultured, cultivated "appreciation" of music—characterizes our age.

Of course, along the way, it should also be noted that this performative "limitation" is typically challenged by many writers on pop music who observe that music is "played" as much as ever it was. How this assertion can be made and in what way (and there are several ways to do this) is beside the point. What is at issue concerns the difference that it makes to be able to read/play a score in the age of precisely non-mechanical but highly technicized—integratedly, as Baudrillard would say—musical production and reproduction. What is thus necessary to underline is that learning to play the piano is a very different enterprise today, even for those who have learned to read music, as one must, to learn to play piano (though it can surely also be done, as it also is done, by ear), than, say, in Nietzsche's day or for Adorno himself, where playing was also the key, sine qua non, to the acquisition of the breadth of music, as Adorno argues and as he himself, Adorno, began in just this way.

Our contemporary engagement with learning to play an instrument is different today where music is broadcast seemingly everywhere and where a seemingly infinite variety of music may be had at will—and this is the socio-phenomenological point of departure for Bennett's *On Becoming a Rock Musician*—as opposed to a world where music would have been limited to live performance of a specific musical work, be it as heard on the street or folk festival, in church across the variations of the liturgical year, or in private, or chamber settings, or the opera, or concert hall. In this world, the individual only had access to a piano and a score, or even, because this is the point of reading music, a score alone. We have already cited Adorno on this theme and here we note his hermeneutic reflection that "our entire awareness of a musical *context* is mediated through the written music."[45] Thus just as today one may have the sense of "meeting" a colleague by

---

see Adorno's (with the assistance of the same George Simpson, whom Ernest McClain recalls as having been hired as his linguistic assistant) "On Popular Music" [1941], in Simon Frith and Andrew Goodwin, eds, *On Record: Rock, Pop, and the Written Word* (New York: Pantheon, 1990).

[45] Adorno, *Towards a Theory of Musical Reproduction*, 160. Here we note that this focus on reading the score also includes what one might call the esoteric Adorno, the "ideal of silent music making ..." Ibid., 2. This always presupposes the high contextual (thus Adorno here highlights "musical *context*") hermeneutic of reading, especially of reading music, as Adorno goes on to say that "in the strictest sense," here with reference to "gazing" upon a Beethoven sonata, "a movement by Beethoven looked different 100 years ago to

way of having read his or her works, even in advance of meeting him or her in person, or indeed of having some sense of Twitter "friends" online, whose tweets give one a sense of the person, so too it could rightly be said that Nietzsche had "encountered" Wagner well before he met him in person, simply by reading and playing his music.

This is not unlike the familiarity that every reader may suppose she or he has with a popular author, and we may call this the "Harry Potter effect,"[46] dependent as that effect was for its force upon familiarity. Everyone who read Rowling's *Harry Potter* series knew the story before the film unfolded, to the great benefit of the movie experience. And this Harry Potter effect fairly conspicuously, if and to be sure seamlessly, affected the story itself. Following the appearance of the first film, Rowling would and perhaps could not but write her later stories as informed by the canonization of her characters on screen, becoming herself a screenplay author in time. Thus the realization of the *Harry Potter* novels in film enacted a mass phenomenon (that is the effect of the Hallelujah effect), reinforcing the same common character or brand. At issue here is nothing like de-mystification. The only point is that the same phenomenon is on offer in and as the culture industry itself as this drives music recordings and tours.

What Adorno calls a cultivated musical analysis separates readers today from authors who write on music like Günther Anders, the phenomenologist of music and technology, along with Nietzsche, who is, if anything, more difficult to understand than Adorno, just because Adorno seems recondite and Nietzsche seems unrecondite, which apparent ease of access is also the achievement of what Nietzsche called 'style.'

In this sense, we can hardly begin to understand what Nietzsche might have meant by "the spirit of music," or indeed how he might have meant his much-cited claim that "without music, life would be an error,"[47] that is to say, a "mistake," which he varied by adding, as he did in a letter to his friend Peter Gast: "a tribulation, an exile,"[48] just because, and this is an exactly phenomenologically eidetic, experiential point, we increasingly cannot imagine what he meant by music—the music that would have *sounded*, as Adorno says with reference to a Beethoven sonata, "different" a hundred years ago. Thus by saying this, I do not

---

how it does today, and therefore also sounded different" (189). For Adorno here, "the written notes hardly have less of an independent life than what they represent" (ibid).

[46]   Patrick Heelan, in a lovely public remark, declared, very Irishly, after his reading of *Harry Potter*, that the author herself was Harry Potter. This was, as some have said, and because Heelan was a teacher of mine in my college years, merely a way for him to get to be Dumbledore. But the author, knowing that she was not indeed Harry Potter, recognized the universality of the claim: Harry Potter's everyman charm is that everyone is Harry Potter.

[47]   Friedrich Nietzsche, *Twilight of the Idols*, "Mixed Maxims," § 33, trans. Richard Polt (Indianapolis: Hackett, 1997).

[48]   "Das Leben ohne Musik ist einfach ein Irrthum, eine Strapatze, ein Exil." Nietzsche, letter to Gast [Heinrich Köselitz], 15 January 1888, KSB, 8, 232.

mean music in the sense of Nietzsche's classical philologist's invocation of the "spirit" of music, that is to say, music as written as word (in ancient Greek), and score, *music in the written word* as well as music as transcribed: as *logos*, which, as we shall see, Nietzsche meant as literally, as rigorously as you please, but just and only ordinary, heard music, the kind of music that Socrates practiced at the end of his life, although to be sure, Plato tells us that Socrates was only hedging his bets, purely ironically, and on the hermeneutic side of safety.

Rather than the spirit of music that traces the birth of the ancient tragic work of art in all its mystery, let us take Nietzsche to be speaking as we have been speaking here—on Socrates's safe side again—of music made and heard: felt music, lived music, music in its popular sense for him in his day. It is this same encounter with lived music, in all its varied dimensionality, that is increasingly lost to us as children of the age of music in the era of technical reproduction, which means that we need "know" nothing about playing, or even making *recordings* of, music to have access to music or to be able to enjoy it. The sound of music, the sound of its sound, is increasingly the same. And instant access and that acoustic phenomenon that physiologists call accommodation is part of this. Nor, although this is a different and perhaps more abstruse point, do we need to wait on particular occasion for it, in church, or at a concert, or passing a street musician. Thus, all the time, at will, and quite apart from the constant stream of music in US supermarkets and restaurants and so on, we have music on command, tucked into our pockets, or strapped to our arms, slipped into knapsacks and handbags, on command in our living rooms and offices, as online streaming, and so on. By contrast, it was not qua recorded, and not qua radio or television music broadcast, and certainly not as downloaded, whether legally—the way Steve Jobs wants you to, commanded in life as in death, over the rightly maligned iTunes—or illegally, however other way, that Nietzsche himself *knew* the music that he knew. In this sense, he heard his music, he could "listen," as he writes in his *Zarathustra* (and the warning is correspondingly meaningless for today's readers) "with his eyes," that is by reading a score. This reading is the spirit converse to which Schopenhauer attests, as Nietzsche cites him. But in this case, this is not merely a familiarity with the temperament of the composer; this is an encounter with "the" music itself.[49] Thus Nietzsche's access to music was by reading it and by playing it, "realizing" a score in this way or by hearing it performed in his presence by musicians physically present to him on instruments present to him and—this is the reference to space— to his surroundings. There is a lot said here and a lot that many will be prepared to dispute, arguing that, as we have already discussed, the aural achievements of digital recording practice, given what we should now name the "ubiquity of digital music" and our concommitant acoustic accommodation to digital music

---

[49]   This is at the heart of Adorno's provocative claim that "It is conceivable that Beethoven actually wanted to go deaf—because he had already had a taste of the sensuous side of music as it is blared from loudspeakers today." Theodor Adorno, *Beethoven: The Philosophy of Music*, trans. Edmund Jephcott (Stanford: Stanford University Press, 1988), 31.

reproduction, is music all the same. But leaving this dispute to whatever side one wishes to take on the matter, what is not in dispute is that Nietzsche, like Adorno, knew his music by heart, in a bodily, performative capacity—given that Nietzsche was celebrated as a performer, and given too, and *ceteris paribus*, Adorno's personal deprecation of his own performative skill (others dispute this). What is required for such a capacity is Adorno's emphasis on listening in *Current of Music* and *Towards a Theory of Musical Reproduction*, and so on. This "musical" currency, as it was for Nietzsche and for Adorno who witnessed its changing, differs from the way we know it as consumers today.

Nietzsche would have argued that the ancient Greeks were musical with every thought they thought, every word they spoke, because of the nature of their language and thus their relation to their language (it remains to be explored whether this relation affected their relation to ideas, as McClain has argued). But today, whether we are musically attuned, or talented, or not, we have, or we *can* have, music, heard music, anywhere we wish, to whatever end we wish.

My point will be that this is increasingly not regarded as constituting real change; certainly not as making any kind of difference that makes a difference. Indeed, it is the basis for Tagg's elaboration of the reasons that popular music is incontrovertibly beyond the purview of musicological analysis. As Simon Frith points out: "Most rock musicians lack formal training, and so do all rock commentators. They lack the vocabulary and techniques of musical analysis, and even the descriptive words that critics and fans do use—harmony, melody, riff, beat—are only loosely understood and applied."[50] H. Stith Bennett makes the same point rather more sympathetically, but just as emphatically, in his chapter, "The Realities of Practice," in his *On Becoming a Rock Musician*.[51]

Bennett's point is that, contrary to the star effect that often seems to be the way that such things come to pass, an appearance many popular musicians cultivate for their own part (here k.d. lang is as good an example as anyone), everything in fact is a matter of practice, *in spite of* the limitations of an otherwise established musical tradition.[52] The point, by contrast, as Bennett argues, is to manage to go

---

[50] Simon Frith, *Sound Effects* (London: Constable, 1983), 13.

[51] Bennett, "The Realities of Practice." Note that this chapter from Bennett's original book, *On Becoming a Rock Musician*, is also reprinted in Frith and Goodwin, eds, *On Record*, 185ff., and those who refer to Bennett today tend to know of his work from this context.

[52] Adorno, who reprises the notion of music as the art of time, plays with the typical cliché of capitalism, time is money: "In capitalism, where working time is exchanged as a commodity, all musical interpretation ... tends to suffer from insufficient rehearsal through lack of time." Referring to opera in particular, Adorno writes that: "Most performances take place at the point where the rehearsals should begin. Reaching a consensus and functioning at a basic level takes the place of genuine presentation." Adorno, *Towards a Theory of Musical Reproduction*, 121. In this sense, quoting the conductor Ludwig Rottenberg's remark, "Ghastly, carry on," would for Adorno have been anything but a joke.

from *forming* a group to getting one's first gig, and "practice" is the only way to get there. Indeed, getting to practice turns out to be the point at the start (and it is in part the reason that agents and managers and record companies come to be indispensable):

> One of the perennial signs of a group in trouble is the absence of members from called practices, for when there is "something better to do" the special nature of the commitment to rock music is bastardized. Groups are founded on the commitment that *nothing comes before music*. When group members fail to show up for practice they are doing more than breaking their commitments to the other members in the group. Their absence demonstrates that something means more than music—that in short they are not *musicians*. The ability of an individual to schedule everyday activities around the schedule of band practice is the ability of the group to exist.[53]

Bennett's observation applies at the start, but some parts remain essential throughout a musician's career. And this sheds worlds of light on k.d. lang's insistence on keeping to what she calls a "monastic existence" on the road. For all the claims that she had a girl in every port, for all the fans' speculations about her club life, and her relationships to this or that person, what matters is a certain solitude, and for lang, the expression of that is in her affirmation that, as she says, she likes to sleep. Alone—and that is to say: no matter whether she happens to have or not to have a girlfriend.

For Bennett, what is at stake is a matter of integration with the group as such, but also, in terms of music, with the music of other groups, other established players. This is in part because the kind of gigs that a group first gets will be in locales where new compositions will not be exactly welcome, but also because the access to music is access to an extant group. One does not "become" a rock musician by inventing a new genre; rather one becomes a rock star by playing along, quite literally, physically, with extant music, "the music," as Bennett helpfully hypostaticizes it for us. Thus it is grist for the mill of his anti-musicological musings above that for the most part the music played, the songs "gotten," to use Bennett's terminology, are not acquired as they are for formally or classically trained musicians (and note the difference here with the very formal or classical acquisition that made all the difference for Cale's interpretation of Cohen's *Hallelujah*), by way of sheet music. This worked for Nietzsche's performance practice in the nineteenth century, and the point that Bennett makes, as must be underscored, is that it is increasingly irrelevant today. Bennett's point, like Frith's point, is thus that many rock musicians cannot read music in any case. Significantly, Bennett adduces a counter-argument, pointing to the existence of sheet music for rock songs to argue that these are often

---

53   Bennett, "The Realities of Practice."

generated after the fact;[54] not only that, but, as he here reflects in a fashion that conforms with both Tagg's and Frith's points above, "rock musicians tend to play in ways for which conventional notation does not exist."[55]

My own experience of analyzing k.d. lang's *Hallelujah*, which Bennett calls the "getting" of the song, attests to the phenomenological distinction to be made between the aural electronic experience of the song and the score.[56] Thus it is important to emphasize that Ernest McClain needed sheet music even to begin a discussion with me because, now in retrospect, I realize that I had bracketed the written music (this is also why I wrote to McClain in the first place, not to check my "reading," but in place of such an encounter with the score) because I, of another generation, with a different relation to today's popular music, simply opted to listen, again and again and again, to the song, and indeed to different takes of the song, its many profiles, and in as many variations of the same as I could find in downloads, on YouTube, and, very officially (I own a lot of *Hallelujahs* now) on iTunes.[57]

And yet, as a university professor who happens to teach in the vicinity of Lincoln Center, thanks to Juilliard and sometimes thanks to the New York City ballet, some of my students over the past two decades have also been performing artists. Mostly I would learn of this as they warned about likely absences. But in some cases, some of my students who were musicians spoke with me about music (none, as far as I could tell, were Cohen or k.d. lang or even Schoenberg or Beethoven fans). Some told me that they could not read music and at least one student found that deficiency worth worrying about, again and again, but not, and this is consonant with Bennett's point regarding utter dedication, to the extent that he remedied this lack (although I did bring this up, in a helpful professorial fashion, as a possible remedy or solution for him). But the key point here, as this also holds for many popular performers today, and as Bennett outlines, is that "recorded songs are not *gotten* through the usual mode of audience exposure, but by the specifically defined event of copying a recording by playing along with it and using the technical ability to play parts of it over and over again."[58]

For Bennett—and Adorno would concur—the very fact that "it is possible to learn to play this way attests to the simplicity of The Music but it is also indicative of the results of a private human–machine interaction where the human is in

---

[54] This claim corresponds to McClain's observation with respect to the differences between the various scores that I was able to acquire for him.

[55] Bennett, "The Realities of Practice," 191.

[56] Classic on this is the Polish phenomenologist, Roman Ingarden, *The Work of Music and the Problem of Its Identity*, trans. Adam Czerniawski (Berkeley: University of California Press, 1986), particularly his chapter "The Musical Work and Its Score," 34–40. See also, for an overview, Edward Lippman's useful discussion of "The Phenomenology of Music," in his *A History of Western Musical Aesthetics* (Lincoln: University of Nebraska Press, 1992), 437–69.

[57] Bennett, "The Realities of Practice," 191.

[58] Bennett, in Frith and Goodwin, eds, *On Record*, 188.

precise control of the stimulation the machine gives."[59] That would be the iPod, -Pad, -Phone; that would be YouTube, for Bennett, that would be a record—or a tape or a cassette, and so on. And if learning to play to the recording is not the only way for pop and rock musicians to learn to play, what is standard is that the recording, which Bennett calls the "electronic god," remains the ideal: the goal is to "play it 'just like the record.'"[60]

Musician friends and colleagues teaching music have also made the same point: students auditioning at Juilliard notoriously attempt to audition by playing, not a set piece, but rather "the" standard recorded piece. Thus Roman Ingarden's point is that the musical work cannot be identified with its score because of the issue of performance and of its conscious, intentional constitution for the composer (this noetic reflection goes back to Plato and the Stoics), as well as the consciousness of those experiencing it. Edward Said makes a related but by no means identical point with respect to a particular performance by Alfred Brendel.[61] Bennett's own point here in his text then, like Frith's point above, like Tagg's point, and albeit indirectly, like Said's point, is that the musicologists cannot but be speaking to themselves. Already in 1981, Bennett warns us that such analyses have tended to have had little to do with actual practicing musicians, playing to the record, or these days to their portable studio computer program, whether it be just an ad hoc internet connection to YouTube, or Audacity, or the conspicuously obviously named GarageBand.

Adorno's reflections include Ingarden's, but he makes the broader point regarding music as writing, as playing, namely "as the music for which the text stands. Reflection upon text, notation, elements of the text is only necessary because this 'music' is neither self-evident as such nor immediately given, nor unambiguous."[62] For Adorno, who also seeks to raise the question of the

---

[59]   Ibid., 189.

[60]   Bennett, "The Realities of Practice," 190. But of course this is a complex point, as not all musicians traditionally could read music, and indeed part of the tradition of classical formation is improvisation—in which quality Nietzsche excelled, as did, as is often cited in proof of his virtuosity, Beethoven, who managed as a young man to impress even Mozart. See, again, Goehr's account of performance practices in her magisterial *The Imaginary Museum of Musical Works*, and her forthcoming essay on improvisation, an advance copy of which I thank her for permitting me to read, "On Broken Strings," which she presented at the start of her own 2011 Fall Aesthetics Colloquia at Columbia University, and which she reprised here and there, most recently in my presence in July 2012 at the meeting of the Royal Musical Association Music and Philosophy Study Group at King's College in London.

[61]   See Edward W. Said, *Musical Elaborations* (New York: Columbia University Press, 1991), 79f. Of course, this is a contest between variations and transcriptions, and Said's point is the literary theorist's and amateur's point; it is thus not Adorno's point, paradoxically it is not protestant enough for that, as Gadamer once emphasized, as it does not attend to the ear.

[62]   Adorno, *Towards a Theory of Musical Reproduction*, 68–.

relation between "musical notation and writing,"[63] the musical text is not "a set of performance instructions," but "rather the notation of something objective, a notation that is *necessarily fragmentary*, incomplete, in need of interpretation to the point of ultimate convergence."[64] Here, the interpreter may wish to wring his or her hands, especially if one is not willing to take up the challenge of hermeneutics. From the Anglophone, particularly the American, perspective, the virtue—we may call this "the Strunk and White effect"—of clarity trumps almost everything else. Hence, after coaxing Adorno to come to America to join the Princeton Radio Research Project (on Peter Felix's behalf), Max Horkheimer also carefully cautioned him, in a letter composed on Christmas Eve, 1937: "try to speak as simply as possible. Complexity is already suspect."[65] Of course, this would be an impossible request to make of Adorno, and an analysis of this complexity rewards further reading in the political context of the Princeton Radio Research Project, as some have already begun to explore it.[66]

But if, as Bennett suggests, the musicologists wind up speaking to themselves (and we can extend this, always *ceteris paribus*, to any theoretical analysis), it is important to note that the distinction, like a good many such distinctions, has a radical reciprocity. For the key point for many listeners or "consumers" of music (or, as her critics often say, of k.d. lang herself) is to mark oneself thereby as different.[67] This marking is also characteristic of what is needed, a branding for the pop/rock musician. Thus one appeals to the excluded group, and the most common trope of all is the claim to be, as everyone claims to be, different. Thus, like every fan, every pop musician too, not only k.d. lang but Prince and Michael Jackson and Lady Gaga and indeed Leonard Cohen, asserts their own uniqueness. None of them want success, so we are told, unless it be that that success arrive on their own terms.

It is the sameness that remains the most striking, and this point cannot but be at the heart of a book written about a cover of a song with the biblical force of

---

[63]   Ibid., 3.

[64]   Ibid., 3. My emphasis.

[65]   Lorenz Jäger cites this letter in his *Adorno: A Political Biography* (New Haven: Yale University Press, 2004), 107.

[66]   See, to begin with, Thomas Y. Levin with Michael von der Linn, "Elements of a Radio Theory: Adorno and the Princeton Radio Research Project," *The Musical Quarterly* 78/2. (1994): 316–24.

[67]   That this also applies to consumers and fans is a long-standing point in the analysis from the side of communication theory and media studies. Its problems are also patent as one can see in reading Neil Postman and indeed Baudrillard, and above I have already cited the useful analyses offered by Patricia Aufderheide, "Music Videos: The Look of the Sound," *Journal of Communication* 36/1 (1986): 57–8; Marsha Kinder, "Music Video and the Spectator: Television, Ideology and Dream," *Film Quarterly* 38/1 (1984): 2–15; and James Boyle, *The Public Domain: Enclosing the Commons of the Mind* (New Haven: Yale University Press, 2008).

"hallelujah." And of course, as anyone who has grown up in a North American or, indeed, European culture knows, this is very much what Adorno and Horkheimer called the "freedom to be the same."[68]

This is part and parcel of the effect of "consuming" the music that the music industry has on offer: and the same tension can also be seen in the now-ongoing clashes between informal video posts and "official" video posts of music performances. "Permissions" for such videos are always about profits for the recording companies and, as already noted with regret, rarely accrue to the artist. At the same time, this proprietary sensibility conflicts with the technological ease of dissemination made possible by video recordings posted to YouTube, shared on Twitter and Facebook, and so on. A certain amount of this enhances the marketing of the brand and hence is tolerated. Thus, this is the darker side of toleration: toleration as such does not preclude the option of later punitive litigation. As Oscar Wilde was among the first to notice, any news *is* good news when it comes to getting the attention of the public. But beyond a certain amount and one is bound to have already come across dead video links on YouTube, often including horror stories, real for all that, of prosecution, fees, and incarceration—fear of which led, in the exactly parallel case of academic publishing, to Aaron Swartz's suicide.

The issue here is part and parcel of what corresponds to consuming the products of the culture industry on what are inevitably the terms of that industry. Creating a market, "creating" consumers, and indeed a certain political climate that can seem indistinguishable from oppression, for all its passivity on the level of the citizen, is and has been the point of the culture industry all along: this is why the radio works so well as an instrument for political propaganda, and it is why musicians to this day hope for nothing so much as airtime, though the meaning of that term is becoming more fluid. What is at stake is literally the manufacture of taste, a universal taste, so that, however many upcoming new musicians there may be, playing as they may be at this very moment in a garage in Pomona, that would be New Jersey rather than an LA suburb, or a basement in Manhattan, Kansas, or downtown San Diego, not to mention Manchester, England, we hear only the barest fraction of the same. This limiting standardization is the point for the music industry: "Nothing really new is allowed to intrude, nothing but calculated effects that add some spice to the ever-sameness without imperiling it."[69]

Nor do we seem to mind that sameness, in fact, and this is the recurrent point made by Adorno, Horkheimer, Anders, and, of course, Marcuse, though,

[68] Max Horkheimer and Theodor W. Adorno, *Dialectic of Enlightenment: Philosophical Fragments*, trans. Gunzelin Schmid Noerr (Stanford: Stanford University Press, 2002), 136.

[69] Theodor Adorno, *Introduction to the Sociology of Music*, trans. E.B. Ashton (New York: Seabury Press, 1976), 26. The same point is emphasized in Horkheimer and Adorno's *The Dialectic of Enlightenment*: "Not only are the hit songs, stars, and soap operas cyclically recurrent and rigidly invariable types, but the specific content of the entertainment itself is derived from them and only appears to change. The details are interchangeable" (125).

importantly, just this redundancy is not emphasized by the newer representatives of communicative discourse, even on the topic of the same. New digital enthusiasts, communications and media theorists, tend instead to insist in their analyses that such sameness is overstated and that there is no such calculative standardization. Nothing but proliferation and diversity abounds.[70] The recording companies could not be happier that the scholars are persuaded of this.

Facing the Radio: A Sound "Larger ... Than the Individual"

The great majority of us do not notice—or if we do, we are inclined to dis-attend to—the digital character of music beyond occasional worries about mp3 formats when we are (if we ever are) copying our CDs for playback on our computers or iPods/-Phones/-Pads, what have you, and which most of us—to the entrepreneurial joy of the late Steve Jobs and Amazon's Jeff Bezos—simply do not do.[71] In this latter case, if we use an iPod or some such i-version, rather than some other mp3 player, the source interface in question, that would tend to be iTunes, streamlines the

---

[70]   Thus the brave, new and very vaunted Web 2.0 becomes the now to be promoted Humanity 2.0. Digital humanities replaces the old-fashioned kind, media studies gives way to newer rubrics (anything to enhance the idea that the new scholarship is the latest and greatest and the only thing worth citing, while the old scholarship is dated and faded and exactly not to be noted), and off we sail into the glowing light of the newly "transhuman" condition.

[71]   This point is the other side of sampling and it is the reason that remastered recordings bring out what is otherwise not in extant recordings. In addition to the authors cited in the first chapters above, see, in particular, Alf Björnberg, "Learning to Listen to Perfect Sound: Hi-fi Culture and Changes in Modes of Listening, 1950–80," in *The Ashgate Research Companion to Popular Musicology*, ed. Derek Scott (Farnham, Surrey: Ashgate, 2009), 105–30, as well as Andrew Goodwin, "Sample and Hold: Pop Music in the Age of Digital Reproduction," in Frith and Goodwin, eds, *On Record*, 220–34, and, for perspectives on the historical range of this development, the contributions to Hans-Joachim Braun, *Music and Technology in the Twentieth Century* (Baltimore: Johns Hopkins University Press, 2000). There is no lack of those who defend the value of less is more and the point that a difference that makes no difference is no difference, arguing that it is "difficult—and sometimes impossible—to tell the difference between a CD recording and an mp3 if someone is listening to mp3s in noisy environments, through poor quality speakers or earbuds, or in cases where a high quality encoder or high bit-rate was used to make the mp3 file." Jonathan Sterne, "The Death and Life of Digital Audio," *Interdisciplinary Science Reviews* 31/4 (2006): 338–48, here 339. Note that the audiophile's appeal to experience is here dismissed as metaphysical, at the same time as the very empirical and precisely quantifiable loss of information is dismissed in terms of the level of resolution that can matter. Here we may be reminded of those who contend that we cannot hear overtones/undertones because, to be sure, recording instrumentation cannot (always) pick up the same. Yet over/undertones are heard, when they are heard, only under particular conditions; when they are heard, they are heard bodily and not only with one's ears, physically/physiologically speaking.

Figure 7.2   Telefunken Arcolette, 3W 1928/29. Photo: © Ralf Kläs.

process, and the same applies, *ceteris paribus*, when we convert our CDs ourselves. And I should not need to remember that listening to YouTube also means listening to one's laptop speakers or computer sound system (and then there would be the earphone issue), with or without a digital audio converter, and so on. Most of us are inclined to defer to whatever is on hand or easiest (that is to say that we often "live" with the limitations of the means we have for getting and hearing music; some more inept users do this more than others, but *everyone* does this) or otherwise said, we sidestep rather than learn the necessary techniques (and there are usually a number of such) that would be required to supersede or overcome the same. This *accommodation* to technology is sometimes called "subverting" technology by ingenious (and seemingly non-critical) scholars.

In addition to the challenges and frustrations of such technical issues, including everyday work-arounds as well as more elegant solutions—whether it be a must-have gadget or app, that is, an add-on extra, at extra cost and sometimes requiring extra know-how—there is the substantive thematic of the Princeton Radio Research Project as Adorno contributes to it (indeed, as he directs this same project in a less than easy alliance with Lazarsfeld),[72] as we can read in Adorno's

---

[72]   Adorno published his own material on this project; see Theodor Adorno, "The Radio Symphony: An Experiment in Theory," in *Radio Research*, ed. Paul Lazarsfeld and Frank N. Stanton (New York: Duell, Sloan, and Pearce, 1941), as well as his "A Social Critique of Radio Music," *Kenyon Review* 7 (1945): 211–13. See, for a useful account, Levin and von der Linn, "Elements of a Radio Theory," but see, too, Robert Hullot-Kentor's introduction to Adorno, *Current of Music*, 7–69. For a general discussion, see David Jenemann, *Adorno in America* (Minneapolis: University of Minnesota Press, 2007).

Figure 7.3   Telefunken Type 50 1931/32 Photo: © Alois Steiner.

posthumously published *Current of Music: Elements of a Radio Theory*, a title which ought indeed to have been the *problem of radio*.

The "radio problem" includes the phenomenon, both political and cultural, of radio broadcasting per se, and in Adorno's day what was at issue was specifically what Bernays called the "crystallization" of "public opinion" as the world was at war, as it of course continues to be, if not in the same way. This also includes questions of propaganda and indoctrination, as well as advertising and marketing, all in addition to the broad scope of contemporary media.[73] Adorno himself, and for his own part, is following a larger research project originated by a number of thinkers in the 1920s and 1930s in the extended wake—and among scholars of musical aesthetics, this shows no risk of diminution—of Walter Benjamin's reflections on the transition from original art, as it were, to art in the age of mechanical reproduction, and it was this character of reproduced, repeated, echoed art that Adorno thematizes in his discussion of what he named the "physiognomy" of radio (a terminological discussion which can seem dissonant until one reflects that Adorno, writing in New York in 1938–41, happens to be offering a specifically, avowedly phenomenological study of radio, and that phenomenological exploration included the look of the radio set itself, its dial, its tuning knobs which permit one to influence and, by way of the arch cybernetic signifier, namely *negative feedback*, to "feel" its reception,[74] and

---

[73]   See, again, Babich, "Adorno on Science and Nihilism, Animals, and Jews."

[74]   Even today's iconic radio brand, Bose, sells this same prowess in reception, an excellence that works to just the degree that the antenna is the power cord, a design move that solves the problems of wireless broadcast in the best way, by means, as users of cable and FIOS broadband already know, of a wire.

this is its "face" (see Figs. 7.2 and 7.3), its "voice," as Adorno goes on to analyze it throughout).

Adorno begins by drawing upon Paul Bekker's historical study of the symphony,[75] noting Bekker's definition of its "power to build a community" (*gemeinschaftsbildende Kraft*). It is instructive to note that Bekker's claim that one cannot understand symphonic form without attending to its social function (it is not cited as such) informs Leon Botstein's analysis of the orchestra, particularly given the very context that Adorno himself foregrounds.[76] For Adorno, what is symphonically at stake is not the nineteenth-century ideal "that music or art in general, can 'create community',"[77] but rather—and, instead of "some mystical social power,"[78] that it makes all the simple, matter of fact difference, sheerly acoustically speaking—that "it is supposed to be listened to by a community and in a large room."[79] Adorno's point is that the audience and the space makes all the difference (and it is worth keeping Adorno's constant attention to Kant in mind when we reflect on this).

Thus he writes—and it is worth citing this at length, as the point bears on our analysis of performance practice in a concert setting (the second sentence in particular, even if inherently esoteric on Nietzsche)—that:

> The interconnection of parts must be particularly intense because much more drastic means are necessary to hold the attention of a group instead of a few expert amateurs in a room. The material involved appears to represent the self-expression of individuals much less than it aims at objectivity within which individual differences could be sublated. Furthermore, in musical works directed to larger audiences the extension in time must be handled completely differently from music which aims at intimacy because it is more difficult to sustain the concentration of masses than of expert listeners.[80]

---

[75]   Adorno, "Radio Physiognomics," in *Current of Music*, 73–200; see, in particular, 86ff, which engages (along with Adorno's usual brand of qualification and reservation) Paul Bekker's *Die Sinfonie von Beethoven bis Mahler* (Berlin: Schuster & Loeffler, 1918). See also Adorno on Bekker in *Beethoven*, 118ff. For a preliminary account of Bekker, see Christopher Hailey, "The Paul Bekker Collection in the Yale University Music Library," *Notes*, 2nd series, 51/1 (September 1994): 13–21, as well as Nanette Nielsen, "*Sein oder Schein*?: Paul Bekker's 'Mirror Image' and the Ethical Voice of Humane Opera," *The Opera Quarterly* 23/2–3 (Spring–Summer 2007): 295–310.

[76]   See Leon Botstein on symphonic form and spatial expression in his "Sound and Structure in Beethoven's Orchestral Music," in *The Cambridge Companion to Beethoven*, ed. Glenn Stanley (Cambridge: Cambridge University Press, 2000), 165–85, in addition to Adorno, as already cited above.

[77]   Adorno, *Current of Music*, 87.

[78]   Ibid.

[79]   Ibid.

[80]   Ibid., 88.

This focus on symphony is not a formal one; it is a "reproductive," as Adorno uses the term, that is again: a resonant or sounding focus. Thus sensual, the material in question involves both spatial and temporal elements. In just this context, Adorno refers to the hermeneutically philosophical musicologist, Thrasyboulos Georgiades, explaining in Adorno's *Vers une analyse des symphonies*, included in his *Beethoven: The Philosophy of Music*, that:

> From the basic material, the symphony spins out non-identical elements in time, just as it affirmatively discloses identity in a material which in itself is disparate and divergent. Structurally—as Georgiades too has stressed—one hears the first bar of a classical symphonic movement only when one hears the last, which redeems the former's pledge.[81]

This is where Adorno also speaks of what he here calls "the illusion of pent up time."[82] Symphonic works, as Adorno metaphorically explains in *Current of Music*, "transform the time element of music into space."[83] In particular, Adorno details the technical transposition of the symphony performance to the radio, where it makes all the difference, of course, that radio then and now sometimes transmitted "live" (rather than *recorded*) performances, which were nonetheless, and again *ceteris paribus*, still a matter of transmission or mediation. And this reflection informs his analysis: for the listener is face to face with the radio, just as one is face to face with one's loudspeaker—thus Adorno refers to the suggestive RCA/Victor logo, "his master's voice"—as it is this use of the "voice" that seems to frame Adorno's own reflective question, "What is the significance if a listener knows a symphony only with the specific characteristics of the 'radio voice'?"[84]

For Adorno, this effectively performative reality makes all the difference for the radio listener; and by extension the YouTube listener (and I would argue that the iPod/smartphone listener, with earphones or a Bose speaker set-up, only takes this to an ultimate extreme) "generally finds himself in a small room, whose acoustic conditions are incomparable with those of a real symphonic performance."[85]

Adorno's point is that, in addition to the work of the studio sound engineer, one has oneself to work on one's own music, which, according to Adorno, one happily does. Adorno's point (and this is why his analysis is a dialectical phenomenology, as well as a cultural criticism and psychoanalysis of the consumer) is that one is not unaware of the impotence, the pointlessness of this work qua project. As Anders noticed that one observes the mediation of one's participation at a distance, in his earlier cited example of watching a religious service on television in his

---

[81] Adorno, *Beethoven*, 119.

[82] Ibid.

[83] Adorno, *Current of Music*, 88.

[84] Ibid., 89.

[85] Ibid.

1956 book *Die Antiquiertheit des Menschen* (*Obsolescence of the Human*), so too for Adorno, in the classic radio context, the radio listener:

> knows he cannot really influence the phenomenon; so he substitutes for this influence the ideal of doing as good a job as possible. Instead of being able to do something against the mechanism when such an attempt would be futile, he wants to do something with the mechanism and identify himself with this attempt at the expense of what he is allegedly pursuing. Good reception becomes a fetish.[86]

The traditional listener has to tune the set: this is the physiognomic dynamic. But this same tuning effort is ultimately bootless for, in fact, it wins little by way of improvement and one is always at the mercy of the limits of the technology in question. This does not mean that one eliminates the equivalent of twirling dials, and the auto-seek on a car stereo allows one to browse at the touch of a button. But the car-bound radio user continues to stop the station that is playing, just in case there is something better on another station, which, for Adorno, translates to the desire to seek further. Apart from the desirability of a phenomenological sociology of car radio listening practice, the technological issue, as Adorno sought to address it, remains in play today. Whatever one's audio set-up, no matter how sophisticated, and even if at some level one has inevitably to tolerate the mechanical limits of one's set-up and to conform to it, the user still lays claim to a certain "tuning."

Thus, Alf Björnberg rightly notes that, despite the almost universal tendency to refuse Adorno's critiques owing to "their strong normative aspect," for Björnberg, Adorno nonetheless offers "some important insights into processes of change affecting music-listening as a result of technicalization and mediaization."[87] This attention to mediation per se, and to the overarching physical, physiognomic, and socio-cultural circumstances of the same, means that Adorno adverts, as many do not, to what Jacques Ellul called, even if this is ill-understood, *technological autonomy*, or what, and of itself, that is, all by itself, the technological reproduction of music does to music. But this attention to mediation also affects thinking on mediation. As Heidegger argued, technology as such, including Ellul's term *technique*, influenced both the possibility of questioning as such and in general and thereby the possibility of what he called a "free" relation to technology itself. Hence, although Adorno would not be pleased to put it this way, the very technological set-up of the radio (and here we may substitute stereo receiver/

---

[86]   Ibid., 102.

[87]   Alf Björnberg, "Learning to Listen to Perfect Sound." In addition to Adorno, Björnberg responds to Jonathan Sterne's "philosophy of mediation," here emphasizing the parsing of fidelity as a matter of "'faith in the technology', a sort of contract between the listener and the technology." Ibid., 108. Here the reference is to Jonathan Sterne, *The Audible Past: Cultural Origins of Sound Reproduction* (Durham, NC: Duke University Press, 2003), 218 and 219.

digital audio components, five-speaker surround sound set-up, or single soundbar, or what have you) is what Heidegger analyzed as the technological *Ge-Stell*.

But Adorno, who, unlike Heidegger, never made one point when he could make two or 20 simultaneously, argued that this already renders the very sociological project of the Princeton Radio Research Project bootless, and thus Adorno already, *avant la lettre* (not really, as it was already in the air at the time, as we have already cited both Bernays and Anders), challenges rational choice theory as he does so, a challenge which cuts to the critical scientific heart of social research, that is, the social sciences as such. Thus Adorno argues, calling it a "hunch," which he further clarifies as drawn from "personal observation and experience," that "people who are dealing with radio do not behave so 'rationally'."[88] And he refers here, in addition to the fetish efforts undertaken with getting better reception, to what has to count as the proto-phenomenon, at least in Adorno's analysis, of channel-surfing, which Adorno regards as fundamentally undertaken for its own sake:

> People twirl the dial for the sake of twirling. They turn the dial until they get a new station and as soon as they get it, or as soon as they know they can get it, they change it again and try anew with a different station.[89]

For many who study media today, in all its newer manifestations, especially digital, transhuman, and so on, this becomes a point of contact for the science du jour, not empirical research, that is, Lazarsfeld's positivistic sociology, but cognitive science, complete with brain scans. This is the hunt, search and find, and it is the secret to Google's success, and it is the reason, perhaps, but only time will tell, for the current dismay at the revelations that one's internet is not, if it ever was, what one imagines it used to be.[90]

This is the point of Adorno's further claim that one includes oneself by adjusting the radio's settings. That is to say, one fits oneself to the radio set, measured to what is not to one's measure. Thus Günther Anders, in his own very phenomenological convergence with critical musical theory, points out, as we have already cited this

---

[88]   Adorno, *Current of Music*, 156.

[89]   Ibid., 157.

[90]   And there are massive political (and personal and social) implications. See, again, Jaron Lanier, *You Are Not a Gadget: A Manifesto* (New York: Vintage, 2011); Eli Pariser, *The Filter Bubble* (Hassocks: Penguin Press, 2011); as well as Lee Siegel, *Against the Machine: Being Human in the Age of the Electronic Mob [How the Web Is Reshaping Culture and Commerce—and Why It Matters]* (New York: Spiegel & Grau, 2006); but also, in addition to others, Evgeny Morozov, *The Net Delusion: The Dark Side of Internet Freedom* (Jackson, TN: Public Affairs, 2011); as well as contributions to Jussi Parikka and Tony D. Sampson, eds, *The Spam Book: On Viruses, Porn, and Other Anomalies from the Dark Side of Digital Culture* (Cresskill: Hampton Press, 2009). See, for background and far more broadly, Mark Minasi, *The Software Conspiracy: Why Companies Put Out Faulty Software, How They Can Hurt You and What You Can Do About It* (New York: McGraw Hill, 1999).

description, the ghostly or spooky character of radio music, assuming radio as a fixed broadcast that one could hear streaming from different apartment window to different apartment window as one strolls along a city avenue.[91] But above all, for Adorno, now in the privacy of one's own room, one confronts the problem of volume, and Adorno's point runs counter to the ideality of the ethos of surround sound, the notion that one can recreate the there-being, the being-there of the concert hall. "The same would not be the same."[92] And Adorno's reasons are as ontically phenomenological as all get out, regarding a room as a sounding board, as musicians do:

> A sound tolerable in a big room would be offensive in a small one. A normal forte, with all its roundness and quiet strength would immediately sound like an assault, like the forbear of a catastrophe. Whoever has twirled the volume control of his radio can testify to the shock he experiences as soon as he tries loud sounds in his apartment.[93]

Adorno's point is far from dated, and the same "shock" that Adorno notes has today reached levels he might have been hard pressed to imagine. Currently the shock, more particularly a sound shock, is used deliberately, precisely for the reasons that Adorno outlines, as an attention-getting device. Today's recording artists (or their engineers or marketers) *determine* the sound level of their own songs, just as television commercials *vary* (just to counter the physiological phenomenon of accommodation) the volume of their broadcasts in order to contrast with the sound level of regular programming. Thus Adorno's analysis here can remind us that with technologically mediated or transmitted music we are dealing, musically speaking, with what Adorno characterizes as "an entirely new phenomenon."[94]

Adorno's point is meant phenomenologically, specifically with reference to what it is that makes a symphony a symphony per se. Thus Adorno argues for the notion of the "volume" of symphonic sound, using the analogy of the difference between an architect's model of a cathedral and the cathedral itself, as all about measure or proportionality. Using this classically metaphorical relationship—one, indeed, that has echoes of both Cicero and Pseudo-Dionysius—Adorno goes on to contend that:

> if the proportion to the body of the beholder is modified, that which gives the cathedral its luminosity falls away. Similarly the synthetic power of a Beethoven symphony depends at least in part on the volume of the sound. *Only if this is*

---

[91]   Anders, "Spuk und Radio."
[92]   Adorno, *Current of Music*, 89.
[93]   Ibid., 90.
[94]   Ibid., 90.

larger, as it were, than the individual is he able to reach the interior of the music through sound's gateway.[95]

The question of a sound that is larger, in this sense meaning not acoustically louder in terms of acoustic sound level, but "larger, as it were, than the individual," first becomes a question, as Adorno emphasizes in his analysis, when it comes to a symphony broadcast, precisely as this is "a symphony acoustically adapted to the conditions of a small room."[96]

As I have noted, the issue goes beyond symphonic form but concerns what is fundamentally the question of media, given the immediacy, and this is how Adorno rightly characterizes it, of media today.

Then and now.

Sensual and Atomistic Listening: The Gourmand

For Adorno, the kinds of elements that are for us today the most compelling elements in the experience of music (and Adorno, like Nietzsche, had real problems with the fixation on "experience," sometimes called "lived-experience," that both of them characterized as nineteenth century), namely, "sensual listening" and what Adorno analyzed as the kind of "atomistic listening" that first becomes a possibility as such with recorded music, in other words, with music in the age of technologically mediated reproduction, that is everything that was for Benjamin a key part of the visual artworld, was for Adorno relevant to music as well. What struck Adorno, what he took from Benjamin, which was why Adorno held to Benjamin's focus on the aura of the original, was adumbrated by way of phenomenology (thus to be distinguished from the extraordinary animus that Adorno had toward what he termed existentialist analysis, which we might today regard in terms of hermeneutics, as well as, if in a more patent fashion, Heidegger's hermeneutic phenomenology). For Adorno, the growing dominance of recorded music threatened musical understanding. Making a point that can seem to be the mirror image of the point that Bennett makes, Adorno reflects that "sensual listeners are always ready to denounce anything which they consider highbrow."[97] At the same time, Adorno also argues that one cannot analyze music with reference to so-called high culture, but must always and also

---

[95]   Adorno, *Beethoven*, 120. Emphasis added. See, for the background reference to "the" music here, in this case the "unuttered harmony," Pseudo-Dionysius, that is, Dionysius Areopagita's Heavenly Hierarchy, *De caelesti hierarchia*: Pseudo-Dionysius, *Pseudo-Dionysii Areopagitae de Caelesti Hierarchia in Usum Studiosae Iuventutis* (Textus Minores, vol. XXV), ed. Petrus Hendrix (Leiden: Brill, 1959).

[96]   Adorno, *Current of Music*, 91.

[97]   Ibid., 97.

include a review of "the kind of musical material consumed by the majority of all people."[98]

Both perspectives are required because anything less would fall short of Adorno's critical social theory.

Because the radio broadcasts a live performance (the case in question for Adorno concerned the transmission of radio symphonies which were not initially broadcast on the basis of recordings but, for reasons of all kinds, initially engineering concerns but also social, political, and technical, were broadcast live, from in-studio orchestras, which is indeed still done on television and radio today), it:

> is, at the same time "the same" and "something different" from the original. This complexity gives rise to the thought that the radio symphony is a sort of "reproduction" of an original in the same sense that pictures are reproduced. The sound received over the radio in a private room is not only physically a reproduction of the live music played in the studio. Being built out of the elements of the "symphony as such" and the alteration it undergoes by broadcasting, the phenomenon in itself has the innate characteristics of reproduction just as a print has certain innate qualities of reproduction beyond the fact that it actually reproduces the original. The print not only reproduces the original, but even phenomenally "looks like a reproduction". The same holds for the radio symphony.[99]

For Adorno, the issue will be all about the differences that we cannot perceive because we have not cultivated the capacity to do so. Our lack of culture may mean that we do not mind what we cannot grasp, but it is no less a lack of culture. As Adorno explains, and here his point is straightforwardly technical: "A symphony of the Beethoven type, so-called classical, is one of the most integrated musical forms. The whole is everything, the part, that is to say, what the layman calls the melody, is relatively unimportant."[100] When Adorno writes in this way, he alienates many sophisticated and sensitive readers on music and culture. Yet by jumping to condemn him to show the breadth of our own musical sensitivity, proving that we "like," as Facebook says, jazz, rock, pop music and its culture, and thus affectively disposed, we defend jazz, say, from Adorno's condemnations, and so on, we also run the risk of missing the point that he is arguing.

---

[98]   From Adorno's *Zum Anbruch: Exposé, Gesammelte Schriften* 19, ed. Rolf Tiedemann and Klaus Schulz (Frankfurt: Suhrkamp, 1984), 601–2. Cited here from Levin and von der Linn, "Elements of a Radio Theory," in Levin's translation, here 317.

[99]   Ibid. Cf. Adorno, "The Radio Symphony," as well as Adorno, "A Social Critique of Radio Music." See too, more generally, Greg Milner, *Perfecting Sound Forever: An Aural History of Recorded Music* (New York: Faber and Faber, 2009).

[100]   Adorno, "A Social Critique of Radio Music," in *Current of Music*, 211.

At the same time, it is also the case, as he observes, that today, and increasingly, we have developed "the tendency to listen to Beethoven's Fifth as if it were a set of quotations from Beethoven's Fifth."[101] As Adorno analyzes this, we listen to symphonies today the way we listen to popular music or jazz—Adorno's own point of reference here is Berlin's or Frankfurt's Parisian night club jazz, import jazz, as well as the jazz of the big band era in New York.

The problem for Adorno's insight here is that, so far from being an end in itself, in his day as in ours, music "has become a means."[102] And as this same issue also concerns Nietzsche in his own analysis of Greek music drama, Adorno analyzes this in a good Marxist spirit as meaning that it has become "a fetish," which last is further defined, in an addition to the text in a painfully obvious but still helpful fashion, as "something adored with ... no immediate relation to its actual being."[103]

Thus that music "is" a commodity; having become such, music, for Adorno, has "ceased to be a human force and is consumed like other consumer goods."[104] For pop musicologists, theorists, and critics, these are fighting words and newer readings emphasize, pretty much in so many words, that one can perfectly well have one's cake and eat it too. The sentiment is laudable but often amounts to the claim that the commodity form is unproblematic—*Mikey likes it*, as a television commercial for a certain breakfast cereal once repeated. So there.

If Jonathan Sterne (and others) argue that an mp3 recording is as good as anything else, because, in effect, one probably could not tell the difference anyway, Mark Katz crowns the argument of his study of today's recording technology, *Capturing Sound*, with a paean to teenage inattention—not unlike a parent fascinated by the oblique appeal of his child (Plato once warned us of this political danger and he allied nepotism to despotism, if it is also true that this warning has not made one bit of paedagogic difference in more than 2,000 years). Indeed, Hollywood, a consummately incestuous industry, cannibalizes itself to this day. For all the reader knows, Katz may be talking about his son or he may be charmed by his younger self's seeming capacity for performative distraction and performative competence, or by his observation of these properties in his students, and so on. After paying precise attention to the boy, the same attention that the boy does not condescend to lend to anything else (no matter whether, in Katz's blow-by-blow report, wandering across campus, writing a term paper, atomistic style, driving to the airport, flying home, listening or, better said, not listening/not responding to his solicitous parent's hopeful queries, and so on), Katz's point comes back to the music (and to keep the issue of the commodity form, what movie, what commercial works or could work without it?):

---

101 Ibid., 211.
102 Ibid., 211.
103 Ibid., 208.
104 Ibid., 208.

> At no time did our subject listen to music with his undivided attention. At no time did he hear music in an even remotely quiet environment. At no time did he hear music played through speakers or headphones of anything but the lowest quality. And[105]

[here, one should note, the boy is idyllically described as "the young man," and as already noted, this would be the moment of Katz's "son envy"]

> at no time did any of this trouble the young man. It is fair to say that a great deal of recorded music today is heard under similarly compromised conditions and that many of those hearing music in this way neither notice nor care.[106]

Katz thus characterizes our era, tellingly enough, as effectively "post-fidelity," as it were, and he is not wrong.

We adjust our expectations to the medium in question.

If an mp3 is, at best, "near CD quality," no matter. If a CD is already distant from the hi end quality of hi fi audio, no matter; we cannot tell and we certainly do not mind in any case. Less is more.

And this "less is more" is exactly what today's theorists, such as Jonathan Sterne and others, call to our attention. Contra Adorno. Thus many authors have observed that mediated music, however it be mediated, is still music, that one "still" gets and even more: the sheer fact that one *can* get an extraordinary amount out of very little indeed. The music industry has known this from the start, and it is why Adorno speaks of the "culinary" qualities of music which he characterizes in terms of the very paradox to which Katz above has recently adverted, albeit *without*—and to be sure because this would be the last thing that the father/author would do (and his publisher thanks him for it)—taking account of Adorno's analysis in Katz's concluding chapter. The culinary is a delicate way of referring to a gourmand's sensibility, and the YouTube effect gives us a virtual or, even better said, effective smorgasbord of anything and everything: if this or that is not particularly "good"—no matter; we have already adjusted our expectations to our cellphone, our tablet, our PC. The range of choice and the direct and immediate access to variety more than make up for that.

For Adorno, what is at issue is a contradiction, and he notes as he points to it that "a theory whose aim is consistency would try to smooth away"[107] the same contradiction, leaving it as an ultimate surd, but that, for Adorno, also means not engaging it:

---

[105]   Mark Katz, *Capturing Sound: How Technology has Changed Music* [2004] (Berkeley: University of California Press, 2010). See, too, for a more historically rigorous treatment of this same subject matter, Milner's *Perfecting Sound Forever*.

[106]   Katz, *Capturing Sound*.

[107]   Adorno, "Radio Physiognomics," 187.

Radio lessens the sensual charm, richness, and colorfulness of each sound; but because the whole becomes less apparent due to this lack of articulation by neutralized sound colors, the listener is forced to devote his attention to the isolated details. Thus listening becomes more sensual in spite of the decrease of its sensual qualities.[108]

Adorno compares this to sexuality and it is, for him, the heart of his analysis of popular light music, and it bears, for him, on the problem of time in music which he takes in a Kantian aesthetic modality. Music for Adorno "plays" with time. "Culinary music" (that is, playlist music, the music of one's own personal life-soundtrack), by contrast, does no such playing. Instead it fills time and indeed, as such, it first becomes what is needed for a soundtrack of whatever kind, radio drama, commercial spot, film music, television music-over, background music in general, including the kind of music that gets people through the day.

For Adorno, this soundtrack quality, as we may call it more generally, is "a tension which is supposed to be pleasant in itself, regardless of what it leads to in time."[109] And Adorno's point is that the use is not unrelated to the technological means of musical reproduction. Every studio effect is part of this, and thus he argues that it "fits in with the use of stimulating chords as mere sound effects without relation to the proper development in time of the music in which they appear."[110] Add to that proper contrast, as in a decent meal,[111] "they must be different against the background of well-known and ordinary effects,"[112] and at the same time, and this is a gourmand's point, "they must not be too unusual and never shock the listening to deprive him of his 'tasting' pleasure."[113]

Newer critics disagree, often by simply passing over Adorno's analysis (all the while, as observed above, insisting that, like the world, Adorno is too much with us). For me, here, what is of interest is that Adorno argues that what goes missing is the *extraordinary* possibility of music in itself and as such. Note that it is not for Adorno a matter of genre; thus he argues that the so-called "culinary" tendency is already at work in the century before his own, beginning with Wagner (Adorno takes the reader to a critical, etymological analysis of the word *Wonne* as favored

---

[108]   Ibid.

[109]   Ibid.

[110]   Ibid.

[111]   Adorno's reference here is to Deems Taylor, "The Scorned Ingredients," in *Of Men and Music* (New York: Simon and Schuster, 1937). It would be intriguing, but it is beyond the limits of this study, to compare this with Jean Anthelme Brillat-Savarin, *The Handbook of Dining; or Corpulency and Leanness Scientifically Considered*, trans. L.F. Simpson (New York: D. Appleton and Company, 1865), originally published as *Physiologie du goût ou Méditations de gastronomie transcendante. Ouvrage théorique, historique, et à l'ordre du jour, dédié aux gastronomes parisiens* (Paris: Charpentier, 1825).

[112]   Adorno, "Radio Physiognomics," 187.

[113]   Ibid.

by Wagner) and arguing that by the time one reaches "a composer like Tchaikovsky the change from specifically expressive to 'culinary' means has already become totalitarian."[114] Puccini too: "A relation between today's light popular music and so-called serious composers like these could easily be shown."[115]

Adorno's point has a good deal to do with taste,[116] if the term "culinary" had not given this away, and thus rather a lot more to do with his own judgments,[117] but it also has to do with the musical work of art, a point that is more interesting in the present context where we are all quite familiar with, and most of us are well-persuaded by, the points made by Katz and many others.

Thus Cohen's "broken" hallelujah works on us as a double entendre, doubly so, and on every level. No matter the scratchy records, no matter the dismal speakers, no matter how poor the voice—which, as it turns out, we also enjoy, to the "golden" advantage of both Bob Dylan and Leonard Cohen—it transpires that, however mediated, what we still "hear" turns out to be something that on more occasions than not transports us, and it seems by the light of day impossible that it should do so. What seems to be at stake is not unlike the undertones of Riemann's schematism, tones that, so the musicologist argues, cannot be heard, even if otherwise competent ears claim that they can (because, literally and technically speaking, *they are not there*, because, and this clinches it, our recordings tell us so).

Thus when Adorno tells us—quite correctly, and it is important to note, *pace* eager contrarians, that Adorno's analysis is not "mistaken"—that all this is the work of the studio engineer, the radio engineer, all this is to be combined with the work of human consciousness—this will be the notion of entrainment with which we began, *your brain on music*, as David Allison draws on late nineteenth-century cognitive psychology for his own illumination of Nietzsche's engagement with music in the first chapter of his book, *Reading the New Nietzsche*.[118] We need both to hear what Adorno is saying and to go beyond it, if to say this will also mean that we need to go back before it as well. What is commonly done by many newer readings is simply to skip Adorno, as

---

[114]   Ibid.

[115]   Ibid., 188.

[116]   Intriguingly more radical kinds of molecular cuisine today have indeed gone in just the direction that Taylor, who was by no means as radical as Adorno, invoked, writing as he did (and as Adorno cites him to disagree with him): "'Now many modernist composers and their advocates remind me of a cook who should suddenly tire of doing things with the same old flour and salt and pepper and beans and lamb chops and should forthwith proceeed to invent dishes composed of benzene, shavings, quinine, oyster shells, and crankcase lubricants." Ibid., 194, citing Taylor, *Of Men and Music*, 86.

[117]   Thus Adorno observes that "the use of discordant tones likely appealed precisely in isolation to avant-garde composers." Ibid., 196 ff.

[118]   David B. Allison, *Reading the New Nietzsche* (Lexington: Rowman and Littlefield, 2001).

already noted above, just as one increasingly skips a reading of Heidegger in today's readings of technology, even—or, so one should say, especially—those concerned with media, just as, for more than a hundred years, classicists simply dispensed with reading Nietzsche as a classicist in their own ranks. I am not doing that here very deliberately, and I realize that I have been thereby and all along running the risk of rendering my own account more difficult in the process. And yet, I argue that scholarly reflection can only see the past with great difficulty and, because it can dispense with no part of it, is in grievous need or lack, lacking philology, as Nietzsche once lamented, and, as Heidegger echoed in his reflections on need, lacking reflection or critical thought.

So too Adorno, I would argue. And hence in Adorno's "A Social Critique of Radio Music," despite his constitutional antipathy to Heidegger, we find Adorno posing a number of Heideggerian questions. Taking the Princeton Radio Research Project at its word and assuming (which is quite a large assumption, given the political circumstances of wartime, and again I note that the same circumstances apply for us today)[119] that the project is benevolent, Adorno contends that the question can be posed: "How can good music be conveyed to the largest possible audience?"[120] To ask this question requires that one ask: what counts as good? Adorno has an answer, for example, Beethoven, but even assuming this, as he reminds us that he does, questions still remain: "Is it not possible that this music, by the very problems it sets for itself, is far away from our own situation?"[121] This first question is already the key to a critically historical reflection. Beethoven's music is not simply a work but already a tissue of contexts, contests, tensions. And the more one knows about music, the more— Adorno never tires of repeating this—*the more* one knows about Beethoven's music as music. And Adorno adds to this the still relevant problem of acoustic accommodation, musical saturation, asking if it is not so that, as he writes, "by constant repetition, it has deteriorated so much that it has ceased to be the living force it was and has become a museum piece which no longer possesses the power to speak to the millions to whom it is brought."[122]

The concern for Adorno has to do with the stultifying effect of the culture industry, and it is not enough to counter: simply because one does not mind, as in the above illustration of a college student, real or imagined, travelling home on spring break, who happens not to mind (literally so in this case) this particular stultifying effect of the music industry.

---

[119] And to be sure and intriguingly, this same political sensibility informs Laurie Anderson's artistic work.

[120] Adorno, "A Social Critique of Radio Music," 205.

[121] Ibid.

[122] Ibid. Here, because this last is exactly the social issue of the difference between approbation or so-called appreciation and musical understanding, Adorno appends emphatically: "though those millions may express enthusiasm about what is brought to them by their announcer."

Thus Adorno poses the phenomenologically adumbrated question of whether "a symphony played on the air" remains or does not remain "a symphony?"[123] And we note that we already suppose we have our answer (or else that some expert has the answer), thus the references noted above to the interventions of the recording industry. And we could go further, as today's musicologists do seem to have all the answers (if only because academics, especially academically established musicologists, like art historians, tend to produce "answers" rather than questions).

For his part, again, Adorno asks:

> Does a symphony played on the air remain a symphony? Are the changes it undergoes by wireless transmission merely slight and negligible modifications or do those changes affect the very essence of the music? Are not the stations in such a case bringing the masses in contact with something totally different from what it is supposed to be, thus also exercising an influence quite different from the one intended.[124]

Indeed the difficulty here is that all these elements require distinct investigation and an integration of the results, just as a preliminary. And this is difficult to do precisely because those of us interested in music, music lovers, pop fans, scholars, all tend to come to the music that we come to these days first and foremost via broadcast media: via radio or as recorded to be broadcast, whether over the air or via one's stereo set-up, as a phonograph or else tape, reel-to-reel being like, and again quite different from, cassettes, CDs being like, and again quite different from, the today more or less ubiquitous mp3 in its various versions.

Adorno's phenomenological point here does not speak to the differences between different kinds of musical media. The point is the difference between direct musical perception, instrumental performing or listening to a performer perform, on whatever instrument, including voice, wherever, in a church, intimate or relatively small setting for concert or chamber music room, or a symphony hall designed for an orchestral experience, just as, so we recall, whether we have been there or not, Wagner spent every bit of every influence he had gained to build Bayreuth for the sake of what he very exactly named the *Gesamtkunstwerk*, which required a consideration of everything and everything.

We know none of that and increasingly it no longer makes sense to us to reflect upon the difference made by such seemingly disparate things. Thus authors who study recorded sound argue, more or less uniformly, and do so even after paying lip service to the notion of recording consciousness (sometimes to the extent of borrowing Bennett's terminology without saying so and renaming it as some other sonic/phonographic "consciousness"), that widespread fears (presumably to be

---

[123]   Ibid. But we may note that we broadcast opera to this day. And record companies specialize in live recordings of rock concerts and folk music events. Can't all that be successfully mediated? What is mediation?

[124]   Ibid.

traced back to Adorno alone) that recording "changes" the way that people interact with music are simply unfounded.[125] Thereby such readings mean to eliminate the basis for Adorno's question by excluding it in advance. This, however, is a move of convenience which may serve one author well enough for his own purposes, but it remains baseless; assertion of this claim does not make it true and above all it does not mean that questions do not remain to be asked.

Later, I will note that it makes all the difference for Nietzsche's own experience of his own then-contemporary music that he experienced that music for the most part by playing it as he did play it himself, that is to say, Nietzsche did not hear music otherwise than by eye, sight-reading as we still say, and thus by ear and by heart. And if we trust, and I do, those who spoke about his talents as a pianist, his interpretive, improvisational, performative talents were genial enough to count as his genius for many who heard him, including Wagner. In the absence of recordings, in the absence of radio (never mind television or YouTube), the *only* way in Nietzsche's day to hear music was to hear performers performing music on musical instruments or, and more immediately and more commonly, to play it oneself. Thus Nietzsche the school boy, in addition to requests for sausages and socks, would also ask for musical scores. And his relation to those scores, just in order to have a relation in the first place, could not but require more of his attention, bodily, mindfully, than can be imagined by Katz's college student as we met him above.

The same experiential involvement, the same hermeneutic encounter with music is also a prerequisite for the kind of "spooky" experience of music from nowhere as Anders described it, and as Adorno took over this account for his own encounter with New York and the same sounds floating from one window to the next.[126] We do not think that we experience this as "ghostly" or "spooky" in Anders's sense any longer. But to say that we do not experience it as such is to make Anders's point: for we thereby become, because we make ourselves into— exactly all by ourselves, and just this autistic condition matters—each of us quite individually, mass consumers.[127] Anders should be noted here as articulating what becomes the key insight not only of McLuhan and Baudrillard, as well as Marcuse,

---

[125] This is like, no, it is the same as, the scientistic advertising claim (this is not science) that GMO crops are "the same" as non-GMO crops; that high-fructose corn syrup is the same as any other kind of sugar, that sugar is sugar, repeating the nutritional absurdity that dominated the twentieth century, that a calorie is a calorie. Easy to calculate, and this indeed is why it held such a purchase as a model in nutrition science, but was physiologically baseless.

[126] Rainer Maria Rilke gives the example in the first of his *Duino Elegies* of the assignment [*Auftrag*] that it is to hear a violin playing from an open window. See Rainer Maria Rilke, *Duineser Elegien. Die Sonneten an Orpheus* (Stuttgart: Reclam, 1997), 8. Given the time period, one might reflect further on this allusion.

[127] See Günther Anders, "The World as Phantom and Matrix: Philosophical Reflections on Radio and Television," in his to date and unfortunately still as yet un-translated, *Die*

but of other political readings of the media. As Anders argues in 1956 on the basis of his experience working far behind the scenes in Hollywood itself (Anders was unlucky enough to have been one of the Frankfurt school theorists *not* to have been employed during or after the war by a university, or a federal project, or an institute of some kind, and hence he worked at odd jobs in America, including a longish stint cleaning television and film set props and costumes), the consumer becomes quite voluntarily the one who works on producing himself as a consumer in the image of mass media. Thus we may cite Anders's provocative section title: "Mass consumption today takes place solipsistically. Every consumer is an unpaid homeworker for the manufacture of mass humanity."[128] For Anders, there is in consequence every difference between film and television, and the difference has everything to do with place, location, the where of the event. As Anders puts it, conscientiously varying the classical ideal of the moving power of religious faith (and the mountain), "the event comes to us, we don't go to it."[129] We have already noted the significance and power of the solitary appeal of MTV as it continues seamlessly in another form of the same streaming video, as we analyzed YouTube above. Today, we happily do the work of wiring our homes for speakers to ensure this same "wireless" streaming, and it is the de facto allure of the mp3 player/iPod that some techno-futurists are predicting will soon be embedded, cyborg that we all are, very physiologically into our jawbones or skulls. Sensible as marketers would appear to be to this ambition, it is not for nothing that some currently popular earbuds have "Skullcandy" as a brand name.

The experience of music across space and time, as Adorno reflected on the inevitable change in music qua temporal art, has to do with what he calls, as we have seen, the physiognomics of radio per se, which Adorno characterizes, specifically, as the "radio voice," thus the spatial disconnect is already at work "within the private room."[130]

This difference between radio music and a direct experience, playing for oneself, composing for oneself, listening to others playing in a given space or hall, or in a market square or on the street, to performers who did the same, made a difference for Adorno himself, and this indeed was the case for some of the musicians who first played on the radio to begin with.

At issue is mass production, mass consumption. "We live," as Adorno tells us, not that we need reminding, "in a society of commodities." As Adorno articulates it, this is "a society in which production of goods is taking place, not primarily to satisfy human wants and needs, but for profit."[131] This point, the profit point, makes all the difference in the music industry, for consumers and artists alike.

Antiquiertheit des Menschen, Bd. 1: Über die Seele im Zeitalter der zweiten industriellen Revolution (Munich: Beck, 1987 [1956]), 99ff.

[128]   Anders, *Die Antiquiertheit des Menschen*, 101.
[129]   Ibid., 110.
[130]   Adorno, "The Radio Voice," in *Current of Music*, 499f., here 550.
[131]   Adorno, "A Social Critique of Radio Music," 206.

Key to this is what follows from this same profit point, given our current and now longstanding capitalist society, namely "monopolized mass production of standardized goods," always and generally a trend but nowhere so particularly concentrated (think only of the power of the recording industry) as in "the communications industry."[132]

Music becomes a commodity in a capitalist society, a commodity engendering what Adorno calls "commodity listening," which listening he compares with the ease of a pancake mix "extended to the field of music."[133] The idea is "to dispense as far as possible with any effort on the part of the recipient, even if such an effort on the part of the recipient is the necessary condition of grasping the sense of the music."[134] We think not, we suppose, but Adorno's counter is that this thinking not is indistinguishable from our tendency to suspend "all intellectual activity when dealing with music."[135] To this uncritical reception, Adorno adds what he calls "standardization," which exists, as he observes, despite the fact that on the technological level, that is, given both radio and recording technology, there is no need for it. Hence, rather like today's print journalism and television news programs, Adorno points to the "haunting similarity between most musical programs, except for the few non-conformist stations which use recorded material of serious music; and also the standardization of orchestral performance, despite the musical trademark of an individual orchestra."[136]

This is a typical move for Adorno; the reader who might have sympathy with his point is alienated by successive turns: first he addresses the light classical music stations of his day, but then adds "serious" classical music as well. And then, as if to guarantee the esotericism of his point, he adds to the list, "above all," as he hardly needs to say, "that whole sphere of music whose life-blood is standardization: popular music, jazz, be it hot, sweet, or hybrid."[137]

All in all, Adorno's point is a social one. For no matter what radio station one listens to, no matter the kind of music one programs for oneself, and it is essential to underscore this point as we now ourselves increasingly do for and to ourselves, this is Anders's "homeworker" point, the "work" that the radio once did *for* us *by* ourselves *upon* ourselves, no matter what music one listens to, radio music's

---

[132]   Ibid., 207.

[133]   Ibid., 208. Adorno does not speak of frozen, that is, toaster pancakes, but this too would only extend and thus confirm his claim.

[134]   Ibid., 208.

[135]   Ibid.

[136]   Ibid. Leon Botstein borrows this point in an essay on repertoire, and Hans-Georg Gadamer makes a related point with reference to the resistance of concert music aficionados to anything but the old standards, whether this excludes new compositions, or indeed the great bulk of the compositions, and even the composers, of the past.

[137]   Ibid., 209. György Markus gives his own analysis of the complicating dimensions of Adorno's apparent elitism in "Adorno and Mass Culture: Autonomous Art Against the Culture Industry," *Thesis Eleven* 86 (August 2006): 67–89.

"ideological tendencies," as Adorno expresses this, tend to realize themselves. Thus "music under present radio auspices serves to keep listeners from criticizing social realities."[138]

For Adorno, the problem is the consumer illusion per se. Given "the standardization of production" in the music industry, here on the radio, "the listener virtually has no choice."[139] Thus pop music is *pop* music. And Adorno goes on to cite sociological study after sociological study, showing that, although "it might appear that radio, by a kind of Darwinian process of selection, actually plays most frequently those songs that are best liked by the people and is, therefore, filling their demands,"[140] this is not the case once one considers that, as Adorno emphasizes, "the 'plugging' of songs does not follow the response they elicit but the vested interest of song publishers."[141] In other words, as he writes with Simpson, speaking of then-popular Benny Goodman and Guy Lombardo: "Popular music commands its own listening habits."[142] Following this command and the industry associated with producing it "on demand," as we say today, the listener becomes "enraptured with the inescapable."[143]

This continues (and belies) the efforts expended by k.d. lang and her managers to have her fans call radio stations and request more airplay. And k.d. lang might do better (and has perhaps already done so, as I write this) to take that issue up with Nonesuch, her current recording company. Leonard Cohen can testify to some of the limits of such negotiations, in his case with SONY.[144] From the point of view of the recording company, the artist is no more than a widget and one widget among many. The recording company promotes some recordings and not others for reasons that have only to do with profit, period, paragraph. The artists promoted turn out to be more rather than less incidental to that aim.[145] As may

---

[138]   Nor, of course, has this changed since Adorno wrote it.

[139]   Adorno, "A Social Critique of Radio Music," 212.

[140]   Ibid., 213. Bourdieu's study of class distinctions in musical taste would only confirm this point, while pointing to crucial social differences, that is, Bourdieu's meaning of "distinction."

[141]   Ibid. Adorno is referring here to Duncan MacDougald, "The Popular Music Industry," in *Radio Reseach 1941*, ed. Paul Lazarsfeld and Frank Stanton (New York: Duell, Sloane, and Pearce, 1941), 65–109.

[142]   Adorno, "On Popular Music," in *Current of Music*, 423.

[143]   Ibid., 426. Cf. with regard to what Adorno calls "structural standardization" and standard reactions, what are popularly called "response mechanisms" (417).

[144]   This was to be sure, along with my own pained experience in seeking such permissions, the reason for citing Robert Kory's cautionary advice to me above.

[145]   Thus, to my frustration, and contributing indeed to personal financial stress, it was the author of this book, not the publisher, who paid SONY (and Random House) for the privilege of citing Cohen's work in this book. And as this is a non-trade, non-commercial, but all-too-academic book, it exemplified fair use, if anything is fair use. But what matters here is to note that the money paid did not profit Cohen.

be seen in Marcuse's analysis in his *One-Dimensional Man*, and as can also be traced in Baudrillard, the illusion of consumer choice continues to function as the animating illusion of capitalist society, especially in the music business. As Adorno writes:

> The identification of the successful with the most frequently played is thus an illusion, an illusion to be sure that may become an operating social force and in turn really make the most played a success because through such an identification the listeners follows what they believe to be the crowd and thus come to constitute one.[146]

Of course, this is the point of advertising and this is the way that propaganda functions, and this point will be expanded upon with Max Horkheimer in *The Dialectic of Enlightenment*. Here Adorno continues, using the example of the parallel with advertising the "difference" between gasoline stations:

> The less the listener has to choose, the more he is made to believe that he has a choice: and the more the whole machine functions only for the sake of profit, the more must he be convinced that it is functioning for him and for his sake only or, as it is put, as a public service.[147]

Consuming/Advertising

Once again, as we recall Adorno's phenomenological analysis of musical sound, the "symphony" as such does not, *because it cannot*, work in a small room. This "not working" is not a defect of radio or today's sound equipment. That is, it is not because the sound engineers have not gotten it right. As Adorno writes: "No technical process can obliterate the loss of all this on the radio."[148] Commentators, in deft fealty to the gods that be, that is, to technology and to industry, are always quick to suggest that in the interim, things have changed. But Adorno's point remains. Indeed, and this is the key to Adorno's insight, as it also happens to be Günther Anders's insight, this corresponds to the musical point of over- and undertones as these are experienced in space and time, as you are—or as you are not—in a specific symphonic space, "larger," as Adorno put it, "than the individual."[149] Note that this refers to the body, to one's bodily habitation in, being in space, which Adorno invokes when he speaks of the "acoustic and social conditions of listening."[150] This is as complex a point as any that Adorno makes;

---

[146] Adorno, "A Social Critique of Radio Music," 214.
[147] Ibid.
[148] Adorno, *Beethoven*, 120.
[149] Ibid.
[150] Ibid.

this has to do with Beethoven, just because of the historicality of his works, works that are not, as Adorno says, "self-sufficient," and hence works that are not "indifferent towards the time."[151] Vulnerable as a result, "they are susceptible to that which is allegedly inflicted on them from outside."[152] Instead of whatever music was, and reminiscent of Anders's spectral convention, "only as ghosts can the dissociated works survive their own downfall."[153]

Note that the phenomenological stake here at issue has nothing to do with over- and undertones per se—although, as Nietzsche already did argue with respect to Riemann, one might go on to make just this argument, provided one can imagine doing so, via either Adorno or Anders. Headphones, and some will argue this quite heatedly, change this a bit, but to make such an argument assumes as its point of departure that one hears with one's ears, alone, that is to say, and not with one's body, not one's skin, and thus not attuned to the space around one, not with one's eyes, and also not with one's mind. This is the point that Anders makes when he argues against those who reduce technology to a mere "means," whatever it might mean to be a mere means, given everything that is involved with mediation in general. As an argument against those who refuse the insight into the autonomy of technology, Anders is unmatched in anticipating the claims of those who suppose it possible to use "correctly" or rightly or, and Anders argues that this is the same, to "subvert" technology for one's own purposes. For Anders, all this is sheerly "illusionary."[154]

Using a counter-argument seemingly made to order for public broadcasting or educational TV, Anders reflects that if one "participates" in a religious service by watching it on TV, the most significant aspect of the experience of any such an explicitly virtual participation will be precisely that one is *not there*, "not participating"[155] in the service. Thus Anders points out that in addition to what impresses us about a televised religious service on an individual basis, there will also be what impresses us phenomenologically, *whether we notice this or not*, namely the very *that* that we are not there. Instead of a communitarian event, a participating presence alongside others (and we see that Heideggerian language, just as Adorno recognized, is here indispensable), so, Anders argues, we "consume" the image of the religious service, which he calls, in an observant Lutheran sense, as indeed here in an observant Jewish sense, a "picture-book effect"—one experiences the religious service as broadcast, as picture, just as one experiences the world not by being in the world but, and this is the context of Anders's argument, via one's television receiver or, as we may add today, cable or internet network.

Anders's religious example is an incarnate but still spiritual one. If Adorno is much more profane for his part, the parallel between the two remains. Arguments countering Adorno's claims by pointing to advances in today's technology, much

---

151   Ibid., 122.
152   Ibid., 122.
153   Ibid.
154   Anders, *Die Antiquiertheit des Menschen*, 99.
155   Ibid., 100.

like arguments countering Heidegger's insights into technology by adverting to the exactly commercial claims made on behalf of supposed technological innovation, that is to say, the supposed differences between Heidegger's experience of technology and technology "today," do not sidestep this point. On the contrary, especially if we bring in Anders's reflections as well, noting that today's recording technology is exactly of a piece with the habits of listening to which both Anders and Adorno advert, and hence do not counter Adorno's claims.

But there is more, and this is where we need to read Adorno's philosophy of music as a phenomenological aesthetics of music: to have a full orchestral experience, in Adorno's sense, to hear a symphony composed as such and as it should be heard, and in order to hear it as such, require one's physical presence and one's informed, listening attention, as Adorno likes to emphasize both the intellectual work involved but also the physiognomy of the concert hall. The hall is a sounding space; one can reproduce it, but when one does so, engineering the sound of sound, as we discussed above, Anders's point, as we have developed it above, is that the listener will notice this lifelike sound, this concert-hall sound, this "as if." And we may replace Adorno's twirling of the dial with the audiophile's search for a sweetspot, together with the engineers' specs for the same, and add to this the very physiological effects of accommodation, so that, after a while, we find that instead we listen only for what we have become accustomed to hear. And as Bennett says, the song we sing becomes the song we hear on the radio or YouTube. Adorno adds, to illustrate the difference that this makes before its jading passes from any possible memory, the external architecture, the physical space, together with the rules or the "praxis" of the concert hall itself. Thus, to use Adorno's example to conclude this chapter, when one is called out, as a physician might be, from the space of a concert to the lobby, the physician can still hear in the distance what he was once part of—and after the intermission can return to—in quite a different way than a latecomer standing in the same lobby can hear the same music at the same physical remove. Note that stepping outside a concert to the lobby from which one can still overhear the music in the hall is exactly not the same as the experience of leaving a lecture or a concert to answer a cellphone. And this is for the same reasons of conscious intentionality. Consciousness is always consciousness of something, but it is never consciousness of everything simultaneously and in the same way. The intentional difference of the work of attention is what makes all the difference in space and time.[156]

---

[156] Adorno refers, as we have already noted above, to Bekker's vision of the community-forming power of symphony, arguing that this only works in a traditional symphonic space and not, although one might have expected this, on the radio; and he argues that this takes place by means of the "power of symphonic contraction of time which annihilates, for the duration of the performance, the contingencies of private existence, and transfigures the individuals," not, as he argues, "into an actual community with others no matter contingent differences but the awareness of the idea of such a community." *Current of Music*, 510.

Interlude

As we have seen in analyzing Cohen's *Hallelujah*, analyzing Adorno's ultimate sympathy for and with Anders's ghosts, there is no way to get around or to avoid metaphor or its admixture. Accordingly, one can suppose, and traditionally one has supposed, that talk of music in philosophy is all so much poetic metaphor. Nietzsche, as we shall see, lectured on the relation between music and word, and included these reflections in his book on Greek tragedy, including there his analyses of Beethoven and Schiller.

But Adorno reminds us that it remains problematic to think of words about music, talking of music. We seem to be inevitably entangled in metaphors speaking of music, where "even the legitimate technical vocabulary of Western music is rooted in metaphor, and the metaphoric roots are still in evidence."[1]

Here we take up a few words on metaphor and poetry, but the key concern is an exploration of the Greek notion of *mousiké techné*.

---

[1]   Marion A. Guck, "Two Types of Metaphoric Transfer," in *Metaphor: A Musical Dimension*, ed. Jamie C. Kassler (Sydney: Currency Press, 1991), 1–12, here 2. Guck cites, for example, images of space and references to movement or motion in musical discourse. See, likewise on the notion of metaphor and music, with specific reference to Nietzsche, Detlef Otto, "Die Version der Metapher zwischen Musik und Begriff," in *Centauren-Geburten: Wissenschaft, Kunst und Philosophie beim Jungen Nietzsche*, ed. Tilman Borsche, Federico Gerratana, and Aldo Venturelli (Berlin: de Gruyter, 1984), 167–90, and more broadly in his *Wendungen der Metapher: zur Übertragung in poetologischer, rhetorischer und erkenntnistheoretischer Hinsicht bei Aristoteles und Nietzsche* (Munich: Fink, 1998).

Chapter 8
Mousiké techné

On Philosophy and the Poetic Practice of "Music"

Leonard Cohen's *Hallelujah* is above all a poem, and that is to say that in all its verses and variants, it is one poem, it is one song.[1] And if Cohen's poem makes the song of praise, his song, reflecting on the song itself, the secret chord, other poets likewise invoke music, and in this chapter we shall see that even philosophy is included among the arts, all of which, according to Pater, "aspire" to the condition of music.

Wallace Stevens plays on the allusive image of music in a variety of his poems, deploying a poetic reading of the kind I have called "concinnity" in his invocation of musical concepts and devices. In *Peter Quince at the Clavier*, Stevens echoes the shadowed silk of Herrick's *Julia*, working with the onomatopoeia that is the music of words: the colored liquefaction of her clothes:

> Just as my fingers on these keys
> Make music, so the self-same sounds
> On my spirit make a music too.
> —Wallace Stevens, *Peter Quince at the Clavier*

Where, using the example of Goethe's word-tone poem, *Über allen Gipfeln ist rüh*, Lipmann points out that the power of a poem can work to leave music impotent, this is most often not the case and thus Nietzsche's metaphor is that of the son seeking to give birth to his father.[2] Just as Hölderlin will say of his own poem, including the conversation of the whole of humankind in the process, *soon we shall be song*, Stevens's *Peter Quince at the Clavier* apostrophizes the achievements of the poet as musician, repeating the same strain with the same colors, using words that do not go beyond music as much as they pretend to, reflecting "the serenade / Of a man that plays a blue guitar" (Stevens, *The Blue Guitar*).

Distant as he is from the essence of music, Stevens approximates an aspect that is qua poetry, essentially musical all the same: "feeling," as Stevens will say, not

---

[1] Leonard Cohen, *Stranger Music: Selected Poems and Songs* (Toronto: McClelland and Stewart, 1994).

[2] Edward A. Lippman, *The Philosophy & Aesthetics of Music* (Omaha: University of Nebraska Press, 1999), 70.

sound.[3] But the sound of the words in question belies the claim and thus Stevens can catch a philosophical rhythm echoed by Ezra Pound's plain-chant suggestion, "End fact. Try fiction," in his poem, *Near Perigord*.

In Stevens's resonance, this rhythm is the round, a musical turning:

> … Perhaps,
> the man-hero is not the exceptional monster,
> But he that of repetition is most master.
> —Stevens, *Notes Toward a Supreme Fiction*

Before such recent American and overtly philosophically minded poets (thus we have noted that Stevens was intrigued by Heidegger), it was the philosophical Shakespeare himself (whether he was "Lord Bacon," as Nietzsche liked to tease, or somebody else) who wrote of the music of music, where a life disjoint in time, or out of tune with itself, kills the beauty of active or heard music:

> Music do I hear?
> Ha, ha! Keep time. How sour sweet music is
> When time is broke and no proportion kept!
> So is it in the music of men's lives
> —*Richard II*, Act 5, sc. 5:41–44

The souring of true or "sweet" music (as Shakespeare expresses it with an uncanny, all-too-Classicist's allusion)[4] transpires as a result of "the music of men's lives," lived through kept time and measure. This measure, like all beauty, is inexpressibly precise, and so, with Heraclitean, Pythagorean precision, our classically mannered Shakespeare continues to remind us of the consequences of lost restraint, shattered measure:

> Take but degree away, untune that string,
> And hark what discord follows!
> —*Troilus and Cressida*, Act 1, sc. 3:109–10

---

[3]   Thus Macquarrie and Robinson cite the German proverb, "Wer nicht hören kann, muss fühlen." (That is to say, "he who cannot heed must suffer.") Martin Heidegger, *Being and Time* [1927], trans. John Macquarrie and Edward Robinson (New York: Harper & Row, 1962), translators' note 2, 207. Manifestly, although Macquarrie and Robinson do not allude to it, this proverb itself derives from the biblical word to the wise, so influential for Nietzsche, *Wer hören kann, der höre* [Whoever can hear, let him hear]. See, on Stevens and Heidegger, Thomas Jensen Hines, *The Later Poetry of Wallace Stevens: Phenomenological Parallels With Husserl and Heidegger* (Cranbury, NJ: Associated University Presses, 1975). While Frank Kermode in one field and Simon Critchley in another have repeated Hines's analysis, Hines remains both timely and useful, for his attention to his own predecessors on the one hand and to related literature on the other.

[4]   It is this kind of allusion that has seekers of the "true Shakespeare" guessing at identities closer to Francis Bacon than to any ordinary master of the village of Hamden, Miltonian qualities immortalized in the absence of mortality by Thomas Grey.

Shakespeare's Pythagorean, Platonic word for what he calls "the music of men's lives" recalls the Athenian, Platonico-Aristotelian ideal of a musical ethos, the ethics of music, the ethical that is music.

In earlier chapters, I began to frame the question of Nietzsche's *Birth of Tragedy out of the Spirit of Music* for the sake of what Nietzsche calls the "becoming-human of dissonance," which I shall take up in the final chapter. Towards this same end, in the current chapter, as this book moves towards a discussion of the role of Beethoven in Nietzsche's first book, this question takes us to Plato's Socrates and his invocation of music, as well as Nietzsche's Pindar and Heidegger's Hölderlin (which is also Adorno's paratactic Hölderlin), to frame an effective or working musical stylistics of the word as word.[5]

As we read, for Hölderlin, here in the seventh stanza of his poem, *Friedensfeier*:

This is a law of fate, that each shall know all others,
That when the silence returns there shall be language too.[6]

Heidegger's reading of Hölderlin's *Friedensfeier* reverses the order of the poet's words in order to echo the beginning of the eighth stanza of the same poem in celebration of peace:

Much, from the morning onwards,
Since we have been a conversation and have heard from one another
has human kind learnt; but soon we shall be song.[7]
—Hölderlin, *Friedensfeier*

In the same locus, Heidegger cites the resonance of song and silence in Nietzsche's Zarathustran converse with his soul: "*that I bade you sing.*"[8] This is Nietzsche's word to the poet, as Stefan George heard it, as George is the poet who lends

---

[5]   Thus Martin Heidegger recalls Friedrich Hölderlin's elegy, *Bread and Wine*: "Why are they silent, too, the theatres ancient and hallowed? / Why not now does the dance celebrate, consecrate joy?" (stanza vi) at the beginning of Heidegger's essay "Words." For Heidegger, "The word is withheld from the former place of the gods' appearance, the word as it was once word." Trans. Joan Stambaugh, in *On the Way to Language*, trans. Peter D. Hertz (New York: Harper & Row, 1971), 139.

[6]   "*Schicksalsgesetz ist dies, daß alle sich erfahren, / Daß, wenn die Stille kehrt, auch eine Sprache sei.*" From Hölderlin's *Friedensfeier*, quoted in Heidegger, "On the Nature of Language," in *On the Way to Language*, 78.

[7]   *Viel hat von Morgen an, / Seit ein Gespräch wir sind und hören voneinander / Erfahren der Mensch; bald sind wir aber Gesang.* From *Friedrich Hölderlin: Poems and Fragments*, trans. Michael Hamburger (Ann Arbor, 1966), 439. Cited in Heidegger, "On the Nature of Language," 78.

[8]   Ibid. Heidegger cites Nietzsche's *Thus Spoke Zarathustra*, "The Great Longing." See, also, Nietzsche's preface to *The Birth of Tragedy*.

Heidegger his own motto of song, and here, for the sound of it, we need the German words of George's poem:

Was ich noch sinne und was ich noch füge
Was ich noch liebe trägt die gleichen züge.
[What I still ponder, and what I still frame,
What I still love—their features are the same.]
—Stefan George, *Song*

For Heidegger, following George, who, as poet also and for his own part, follows Hölderlin, precisely as both George and Hölderlin see themselves in a conscientiously antique mode, the poet "sings, and song remains discourse."[9]

I argue that a reflection on the nature of this poetic singing exchange or discourse recalls the Greek origin and meaning of *mousiké*. In discourse, the reciprocity of conversation is key. Music in this sense (and this rejoins Stevens and Shakespeare with Adorno's architectural imagery of symphonic space) requires a response, utterly public, essentially resonant.

Towards a Musical Praxis in Philosophy: Playing Temperament and Thought

What Plato called μουσική τεχνή, the art of music, included all the arts. The "practice of music" thus included philosophy itself, understood as "a" music, mathematically understood as art or technical practice.[10]

Metaphors for this musically ordinal expression are found in both Pythagoras and Heraclitus. Peter Kingsley lends power to his otherwise mystagogical bent as he calls attention to the "sound" of the syrinx in Parmenides's strikingly vivid description of the chariot wheels that take him on his journey "beyond the gates."[11]

---

[9]   Ibid.

[10]   See, especially, Martin L. West, *Ancient Greek Music* (Oxford: Clarendon, 1992); as well as Warren D. Anderson, *Music and Musicians in Ancient Greece* (Ithaca: Cornell University Press, 1994); and, for a perspective including the culture of ancient Rome, Giovanni Comotti, *Music in Greek and Roman Culture*, trans. Rosaria V. Munson (Baltimore: The Johns Hopkins University Press, 1977). In addition, see Lewis Rowell, *Thinking About Music: An Introduction to the Philosophy of Music* (Amherst: University of Massachusetts Press, 1983); Wesley Trimpi, *Muses of One Mind: The Literary Analysis of Experience and Its Continuity* (Princeton: Princeton University Press, 1983); and, more rigorously, Amy M. Dale, "Words, Music and Dance," in *Collected Papers* (Cambridge: Cambridge University Press, 1969), 156–69.

[11]   Kingsley has moved to the exoteric beyond the esoteric and well beyond academic Straussianism. See Peter Kingsley, *In the Dark Places of Wisdom* (Inverness: Golden Sufi Press, 1999), as well as the chapter on Nietzsche's use of chaos below. See, too, P.A. Meijer, *Parmenides Beyond the Gates* (Leiden: Brill, 1997).

In the case of Heraclitus, we recall his cautionary words regarding the merits of the hidden attunement, the backstretched connexion that is also the secret of variance in harmony, as Plato also claims through Socrates and as McClain argues.[12] More generally, more exoterically, Pythagoras held that both mathematics and philosophy derive from the structural nature of music. With the same regulative measure following from an understanding of the political/ethical effects of musical tuning, Plato sought to construct an ideal musical city on the same well-tempered measure as foundation. The philosopher Reiner Schürmann is one of the most recent to have explored the architectonics of this musical metaphor in his posthumously published *Broken Hegemonies*,[13] and it also appears in Antonio de Nicolàs's study of the Vedic tradition in his *Avatara*.[14] In the same fashion, Aristotle invoked the ethical ideal of musical harmony (*Nicomachean Ethics*, 1131a–1134b).

Despite today's best intentions toward multiculturalism, indeed in spite of internet and networked connectivity, we are as closed a culture as only a monological culture of the book can be (and we remain a book culture, even as we become those who "read" nothing further than internet posts, blogs, tweets, and texts. That is, the move away from the physical book to digital media enriched with sound, color and light is not a return to an oral culture but only *otherwise* mediated in Anders's sense of an otherwise, differently textured, texted, keyed, traced, but still text culture. As the classical philologist Albert Lord emphasized, a book culture (substitute tweet or text or podcast or video culture, if you like) is inherently closed. Yet openness of an oral culture is foreign to us. It is because we are so very monolithically text (letter, law) oriented that—so Lord contends, needing as he did already so many years ago to make the point of what it is to try to understand a culture thousands of years *distant* from us, other than our own, that would be the Greeks separated from us by an utterly different linguistic-acoustic sensibility (Nietzsche attempted to convey this by speaking of the "spirit," the breath of music)—"we are not accustomed to thinking in terms of fluidity. We find it difficult to grasp something that is multiform. It seems ideal to us to construct an ideal text or to seek an original, and we remain dissatisfied with an ever-changing phenomenon."[15] An oral culture is mutable, constantly and consciously recreated and because of this it is open. Against the fixed ideal of *prosaic* literality, made more rather than less profound in the newer, multimedia expressions (double-media, music-as-vision expressions: in YouTube videos, computer games, along with graphic and sonorous varieties of internet or streaming connectivity), the ideal of music is itself a playing attunement.

---

[12] See Ernest McClain, *The Myth of Invariance: The Origin of the Gods, Mathematics and Music from the Rg Veda to Plato* (York Beach, ME: Nicolas Hays, 1976).

[13] Reiner Schürmann, *Broken Hegemonies*, trans. Reginald Lilly (Bloomington: Indiana University Press, 2003).

[14] Antonio de Nicolàs, *Avatara: The Humanization of Philosophy Through the Bhagavad Gita* (York Beach, ME: Nicolas Hays, 1976).

[15] Albert B. Lord, *The Singer of Tales* (Cambridge, MA: Harvard University Press, 1960), 100.

In this vein, Michael Chanan connects social-theoretical observations about practice with Bakhtin's reflections on the dialogical nature of music and all sign systems in general.[16] Elsewhere, I have also argued that the practical art of hearing in a philosophic mode as itself a modality of thought is a dialogical art of attuned or musical listening.[17] For philosophy, such listening or playing attunement can be, as at least Heidegger supposed, following Nietzsche, the opening of thought towards a musical ethos, assuming that such is possible at all.[18]

Musicology contra the Music of Music: Metaphor and its Discontents

We recall the culture of the concert hall and we should also keep in mind Adorno's more complicated reflections—sounding board reflections, as I would call them, remembering the power of the cello and contrabass among the string instruments—on the role of the symphony hall in the sound of the symphony as such. At the very least, one can say that in the concert hall, we have to do with so-called "real" music, no matter whether popular or classical. Bracketing the debate on high or low culture, we may invoke the Horatian poignancy already noted at the outset in which Walter Pater famously declares that "*All art constantly aspires to the condition of music.*"[19] Pater's insight is typically taken to signify the tragic condition of art as such, precisely as it inevitably fails this ambition, and Adorno may be read as a series of aphorisms on this same failure. Indeed, Nietzsche also claims, following Schopenhauer as he does so, that "music" *articulates* inexpressibility itself, giving it breadth and form, life and time. In this way, Said articulates the paradox of Adorno's reflexive critique as corresponding, as we have seen, to "a serious appraisal of how music manages in spite of everything to preserve its reticence, mystery, or allusive silence."[20]

---

[16] Chanan recalls the Barthean ideal of polysemy, where it is music that "provides the very model of a discourse which is composed of simultaneous voices." Michael Chanan, *Musica Practica: The Social Conventions of Western Music from Gregorian Chant to Postmodernism* (London: Verso, 1994), 39.

[17] These arguments run indeed throughout my publications.

[18] See Barthes, in Chanan, *Musica Practica*. Similarly, Edward Said, *Musical Elaborations* (New York: Columbia University Press, 1991), 88, cites Gramsci's expression of the "muscular-nervous," referring to Foucault in order to make the same point vis-à-vis practice in addition to Said's own account of his playing skills, and Kathleen Higgins highlights her own musical experience as pianist. See Kathleen Marie Higgins, "Musical Idiosyncrasy and Perspectival Listening," in *Music and Meaning*, ed. Jenefer Robinson (Ithaca: Cornell University Press, 1997), 83–102.

[19] Walter Pater, "The School of Giorgione," in *The Renaissance* (Oxford: Oxford University Press, 1986), 86.

[20] Said, *Musical Elaborations*, 16.

For expert writers on music, as we recall McClain and others, music sings the "song itself."[21] What matters here is metaphor, for Nietzsche, music and word, speaking of music, as we have throughout been reflecting on Leonard Cohen's language of David's "secret chord." In this spirit, the scientifically sophisticated musicologist Robin Maconie is at pains to qualify the claims of music's "inexpressibility" in the hierarchization of music, from Socrates throughout the music theory of antiquity and through the Renaissance. Maconie draws on tradition for this modernist point, invoking Boethius's "right"[22]-minded distinction between "three levels of musical understanding. At bottom, *musica instrumentalis*, above that, *music humana*, and at the top, *music mundana*."[23]

Maconie's demythologization of the "music of the spheres" works allegorically. Thus he reduces the realm of music to a technical achievement of musicological expertise: "what Boethius is saying is that what an instrument-maker (or recording engineer today) would call sound quality is different from what a professional musician would call a musical performance and a composer (or connoisseur) would

---

[21]   See, once again, Ernest McClain, *The Pythagorean Plato: Prelude to the Song Itself* (York Beach, ME: Nicolas Hays, 1978). More recently, just in the context of metaphor and association, Jay Kennedy, cited below and again in the concluding chapter, has claimed to have discovered a hithertofore unprecedented musical construction in Plato. This is a clear exaggeration, given McClain's *The Pythagorean Plato*, and not less, perhaps still more likely, given John Bremer's *On Plato's Polity* (Houston: Institute of Philosophy, 1984), reprised and clarified in a subsequent article, "Some Arithmetical Patterns in Plato's *Republic*," *Hermanathena* 169 (Winter 2000), 69–97, as well as Graham Pont's "Analogy in Music," as well as Árpád Szabó, both of which I cite and discuss below. The tendency to blindered research, and therefore and correspondingly permitting more convenient "discovery," has a good deal more to do with the politics of scholarship (who we cite, who we do not cite, and when I wrote to Kennedy about his citation practice, he was frank in replying that in his opinion the scholarly mill sieves only the "best" while leaving the chaff—an opinion that Oscar Wilde famously inverted and Nietzsche in his day likewise disputed, as he argued that there seems to be "more likelihood that a bad book will be preserved than a good one," (KSA 7, 9 [203], 481), merely judging here, in his context, from the seeming standards of academia.) Nevertheless, the practice outlines what counts as knowledge inasmuch as the fate of the non-cited is to disappear from the scholarly horizon; it is a self-referred and hence-confirming conviction. See also, in the context of the politics of academic or university philosophy, especially analytic philosophy, as Kennedy's point justifying his scholarly non-reading is as analytic as was his formation, Babette Babich, "On the Analytic-Continental Divide in Philosophy: Nietzsche's Lying Truth, Heidegger's Speaking Language, and Philosophy," in *A House Divided: Comparing Analytic and Continental Philosophy*, ed. C.G. Prado (Amherst, NY: Prometheus, 2003), 63–103, and my recent interview, "An Impoverishment of Philosophy," *Purlieu* 1/3, special edition: *Philosophy and the University*, ed. Dennis Erwin and Matt Story (2011): 37–71. I take up this theme again below as it bears on Nietzsche and, indeed, Riemann.

[22]   Robin Maconie, *The Concept of Music* (Oxford: Clarendon, 1990), 11.

[23]   Ibid.

recognize as sublimely inspired musical invention."[24] For his own part, Adorno has spent a lifetime looking at the relationship between music and language, but above all at the language of music as such, as its own discourse:

> many of the most perfect melodies sound like quotations. Not like quotations from other pieces of music, but rather as if they had been taken from a secret musical language from which the ear picks out snatches here and there, which it does not even understand.[25]

On this level, despite his opposition to Adorno, Said concurs, recounting his perceptual identification of musical transcription of Brahms's String Sextet in B Flat, referring to a Carnegie Hall performance by Alfred Brendel. In his phenomenological account of the musical object, Said realized that he heard the transcription as such, although he was unfamiliar at the time with Brahms's own transcription, and one that Brahms, as Said discovered, frequently performed. Thus for Said, the compelling rarity of the piece, known in other "variations," educed an array of associative constellations, all reminiscences of music "past" in Said, including not only a Proustian core but also the "unstable or inexpressible, aspect of his music, the music of his music, which I think anyone who listens to, plays, or thinks about music carries with oneself."[26]

If Adorno's critiques of the fragmentization of music—as the attunement to the melody of music, as he denigrates it in his reflections on the fetish character of modern music, in all its intensification post-MTV and with the various YouTube options to be found and heard (and hummed, to put Adorno's spin on it)—apply in the popular context, Said's reflections do not preclude the applicability of Adorno's criticisms.[27] And where Adorno and Nietzsche come together, what is at stake is a specifically practical community. This community is that of a musical cultivation as this is common to those with the capacity to play, to compose, and perhaps most importantly to think of music as players/singers/composers do. It goes without saying that this proficiency, as Adorno argues and as H. Stith Bennett, for his own part, illustrates by inversion, is increasingly threatened, not by the average listener but exactly by expertise. Adorno's enduring contribution to the discussion of music—and he takes this esoteric turn from Nietzsche—is to find more philistinism in the expert afficionado or enthusiast than in the ignorant. It is atomization into sheer consumption which turns us into the kind of childish competitors who, in Adorno's critique, prized their capacity to function as what

---

[24]   Ibid.

[25]   Theodor Adorno, *Quasi Una Fantasia: Essays on Modern Music*, trans. Rodney Livingstone (London: Verso, 1992 [1963]), 25.

[26]   Said, *Musical Elaborations*, 93.

[27]   Theodor Adorno, *The Culture Industry: Selected Essays on Mass Culture* (London: Routledge, 1991).

he called—already seemingly criticizing Said's Proustian example in advance—tone-thief detectives.[28]

On the Birth of Music in Ancient Greek *Mousiké*

Μουσική, according to Liddell and Scott's *Greek–English Lexicon*, is defined as "*any art over which the Muses presided*, esp. *music or lyric poetry.*"[29]

In the field of music and theory, and in express connection with its relevance for philosophy, the hermeneutic musicologist, Thrasybulos Georgiades, who we have already encountered in connection with Adorno's discussion of the temporality of the symphony, and who also plays a role for Carl Dahlhaus and most particularly for Gadamer,[30] underscores the difference that such a breadth makes for understanding music in ancient Greece. Both prose language and poetry derive from the exactly, comprehensively musical complex of *mousiké* (μουσική).[31] The independence of prose and poetic language from the musical as such is only the

---

[28] This is not unlike Arnheim's argument contra formalism in art, with reference to the "consumers" of concerts, art galleries or the theatre: "If they talk about what they just saw or heard, as they sometimes do, they will hold forth on what is good and what is bad, who imitates whom … or that the second aria is too fast or that the last act betrays the latent homosexuality of the author. All these critical observations are presented with a chilly detachment that makes it perfectly clear that the speaker cannot have been in recent communion with Beethoven or Shakespeare, Verdi, or Matisse. The pose coveted by our young intellectuals is no longer that of the stirred lover of the beautiful but the poker face of the critic who sniffs and judges." Rudolf Arnheim, "Form and the Consumer," in *Toward a Psychology of Art: Collected Essays* (Berkeley: University of California Press, 1966), 12–13.

[29] Definitions and source references quoted from *An Intermediate Greek–English Lexicon, Founded Upon the Seventh Edition of Liddell and Scott's Greek–English Lexicon* (Oxford: Clarendon Press, 1889), 520. For Homer, the art of the Muse embraced the broadest range of the fine arts as eloquence or cultivation in general. And for Pericles, to be μουσόμαι, meant to be educated or cultured. Thus μουσικός characterizes one who is "skilled in music" but also "generally, *a votary of the Muses, a man of letters and accomplishment, a scholar.*" Ibid. Giovanni Comotti further elaborates the broad scheme of music in antiquity: "in the fourth and fifth centuries B.C., the phrase *mousikos aner* would be used to indicate an educated man, able to comprehend poetic language in its entirety. The unity of poetry, melody, and gesture in archaic and classical culture made the rhythmic-melodic expression contingent on the demands of the verbal text. The simultaneous presence of music, dance, and word in almost all forms of communication suggests also the existence of a widespread musical culture among the Greek peoples from the remotest times." Comotti, *Music in Greek and Roman Culture*, 5.

[30] See Thrasybulos Georgiades, *Musik und Rhythmus bei den Griechen. Zum Ursprung der abendländischen Musik* (Hamburg: Rowohlt, 1958), as well as Carl Dahlhaus, *Between Romanticism and Modernism: Four Studies in the Music of the Later Nineteenth Century* [1974], trans. Mary Whittall (Berkeley: University of California Press, 1980).

[31] Georgiades, *Musik und Rhythmus bei den Griechen*, 52–3.

most obvious coordinate of the similar separation of "music alone" (the very idea) from the whole complex of its origins in *mousiké*. This complex is what makes it possible to understand the otherwise irremediably paradoxical, or at best metaphorical, meaning of *mousiké* in its formative, ethical sense. This "ethical functionality" is, qua ethos, the precondition for the very political transformation for which Nietzsche argues in the second half of *The Birth of Tragedy*, and it is indeed the defeated object of a completely successful philosophical and cultural siege, a success which renders the accomplishment invisible because, as Nietzsche reminds us, a successful achievement is always invisible or transparent.[32]

For Georgiades, the term *mousiké* reflects the resources of the Greek mind intrinsically linked to this same broad musicality, but it also expresses the *Eigenart* or essence of each work in particular. It is for this reason that in its grammatical form, *mousiké* is not substantive but primordially or prototypically adjectival, belonging to the muses.[33] Because music articulates itself as an activity in play, in

---

[32] Cf. Friedrich Nietzsche, *On the Genealogy of Morals* I: 8; Nietzsche, KSA, vol. 5. Tracy B. Strong also argues this, very differently but persuasively, in his *Nietzsche and the Politics of Transfiguration* [1974] (Berkeley: University of California Press, 2000), and also in his chapter on Nietzsche in *Politics Without Vision* (Chicago: University of Chicago Press, 2012), pp. 57–90.

[33] "*Es bedeutet 'musisch', 'auf die Musen bezogen'.*" Georgiades, *Musik und Rhythmus bei den Griechen*, 45. Of course, not every account of music in antiquity admits such a broad connection to the Muses and to culture in general. A critical exception is Warren Anderson in *Music and Musicians in Ancient Greece*, a book dedicated to delineating what Anderson takes to be the "truly" musical. Anderson seems to understand the specifically sounding essence of music in a quasi-autochthonous sense, as the "amateur musician" opposed to the expert theorist or *philosopher*. The opposition that Anderson proposes finds an instrumentally sounding music in rather determined distinction to the extreme variety of ancient references, where these references do not reflect the difference between the amateur and the professional musician as this difference is understood in today's musical culture. Anderson's focus on just the music that one might play (his book might also have been titled "Musical *Instruments* and Musicians in Ancient Greece"), while (very!) laudable on many accounts, misses the ancient breadth of the term exemplifying instead the monologically modern and very Western distinction between music and language. Yet even Anderson concedes the broad referentiality of antique music where he notes, with careful reference to Plutarch (and thereby, at least in the Spartan context, of the virile activity of music as Terpander expresses it), that "*Mousa* stands for music and poetry in all their manifestations as essential cultural expressions of the city-state." Anderson, *Music and Musicians in Ancient Greece*, 64. But Anderson outdoes Nietzsche in repeated references to Socrates's rabble origins (Socrates was a stonecutter's son). The claim that Socrates hated music because he did not understand it would be better if Anderson had only worded it in this wise, reminiscent as it would have to be of Nietzsche's verdict on the death of tragedy, which he argued to have been due to a failure of understanding on the joint parts of Socrates and Euripides. As it is, Anderson inserts a genteel, dissonantly Victorian vision of ancient Athens, with the well-born Plato expertly playing in a chamber music trio on a five or seven-stringed lyre, with his high-born companions on the syrinx or aulos. It is unclear that

its very primordial essence, "music" can never be a finished, objective, or fixedly given work.[34] This active dimensionality reflects the unique character of the Greek language.

Where an intrinsically Western perspective "presupposes the field of tension which formed between the word and art, between language and music," Georgiades argues that "the *musiké* of antiquity ... does not recognize this distinction."[35] This non-recognition is key. Because art and truth formed "an indissoluble unit" for the ancient Greeks, Georgiades argues that it is misleading to translate μουσική "simply as music," contending indeed (and this contention should be extended to the whole of what we call the arts) that it "cannot even be termed 'art' in our sense."[36] Warren Anderson also concurs: the modern word "music" fails "to render *musiké*. The Greek term designates here the oral training in poetry—sung to lyre accompaniment or recited without it—that had for so long been the means of transmitting the values and precepts of Greek culture."[37] Our tendency to limit what counts as music to the "organized" art of sound obscures the equiprimordial sense in which *musiké* was the enabling element of intellectual or spiritual education, figuring as the determining force of both individual and societal character (ethos). The ethical character of music works, at least for interpreters such as Georgiades, because of the essentially, literally musical difference that Georgiades constantly emphasizes between the language of archaic Greece and contemporary Western languages.

The fundamental musicality of antique Greek resides in the tonic interval of fixed time: long or short, and this is also what Georgiades names its static or, as he says, *masked* dimension, in a parallel that Nietzsche also underlines with the fixed expression of the masks of ancient Greek theatre. For Georgiades, as for Nietzsche, it is just the inflexibility of archaic Greek that compels the speaker/ hearer's active or ethical engagement. Nevertheless, as Martin West's own emphases reveal, the tendency in more recent studies is to represent music in antiquity on the model of music in contemporary contexts, that is, as a separable and distinct *accompaniment*, supplement, or extra, corresponding to extant written texts preserving what we recognize to be music notation. This tendency in West is expressed without reference to Nietzsche's researches in lyric (a regrettable

---

music playing counted as such a class-based diversion, or even that "facility" with musical instruments would have been limited to the upper classes the function and status of flute players in the *Symposium* or comedy contradict this assumption of music-lesson culture.

[34] Accordingly, a "musical education" is only dynamically possible "through musical activity." This is the ideal of " '*Musische Erziehung durch musische Betätigung*'," Georgiades, *Musik und Rhythmus bei den Griechen*, 45.

[35] Thrasybulos Georgiades, *Music and Language: The Rise of Western Music as Exemplified in the Settings* [1974], trans. Marie Louise Göllner (Cambridge: Cambridge University Press, 1982), 134.

[36] Ibid.

[37] Anderson, *Music and Musicians in Ancient Greece*, 143.

omission, given West's own research on Greek lyric poetry), but rather with specific reference to the *Documents of Ancient Greek Music*, which West bases on his co-editor's earlier and, in Nietzsche's historical sense, literally "monumental" 1970 study of ancient Greek melodies.[38] This valuable collection is inevitably limited to the remaining exemplars as we have them of specifically musical notation, and all of these are fairly late. Arguably, it would seem that, rather than lament what we do not and cannot know, scholars take the bits we do have and fixate their studies upon them. For his part, however, Nietzsche repudiated this tendency even in his day, beginning with his inaugural dissertation.[39]

West is careful to remind us that this representation is overwhelmingly occidental. For West, we need all the resources of ethnomusicology to approach the Greeks, whose music is not merely non-Western but still more foreign and, most fatally of all, inevitably, incorrigibly silent.

On Georgiades's account, if the "Western verse line is not a musical but rather a linguistic form," the musical-rhythmic structure of the ancient Greek verse line, by contrast, reflected the music of the language: "The ancient Greek word comprised within itself a firm musical component. It had an intrinsic musical will."[40] Because "individual syllables could be neither extended nor abbreviated,"[41] the Greek language was expressed in consummate, completed time. "The rhythmic principle of antiquity is based not on the distinction between the organization of time (the measure, system of accents) and its filling in (with various note values) but rather on intrinsically filled-in time."[42] For this reason, music was indistinguishable from speech. Yet because of this inextricably compound character, *mousiké* could have the edificatory powers that Plato attributes to it. The speaking subject was engaged not only as a speaker but always also as an active listener. Because of this doubly aspected engagement of attentive articulation, ancient Greek presupposed a community and possessed a community-building power nearly impossible to

---

[38]   See, accordingly, Egbert Pöhlmann and Martin L. West, *Documents of Ancient Greek Music: The Extant Melodies and Fragments Edited and Transcribed with Commentary* (Oxford: Clarendon Press, 2001). This art book-sized collection builds upon Pöhlmann's *Denkmaler altgriechischer Musik. Sammlung, Ubertragung und Erlauterung aller Fragmente und Fälschungen* (Nurnberg: Verlag Hans Carl, 1970). But as Amy Dale notes in *The Lyric Metres of Greek Drama* [1948] (Cambridge: Cambridge University Press, 1968), "most of the evidence, and it is little enough, which can be gathered as to the relation of music and metric is of too late a period to help our understanding of Greek drama." She is in accord with Nietzsche here and she clarifies her point: "No material evidence survives from pre-Hellenistic times" (2).

[39]   I discuss this further, along with the abundance of literature, in an earlier discussion of these themes in Babette Babich, "The Birth of Tragedy: Lyric Poetry and the Music of Words," in *Words in Blood, Like Flowers: Philosophy and Poetry, Music and Eros in Hölderlin, Nietzsche, and Heidegger* (Albany: State University of New York Press, 2006), 37ff.

[40]   Georgiades, *Music and Language*, 4–5.

[41]   Ibid., 4–5.

[42]   Ibid.

imagine today. For Georgiades, this implies a fundamental ethic of responsibility which dares him to claim that the effect of a Hitler would have been impossible in ancient Greece.[43] But only the linguistic constitution of ancient Greek *mousiké* ensures such discrimination and thereby supposes such an ethical claim. After song has emptied its spirit in writing, breathing breath into bare bones, as Ivan Illich puts this with considerable insight and as Anne Carson also underlines,[44] rendered as prose (distinct as such) and poetry/music (distinguishable as such), there is no prose, philosophy (not even Levinas's, perhaps especially not Levinas's), no poetry that can be proof against such use/abuse. The development of prose out of music separates music and text—it is no accident that this begins with the institution of writing whereby the text is liberated from its originally musical expression in the full measure of time.

For these and other reasons, we can say that in general terms, μουσική functions only within the complex of ancient Greek culture. For this reason, Amy Dale could explain, contra a particular aesthetic tradition, that "Classical Greek needed no Wolfian doctrine of 'poetic supremacy' because song, with its dance, [that is to say, music] was a function of the words themselves when they were alive—that is in a performance."[45] For Dale, the performance as such, itself an epiphany of Greek culture and its communal foundation, demanded everything society had to offer it. As a performance, the musical event, the event of "words, music and dance," required a staging and a consummate celebration:

> one great occasion in all its bright splendour, its αγλαία, round an altar, or in the orchestra, or processionally ... With the passing of the kind of society which required and supported public performances of this kind, the living art of this supple polymetry soon perished; it shrank and petrified into the words on paper, so unskillfully preserved that even the proper ordering of the phrases quickly faded from memory.[46]

---

[43]   Georgiades, *Musik und Rhythmus bei den Griechen*, 48. The political question which can be posed against any philosophical text after the unspeakable (now in the antique Greek sense) experience of the Second World War—or whether on its basis a Hitler could or could not be countenanced— as the ethical touchstone that rates a Levinas above a Heidegger, becomes a somewhat more fruitless one on this reading.

[44]   Cf., in addition to Lord, *The Singer of Tales*, Ivan Illich, *In the Vineyard of the Text: A Commentary to Hugh's Didascalicon* (Chicago: University of Chicago Press, 1996), as well as Anne Carson, *Eros, the Bittersweet* [1986] (Normal, IL: Dalkey Archive Press, 1998).

[45]   Dale, "Words, Music and Dance," 168.

[46]   Ibid. Gary Tomlinson points to the difficulty inherent in the metaphorical language implicated in such an ethical (versus cosmic) ideal of harmony, in a chapter entitled "Modes and Planetary Song: The Musical Alliance of Ethics and Cosmology," in his *Music in Renaissance Magic: Toward a Historiography of Others* (Chicago: University of Chicago Press, 1993).

Thus Nietzsche continues to emphasize the role of dance and performative representation of the music, the words, as that was, for him, ineluctably the totality of the work of art, including the entirety of the polis, politics, culture, society, and art and religion, philosophy included.

Philosophy as the "Highest" Music: The Technical Case of Socrates

Pythagoras's esoteric, allopathic concept of musical harmony between world and soul makes "music" the soul of philosophy.[47] In his *Republic*, Plato agreed with traditional wisdom concerning the consequences of any changes to the musical modulation of the state: "when the modes of music change, the fundamental laws of the state always change with them."[48] Where writing (just because it is writing) underlines what is no longer a universal practice,[49] Plato's expression of philosophy as a kind of music invokes a very traditional conception of music. As the love of wisdom or theory, philosophy installs itself precisely in the place of music as the highest or noblest kind of music. And it is in this same correspondent, musical company that the idea of the musical practice or ethos of philosophy is more than a matter of metaphor.

In apparent tension with the negative judgment on music rendered by the *Republic*, the question of the right relation between music and philosophy is addressed in the *Phaedo*, which is also the question of the primacy of philosophy over poetry or music. Music, in all its breadth as *mousiké*, could be regarded as constituting a danger to philosophy qua highest music, that is, beyond popular music and poetry, threatening the Socratico-Platonic claim for the way of life understood as a matter of ratiocination: that is, the uniquely ethical dominion of philosophy as the project of conceiving and living a well-ordered or examined or good life.[50] As the greatest of erotics, in Nietzsche's words, an ironic Socrates

---

[47] According to Theon of Smyrna, the Pythagoreans called "music the harmonization of opposites, the unification of disparate things, and the conciliation of warring elements … Music, as they say, is the basis of agreement among things in nature and of the best government in the universe." *Mathematica*, I.

[48] Plato, Rep. 4, 424c. "Damon," as Lewis Rowell writes, "one of Socrates teachers, was one of the earliest authors to suggest a specific conception between music and the formation of the human character." Rowell, *Thinking About Music*, 51.

[49] For a discussion of the issues at stake, especially in analytic aesthetics and beyond the similarly relevant debate on performance practice, see Lydia Goehr, *The Imaginary Museum of Musical Works: An Essay in the Philosophy of Music* (Oxford: Oxford University Press, 1992).

[50] See Alexander Nehamas's well-ordered argument, beautifully placed rhetorically speaking or, as an intellectual, as an op-ed contribution to the *New York Times*, that either video games and television present no danger to the soul and no risk of inciting criminality, or else that Plato's ban on Homer and Euripides might have had some merit. Nehamas, "Plato's Pop Culture Problem and Ours," *New York Times*, 29 August 2010.

left the world whatever music he had created, of whatever kind, without a text, but what he did do through Plato was to call philosophy the "highest" music in a teasing gesture.[51]

Socrates, the amateur sleuth of the good, claiming incompetence and distraction as a ruse to convert his interlocutors (on the model of the late Peter Falk's philosophically fascinating constitution of television's "Columbo"), was notoriously fond of seemingly vulgar allusions and common oaths,[52] as well as banausic or pedestrian examples. Thus the immortality of the soul is the theme of the *Phaedo*, where Socrates recounts his eleventh-hour musical exercises. And soul or not: the dialogue is all about the body—beginning and ending with strikingly graphic descriptions.

The pathos of the body includes pain and feeling, especially sensual, erotic feeling, and hence the conjunction of pain and pleasure. To seemingly illustrate this, the dialogue begins with Socrates sending off his wife, so to spare himself (so we are told) the unseemly sounds of her anguish. Scholars are quick to advert to the typically ironic foreshadowing of the later lamentation of Socrates's manly disciples at the dialogue's conclusion, but scholars ignore the crucial bodily detail of Xanthippe's support of Socrates's last earthly night (the dialogue begins with his male friends waiting impatiently for morning light for his jailors to permit entry).[53] It is in this relational and erotic bodily context that Socrates's fetters are loosened and Plato offers us the sight of Socrates rubbing his legs (a dissonant, homely image, not unlike the paradoxical picture of Heraclitus surprised by his admirers with his back to the kitchen stove—and it is relevant to note in passing that Heraclitus is positioned to see his visitors approach, take note of their embarrassment, and urge them to stay, despite having come upon him seemingly indisposed: echoing Thales, "There are gods," said Heraclitus, "even here.")

In this same physiological context, we are presented with so many details of Socrates's death that it is possible to reconstruct the ancient aetiological

---

[51]   Socrates's literary "silence" is also what saves him from stasis. As Adorno writes, "music and literature alike are reduced to immobility by writing." Adorno, *Quasi Una Fantasia*, 295.

[52]   Scholars, however, have recently begun to pay attention to the significance of his "by the dog" as an invocation of Hecate and Cerberus, and thus of the significance, as if this needed to be otherwise adverted to, of philosophy's role in crossing the boundaries between this life and the next. See, for a discussion of Hecate in the context of Empedocles, including a range of additional references, Babette Babich, "Le Zarathoustra de Nietzsche et le style parodique. A propos de l'hyperanthropos de Lucien et du surhomme de Nietzsche," *Diogène. Revue internationale des sciences humaines* 232 (October 2010): 70–93.

[53]   The gentleman's club or (male) biased conviction that Socrates had nothing to do with Xanthippe is questionable. We note that Socrates was once a student of Diotima and add that he was at his age both married and blessed with *young* sons—the very ones that he invoked during his trial under the ruse of not mentioning their vulnerability or youth.

understanding of herbal pharmaceuticals, nor need we advert to the typically scholarly blush that awaits any reference to the precise place where the poison rises, to call forth Socrates's last words referring to a rooster as a debt for healing.

Socrates confesses that he was, throughout his life, persistently visited with the same unusual dream figure, repeatedly uttering an imperative caution. The oneiric warning never varied: "make music" (*Phaedo*, 61a).[54] Thus Socrates tells us in Plato's dialogue that he had always assumed that, because philosophy itself represented the apex or culmination (*hé megisté mousiké*) of the musical arts (61a), he had always already been in compliance with the dream's command, dedicated as he was to philosophy. The recurrence of the dream—and note here that such an invocation is itself a *literary conventionality*—brought him to rethink his lifelong interpretation of philosophy as music in the highest sense.

In an ironic gesture of superstitious appeasement, recollecting the pious preoccupations of Cephalus in the *Republic*—the locus classicus for Plato's most stringent political regulation of music—Socrates then says that he casually turned to practice "music in the commonly accepted sense": composing a hymn of praise to Apollo, together with a few common verses (construed from Aesop's fables).[55] As the parallel with the *Republic* suggests, it is not difficult to extend this observation of Socrates's very musical achievement to the composition of the dialogue as playing "the song itself."[56]

---

[54]   The command was the literal: "O Socrates, make and practice music." *Phaedo* 60e. We may assume that the god of the dream could be named Apollo, as we are justified in so doing by way of metaphor (as the dream-god par excellence) or else metonymy (the Apollo who held state executions in abeyance for the duration of his feast).

[55]   The ironic point is that, in a Platonic scheme, such a routine rendering of "real" music or poetic composition necessarily limits the poet to the unreal world of myth or fable. The joke equates Aesop with Apollo. Or perhaps, as Socrates is said to resemble Marsyas, Aesop is better equated with Dionysos.

[56]   Cf. Plato, Rep. 531a–532c. By quoting these esoteric lines from the *Republic*, I also invoke the elegant referentiality of the subtitle to McClain's *The Pythagorean Plato: Prelude to the Song Itself*, which I have cited above. There are important reserves concerning the exactly metaphorical limits of this expression of the force of analogy *itself* as what Graham Pont applauds as an identification of "the *analogia* or proportion of 6:8:9:12 and the three means it encodes, arithmetic, geometric, and harmonic" to show "how Plato applied the precise mathematics of tuning and temperament to the quantitative modelling of political systems and the fine attunement of the ideal city-state." Pont, "Analogy in Music: Origins, Uses, Limitations," in *Metaphor: A Musical Dimension*, ed. Jaimie C. Kassler (Basel: Gordon and Beacon, 1994), 195. See too, again, John Bremer, *On Plato's Polity*, as well as his "Some Arithmetical Patterns in Plato's *Republic*," both cited above. My own reservations respond to Georgiades's broader reading, a reading which would not subsume the ideal of musical harmony to the mathematics or "rationality" of the same, just where mathematics and rationality begin from that harmony and not the other way round—as well as to Árpád Szabó, *The Beginnings of Greek Mathematics* (Dordrecht and Boston: Reidel, 1978), whom Pont himself cites: 132 ff. For the contrary emphasis, see Robert Brambaugh,

Applying a formally mathematical analysis of the structure of the dialogues themselves, McClain has already given us an important application of Stesichorus's own analyses, an analysis of the same computational kind, so it has been argued, that may be applied to other texts, especially the Bible, but also the Babylonian epic of creation, in addition to, as Nietzsche argues, lyric poetry in Greek and, especially if one wishes an acrostic connection, as Walter Schmid has also argued, in Latin.[57]

To take the Socrates of Plato's *Phaedo* at his word is to invert the order of indebtedness, which is its final irony. There is no challenge to the conception of philosophy as the highest music in the ultimate recourse to everyday musical kinds. Indeed, the point of the conclusion is reinforced by the lyre lessons that West tells us that Socrates takes at the end of his life, because, as West also tells us, like champagne to us, for the Greek, "Music is constantly associated with celebration."[58] Given the Platonic representation of the body as the prisonhouse of the soul, Socrates's causal reflection on the relation between pain and pleasure, at the moment of his preliminary liberation from his fetters at the start of the dialogue, is then argued to foreshadow the ultimate Platonic ideal of liberation from the illusions of earthly life. And we find a similar parallel between the practice of

---

Plato's Mathematical Imagination (Bloomington: Indiana University Press, 1954), and see too, for a recent account, ignoring as it happens to do almost all of this earlier scholarship and much more besides, Jay B. Kennedy's "Plato's Forms, Pythagorean Mathematics, and Stichometry," *Apeiron* 43/1 (2010): 1–31. Kennedy's analysis is effected not by philological but by cybernetic means, that is, computer coding of the database retrieval kind, not taken for granted courtesy of the *Thesaurus Linguae Graecae* but also (online) *Perseus*, and so on. Hence, Kennedy does not refer to scholarship as a matter of course, given his own research methodology. The weakness of such a "digital humanities" approach in the case of ancient texts (and it is instructive that the late Friedrich Kittler would never have endorsed such an approach) is that it depends upon the exact precision of prior philological work, not to mention its reliance on the TLG and other databases. For a musicological reply, see John McCay and Alexander Rehding, "The Structure of Plato's Dialogues and Greek Music Theory: A Response to J.B. Kennedy," *Apeiron* 44/1 (2011): 359–75.

[57] See, for this, Schmid's theory of prose rhythm in Sallust: Walter Schmid, *Frühschriften Sallusts im Horizont des Gesammtwerks* (Neustadt/Aisch: P. Ch. W. Schmidt, 1993). For an overview, see Gregor Damschen, "Das lateinische Akrostichon. Neue Funde bei Ovid sowie Vergil, Grattius, Manilius und Silius Italicus," *Philologus* 148 (2004): 88–115. Kennedy, as mentioned above, offers a recent contribution to this discussion from the side not of numerological musicology or studies of the Bible, but philosophy. Yet Kennedy misses a good deal with his assumption that his contribution is without precedent, as he claims. On the level of traditional musicology, see, again, McCay and Rehding, "The Structure of Plato's Dialogues and Greek Music Theory." At the same time, we have already noted, and this will matter when it comes to Nietzsche, that the supposed "scores" are limited to comparatively late instances. We have no such "scores" from Plato's era, much less before that and this textual lack bears on Nietzsche's own argument on music and word as he holds, in a nutshell, that the text *was* the music, qua writing of sound, that is phonetic writing.

[58] West, *Ancient Greek Music*, 14. West refers to Socrates's tutelage in the lyre on page 26, citing Plato, *Euthydemus* 272c.

music qua popular or esoteric celebration, sacrificed by way of expiation to the healer god, Apollo, the dream god or the leader of the Muses, Musagetes,[59] and the rooster that Socrates asks Crito to sacrifice to the vulgar or people's god of healing, Asklepius.[60]

In accord with Greek tradition, Socrates appeals to the popular practice of music. Thereby he exploits an exoteric image for the sake of his most consistent account of the priority of soul or pure form over body or sullying matter. But if we have not learnt from Nietzsche's genealogical method, then perhaps we can remember Freud or else Lacan, masters of psychoanalytic suspicion, who suggest that the secret of the secret is always betrayed in such an overtly provocative manner. Nietzsche goes further here as he suggests that we might, after two millennia, begin to wonder about the possibility of a Socrates who might have lived a different life, one dedicated not to philosophy, proclaiming it the superior or higher path, a kind of *Übermusik*, but much rather to music itself.

The Thinker's Concinnity: On Nietzschean Discrimination and Resonance

Below, I focus on Nietzsche's notion of the "becoming-human of dissonance" as he discusses it with reference to Beethoven at the culmination of his first and most important book, particularly considered with respect to music. Here, I offer a first revision of a more general question of Nietzsche and music, particularly with regard to his writing. In this sense, I hardly oppose the claim that Nietzsche may be regarded as the philosopher most often associated with music.[61] Yet we have already seen that this kind of claim to uniqueness can discount the role of music for other thinkers, quite apart from their affection for it. For apart from music, Heraclitus is unthinkable, as is Pythagoras, and then there is Augustine's important recourse to musical metaphor and verse metrics in his explication of time in his

---

[59]   Richmond Y. Hathorn, *Greek Mythology* (Lebanon: American University of Beirut, 1977), 162. Hathorn was my first Greek teacher and I dedicated an earlier version of this current chapter to his memory.

[60]   The contrast between the world of images and the world of ideas, between pious petition in the face of bodily sickness (Asklepius) and the new program of scientific theoretical medicine represented by the followers of Hippocrates, deserves further investigation.

[61]   For a philosophical discussion of Nietzsche and music, see my treatment of Nietzsche's concinnity in the Introduction and Chapter One of Babette Babich, *Nietzsche's Philosophy of Science: Reflecting Science on the Ground of Art and Life* (Albany: State University of New York Press, 1994), as well as, and for greater musicological rigor, the many books and essays by Friedrich Love, Roger Hollinrake, Curt Paul Janz, George Liebert, Bruce Ellis Benson, and so on, among a great many other names. I offer a bibliography dated up to 1996 in "Nietzsche and Music: A Partial Bibliography," *New Nietzsche Studies* 1/1–2 (1996): 64–78.

Confessions.[62] Indeed, as our reference to Maconie has already made plain, we cannot think of Boethius apart from music, and Nietzsche himself takes pains to highlight the role of the troubadour, whom he calls the "knight-poets" to describe their contribution to Europe in general and indeed to school philosophy, especially as Peter Abelard exemplifies this. Schopenhauer too built his metaphysics on a parallel to music "alone," as the title to Peter Kivy's book has it, and the previous chapter already illuminates, as if this had needed doing, Adorno's connection with music (here we skip Stanley Cavell as claimant for the same reasons that we could also include Paul Feyerabend, Stanley Aronowitz, and none other than Ludwig Wittgenstein). Indeed, with reference to Adorno and Günther Anders, we already had cause to note that Husserl's phenomenological analysis is indebted to Stumpf's psychology of musical experience.

Still, Nietzsche is a special case and we are told that Nietzsche's entire life was entranced, captivated [*umgreift*] by music.[63] Nietzsche very explicitly says that one should read his own writing *as* music and his philological focus as scholar involved nothing less than the coordination, in measure and rhythm, of the music of the ancient Greek word.

Rhythm and meter in the classicist's sense is one thing to be sure, and I have emphasized, as others are increasingly doing as well, that we need to pay attention to this. But how are we to read Nietzsche's advice that we count his *Thus Spoke Zarathustra*, his major work as popularly received, *exactly* as music? As a symphony—as he writes to his composer friend Heinrich Köselitz? How do we begin to parse this un-book as a book of parables, modeled, as we are instructed by so many commentators, on the gospels or, as I have recently argued, on Lucian's parodies?[64] *Zarathustra*, a symphony? A symphony in what sense? How is this a "music"? Maybe we would do better to read Nietzche's *Zarathustra*, as Ernst Bertram and Angèle Kremer-Marietti tell us, as modeled on Wagner's antichristian musical *Ring*?[65] If I could allude to the poets at the start of this chapter, I might go on to argue in Plato's spirit, and certainly McClain argues in this spirit, that the gospels too might be considered a kind of music, and the Bible itself, especially the psalms, certainly David's songs, can be counted as music, secret and not. Perhaps, as Nietzsche also adverted to, the consummate style of the New Testament is written as if designed to be a book for everyone. Thus Nietzsche simply imitated that *allerwelts* design, down to part of the subtitle for his book, *for all*, as this also

---

[62] See, on Augustine and the measure of time, Peter Janich, "Augustins Zeitparadox und seine Frage nach einen Standard der Zeitmessung," *Archiv für Geschichte der Philosophie* 54 (1972): 169–86.

[63] Curt Paul Janz, "Nietzsche Verhältnis zur Musik seiner Zeit," *Nietzsche-Studien* 7 (1978): 308–26.

[64] Babich, "Le Zarathoustra de Nietzsche et le style parodique."

[65] See, for one such, Ernst Bertram, *Nietzsche: Attempt at a Mythology*, trans. Robert E. Norton (Champaign, IL: University of Illinois Press, 2009).

describes a book like the New Testament, a book for everyone, while undercutting that description at the same time: *for all and none*.

To give the question of the self-declared musicality of Nietzsche's texts another edge, how do we read Nietzsche's claim in his self-criticism of his first book, as this descriptive assertion could catch the exactly poetic sensibilities of Stefan George: "it should have *sung*, this 'new soul'—and not spoken!"[66]

To answer these questions, I have noted that I lay claim to a complex metaphor, in the somewhat conceptually disjoint term, "concinnity."[67] I use the word in its harmonic musical sense, largely affine to the sense of the Latin *concinnitas* as rhythmically attuned diction. It is *concinnity* that resounds in the well-rounded or happy phrase. And the architectural sense of *concinnity* belongs to or is part of the originally rhetorical term employed by Cicero and Seneca to indicate the successful musicality of expression.[68] But where one may speak of music as liquid architecture and where Nietzsche, not unlike Adorno, as we have seen above, insisted on architectural resonances to describe his own definition of the *grand style*, the term "concinnity," as I employ it here and elsewhere, recalls its own traditionally architectural meaning, in addition to its rhetorically musical sense.[69] This properly

---

[66]   Friedrich Nietzsche, BT, § iii, KSA vol. 1, 15.

[67]   See note 61 above.

[68]   For concinnity in music, see, in general, Jan La Rue, *Guidelines for Style Analysis* (Michigan: Harmonie Park Press, 1992, 1997). "Concinnity" is a rhetorical term employed by Cicero (*Orator*, 19.65; 24.81; 25.82) and Seneca, and by Alberti in a musico-architectural context (see the note below). In a mechanical extension, Graeme Nicholson uses the term "concinnity," as well one might, in a carpenterly sense to express the fitting and jointure of Heidegger's use of the German *Fug* or *Fügung*, as in mortise and tenon, or coordination of the organs of human sexual expression. Nicholson, *Illustrations of Being* (Atlantic Highlands: Humanities Press, 1992), 272–3. It is also used as a term for facilitating concourse in urban transportation studies and has been utilized in descriptions of Hindu ethics.

[69]   According to Vitruvius, music was among the essential formational requisites for the practice of architecture, and listed the following desiderata: "Let him be educated, have skill with a pencil ... have followed the philosophers with attention, understand music ..." (1.1.3). Such a knowledge of music was useful for practical (mostly military) reasons: "Music, also, the architect ought to understand so that he may have knowledge of the canonical and mathematical theory, and besides be able to tune balistae, catapultae, and scorpiones to the proper key" (1.1.8), where the "correct note" heard by the skilled workman served as a kind of acoustic level. The same understanding would ensure the sounding proportions of theaters, together with the "bronze vessels (in Greek ἠχεῖα) which are placed in niches under the seats in accordance with the musical intervals on mathematical principles. These vessels are arranged with a view to musical concords or harmony ..." (1.1.9), where such an arrangement evidently served to amplify the actor's voice. Vitruvius's assumption of the importance of music for architecture is echoed in Alberti's claim that the intellectual edification is inspired by "lines and figures pertaining to music and geometry." Alberti, *De re aedificatoria*, VII, chapter 10, cited in Rudolf Wittkower, *Architectural Principles in the Age of Humanism* (New York: Norton, 1971), 9. Wittkower explores the role of "Harmonic

architectural significance originates with Alberti's definition of concinnity as the coordinate harmonization of naturally divergent or contrasting parts.[70]

The need for such a "musicality" in reading and thinking is not figurative or allegorical, and so able to be conceived as an isolated interpretive turn, but a firstly literal, textually explicit prerequisite for a triadic resonant hermeneutic of the aphorism written as Nietzsche writes, and he declares that he so writes, in a reader-ironizing counterpoint. And on Nietzsche's author's or composer's side, such a musical or aphoristic style supports or enables an account of the world without truth, without event, without remainder.[71] Yet most immediately relevant because most pernicious, this same musicality leaves his text (deliberately) liable to

---

Proportion in Architecture," and Palladio's conventions in particular, at critical length. For Wittkower, Alberti's claim can only be understood if we recall that, for Alberti, "music and geometry are fundamentally one and the same; music is geometry translated into sound, and that in music the very same harmonies are audible which inform the geometry of the building." Ibid. Maconie, captivated by the literal interpretation of such a notion, is more emphatic than Wittkower when he declares that "The Palladian interior can be considered in precisely the same terms as a recording studio," save that the studio designer seeks to avoid those eigentones that Palladio sought to generate. See Maconie, *The Concept of Music*. Wittkower, however, notes that such resonant notions for the theory of proportional design are out of style, where he cites the substance of Julien Guadet's critical reserve in *Eléments et théorie de l'architecture*, concerning "je ne sais quelles propriétés mystérieuses des nombres ou, encore, des rapports comme la musique on trouve entre les nombres de vibrations qui déterminent les accords." For Wittkower, if Guadet's sobriety is beyond reproach, the problem remains: "*Les proportions, c'est l'infini*'—this terse statement is still indicative of our approach. That is the reason why we view researches into the theory of proportion [that is: musical or harmonic proportion—BB] with suspicion and awe. But the subject is again very much alive in the minds of young architects today, and they may well evolve new and unexpected solutions to this ancient problem." Wittkower, *Architectural Principles in the Age of Humanism*, 154.

[70] "Atque est quidem concinnitas munus et paratio partes, quae alioquin inter se natura destinctae sunt, perfecta quadam ratione constituere, ita ut mutuo ad speciem correspondabat." Alberti, *De re aedificatori libri decem* IX/5 (1962, 815). Cited by Paul von Naredi-Rainer, *Architektur & Harmonie, Zahl, Maß und Proportion in der abendländischen Baukunst* (Cologne: Dumont, 1982), 23. In this same context, beyond the reference to urban transport and Hindu ethics (here note 68), Naredi-Rainer also notes Luigi Vagnetti's comprehensive investigation of the word "concinnitas" and its verbal affinities which apparently may be taken as far as the word cocktail. See Vagnetti, "Concinnitas, riflessioni sul significato di un termine albertiano," *Studi e documenti di architetura* 2 (1973): 139–61.

[71] Thus a specifically musical temperament is required just to follow (to read) Nietzsche in his textual ventures. Without a musical reading, Nietzsche offers only contradictions and logical infelicities—at best a kind of poetry for philosophers with a taste for it, at worst, sheer nonsense. Nietzsche quite literally plays philosophical perspectives upon philosophical perspectives, along with conceptual terms. It is thus for the sake of winning the great part of Nietzsche's philosophy that a resonantly musical reading is needed. Within such a dispositionally resonant interpretation, oppositions or contrasts

misunderstanding through simplistic or shortsighted or flattened and consequently inadequate readings.

As I have sought to show elsewhere on more than one occasion, mis- or short readings exemplify the connection between the aesthetic nihilism that inheres in the pathos of truth and the interpretive truth of truth, the truth of illusion, or the truth of the world as will to power.[72]

The elusiveness of Nietzsche's style derives from the specifically Heraclitean— and intrinsically musical—tension of his aphorisms. By virtue of this literally compositional tension, I have argued that the aphorism can—and must—be read against itself.[73] In other words, Nietzsche's aphoristically composed text plays upon both sides of the listening/reading dynamic. A "musical" reading is advantageous for the interpretation of any poem, rhyme, any joke—but such a musicality is especially needed for Nietzsche's aphorisms. Falling short of the aphorism's music, the prosaic reader, deaf to the resonance of the text, like Socrates's uncomprehending vision of the music of tragedy, not only fails to "get it," as we say, but as a failure unawares, such an error is effectively incorrigible.

This does not mean that Nietzsche will not be understood. To the contrary, everyone believes they understand him. How hard could it be? Thus it seems no great philosophic achievement to "get" a sense of Nietzsche's meaning—in pointed contrast, for example, with Kant. Despite Nietzsche's hyperbolic anxiety regarding his posthumous reception, it would seem a simple matter to understand or read Nietzsche. And nearly every newspaper pundit, like every university instructor, has no hesitation in laying a claim to saying what Nietzsche means. And there is truth in this common sense conviction that one understands Nietzsche. Every Nietzschean aphorism has at least two points (if not indeed more). This characteristically Nietzschean excess permits most readers to come away with at least a partial notion of the text. This means that Nietzsche's esotericism is an inclusive, rather than exclusive, one.

The musical dimensionality of Nietzsche's aphoristic style is consequently capable of instigating an ironic reversal or provocative inversion of best intentions in the reflective spirit of esoteric Protestantism. Thus, for example, bristling in a forest of related aphorisms in *Beyond Good and Evil*, Nietzsche warns: "He who fights with monsters should look to it that he himself does not become a

---

evident in the conceptual independence of the pairs truth/science and genealogy/morals can be heard as posed in accord.

[72]   As already noted, I have a book to illustrate this point with regard to the philosophy of science and the epistemic and methodological significance of Nietzsche's thought for this tradition: Babich, *Nietzsche's Philosophy of Science* (cited above). Here I seek to illustrate the musical (philosophical) reading of an aphorism by contrast with a flat or literal approach.

[73]   See Tracy Strong's introduction to Richard Polt's translation of Nietzsche, *Twilight of the Idols* (Indianapolis: Hackett, 1997), vii–xxx, for his own expansion on my original point here.

monster. And when you gaze long into an abyss, the abyss gazes into you."[74] Without hearing its resonantly rhetorical "English," without a specifically attuned or "musical" reading, the reader may catch Nietzsche's reference to monsters and the danger of the abyss while missing his emphatic melancholy. However, to take Nietzsche's words flatly or atomistically, as logically ranged terms and not as the reticulated elements of a provocatively framed aphorism, is to obscure their inherent backwards (and rhythmically musical) reflex. And it is no accident that a number of readers offer interpretations assuming that the monstrosity of the abyss is a specific or accidental, and hence avoidable, enemy, and that the point of the statement is tactical avoidance rather than the inevitable entanglement of engaging corruption or evil. The threat of the abyss thus becomes another threat to modernity, something else to be banished with the light, like a monster lurking in the closet, or a fault to be paved or smoothed over with the landfill of "values."[75] But for Nietzsche—and this is the Kantian dimension that would most intrigue Heidegger—the knower's confrontation with the abyss always admits the abyss in the knower. All engagement is relational. Like the backwards and forwards relationality of Nietzsche's reconstruction of the human subject poised by rather than merely posing the object of judgment, there is a coordinating movement inherent in the progress of verse and music. Correspondingly, and this is important, a musical reading is impossible unless the reader holds with—as one must with a poem or a piece of music—the beginning through to the end. Thus of Nietzsche's Zarathustran "symphony," composed as he composed it for all *and* for none, he would claim in his *Ecce Homo* that "it be ranged under music."[76] Indeed, one should be able to say, and Nietzsche did say as much at the conclusion to his preface to his polemic, *The Genealogy of Morals*, that this claim would be "clear enough" if one has taken care to read it, in this case, to hear it, in the context of his prior writings.

A similar interpretive dynamic accounts for the typically flattened reading of the warrior's maxim listed at the start of *Twilight of the Idols*: "From the military school of life," which continues"—What does not kill me makes me stronger."[77] Here, the prose or routine reading overshoots the emphatic prelude as context: one reads Nietzsche's contention as a literal and literally prosaic truism. Nietzsche, one takes it, says the same thing as any military or personal sports trainer might say: what doesn't kill one makes one stronger. This also includes a challenge against the declaration. And the title of the maxim, the one for whom such a personal rule might be supposed, offers a backwards echo: from such a perspective on strength

---

[74]   Nietzsche, BGE. The German is useful here: "*Wer mit Ungeheuern kämpft, mag zusehn, dass er nicht dabei zum Ungeheuer wird. Und wenn du lange in einen Abgrund blickst, blickt der Abgrund auch in dich hinein.*" KSA 5, 98.

[75]   Gertrude Himmelfarb, *On Looking Into the Abyss* (New York: Knopf, 1994).

[76]   Nietzsche, EH, *Thus Spoke Zarathustra*, §1.

[77]   See, again, for a discussion, Strong's introduction to Nietzsche, *Twilight of the Idols*.

and intensification, but also compulsion, blind loyalty, and humiliation, it is said, and said from within a military mode, that what doesn't do one in leaves one better off or makes one stronger. Or so the tired veteran hears the tale told from Pericles's Athens to Lincoln's Gettysburg, and still today in everyman's army, everywhere in the world. Nor is it untrue as such; rather, it is only and exactly half true, just as to be half-dead is also to be half-alive. On matters military, Archilochus, reclining on his spear to drink—in a dialectic reflection poised with this very posture—muses on the attunement of two truths held in balance. For the first: "Some Saian sports my splendid shield: / I had to leave it in a wood, / but saved my skin. Well I don't care— / I'll get another just as good."[78] What is then usually rendered in helpful translation as living to fight another day, promises another kind of restitution or payback. The more suitable "leaving-present"[79] that Archilochus threatens for his future return can only be dealt from a mercenary's perspective—beyond the "military school of life."[80] Nietzsche's *Kriegschule des Lebens* captures the brutality of the training ground from the precise advantage of an irony that goes beyond it. This is what Hollywood's successful warrior/soldier, now turned failed California governor, means by the promise: "I'll be back."

Taking up the musical sense of the aphorism keeps both its subject matter and its development as parts of a whole. Thus positions, statements at variance with one another are not simple contra-*dictions* but contra-*puntal* (the terminological contrast need not be taken literally but can be read metaphorically here, as "music"), balanced exactly in their opposition in the backstretched connexion that Heraclitus long ago compared to that found in the (philosophic) bow of life and the (musical) lyre.[81]

---

[78]   Archilochus, *Elegies*, 5, in Martin L. West, *Iambi et Elegi Graeci* (Oxford: Oxford University Press, 1955) and, for the English translation cited, Martin L. West, *Greek Lyric Poetry* (Oxford: Oxford University Press, 1994), 14.

[79]   Archilochus, *Elegies*, 6.

[80]   For another example, in a provocatively brief declaration, a two-point epigram is offered against the iconic image of truth: "'All truth is simple.'—Is that not a compound lie?—." Nietzsche, *Twilight of the Idols*, 23. The epigram undoes itself here overtly but, as may be claimed in every Nietzschean stylistic case, without dissolving the original contrast. And it is this original contrast that matters.

[81]   Once again, I follow Strong's reading of my essay, "On Nietzsche's Concinnity: An Analysis of Style," *Nietzsche-Studien* 19 (1990): 59–80, in his introduction, especially xx–xxii. Cf. my discussion of Nietzsche's style in Babette Babich, "The Genealogy of Morals and Right Reading: On the Nietzschean Aphorism and the Art of the Polemic," in *Nietzsche's On the Genealogy of Morals*, ed. Christa Davis Acampora (Lanham: Rowman & Littlefield, 2006), 171–90.

Chapter 9

The Spirit of Music in *The Birth of Tragedy*: Nietzsche's Phenomenological Investigations of Music and Word

Nietzsche's Phenomenology

If Adorno's critical philosophy of music includes phenomenological elements that scholars have tended to disregard, the same claim may be argued in Nietzsche's case.[1] Indeed, *The Birth of Tragedy* is methodologically conceived as a phenomenology, in the sense in which Nietzsche understands "aesthetics." Hence the "science of aesthetics,"[2] as Nietzsche expresses his project in his first book, is the theory of specifically sensible, felt phenomena. In this fashion, we may trace Nietzsche's "reduction" of conventional assumptions regarding the history of the tragic art form, as well as the history and function of the tragic chorus as a musically poetic performance that can only be understood, so Nietzsche argued, in the total context, that is, political and social and religious, of the life-world of Greek antiquity. Apart from such a phenomenological reading, it can be difficult to understand the critical importance of Nietzsche's counter-arguments regarding the chorus with regard to the "working" dynamic of tragic work of art which Nietzsche famously understands as coming to birth "*out of the spirit of music*." Similarly phenomenological, we might argue, are Nietzsche's genealogical (here we might say genetic) reflections in his *Untimely Meditations* (ranging from

---

[1]   See, for a discussion including both Husserl and Nietzsche in the period running from 1880 and 1890 through 1930 and 1940, Babette Babich, "Early Continental Philosophy of Science," in *The New Century Volume Three: Bergsonism, Phenomenology and Responses to Modern Science: History of Continental Philosophy*, ed. Keith Ansell-Pearson and Alan Schrift (Chesham: Acumen, 2010), 263–86. On Nietzsche and phenomenology, see, for one of the first comprehensive retrospective treatments of Nietzsche and phenomenology, articulated from a Husserlian perspective, Rudolf Boehme, "Husserl und Nietzsche," in *Vom Gesichtspunkt der Phänomenologie* (The Hague: Nijhoff, 1968), 217–37 (Boehme initially published this six years earlier in French as "Deux points de vue: Husserl et Nietzsche," *Archivo di Filosofia* 3 (1962): 167–81). See the further contributions to Élodie Boubil and Christine Daigle, eds, *Nietzsche and Phenomenology: Power, Life, Subjectivity* (Bloomington: Indiana University Press, 2013), including my own "Nietzsche's Phenomenology: Musical Constitution and Performance Practice," in which I specifically engage Boehme; I draw on this essay for parts of the current chapter.

[2]   Nietzsche, BT, §1.

religion, history, education, culture, and politics, and including, well beyond Wagner, his own contemporary musical cultural world), in addition to his critical reflections on logic, perception, and indeed science, just as Nietzsche claims he is the "first" to raise the question of science as such—and here, with respect to the question of science per se, we should think of Heidegger's but also of Husserl's philosophies of science—as a question that is specifically "question-worthy."[3] We have already noted Nietzsche's most "scientific" or scholarly discovery regarding the prosody or musical intonation of ancient Greek,[4] a discovery that also served as the basis for a very literal emphasis on the importance of "music" in *The Birth of Tragedy.* To say that this "discovery" of the "music" in the language of ancient Greek was Nietzsche's discovery does not mean that everyone adverts to this today. On the contrary, Nietzsche's discoveries tend not to be denied by today's classical philologists writing on Greek prosody so much as they are simply taken up and assumed, their origination and significance in Nietzsche's specific context completely forgotten. Nor does it mean that Nietzsche's then-contemporaries grasped or "heard" what he said—be it in his inaugural lecture as a newly appointed professor of classics in Basel, with all of its relevance for the parallels between the stylistic methods of philological discovery and those of natural scientific discovery,[5] or else in *The Birth of Tragedy*—no more so than today, especially perhaps in the case of classics scholars. Hence it is not without reason that we find his Zarathustra seemingly compelled to cry out in frustration: "They do not understand me; I am not the mouth for these ears. Must one smash their ears before they learn to listen with their eyes?"[6] So little was he heard that Nietzsche found himself compelled to offer a first reprise of the claims of his first book ten years later in *The Gay Science*, recalling his initial denigration of Aristotle's telic theory of tragic catharsis in *The Birth of Tragedy*, clarifying that what had been at stake in antiquity was anything but an "attempt to overwhelm the spectator with emotion. The Athenian went to the theater *in order to hear beautiful speeches*. And beautiful speeches were what concerned Sophocles: pardon this heresy!"[7] The problem perhaps endemic to heretical arguments contra the received

---

[3]   Ibid., §ii.

[4]   See Babette Babich, "The Birth of Tragedy: Lyric Poetry and the Music of Words," in *Words in Blood, Like Flowers: Philosophy and Poetry, Music and Eros in Hölderlin, Nietzsche, and Heidegger* (Albany: State University of New York Press, 2006).

[5]   I discuss Nietzsche's inaugural lecture in the first few sections of Babich, "Towards a Critical Philosophy of Science: Continental Beginnings and Bugbears, Whigs and Waterbears," *International Journal of the Philosophy of Science* 24/4 (December 2010): 343–91, and I develop this further in Babich, "On Nietzsche's Judgment of Style and Hume's Quixotic Taste: On the Science of Aesthetics and 'Playing' the Satyr," *The Journal of Nietzsche Studies* 43/2 (2012): 240-259.

[6]   Nietzsche, Z, *Prologue*, §v.

[7]   Nietzsche, GS, §80. Cf. Babette Babich, "The Science of Words or Philology: Music in *The Birth of Tragedy* and The Alchemy of Love in *The Gay Science*," in *Revista di*

view in any field is that ones' contemporaries, rather than hearing or even engaging the argument, tend instead to fall right back to idolatry, in this case, the idolization of Aristotle—and that on the basis of inertia, not argument.

Nietzsche's *genetic* or generative phenomenological approach to philology drove his discoveries regarding the stress ictus—more precisely, regarding what he argued as the absence of the same in favor of musical ictus[8]—in his studies of the prosody of ancient Greek, his studies of rhythm and meter, using, as was commonly conventional, specifically musical notation for the sake of the same. This was no mere metaphor, and the conclusion of his *The Birth of Tragedy*, as we shall see, invokes the technical musical notion of dissonance with particular reference indeed to Beethoven. Constitutively, for the sake of a performative phenomenology, Nietzsche drew upon his own improvisational musical gifts[9] and, like other scholars of his day and ours, he also had recourse to physically archaeological "realizations" or "reenactments."

Thus Nietzsche could contrast the achievement of Greek poetics with the modern ideal of freedom of expression:

> With every Greek artist, poet and writer one has to ask what is the new constraint he has imposed upon himself and through which he charms his contemporaries (so that he finds imitators)? For that which we call "invention" (in metrics, for example) is always such a self-imposed fetter. "Dancing in chains", making things difficult for oneself and then spreading over it the illusion of ease and facility—that is the artifice they want to demonstrate for us.[10]

---

estetica, n.s. 28, XLV, edited by Tiziana Andina (Turin: Rosenberg & Sellier, 2005), 47–78, especially, with regard to specific musical forms, 55ff.

[8] See, again, Babich, "The Science of Words or Philology," and elsewhere. See, too, Friederike Felicitas Günther's monograph, *Rhythmus beim frühen Nietzsche* (Berlin: Walter de Gruyter, 2008), as well as Christian Benne, "Good Cop, Bad Cop: Von der Wissenschaft des Rhythmus zum Rhythmus der Wissenschaft," in *Nietzsches Wissenschaftsphilosophie. Hintergründe, Wirkungen und Aktualität*, ed. Günter Abel and Helmut Heit (Berlin: de Gruyter, 2011), 189–212. In Theodor Adorno's discussion of Greek music and prosody in his *Towards a Theory of Musical Reproduction: Notes, a Draft, and Two Schemata*, trans. Wieland Hoban (London: Polity, 2006), he cites some of the same authors that Nietzsche invokes, particularly Bellermann's 1847 *Die Tonleitern und Musiknoten der Griechen*, but he does not cite Nietzsche here inasmuch as he is engaged with Riemann's *Handbuch der Musikgeschichte*. See Adorno, *Towards a Theory of Musical Reproduction*, 57 and cf. 169ff., as well as his citation of Mocquereau on mimic notation (virga and gravis), "the accents as a way of describing the pitch movement (pictography)" (175). Adorno also notes Coussemaker's 1852 "theory of the origin of neumes in accent-markings (prosody)" (57), and I would argue that Nietzsche's own discussions are indebted to this, particularly his references to color (as indices of tone or sound) in medieval manuscripts.

[9] Curt Paul Janz, *Friedrich Nietzsche Biographie* (Munich: Hanser, 1993) is valuable here throughout.

[10] Nietzsche, HH, *The Wanderer and his Shadow*, §140.

In addition to his attention to the collective Greek work of art, in all its dimensionalities, both historico-philological and monumental as he speaks of the historiological sciences in his *Untimely Mediations*, Nietzsche constantly *mixes* his own concerns, as he sees all these concerns as related. Hence Nietzsche uses the metaphor of musical dissonance to speak of the themes of tragedy as so many variants on "that which is ugly and disharmonic,"[11] but also as "part of an artistic game,"[12] in order to claim that both "music and tragic myth ... transfigure a region in whose joyous chords dissonance as well as the terrible image of the world fade away charmingly."[13] And, as we have noted from the start, there is his metaphor at his own conclusion, of the "becoming-human of dissonance."

In this complex sense, the concluding sections of *The Birth of Tragedy* outline a phenomenological hermeneutics of Greek tragedy as music, heard through Hölderlin's beautifully provocative reflections on Sophocles,[14] and understanding the tragic art form as a resonant expression of "the spirit of music." As Nietzsche here articulates, this spirit emphasizes the sheer possibility that is Beethoven's music as literally performative, in the same way that Adorno also foregrounds in his reflections on performance and play with respect to Berg's Chamber Concerto performed just before his lecture on "The Aging of New Music":

> Incredibly *careful* performance, no one dared to play out a melody, not even the pianist in the 1st variation, and through so much caution without any daring it became inarticulate, muddled, just as laymen imagine modern music to be. Humility and restraint are dubious dangerous virtues in music, just as, if one avoids extreme decisions in life and risks nothing, one can lose everything. In this sense, music making is indeed playing.[15]

As composer, Nietzsche argues that Beethoven's music-making similarly "plays" with the "thorn of displeasure" [*Stachel der Unlust*], which playing Nietzscheproceeds to deploy in order to illuminate the ancient (tragic) art of "transfiguring illusion [*Verklärungschein*]."[16] Key here, as Nietzsche emphasizes, is his reflection that one cannot explain the Greek tragic work of art by arguing that life "really is so tragic" (quite apart then from the question of how life is experienced by other peoples and in other times, and quite apart from the classical

---

[11] Nietzsche, BT, §24.

[12] Ibid.

[13] Ibid.

[14] I refer, of course, to Hölderlin's *Sophokles*: "Viele versuchten umsonst das Freudigste freudig zu sagen / Hier spricht endlich es mir, hier in der Trauer sich aus."

[15] Adorno, *Towards a Theory of Musical Reproduction*, 89.

[16] Nietzsche, BT, §24. Cf. here Adorno's performative notion of "playing," which he also speaks of as the "relationship between mime and music," emphasizing that "[m]usic-making and acting are closely related." Adorno, *Towards a Theory of Musical Reproduction*, 158.

convention of Greek "cheerfulness"—*Heiterkeit*—as Adorno also mentions in his own treatment of the history of Greek notation in musical reproduction).

To put this in other words—and this is related to my earlier reflections on Nietzsche's philosophy of science—Nietzsche poses the question of tragedy, as he sought to raise the conjoined question of both classical philology and science as such, *as a question*. The answer that Nietzsche gives he finds on the model of music and this is the importance of literal or poetic metaphor with which we began the previous chapter. Nietzsche's interest was in the music of antiquity and or as the musicality of ancient tragedy, as opposed to, as is conventionally argued when it comes to Nietzsche's first book, Wagner's musical and cultural program. Thus Beethoven, rather than Wagner, features from start to finish in Nietzsche's first book, as conjoining, as Nietzsche argues there that the ancients also conjoined, music and word in his symphonic work, particularly the Ninth Symphony. Beethoven's musical accomplishment thus seemed as if directly addressed to the focus of the young philological Nietzsche regarding what he also called the "alchemical marriage" of music and word.[17]

At issue was the role of dissonance for Nietzsche, theorist as he was of the Greek ictus.

What is intriguing in Nietzsche's articulation of Beethoven's dissonance (or "discord," as Beethoven's nineteenth-century English translators rendered the term) is that such *Dissonanz* works in a conventionally musical tension. Dissonance is all about the sublimation of harmony, which is to say that it is all about tension and resolution. Thus Nietzsche asks, if one "could imagine dissonance become human—and what else is the human being?—this dissonance, just in order to live, would need a splendid illusion to conceal its own essence with a veil of beauty."[18]

We have seen that a musical aesthetics corresponds to a phenomenological approach, as Adorno also argues when it comes to *Current of Music*, and we have seen that this requirement goes two ways. For phenomenology itself is steeped in music, not only allusively, drawing as Husserl does for his famous analysis of intentional consciousness of what is to come, and what has been, protention and retention, in the singing of a song precisely while singing it; this is Augustine's classic image in his reflections on the measure of song, counting the metrics of verse as we sing, just as we also know that music is the art of time. F. Joseph Smith, a musicologist and phenomenologist,[19] articulates the relevance of music

---

[17]   I discuss this notion of an "alchemical marriage" in Babette Babich, "Nietzsche's *göttliche Eidechse*: 'Divine Lizards,' 'Greene Lyons' and Music," in *Nietzsche's Bestiary*, ed. Ralph and Christa Acampora (Lanham: Rowman & Littlefield. 2004), 264–83. For a more extensive account, connected to Hölderlin, Derrida, and Lacan, see Artur R. Boelderl, *Alchimie, Postmoderne und der arme Hölderlin. Dreis Studien zur philosophischen Hermetik* (Vienna: Passagen Verlag, 1995).

[18]   Nietzsche, BT, §24.

[19]   Smith was disappointed by both professions. More exactly said, and there is a parallel to be drawn with Anders, both professions failed to do him justice, perhaps just

to phenomenology in his still (to date) little noted, *The Experiencing of Musical Sound: Prelude to a Phenomenology of Music.*[20]

I have already adverted to Smith's study above, but here it is important to note that Smith's work illuminates what is not merely a phenomenology of music, but foregrounds—as is rarely done, not even by Roman Ingarden, the more well-known Polish phenomenologist of music—what Smith highlights as phenomenology's explicitly *musical foundations*. In this way, Smith can remind us that Husserlian *Abschattungen*—or profiles—are to be heard as perceptions of sound, soundings, echoings, resonances. For Smith, the critical fact that Husserl dedicates his *Logical Investigations* to Carl Stumpf entails in every literal sense that when Husserl refers to Augustine on time—where, once again, Augustine very famously uses the example of time, the meaning of time, and hence phenomenologically speaking, the instantiation of time consciousness as this is directly given to us in the rhythm and meter of St Ambrose's hymn, citing as Augustine does its *incipit* in eight syllables, alternating long and short—*Deus creator omnium*—but also when singing a given psalm, time unfolding and then echoing, resounding point to point, as protention, and as retention—the metaphor sticks as it does for Husserl, just as was explored in terms of musical consciousness by Carl Stumpf.[21] And Smith

---

because, as with Anders, Smith fell between two stools. And although Smith was one of the founding members of the American Heidegger Society, he also, with a good deal of completely ill-understood anger, withdrew from the society as a founding member. (To say that his frustration was ill-understood is to put matters elliptically. The members of the Heidegger Society—I was there at the time of his submission of his letter—were as bewildered by as they were disinterested in this report of his withdrawal.) Smith's reasons, as it turned out in a later letter that he would send to me, had less to do with Heidegger per se than his own frustrations with the academy itself, which had injured him as a scholar and treated him with the kind of uncommon disrespect that it tends to reserve for thinkers who do not repeat mainstream themes in mainstream ways. As both Adorno and Anders have observed, it is repetition that is rewarded in the cultural collectivity. This contradictory double speak bodes ill for radical thinking, as the current fortunes of critical theory and the Frankfurt School, now in the wake of Habermas, himself no friend of Adorno (and vice versa), illustrate.

[20]   See here, again, F. Joseph Smith, *The Experiencing of Musical Sound: Prelude to a Phenomenology of Music* (New York: Gordon and Breach, 1979). Saying this does not mean that no one cites Smith. He is indeed sometimes cited but *only*, and that is my point here, *in passing*. Scholarship could do with a proper engagement centering on Smith.

[21]   Smith, who published some of Ernest McClain's early articles in a journal he edited, also spends a lot of time sporadically referring to the musicologists who "do the math," as it were, and both McClain and his musicologically distinguished friend and colleague, Siegmund Levarie, were exemplary at doing this kind of math. See, here, McClain's books, already cited above, as well as Siegmund Levarie and Ernst Levy, *A Theory of Harmony* (Albany: State University of New York Press, 1985), in addition to Leo Treitler today. Treitler's *With Voice and Pen: Coming to Know Medieval Song and How It Was Made* (Oxford: Oxford University Press, 2003) forms part of the background context for my discussion of Nietzsche's study of troubadour forms. See Babette Babich,

also invites philosophers of a phenomenological bent to pay attention to what they hear. If all of us can be inclined to think that we *already* do do this, we should keep Nietzsche's Zarathustran words as a gnomic warning, especially in the age of music video and YouTube, as we have explored above: "must one smash their ears before they learn to listen with their eyes."[22]

Nietzsche's Musically Phenomenological Investigations

What we are calling Nietzsche's phenomenological investigations critically drive his explorations of the musical character of ancient Greek,[23] an exploration that is all about the relations between ancient musical dance and musical drama, but ultimately and above all, an exploration of the very literal music of the tragic poem itself, which precisely *phenomenological* hermeneutic depends upon Nietzsche's discovery of the musical resonances of ancient Greek.[24] It is important to note here that, where Heidegger offers us a *hermeneutic* phenomenology, Nietzsche elaborates his own scientific field of classical philology phenomenologically, an adumbration which also includes history and hermeneutics.

For Nietzsche, this means that the very artistic role of the science of philology corresponds to neither that of the artist nor the composer, but and exactly qua performer (thus art in the light of life). The classical scholar of classics in this sense always undertakes or effects a kind of making present or realization (*Vergegenwärtigung*) of the kind one can perform by articulating ancient Greek in the constraints, in Nietzsche's case, in the fully rigorous consideration which he spoke of with reference to the "chains" of rhythm and time—that is to say, out of the spirit of music.

To understand this notion of performance in philology, thereby regarding the philological scholar as a reflective practitioner of classical or ancient philology (Nietzsche's word for this reflectivity was "philosophical," as Erwin Rohde was alone able to see), it is key here to note that Nietzsche was as much a student of Otto Jahn's archaeological or "monumental" philology as he was of Friedrich Ritschl's

---

"Nietzsche's 'Gay Science': Poetry and Love, Science and Music," in *Words in Blood, Like Flowers*, 55ff. Note, without this mathematical focus, Levarie's "Noise," *Critical Inquiry* 4/1 (Autumn 1977): 21–31.

[22]   Nietzsche, Z, *Prologue*, §v.

[23]   See, for a discussion, Babette Babich, " Musik und Wort in der Antiken Tragödie und *La Gaya Scienza*: Nietzsches 'fröhliche' Wissenschaft," *Nietzsche-Studien* 37 (2007): 230–57; I replicate Nietzsche's own illustration below.

[24]   See, again, my own studies: Babich, "Nietzsche's Philology and Nietzsche's Science: On the 'Problem of Science' and '*fröhliche Wissenschaft*'," in *Metaphilology: Histories and Languages of Philology*, ed. Pascale Hummel (Paris: Philologicum, 2009), 155–201, and Babich, "The Science of Words or Philology," as well as Günther, *Rhythmus beim frühen Nietzsche*.

text-critical approach.[25] Indeed, it would be in Jahn's spirit that Nietzsche invoked literally archaeological discoveries to frame his discussion of Greek music drama, reminding his listeners of the difference it makes to know that ancient Greek statues and especially Roman marble copies of the same, now whitened with age (and often with "restorative measures") had not always been so classically "classical" in their aspect. Originally these statues, whether in bronze or marble or terra cotta or wood, had been painted in vibrant, even garish, colors.[26]

Nietzsche's point here with respect to scholarship, scientific and historical, is almost Kuhnian in advance of Kuhn, for paradigms persist and, despite new discoveries, we tend to retain the older, inaccurate image of classical Greece. For this reason, noting the role of prejudice as it tends to be retained in the world of scholarship, oftentimes canonized by personal preference or taste, Nietzsche argues musico-archaeologically, pointing out to his audience that, were the statues on the Parthenon frieze to come to life, not only would they "sing," as he declares, but they would sing in specifically, that means singularly, exclusively, Aeschylean and Sophoclean tones.[27] With this claim for the totality of the ancient work of musical art, Nietzsche underscores a phenomenological practice: representing an ideal project for a scientific philology as a kind of playing with variants, again, not unlike Feyerabend's recommendation for an anarchic scientific method, drawing upon historical scientific practice and with reference to the same Machian empiro-criticism from which Nietzsche also drew. In this same sense, Nietzsche inverted the classicist's motto borrowed from Seneca, arguing at his lecture's conclusion for the imperative value of philosophy for philology, a claim corresponding to his call for the very phenomenological question of philology as a science and above all as a practice.

If the philologist cannot hope, as Nietzsche here argues, to match antiquity with the genius of the poet/composer, what the classical philologist *can do* is to aspire to call upon the ingeniousness of performance or *practice*, attending thereby to the effects of his own practices, and not sparing self-criticism thereby. By recalling

---

[25]   For an overview, including further references, see Lorella Bosco, *"Das furchtbar-schöne Gorgonenhaupt des Klassischen". Deutsche Antikebilder (1755–1875)* (Würzburg: Königshausen & Neumann, 2004), 301ff. I discuss this as well in a number of places, for example, most recently Babich, "Towards a Critical Philosophy of Science."

[26]   See, for additional references and discussion, Babette Babich, "Reflections on Greek Bronze and the Statue of Humanity: Heidegger's Aesthetic Phenomenology, Nietzsche's Agonistic Politics," *Existentia* XVII 5/6 (2008): 243–471, as well as Babich, "Skulpturen und Plastiken bei Nietzsche," in *Grenzen der Rationalität: Teilband 2: Vorträge 2006–2009*, ed. Beatrix Vogel and Nikolaus Gerdes (Munich: Allitera Verlag, 2011), 391–421.

[27]   Nietzsche, "Das griechische Musikdrama," KGW III/2, 18. Nietzsche is here confirming and intensifying a contemporary music critic, noting that, whatever recognition we conceded to the "language of Sophocles," what is most important to recognize is that "we *must* be inaccurate when it comes to Aeschylus and Sophocles, as we really do not *know* them" (ibid). The element of music is lacking.

the music of the tragic art form, Nietzsche was thus able to explain how the tragic poet plays with the "thorn of suffering," as Beethoven plays with dissonance in his setting and indeed in his transfiguration of Schiller's words as tones in the Ninth Symphony, as we shall see that Nietzsche argues in further detail below.

As already noted above, the essential metaphor as Nietzsche deploys it in this classical context was a very musically technical one. Musical dissonance, so Nietzsche would argue, was the operative metrical key to ancient tragedy just to the extent that expressly musical sound was the heart of the ancient art form. For Nietzsche, the goal was not to elicit, contra Aristotle, pity and fear, but rather and precisely for the very aesthetic sake of beauty "to speak well," as we have seen above and where "music directly reaches the heart."[28]

Intoning the tragic poems, one, as it were, *plays*—this is Nietzsche's tragic *Vergegenwärtigung*—the past. Hence Nietzsche as early as his inaugural lecture in Basel, suggested that the philologist disposes over a very scientific "art" as he spoke of it there, as we also know that he conjoins art and science in his first book and throughout his writings. The classicist, for Nietzsche, is thus a "virtuoso," as it were—only as such is he or she able to sight read or sing the "music" of antiquity to life and thus "for the first time to let it sound again."[29] At this juncture, Nietzsche thereby offers a first articulation of the musical dynamic and radical insights[30] of his first book, *The Birth of Tragedy out of the Spirit of Music*.

Nietzsche's resolution of the question of tragedy in his first book was declaredly, and of course literally, musical,[31] taken with a very phenomenological reference to specifically *philological* practice as referring, as it were, "to the words themselves," to spoken Greek as it was sung—for Greek, as Nietzsche maintained and Georgiades, as we have seen, confirms, could *only* be sung or musically declaimed, as he writes—on the tragic stage of antiquity, but not less with reference to the paradoxical question that, for Nietzsche, illuminates the problem of both pleasure *and* pain in ancient Greek tragedy. It is this paradoxical question that takes us to dissonance, a paradoxical echo that begins already with the first lines of *The Birth of Tragedy*, where he speaks of the duplicity of the Apollonian

---

[28]   Ibid., 18–19.

[29]   Nietzsche, "Homer und die klassische Philologie," KGW II/1.

[30]   It must be underscored, with some regret, that we have yet to begin to engage his claim as philosophers; it must also be said that classical philologists remain, if anything, still further away from such engagement, despite the efforts of Pöschl, Arrowsmith, and Lloyd-Jones. Other scholars, such as Most, Cančik, and Porter, are happy to bring Nietzsche into the fold, but they do not see as their task the issue of engaging Nietzsche on music nor indeed on the matter of prosody. And at the same time one must also note that this shows signs of beginning to change. See, for references, Babich, "The Science of Words or Philology," and see too, for additional references as well as a discussion of the methodological relevance of classical philology for science, especially for the structure of Darwin's origin of the species, Babich, "Towards a Critical Philosophy of Science."

[31]   Nietzsche, BT, §22.

and the Dionysian—and most discussions attend to this dyad—which he expresses not only in terms of the antagonistic duality of the sexes and the species resolution of the same, but also in phenomenological terms. This is no mere metaphor, as we recall that Nietzsche declares:

> we shall have won much for the science of aesthetics once we perceive not merely with logical insight [*logische Einsicht*], but with the immediate certainty of intuition [*Anschauung*] that the continuous development of art is bound up with the Apollonian and Dionysian duality: just as procreation depends on the duality of the sexes, involving perpetual strife with only periodically intervening reconciliations.[32]

Indeed, in his later-written attempt at a self-criticism, Nietzsche will emphasize that, for classical philologists concerned with his theme, "nearly everything yet remains to be discovered"[33]

Nietzsche's concluding reflections on "What I Owe the Ancients" in his *Ecce Homo*, written at the end of his productive life, echo his allusion to the phenomenon of "musical dissonance,"[34] recalling his description of the "becoming-human"[35] of such dissonance in the conclusion to his first book. This notion may also be heard in Leonard Cohen's "broken" *Hallelujah*, but it also resounds in elements of k.d. lang's performance practice, as well as with respect to Adorno's, as indeed Anders's, phenomenology[36] of music in the era of not only mechanical but what becomes, electrically, electronically today's digital reproduction.[37] The musical "dissonance" of which Nietzsche speaks, as we shall see in the concluding chapter below, is an explicitly compositional notion, understood in the nineteenth-century context in terms of the play or interaction of consonance and dissonance, which is thus underway, as it were, to what

---

[32]   Ibid., §iii.

[33]   Ibid.

[34]   Ibid., §24.

[35]   Ibid., §25.

[36]   See Brian Kane's discussion of Pierre Schaeffer's *Traité des objets musicaux* (Paris: Éditions du Seuil, 1966), and his *La musique concrète* (Paris: Presses Universitaires de France, 1967), in Kane, "L'Objet Sonore Maintenant: Pierre Schaeffer, Sound Objects and the Phenomenological Reduction," *Organised Sound* 12/1 (2007): 15–24; as well as, on the same theme, Makis Solomos, "Schaeffer phénoménologue," in *Ouïr, entendre, écouter, comprendre après Schaeffer*, ed. F. Delalande (Paris: Buchet/Chastel, 1999), 53–67. Kane's notion of the profiling of the "emergent sound object" (21f) and, in the technological—especially the radio—era, the "acousmatic" reduction of sound to the field of hearing alone" (19), although indebted to Schaeffer as well as Attali and manifestly to Adorno, also seems convergent with Levarie's discussion cited earlier.

[37]   Again, see Arved Ashby, *Absolute Music: Mechanical Reproduction* (Berkeley: University of California Press, 2010), and others.

later comes to be called the "emancipation of dissonance"[38] in studies of early twentieth-century atonal music.

Drawing on nineteenth-century musical theory to make his own case, David Allison invokes similarly nineteenth-century cognitive science and psychology to make the case with regard to the phenomenon of Greek music, in word and culture, emphasizing that Nietzsche draws upon his own experience of the Dionysian as an experience of "a dizzying state of transfiguring ecstasy."[39] As Allison notes, Nietzsche reflects upon his own experience, not of music as inchoate or as beyond word, but rather in the individually dynamic sensed *experience* of musical dissonance, which same ecstatic experience, as Allison cites Nietzsche's reflections at the end of his *The Birth of Tragedy out of the Spirit of Music* (and here we see how much we need Nietzsche's initial, first full title, a title he himself would change, as we shall take up again, in response to the book's lack of initial readers), corresponds to "music" as Nietzsche understood it in Schopenhauerian terms as giving us "an idea of what is meant by the justification of the world as an aesthetic phenomenon."[40] Inasmuch as Nietzsche also specifically invokes the "joyous sensation of dissonance in music,"[41] he refers to Beethoven's Ninth Symphony. Like his earlier *Chorfantasie*, op. 80, Beethoven's "Chorale" Symphony is written to culminate with a chorus. This is not only a musicologist's conception but, as I have already noted, is also on offer in Beethoven's own writings, which writings on composition were influential for *both* Nietzsche and Wagner—although Wagnerians uniformly contend that Nietzsche's observations derive from Wagner (pretty much without remainder) and that is to say from Aeschylus to Beethoven. Again, we need to reflect that Nietzsche also represented his own discovery of

---

[38]   This is the subtitle of Thomas Harrison, *1910: The Emancipation of Dissonance* (Berkeley: University of California Press, 1996). The term is usually attributed to Arnold Schoenberg who uses it in his 1926 essay, "Gesinnung oder Erkenntnis?" in Schoenberg, *Stil und Gedanke. Aufsätze zur Musik*, ed. Ivan Vojtěch (Frankfurt am Main: Fischer, 1976), vol. 1, 211. But see, for a discussion of the origination of Schoenberg's "Emanzipation der Dissonanz," August Halm's turn of the last century *Harmonielehre* (Berlin: Göschen, 1900), as "Befreiung der Dissonanz." See Rafael Köhler, *Natur und Geist. Energetische Form in der Musiktheorie* (Stuttgart: Franz Steiner Verlag, 1996), throughout, but here 230ff. And see, for a recent account on Halm, Lee Allen Rothfarb, *August Halm: A Critical and Creative Life in Music* (Rochester: University of Rochester Press, 2009). Of course, the claims in this regard go even further back in the nineteenth century—see here, among others, Barbara R. Barry, *The Philosopher's Stone: Essays in the Transformation of Musical Structure* (New York: Pendragon Press, 2000)—a circumstance to be expected, given the dynamic between consonance and dissonance; Beethoven discusses just this tension in his own writings on composition, as does indeed, and to be sure, everybody else.

[39]   David B. Allison, *Reading the New Nietzsche* (Lexington: Rowman and Littlefield, 2001), 64.

[40]   Ibid. The change of title to *The Birth of Tragedy or Hellenism and Pessimism* foregrounds the Schopenhauerian connection.

[41]   Nietzsche, BT, §24.

the pitch ictus using musical notation, as well as references to musical works and illustrations drawing upon musical practices. Indeed, when Nietzsche emphasizes in his notes the incomparable difficulty of imagining the experience of ancient tragedy from the modern viewpoint, by way of what we have now seen to be a very phenomenological reflection of the need to consider and bracket the assumptions that go with our understanding of musical works of art, all in order to conceive the performance of ancient Greek tragedy, from the darkness before the break of day, then in the morning light, in the noonday, to afternoon, and evening, one play after another, over the course of several days and nights, but above all and precisely where everyone listening—Nietzsche insists on this—would be expected to catch the least false note, it may well defy imagination. I have already noted that only Father Owen Lee comes close to following Nietzsche's recommendations, without emphasizing these as such, in his valuable *Athena Sings*.[42] Thus in *The Birth of Tragedy* and related lectures, Nietzsche sought to explore the physical and psychological experience, whereby "the 'phenomenon'," as Allison emphasizes it, "of 'musical dissonance,' is the Dionysian state of ecstasy."[43] For Allison, what is at stake involves a phenomenology of musical experience. Thus:

> addressing exactly what the object of music is (i.e., the theoretical model of its subject matter), Nietzsche realizes that its object (*Gegenstand*) is given to us as the content (*Inhalt*) of our own intensely undergone aesthetic experience, our ecstatic states of dispossession. This musically charged state of ecstatic disposition is precisely what he terms "the Dionysian state," and such a state is effectively the entire *field* of experience, shorn of simple subject–object relations.[44]

Allison connects this focus, then, with Nietzsche's further explorations of the "Dionysian" in terms of "the most natural and extreme states of intoxication and frenzy,"[45] and emphasizes that modern studies of musical cognition support the phenomenological insights of Nietzsche's "focus on dissonance as 'the primordial phenomenon of Dionysian Art.'"[46]

---

[42] M. Owen Lee, *Athena Sings: Wagner and the Greeks* (Toronto: University of Toronto Press, Scholarly Publishing Division, 2003). Beyond Lee, see too the still broader insights and political analysis of Nicole Loraux, *The Mourning Voice: An Essay on Greek Tragedy*, trans. Elizabeth Trapnell Rawlings (Ithaca: Cornell University Press, 2002).

[43] Allison, *Reading the New Nietzsche*, 64.

[44] Ibid., 65.

[45] Ibid., 66.

[46] Ibid., 67.

Chapter 10
Nietzsche and Beethoven: On the "Becoming-Human of Dissonance"

"Music about Music": Nietzsche and Beethoven

As Martin Heidegger is fond of foregrounding his esteem for Hölderlin by naming him a poet's poet, Nietzsche too celebrates Beethoven as a composer's composer. Following E.T.A. Hoffmann's cadence of composers, as Nietzsche would seem to echo Hoffmann's 1810 review of Beethoven's Fifth Symphony,[1] Nietzsche contrasts Beethoven with Mozart and Haydn. For Nietzsche, Mozart is a composer who writes music about life, and by contrast Beethoven is said to compose "music *about* music."[2] Thus Nietzsche characterizes Beethoven as a "gathering bee," an interpretive, philologically attuned composer.

If the image of honey resonates in Nietzsche's *Thus Spoke Zarathustra*,[3] the image of the "honeybee"[4] as a kind of parable or tuning fork addressed to the "treasures

---

[1]   E.T.A. Hoffmann, "Beethovens Instrumentalmusik," *Allgemeine musikalische Zeitung*, Leipzig: Breitkopf & Härtel, 1810. Friedrich Nietzsche, HH, *The Wanderer and his Shadow*, §152. The parallel is of course overdetermined beyond Hoffmann inasmuch as, and in addition to others, Nietzsche's own teacher, Otto Jahn, was also the author of a noted biography of Mozart, including, in Volume 2, a classically hagiographical encounter in Vienna in 1787 between the eager young Beethoven and Mozart, who was converted from his initial diffidence by hearing Beethoven improvise on one of Mozart's themes to an enthusiasm of the "pay attention to that one, someday the world will be talking about him" variety (*Auf den gebt Acht, der wird einmal in der Welt von sich reden machen*). In Otto Jahn, *W.A. Mozart, Zweiter Theil* [1856] (Leipzig: Breitkopf & Hartel, 1867), 34. We owe part of our knowledge of Beethoven's exceptional improvisational skills to the very human and very triumphant contours of this vignette.

[2]   Nietzsche, HH, *The Wanderer and his Shadow*, §152. Cf. Adorno's discussion of Mozart, whom Adorno characterizes by the coincidence of his music, "at one with bourgeois subjectivity," by contrast with Beethoven, in whom "the traditional forms are reconstructed out of freedom." Theodor Adorno, *Beethoven: The Philosophy of Music*, trans. Edmund Jephcott (Stanford: Stanford University Press, 1988), 60–61.

[3]   I discuss this in Babette Babich, "Le Zarathoustra de Nietzsche et le style parodique. A propos de l'hyperanthropos de Lucien et du surhomme de Nietzsche," *Diogène. Revue internationale des sciences humaines* 232 (October 2010): 70–93, here 88ff and elsewhere with respect to Wagner in Babich, "Nietzsche's *göttliche Eidechse*: 'Divine Lizards,' 'Greene Lyons' and Music," in *Nietzsche's Bestiary*, ed. Ralph and Christa Acampora (Lanham: Rowman & Littlefield, 2004), 264–83.

[4]   Nietzsche, *On the Genealogy of Morals*, Preface §I; KSA, vol 5.

of the heart" also appears at the start of Nietzsche's preface to *On the Genealogy of Morals*, the polemic written as the sequel to Nietzsche's important *Beyond Good and Evil* which featured the musical subtitle, *Prelude to a Philosophy of the Future*, and which closes, following a penultimate section on the "genius of the heart,"[5] with what he calls "*Nachgesang*," that is, a *Postlude in High Mountains*. Beyond describing Beethoven as a "gathering bee," what Nietzsche means by his references to beehives and honey is complex in and of itself, and we have already begun to unpack some of Nietzsche's complexity in the chapter on *mousiké techné*, together with our previous discussion of Nietzsche's phenomenological investigations.

To frame our discussion of Beethoven, we note that, in addition to Mozart and Haydn, Nietzsche also contrasts him with Schubert as "the ideal audience for a music maker."[6] I note this contrast here as we began by remarking upon Cohen's *Hallelujah* in its illumination through the many covers, especially the musically iconic cover provided by John Cale, and in its musical tuning in k.d. lang's interpretation. For the point from the start, as it has taken us here, is that Cohen's *Hallelujah* is not less music *about* music than it is also about Eros and the spirit, and the combination, as we have seen, is inseparable from its appeal for so many artists and so many applications.

"Music about music," whether it is applied to Cohen's *Hallelujah* song or to Beethoven, reflects what captivates us when it comes to Cohen, and this is in part what I have been calling the Hallelujah effect. Yet we have also seen that it unsettles us, and when it comes to Beethoven, in what can seem an uncannily all-too-familiar fashion, the classicality of the classic, as it were, Nietzsche writes that:

> Beethoven's music frequently appears as a profoundly felt *reflection* upon the unanticipated re-hearing of a long forgotten piece, an innocence in tones [*Unschuld in Tönen*]: it is music *about* music [*Musik über Musik*]. In the songs of beggars and children in the alleyways, by the monotone modes of wandering Italians, at dances in the village tavern or during the nights of Carnival—there he uncovers his "melodies": he carries them together like a bee, in that he grasps now here and now there a sound, a bare interval. They are for him transfigured *recollections* of a "better world: not unlike what Plato thought of his Ideas.—Mozart stands entirely otherwise with respect to his melodies: he does not find his inspiration by listening to music but in the contemplation of life, of the most moving, most *southern* life: he always dreamt of Italy whenever he was not there.[7]

This is a complex constellation and to this we should add what scholars who know these things have told us, for much of the issue when it comes to Nietzsche is already decided, packed up, a done deal. Thus we already "know" that—not

---

[5] Nietzsche, BGE, §295.

[6] Nietzsche, HH, *The Wanderer and his Shadow*, §155.

[7] Ibid., §152.

Beethoven and not even Mozart or Haydn or Bach—Nietzsche *really* loved Bizet[8] or Rossini, and so we are also told, simultaneously at times, that Nietzsche began a Wagnerian and remained one to his death.[9]

As in the great Monty Python sketch of philosophical allegiances and fealties, we know that favoring one musician is often expressed in terms of preferences and competitive favoring, the one over and above or contra another, which is why the football team metaphor remains appealing for philosophy. Whose team are you on, one seems to ask the philosopher, who replies, in language vaguely like a hook-up, which indeed it is, that one "does" Merleau-Ponty or Bergson, or Heidegger (so speaketh the continentals), that one does analytic metaphysics, philosophy of mind, cognitive science, speculative realism (so sayeth analytic style philosophers). Thus the mainstream Nietzscheans vote for Wagner, self-styled outsiders make pitches for the other names that Nietzsche also mentioned and almost no one bothers to mention the Greeks when it comes to Nietzsche and music, despite the rather staring obviousness of the subtitle of his first book (*… out of the Spirit of Music*, to say this one more time) or his insistence that his Zarathustra be counted as music (even to the extent of specifying the kind: a symphony).

Here I have been asking, as I think others might well join me in asking, why Nietzsche writes the things he does about Beethoven? Why does Beethoven make an appearance from the start, and perhaps most significantly for me, now speaking as a Nietzsche scholar, I think it worth asking why Nietzsche writes *as much* about Beethoven as he does? Thus I find it especially important to ask why, in particular, we find an allusion to Beethoven's tones at the conclusion of his first book, just at a time when Nietzsche would have been, this much is biographically incontestable, still thoroughly in Wagner's thrall? Why, then, per contra, do we not find an allusion to *Wagner's tones*, as the rhetoric that describes Nietzsche as a Wagnerian, condemning his first book in exactly so many words, would seem to suggest? Here it is worth recalling Nietzsche's reference to Beethoven's "innocence of tones,"

---

[8] This begins fairly early; see, for example, Hugo von Daffner's pamphlet, *Friedrich Nietzsches Randglossen zu Bizets Carmen* (Regensburg: Gustave Bosse, 1912), as well as John W. Klein, "Nietzsche and Bizet," *The Musical Quarterly* 11/4 (October 1925): 482–505. See, further, George Leiner, "To Overcome One's Self: Nietzsche, Bizet and Wagner," *Journal of Nietzsche Studies* 9/10 (Spring/Autumn 1995): 132–47, but see, too, Benoît Goetz, "Nietzsche aimait-il vraiment Bizet?" *La Portique* 8 (2001), and somewhat obliquely, Sander L. Gilman, "Nietzsche, Bizet, and Wagner: Illness, Health, and Race in the Nineteenth Century," *The Opera Quarterly* 23/2–3 (Spring–Summer 2007): 247–64.

[9] This is the powerful presupposition of many scholars, from Ernst Bertram to Curt Paul Janz, to Tracy B. Strong and indeed to Georges Liébert. In addition to the argument of his book, *Nietzsche and the Politics of Transfiguration* [1974] (Berkeley: University of California Press, 2000), Tracy B. Strong repeats this claim and further extends it to include a reference to my notion of concinnity, in his introduction to Richard Polt's translation of Nietzsche's *Twilight of the Idols* (Indianapolis: Hackett, 1997), vii–xviii, especially xx–xxii.

already cited above from the explicitly Lucian-inspired,[10] that is to say, overtly satirical, concluding section of Nietzsche's *Human, All too Human*, namely "The Wanderer and his Shadow" (the reference to Lucian's Underworld in the pilgrim's or wanderer's shadow usually passes unnoticed). Here, what Nietzsche calls the "innocence of becoming" emphasizes the desirability of redemption or salvation. The same echo resounds in the second edition of his *The Gay Science*, as Nietzsche re-issues it in 1887 with a new fifth section,[11] as Nietzsche always emphasizes the musical challenge that is what he calls, very musically, *the art of ending*, and here too, once again, we meet not an allusion to Wagner but Beethoven once again:

> "We can no longer stand it," they shout at me; "away, away with this raven black music! … [not the] voices from the grave and the marmot whistles as you have employed so far to regale us in your wilderness, Mr Hermit and Musician of the Future! No! Not such tones! Let us strike up more agreeable, more joyous tones.[12]

Note that I am not arguing that no one catches this reference, and Stephen Hinton has also pointed to Nietzsche's emphasis, if indeed in order to point out the difficulty of parsing Beethoven himself, in his genial essay, "Not *Which* Tones? The Crux of Beethoven's Ninth."[13] As Hinton points out, the problem here is a wholly musical, wholly hermeneutic or performative one, and thus it matters to this discussion. For Hinton, when it comes to "the beginning of the baritone recitative 'O Freunde, nicht diese Töne!',"[14] everything turns on how the singer sings the word *Töne*. The singer can sing "the pitches literally, as notated," or else the singer can "add an unnotated but implied appoggiatura on the first syllable."[15] The alternate option is there, as Hinton observes, just because it is indicated in the score itself: "in the versions of the

---

[10]   For a discussion of Nietzsche and Lucian, the second-century CE cynic and satirist, see Babich, "Le Zarathoustra de Nietzsche et le style parodique," and, for a version in English, with fewer references, Babich, "The Philosopher and the Volcano," *Philosophy Today* 36 (Summer 2011): 213–31.

[11]   See Babette Babich, "Nietzsche's 'Gay Science': Poetry and Love, Science and Music," in *Words in Blood, Like Flowers: Philosophy and Poetry, Music and Eros in Hölderlin, Nietzsche, and Heidegger* (Albany: State University of New York Press, 2006), 55ff, as well as Babich, " Musik und Wort in der Antiken Tragödie und *La Gaya Scienza*: Nietzsche's 'Fröhliche' Wissenschaft," *Nietzsche-Studien* 37 (2007): 230–57.

[12]   Nietzsche, GS, §383. To include the original terms of his imagined interlocutors here: "… Nein! Nicht solche Töne! Sondern last uns angenehmere anstimmen und freudenvöllere!"

[13]   Stephen Hinton, "Not *Which* Tones? The Crux of Beethoven's Ninth," *Nineteenth Century Music* XXII/1 (Summer 1998): 61–77.

[14]   Ibid., 61.

[15]   Ibid. See Hinton's illustrations of Beethoven's Symphony Number Nine, movement IV, baritone recitative, mm. 216–236, at 62.

recitative presented earlier in the movement by the lower strings, the appoggiatura is written out."[16] Hinton emphasizes what he calls Beethoven's "irony," but he is also interested in what our interpretations tell us about ourselves, and how we hear such possibilities, whether in the case of scholars, but more importantly in the case of composers such as Wagner, and of course in the case of performance practice. Thus Hinton cites Nietzsche, duly described, together with the entirety of *The Birth of Tragedy*, as "otherwise pro-Wagnerian," as calling attention to just these words—and, as we might say, the tonality of *Töne*—in Nietzsche's "On Music and Word."[17] Nietzsche, as Hinton reflects "is the only commentator to have picked up on the ironic significance of Beethoven's reference to tones, as opposed to words which Wagner found so critical."[18] In what follows, I foreground the nature of the difference that this makes for Nietzsche himself.

Nietzsche on the Words and Music of Ancient Greek

I noted at the outset that Nietzsche's first book, *The Birth of Tragedy out of the Spirit of Music*, continues to be undervalued by Nietzsche scholars inasmuch as such scholars (no matter whether students of literature or philosophy) also tend to suppose the book irrelevant to Nietzsche's overall project, usually citing Nietzsche's own later revision, complete with an appended second preface, "Attempt at a Self-Critique," and a new title, *The Birth of Tragedy or Hellenism and Pessimism*. Thus it is supposed that Nietzsche moves on and his work is divided accordingly into so-called second and third periods. And classicists suppose Nietzsche's first book irrelevant as a contribution to classics regarding ancient Greek tragedy and lyric poetry and ancient music.[19] What is crucial for me is that the dividing of

---

[16] Ibid., 63. See here Hinton's illustrations of Beethoven's Symphony Number Nine, movement IV, instrumental recitative, mm. 7–16 and 81–84, at 62.

[17] Ibid., 66. Hinton, who had been Carl Dahlhaus's assistant at the Freie Universität Berlin, notes this crucial point (rare even within Nietzsche scholarship), citing the Kaufmann translation of Nietzsche's "Music and Word" in Dahlhaus, *Between Romanticism and Modernism: Four Studies in the Music of the Later Nineteenth Century*, trans. Mary Whittall (Berkeley: University of California Press, 1980), 103–19.

[18] Ibid., 67.

[19] James Porter notes that, notwithstanding the quality of Nietzsche's actual accomplishments and despite the potential promise of unrealized but outlined projects (both of which would count as the basis for scholarly esteem in classical philology), "you will look nearly in vain for mentions of [Nietzsche's] name in the definitive histories of the field, even though several of his findings have made their way, often namelessly, into the mainstream of classical scholarship. Thus to Nietzsche must be accorded a paradoxical honor: that of being the least remembered—or most repressed—scholar in the history of classics." James Porter, "'Rare Impressions.' Nietzsche's Philologica: A Review of the Colli-Montinari Critical Edition *Nietzsches Werke: Kritische Gesamtausgabe* ['KGW'] by Giorgio Colli; Mazzino Montinari," *International Journal of the Classical Tradition*

Nietzsche's works also entails that he abandons his initial interest in antiquity and this is demonstrably inaccurate. Nevertheless, the upshot for scholarship is that a great many Nietzsche scholars do not read his first book at all, or if they do, read it as a confession of his relation to Wagner.[20]

Nietzsche's first book, however, as I have shown, is central to his thought, and his philosophy cannot be understood without it. Moreover, I argue contra the tripartite division of Nietzsche's philosophy that he never forsakes the themes of his first book, particularly with regard to the role of music in his thinking. For in this first book, as he tells us, Nietzsche undertakes to pose the question

---

6/3 (Winter 2000): 409–31, here 410. But see, too, Hugh Lloyd-Jones's first-rate account in his "Nietzsche and the Study of the Ancient World," in *Studies in Nietzsche and the Classical Tradition*, ed. James C. O'Flaherty, Timothy F. Sellner, and Robert M. Helm (Chapel Hill, NC: University of North Carolina Press, 1976), 1–15, as well as Viktor Pöschl, "Nietzsche und die klassische Philologie," in *Philologie und Hermeneutik im 19 Jahrhundert. Zur Geschichte und Methodologie der Geisteswissenschaften*, ed. Hellmut Flaschar, Karlfried Gründer, and Axel E.A. Horstmann (Göttingen: Vandenhoeck und Ruprecht, 1979), 141–55, 368–70, and Carlo Gentili, "Die radikale Hermeneutik Friedrich Nietzsches," *Nietzscheforschung* 8 (Berlin: Akademie Verlag, 2001), 333–6. See, for additional references, Babich, *Words in Blood, Like Flowers*, 278ff.

[20]   This is a scotosis that mars what would otherwise have been Ferenc Feher's insightful reading of the relationship between Max Weber's musicological studies and those of Bloch and Adorno in Feher's "Weber and the Rationalization of Music," *International Journal of Politics and Society* 1/2 (Winter 1987): 147–62. In this, Feher follows Lukács and thereby manages to miss both the point and the fundamental substance of Nietzsche; Feher's reason for this is well-meaning, that is, he thereby intends to mark off a fascist proto- or still-Nazi political reading of music from other, "better" varieties, claiming the latter on Weber's behalf. But Feher's mistake is in his summary of Nietzsche's project: "For Nietzsche, it was precisely Socratic rationality, the spirit, and the gaze of the antimusical observer of tragedy, that had undermined and ultimately destroyed the Dionysian qua the musical and had doomed to failure tragedy as a genre. In turn, both music and tragedy would resurrect, through the anti-Socratic, Aryan, and thoroughly anti-rationalist spirit of German music, the music of Richard Wagner" (148). With or without its implicit value judgments, Feher's description articulates what is conventional wisdom for most theorists. For one rather regrettable example of a theorist who knows his way around Riemann and Wagner, but who assumes that a similar conversancy is unneeded in a discussion of Nietzsche, see Leslie David Blasius, "Nietzsche, Riemann, Wagner: Where Music Lies," in *Music Theory and Natural Order: From the Renaissance to the Early Twentieth Century*, ed. Suzannah Clark and Alexander Rehding (Cambridge: Cambridge University Press, 2001), 93–107. Limiting himself to little Nietzsche and limited commentary (just the analytic and high Wagnerian Julian Young and Eric Blondel's fairly unmusical and just as fairly analytic study of Nietzsche and "the body"), Blasius gives himself an author's pass in a parenthesis on his first page: "(Given the almost accidental character of his references to the theorist, I trust that my own misappropriation of Nietzsche is no more irresponsible than that of others)" (93). But, and to the plain extent that Nietzsche's references were not all accidental, Blasius's confidence is unfounded. For my own part, I prefer to be careful with an author who seems as easy or ripe for the picking as Nietzsche does.

of tragedy as he similarly poses the question of science in itself and as such, that is, as he emphasizes the singularity of this achievement (he says that he is the first one to attempt this), *as* a question.[21] In this way, as was demonstrated above in the broader context of Greek *mousiké*, Nietzsche traces the "birth" of tragedy out of the spirit of music, which is to say in the very specific terms of the performance or working of the tragic work of art that Nietzsche also speaks of in terms of the tragic cult and with respect to the entire political and religious economy of ancient Greek society. This will also turn on the question of the role of the chorus and of the tragic spectator for Nietzsche.[22]

Nietzsche's illustrative philological instructions (and we note that he is explicitly didactic, as these are notes for his courses at Basel) remind his students that we today and habitually are inclined to "read with the eyes."[23] By contrast, in his "On the Theory of Quantificational Rhythm," Nietzsche invokes a different physical readerly praxis or performative technique, under the heading "Arsis/ Thesis" (which, as he says, dates back, in its analytic expression, to Horace), differentiated into two kinds of quantifying rhythm, and marked either with the hand or the foot, "by which one indicates the tact interval: *percussiones*," in other words, keeping or "striking time."[24] As Nietzsche explains—and it is to his purpose

---

[21] Babette Babich, "Nietzsche's Philology and Nietzsche's Science: On the 'Problem of Science' and '*fröhliche Wissenschaft*'," in *Metaphilology: Histories and Languages of Philology*, ed. Pascale Hummel (Paris: Philologicum, 2009), 155–201.

[22] See, again, Babette Babich, "The Science of Words or Philology: Music in *The Birth of Tragedy* and The Alchemy of Love in *The Gay Science*," in *Revista di estetica*, n.s. 28, XLV, ed. Tiziana Andina (Turin: Rosenberg & Sellier, 2005), 47–78.

[23] Nietzsche, *Griechische Lyriker*, KGW II/2, 375.

[24] Nietzsche, *Griechische Rhythmik*, KGW II/3, 102. See, for further discussion, Fritz Bornmann, "Nietzsches metrische Studien," *Nietzsche-Studien* 18 (1989): 472–89, as well as Angèle Kremer-Marietti, "Rhétorique et Rythmique chez Nietzsche," in *Rythmes et philosophie*, ed. Pierre Sauvanet and Jean-Jacques Wunenburger (Paris: Kimé, 1996), 181– 95. Kremer-Marietti refers to Marcel Jousse, *L'anthropologie du geste*, II: *La Manducation de la parole* (Paris: Gallimard, 1975) as this develops in Jousse, *Les Récitatifs rythmiques*: *I, Genre de la maxime, Etudes sur la psychologie du geste* (Paris: Ed. Spes, 1930). See, in English, Jousse, *The Oral Style*, trans. Edgard Richard Sienaert and Richard Whitaker [Albert Bates Lord Studies in Oral Tradition] (New York: Garland, 1990). As Kremer-Marietti informs us in her footnote 5, Father Jousse gave a course at the Sorbonne in 1935 on the theme of the psychology of the parable in the Palestinian style of orality, which was subsequently taken up by Etienne Boucly in "La mimique hébraïque et la rythmo-pédagogie vivante," *Cahiers juifs* N 15 (May–June 1935): 99–210. See, on Jousse, with a valuable bibliography, Edgard Richard Sienaert, "Marcel Jousse: The Oral Style and the Anthropology of Gesture," *Oral Tradition* 5/1 (1990): 91–106. With specific reference to Nietzsche, I make a similar point with respect to oral style (although I do not refer to Jousse here), observing that: "It is not Nietzsche's claim (and if he is right, it is not the case) that what has gone missing are the corresponding musical notes to the tragic poems (like the vowels in Hebrew, these would be conventions added only for a later—'more

here to be repetitive—there are two distinct styles or "arts" of keeping time: again, one for visual indication, "for the eye using the hand," and the other "for the ear with an audible tap of the hand, finger or foot."[25]

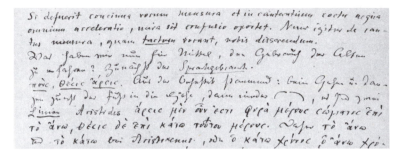

Figure 10.1   Arsis/Thesis Illustration in Nietzsche, *Zur Theorie der quantitirenden Rythmik*. Courtesy of the Goethe Schiller Archive, Weimar.[26]

The point, as Nietzsche emphasizes in his brief disquisition "On the Theory of Quantificational Rhythm," is to avoid the a-historical modernizing of the past, what Butterfield called the Whig interpretation of history, and thus to emphasize the gulf between our own conceptions of rhythm and that of the Greeks. Despite, as Nietzsche writes, "our failing of the ancient rhythmic taste, our failing of the ancient Melos, how much we yearn not to be so deficient," and given what we are

decadent' time, to use Nietzschean language)." Babich, *Words in Blood, Like Flowers*, 47. In addition to Angèle Kremer-Marietti's *Nietzsche et la rhétorique* (Paris: PUF, 1992), see James Porter's chapter, "Being on Time," in his *Nietzsche and the Philology of the Future* (Stanford: Stanford University Press, 2000), 127–66; Pierre Sauvanet, "Nietzsche, philosophe-musicien de l'éternel retour," *Archives de Philosophie* 64 (2001): 343–60; Eric Dufour, "La physiologie de la musique chez Nietzsche," *Nietzsche-Studien* 30 (2001): 222–45, as well as Dufour's *L'esthétique musicale de Nietzsche* (Lille: Presses Universitaires du Septentrion, 2005); and most comprehensively on this theme, Friederike F. Günther, *Rhythmus beim frühen Nietzsche* (Berlin: Walter de Gruyter, 2008). Christophe Corbier's "*Alogia* et Eurythmie chez Nietzsche," *Nietzsche-Studien* 38 (2009): 1–38 offers a very useful reading that detours into an emphasis on dance, important for Nietzsche but which, as Nietzsche emphasizes, carries the risks of our own associations, and it is for this reason that Nietzsche always stresses the *narrowness* of the Greek stage, a constraint that also set the actors, as it were, in a kind of "relief" and, emphasizing the dance in question, not as freely moving, as we assume today, but as more a "beautiful walking than a whirling dance." Nietzsche, KGW II/3, 270. Here one is reminded of Augustine's definition of rhythm as *ars bene movendi* (the science of beautiful movement).

[25]   Nietzsche, *Griechische Rhythmik*, KGW II/3, 102.

[26]   Nietzsche, KGW II/3, 270. See also Babich, "Musik und Wort in der Antiken Tragödie," 235.

missing, precisely such completeness cannot but elude us. For Nietzsche, the only things at our disposal are the artifacts and texts we have, and the key to the texts is to comprehend what is given in language use. This is the advantage of philology, at its highest level, attuned in this case to the differentiation between measure and, in Nietzsche's case, tone.

The point for Nietzsche is that *pous* (the poetic foot) is effectively traced out via two lines: thesis (raising the physical foot) and arsis (lowering the foot), whereby the thesis is not a matter of rhythmic ictus but a measure of time.[27] To grasp this requires that one separate our tendency to conclude that we have to do with an emphatic vocal or stress echo from what is indicated by the measure of time or tempo. For Nietzsche, indeed, what is crucial is time, but the problem here is that "we hardly understand to what end timing would be necessary, as we set the ictus in pronunciation."[28] By contrast—and here we recall the distinction between the stress and pitch ictus as discussed in the previous chapter—"the ancients knew nothing"[29] of our kind of emphatic articulation. Everything turns for Nietzsche upon making sense of this phenomenon, where "the accent is grasped purely as pitch, the rhythmical ictus purely as marcato."[30] Where can we find, he asks, a language that can withhold the elevation of tone from a marked or stressed emphasis or accent? The answer, indeed, will turn out to be only afforded by what he calls the contrast that music makes, and in the process Nietzsche proceeds to distinguish a rhythmic and a pitch ictus,[31] whereby what is at stake is pitch, and thus the arsis, indicated as the upward-moving emphasis (or "*hochbetonte*"),[32] turns out to have a higher tone, in turn corresponding to the shorter intervals.

In this sense, so Nietzsche argued, the scholar's hermeneutic work amounted to a virtual making present of the text of the past, a *Vergegenwärtigung* of the kind

---

[27] Nietzsche, KGW II/3, 272. The point that Nietzsche seeks to make here is a challenging one. As Amy M. Dale explains, without to be sure mentioning Nietzsche, in *The Lyric Metres of Greek Drama* [1948] (Cambridge: Cambridge University Press, 1968), our own usage gets in the way of the concept: "Not only is our aesthetic understanding crippled by the loss of music and dance; there is the further difficulty of training our ear to appreciate, or even to hear, a purely quantitative rhythm. Germanic peoples [this will include English—BB], with their ear accustomed to poetic and prose rhythm in which stress is the dominant factor, have here an all but impossible task, and even in languages like French where stress is weak and fluctuating, the effect of lyrics set to music with equidistant beat is to create a similar demand for 'ictus' as an element in ordered rhythm" (4–5). But, as she points out, and this is also Nietzsche's point: "There is no vestige of evidence that dynamic stress had any structural significance in Greek verse rhythm before the imperial period" (5).

[28] Nietzsche, KGW II/3, 272.

[29] Ibid., 272.

[30] Ibid., 273.

[31] Ibid., 315.

[32] Ibid., 317.

one can perform by articulating, that is, speaking/singing, that is to say, "sight-reading" ancient Greek within the constraints, that is also to say, musically, in the "chains" of temporal rhythm, but also of mimetic dance (and, as noted above, the straitened dimensions of the stage), as well as harmony (including "the correct art of deploying dissonances").[33] As Nietzsche also always reminds us, we need to guess where we do not, cannot, know.[34] And the problem, "the mistake," as he writes, "is to take our music as identical with that of the ancients."[35] And the "enormous chasm" that Nietzsche meant to emphasize between our own sensibilities and those of antiquity? For us, he writes, passion and its intensities, excitement and relaxation rule (Wagner, anyone?), while for the ancients, by contrast, "the delight is in temporal proportionalities."[36]

Tragedy and Music

Before writing *The Birth of Tragedy out of the Spirit of Music*, Nietzsche's other philological and phenomenological investigations of the spirit of music in antiquity thus began with his explorations of the *musical* character of the Greek language as spoken/sung, and it is in this sense that we ought here to understand his reflections on Greek music drama and dance, together with his little illustration of arsis/thesis (Fig. 10.1 above).

In this way, keeping time with one's feet (tapping) derives from ancient Greek musical dancing practice (or *Orchestik*, as Nietzsche writes here).[37] As Curt Sachs

---

[33]   Ibid., 269.

[34]   Nietzsche, KSA 11, 522; 12, 145; 13, 282.

[35]   Nietzsche, KGW II/3, 399.

[36]   Ibid., 401.

[37]   As Dale notes, the reference to dance is vestigial at best: "'arsis' and 'thesis' echo the lift and fall of the dancer's feet." Dale, *The Lyric Metres of Greek Drama*, 2. In a footnote, she further emphasizes caution, before noting that her own discussion will be left to her final chapter: "These terms, obscured as they have been by the varied and contradictory usage of past generations of scholars can only lead to confusion in a modern system of metric." (Ibid.) A number of authors who write on Nietzsche's "Orchestik" manage to leave the Greek origination of the term out of consideration both in reviewing Nietzsche's own writings and in their estimation of its current significance. Thus Axel Pichler, in *Nietzsche, die Orchestikologie und das dissipative Denken* (Wien: Passagen Verlag, 2010), makes a great contribution to dance but excludes an engagement with Nietzsche's own textual focus which is antiquity as a whole, as Nietzsche specifically stresses this collectivity, which whole is also its political significance and which is more noteworthy in Pichler's case as he uses the Greek term than, say, in Georg Stauth and Bryan S. Turner's Weberian and hence less philosophical, and even less philological, account in their wonderfully, but misleadingly, titled *Nietzsche's Dance: Resentment, Reciprocity and Resistance in Social Life* (Oxford: Blackwell, 1988). In addition to Dale's broader study, see Günther's book on Nietzsche and rhythm, *Rhythmus beim frühen Nietzsche*, as an exception, and see too

writes, in accord with Nietzsche's time measure and as opposed to stress: "The metric accents in both poetry and melody followed the so-called quantitative principle, they materialized as long syllables or short ones, not as strong among light beats."[38] Adorno likewise foregrounds ancient dance in the context of his own comments on Riemann "Ad ancient musical notation."[39] This mode of keeping time is suitable for dramatization as a literal coordination: "in the weightier intervals, the dancer brings his foot down."[40] Here Nietzsche explains that what we call rhythm is "a whole drawn from a series of tacts."[41] In the distinction drawn above (Fig. 10.1), we recall that "elevating and setting down are presented for the eye, this is in poetry, in *pous*, *thesis*, *arsis* … while walking and dancing, the foot at first elevated, then lowered."[42] As Sachs explicates, arsis and thesis are dyadic beats: "*arsis*, lifting and *thesis*, dropping of the time-regulating hand or foot; in our words upbeat and downbeat."[43]

Thus the question here is to distinguish a kind of tact that has nothing to do with stress as we know it (this is related to the medieval *recto tono*, which is importantly unstressed and which has everything to do with the communal function of voice in the context of, that is, against the background of, monastic life practice, as Ivan Illich reminds us in his book, *In the Vineyard of the Text*, as this draws on his earlier work on oral and written culture),[44] and we note that we usually signal the unstressed by contrast. At issue is the tone or sound of Greek, and for Nietzsche, this is literally music.

According to the entry in Liddell and Scott, ἄρσις, *ársis* is the "lifting, removal, raising of foot in beating of time,"[45] and Nietzsche's point is that this is, as in music, unaccented, by contrast with the stressed meaning that it has in Latin poetry and in

Günther, "Am Leitfaden des Rhythmus. Kritische Wissenschaft und Wissenschaftskritik in Nietzsches Frühwerk," in *Der Tod Gottes und die Wissenschaft. Zur Wissenschaftskritik Nietzsches*, ed. Carlo Gentili and Cathrin Nielsen (Berlin: de Gruyter, 2010), 107–22. See, for Adorno, *Towards a Theory of Musical Reproduction: Notes, a Draft, and Two Schemata*, trans. Wieland Hoban (London: Polity, 2006), 57.

[38] Curt Sachs, *The Rise of Music in the Ancient World: East and West* (New York: W.W. Norton, 1943), 263.

[39] Adorno, *Towards a Theory of Musical Reproduction*, 57.

[40] Nietzsche, KGW II/2, 102.

[41] Ibid., 103.

[42] Ibid.

[43] Sachs, *The Rise of Music in the Ancient World*, 263.

[44] Illich uses this illustration in his *In the Vineyard of the Text: A Commentary to Hugh's Didascalicon* (Chicago: University of Chicago Press, 1996), to clarify the distinction between various cultures of reading as of scholarly, monastic life, in his commentary on Hugh of St Victor's *Didascalicon*: "They listen to recitations done on one tone (*recto tono*) …" Ibid., 59.

[45] Henry George Liddell and Robert Scott, *A Greek–English Lexicon*, seventh edition revised and augmented throughout by Sir Henry Stuart Jones, with the assistance of Roderick McKenzie (Oxford: Clarendon Press, 1940): "*raising of the foot* in beating time,

Figure 10.2   Arsis/Thesis: A = Arsis, T = Thesis. After Thurmond, *Note Grouping*.
Reproduced courtesy of Marianne Kearns.

poetry as we know it in English, German, French, Italian, and so on, which always exemplifies the stress ictus that Nietzsche argues as untenable in the Greek.[46]

Of course, as a technical term, *thesis* is used in Greek poetry as it is also used musically to signify downbeat notes: James Morgan Thurmond, in his book on piano technique, emphasizes this old (and, reading Nietzsche, it is obviously ancient) technique of *Note Grouping* and points out that, by avoiding the tendency to *stress* the downbeat, one can improve one's playing.[47] Indeed, in a correspondence charmingly coincidental with the current context, characterizing both Beethoven (and Brahms) as the "Greeks of musical art,"[48] Godowsky similarly emphasizes the fundamental rules of interpretation for piano mastery: "There are laws of interpretation. One of them is never to lay stress on a consonance but rather on a dissonance. The stronger the dissonance, the heavier the stress put upon it."[49] It is significant to note Nietzsche's emphasis here (along with his illustration, Fig. 10.1), not only because Nietzsche repeats this point

---

opp. θέσις, *downward beat, Aristox. Rhyth.12.17, D.H.Dem.48, Aristid.Quint.1.13, Luc. Harm.*I, etc."

[46]   "Wenn es Ictus in dem Sprechen giebt—verschieden vom Accent—dann muß der im Verse sich wiederfinden. Aber die Worte haben die verschiedenste Stellung im Verse, bald in der Arsis, bald [in der] Thesis, somit haben sie keinen Ictus. / Giebt es einen Versictus (a), dann gewiß keinen Wortiktus (b). / Wenn es aber keinen Wortiktus (b) giebt, dann gewiß keinen Versictus (a). / Wenn a ist, dann ist b nicht. / Wenn b nicht ist, ist a nicht. / Also giebt es *nicht* a. / Giebt es *keinen* Versictus, dann ist Wortiktus möglich. Wenn es Wortiktus giebt, dann ist Versictus möglich." KSA 7, 4 [7], 90–91.

[47]   Thurmond explains his "theory of *note grouping*" as based on this account: the arsis or weak note (upbeat) of the motive or measure (in an iambic meter) is more expressive musically than the thesis (downbeat), and by stressing "the arsis ever so slightly, the performance of music can be made more satisfying and musical." James Morgan Thurmond, *Note Grouping: A Method for Achieving Expression and Style in Musical Performance* [1982] (Galesville, MD: Meredith Music Publications, 1991), 29. The dynamic or stress ictus by contrast, as Thurmond explains, is set "on the thesis or strong element of the foot" (30).

[48]   Harriette Brower, *Piano Mastery: The Harriet Brower Interviews. Talks with Paderewski, Hofmann, Bauer, Godowsky, Grainger 1915–1926*, ed. Jeffrey Johnson (New York: Dover, 2003), 96.

[49]   Ibid., 98.

throughout his early philological reflections, but also because he returns to it later in life, drawing too upon his own experience as a pianist (and at the outset of this study we noted Nietzsche's remarkable gift for musical improvisation and thus as a performer),[50] and especially in his correspondence with Carl Fuchs, a correspondence concerning music and phrasing with reference to Riemann's study, published in 1882.[51]

In spite of his rather Nietzschean title, Alexander Rehding's *Hugo Riemann and the Birth of Modern Musical Thought* does not progress beyond the routine account.[52] Indeed, although, as noted above, Christoph Corbier mentions the parallel between Nietzsche's early studies and his "long" late-summer 1888 letter to Fuchs, Corbier does not refer to Riemann, although he does give an important but similarly undeveloped reference to Rousseau,[53] in connection with Nietzsche's own philologically pointed distinction between German (that is, then contemporary as well as the high and middle-high traditions) and antique senses of rhythm, and part of the reason for this may be that Corbier's main reference depends on Porter and Most, and this is so in spite of his seemingly broad references to the literature from Bornmann to Dufour and Günther. In addition, where Nietzsche's explicit focus is on the *Gesammtkunstwerk*, as it were, of the ancient musical work of art that was Greek tragedy, Corbier's own interest focuses more on dance than it does on tone. Hans-Joachim Hinrichsen, in a valuably broad discussion including both Nietzsche and Fuchs, begins with an emphasis on the importance of no one less than Hans von Bülow for the renewed theoretical attention to the problem of rhythm dating from the 1880s (citing von Bülow's "Im Anfang war der

---

[50] Improvisation is no mean thing and refers to a quite specific relation to performance, as Lydia Goehr, for her part, develops in a different direction in her "On Broken Strings" (at the time of this writing, still unpublished). With respect to Nietzsche, Beethoven's own reputation for improvisation may be illuminating, and Glenn Stanley tells us that Beethoven "preferred improvisations, which had an artistic status equal to, and perhaps higher than, playing finished works." Glenn Stanley, ed., "Introduction," in *Cambridge Companion to Beethoven* (Cambridge: Cambridge University Press, 2000), 14–31, here 16.

[51] Of course, this correspondence included, inasmuch as Nietzsche (like most of us) always did more than one thing at a time, getting some attention and ideally securing possible gigs for his friend, the composer Heinrich Köselitz, Nietzsche's Peter Gast/Pietro Gasti. See, on Köselitz, Frederick Love, *Nietzsche's Saint Peter: Genesis and Cultivation of an Illusion* (Berlin: de Gruyter, 1991). See again, with the above noted reservations, Blasius, "Nietzsche, Riemann, Wagner: Where Music Lies." Christopher Middleton provides a translation of Nietzsche's correspondence with Fuchs in "Nietzsche on Music and Metre," *Arion* 6/1 (Spring 1967): 58–65. See, too, Damien Ehrhardt, "Aspects de la phraséologie riemannienne," *Musurgia* 4/1 (1997): 68–83.

[52] See Alexander Rehding's epilogue to his *Hugo Riemann and the Birth of Modern Musical Thought* (Cambridge: Cambridge University Press, 2003), 182–5.

[53] "Il est courant, depuis l'*Essai sur l'origine des langues* de Rousseau au moins, d'opposer les langues anciennes mélodiques et les langues modernes accentuées, nées sous l'influence des Barbares." Corbier, "*Alogia* et eurythmie chez Nietzsche," 8.

Rythmus"),[54] and noting Nietzsche's aphorism, *How modern music is supposed to make the soul move*, as including "in nuce" all the lineaments of Nietzsche's Wagner critique.[55] Hinrichsen's reference is offered only in passing and in order to highlight the distinctiveness of von Bülow, and Riemann to be sure, and not to foreground either Fuchs or Nietzsche. Nevertheless, what is significant is that Nietzsche's own aphorism is all about the distinctive gesture of ancient and modern movement of body—and soul and the measure, the time measure as it were, of rhythm. As opposed to both "whirling dance," as seen above, but also as opposed to the Wagnerian "endless melody," Nietzsche writes of the role of rhythm and time: "Earlier music constrained one *to dance*—with a delicate or solemn or fiery movement back and forth, faster and slower—in pursuit of which compulsion the needful preservation of orderly measure compelled the soul of the listener to a continual self-possession."[56] No part of this reflection can be understood without reference to *The Birth of Tragedy* and Nietzsche's "On Music and Word," "The Greek Musical Drama," as indeed his reflections on Greek lyric, Greek rhythm, and so on.

Walking the Music

I have been arguing that the philological foundations for Nietzsche's exploration of *The Birth of Tragedy out of the Spirit of Music* must be taken into consideration, even to the extent that Nietzsche highlights the differences between our own understanding of rhythm and meter and ancient Greek poetic measure. In addition to the *intonation* of Greek, the ancient Greek work of tragic art ultimately constitutes a *Gesammtkunstwerk* in a sense far exceeding that which Wagner had in mind, a sense that only the scope of Nietzsche's studies, of lyric, rhetoric, philosophy, history, including politics and especially religious practice, begins to intimate.[57] If

---

    [54]   Citing Theodor Pfeiffer (1884) and Otto Lessman (1882) for this and discussing von Bülow's influence on Riemann, as well as Riemann's own correspondence with Fuchs, in Hans-Joachim Hinrichsen, "Musikalische Rythmustheorien um 1900," in *Rhythmus: Spuren eines Wechselspiels in Künsten und Wissenschaften*, ed. Barbara Naumann (Würzburg: Königshausen und Neumann, 2005), 141–56. Cf., for complete reference and further discussion, Hans-Joachim Hinrichsen, *Musikalische Interpretation. Hans von Bülow* (Stuttgart: Franz Steiner Verlag, 1999), 238.

    [55]   Nietzsche, HH, §134; Hinrichsen, "Musikalische Rythmustheorien um 1900," 141.

    [56]   Nietzsche, HH, §134.

    [57]   The scope of Nietzsche's philological writings is breathtakingly impressive by any standard. I list here, just to offer a sense of this, some of the titles of his Basel lectures: *Prolegomena zu den Choephoren des Aeschylus*; *Die griechischen Lyriker*; *Vorlesungen über lateinische Grammatik*; *<Hesiod Γένος καὶ βίος Ἡσιόδου. Certamen. Ἔργα>*; *Griechische Lyriker* (in KGW II/2); *AΞIE TAYPE. Zur Geschichte der griechischen Tragödie. Einleitung in die Tragödie des Sophokles. 20 Vorlesungen*; *<Ciceros Academica>*; *Griechische Rythmik*; *Aufzeichnungen zur Rhythmik und Metrik*; *Zur Theorie der quantitirenden*

the term *Gesammtkunstwerk* tends to be associated with Wagner—although it is also associated with Goethe's and Schiller's Weimar—it is perhaps not surprising that some or even the great majority of scholars have contended, even in the face of Nietzsche's philological formation, that Nietzsche could only have drawn the notion from Wagner to begin with. Against the specifically modern notion of "art as art totality," Nietzsche explains that "ancient drama is a grand work of music."[58]

For Nietzsche, what is involved in the tragic musical work of art is music in addition to the collectivity of the culture as a whole and on every level. Thus "the enjoyment and art of hearing were for the Greeks powerfully developed by means of the epic rhapsodes and melists."[59] But rather than serving the German (and still contemporary) function of temporary distraction and entertainment, as both Nietzsche and Adorno lament, the Greek experience of the old tragedies was distinguished by its function of allowing the Greek to "collect himself."[60] Thus the tragedy is and had to be a work of musical art, given what Nietzsche argues, as we have seen, but not less and just because it was composed in Greek.

In addition, we have noted the relevance of dance, which Nietzsche distinguished from the more ecstatic expressions of dance by comparing it to walking, a comparison which, however, would not eliminate its erotic dimension. As Adorno, albeit offensively, as already noted and given the normative exigencies of today's scholarly sensibilities, reminded us in his 1936 reflections, jazz is "directly related to coitus: the walking rhythm resembles the sexual, and if the new dances have demystified the erotic magic of the old ones they have … replaced it with the drastic insinuation of the sexual act."[61] Adorno's associative move here between rhythm, dance, and eros is far from passé, if it also echoes in Nietzsche's first book. Thus it is significant that a similar emphasis, with to be sure a "corrected" tone, also inspires Susan McClary's transgression against the assumed elders of standard Beethoven reception, as detailed in her *Feminine Endings* and as beautifully articulated in the poetry of the late Adrienne Rich, beginning indeed with her title, *The Ninth Symphony of Beethoven Understood At*

Rhythmik; *Rhythmische Untersuchungen*; *Encyclopädie der klassischen Philologie und Einleitung in das Studium derselben* (in KGW II/3). Nietzsche, who would otherwise use the term "Altphilolog" to describe his study of antiquity, includes a footnote in his title detailing the use of the term "classical" (KGW II/3, 341). He goes on in the following volume to Plato and his dialogues and teachings, in the context of which should be read his notes on *The Preplatonic Philosophers*, including a separate course on the dialogues of the same, followed by a *History of Greek Eloquence* (and a supplementary course offering an appendix to the same); a *Presentation of Ancient Rhetoric*; and several courses on Aristotle's *Rhetoric* (in KGW II/4), in addition, indeed, to his studies of Diogenes Laertius.

[58]   Nietzsche, KSA 7, 3 [1], 57.

[59]   Ibid., 57–8.

[60]   Ibid., 58.

[61]   Theodor Adorno, "On Jazz," in *Night Music: Essays on Music 1928–1962*, trans. Wieland Hoban (Chicago: Seagull Books, 2009), 152.

Last As a Sexual Message. Robert Fink's defense of McClary takes up the same emphasis in his own articulation of the theme in "Beethoven Antihero."[62] For his part, Fink not only defends McClary, but also stakes a claim to a nuanced reading of Beethoven's sublime contra Dmitri Tymoczko's "The Sublime Beethoven."[63]

Bracketing (as we really, truly ought to do by now)[64] the traditional and often unreflected antipathy to Adorno's criticism of jazz (which can often amount to an "I like jazz"—and the current author certainly does), the same sexual allusion is also the point of *The Birth of Tragedy out of the Spirit of Music*, as it is born—as Nietzsche emphasizes that it is born—out of the folk dance, that is, the dithyramb as originally articulated for reasons of fertility, in the spring festivals, and thereby foregrounding the erotic connection with Dionysus *and not less* with Apollo.[65]

---

[62]   Robert Fink, "Beethoven Antihero: Sex, Violence, and the Aesthetics of Failure, or Listening to the Ninth Symphony as Postmodern Sublime," in *Beyond Structural Listening: Postmodern Modes of Hearing*, ed. Andrew Dell'Antonio (Berkeley: University of California Press, 2003), 109–53. See, too, Robynn J. Stillwell, "Hysterical Beethoven," *Beethoven Forum* 10/2 (2003): 162–82.

[63]   Dmitri Tymoczko, "The Sublime Beethoven: Did the Composer Share an Aesthetic Principle with Immanuel Kant?" *Boston Review: A Political and Literary Forum* (2000). Contra its title, Tymoczko's essay replies not to Kant but Lyotard. I note in passing that the status of the postmodern remains worrisome for musicologists and other theorists (although the postmodern per se has, by now, lost most of its promising, as well as its threatening, cachet). See too, where he reprises this theme, Robert Fink, *Repeating Ourselves: American Minimal Music as Cultural Practice* (Berkeley: University of California Press, 2005).

[64]   But we are far from this, as was evident in the anti-Adorno focus or theme of the recent Royal Musical Association Music and Philosophy Study Group at King's College London on 20–21 July 2012. Featuring Roger Scruton, Stephen Hinton, and Andrew Bowie to discuss the theme set by Scruton's "Is Adorno a Dead Duck?" the conference showed less progress than the inclusion of supposedly continental philosophers would have promised. In fact, however, very few continental philosophers were on hand. Both Lydia Goehr and Paul Boghossian enjoy a similarly analytic formation (which dominant formation is also why Goehr enjoys an appointment at Columbia and so too Boghossian at NYU). As I sought to underscore in my concluding remarks (I played the bit continental role as opposed to Levinson's grander analytic role), the real issue at the conference was the promise of interdisciplinarity. But this same intrinsic interdisciplinarity (that is, mixing philosophy and musicology) soured philosophers like Scruton and Levinson as they were unused, as mainstream scholars are unused, to being marginalized when it comes to music and to musicologists. No matter how many times Scruton and Levinson insist that they are the key, if not the *only*, philosophers to be heard (and quoted), musicologists seemingly go right on reading Adorno and citing him. Still, progress was made on the analytic front (the point of being mainstream or dominant is that one always wins), and the high point of the conference for Levinson, as he reported in his concluding remarks, was that he heard some references to Levinson amongst the references to Adorno.

[65]   For an insightful discussion of ancient Greek music drama, here in connection with Wagner, see, again, Father M. Owen Lee, *Athena Sings: Wagner and the Greeks* (Toronto: University of Toronto Press, Scholarly Publishing Division, 2003).

Nietzsche's reflections on what he carefully articulates as the "birth" of tragedy work to draw out the *literal* musicality of the ancient Greek tragic poem as such, a phenomenological philology that we have seen to have been dependent upon Nietzsche's discovery of the musical resonances of ancient Greek. What is important is that Nietzsche, like other philologists before him, draws upon music in order to mark the measures of ancient poetry and that he hears this as a performer as well.

In an earlier chapter, I observed that it is because k.d. lang happens to walk the music as she does (pace Adorno, pace McClain) that we might learn something, hear something—better said: that we might guess at something when it comes to Nietzsche and the Greeks, Nietzsche and Beethoven. This walking, as Nietzsche also reminds us, works in the time-space that is the music. Here it is important to add that Nietzsche alludes to Beethoven's music as a creative, inventive artist and highlights that, as a composer, the deaf Beethoven is above all one who *listens*, rather as Schopenhauer hears music,[66] as Nietzsche recalled Beethoven's Platonic *"recollections* of a 'better world.'" Beethoven's "music about music" thus turns out to be harder to parse in Nietzsche's characterization, even as contrasted with Mozart's "music about life," than it may have seemed at first sight.

It is important to add here that Nietzsche also refers, no less theoretically, to Beethoven's early nineteenth-century *Harmonienlehre* of dissonance and consonance,[67] alluding to compositional notes he took to be Beethoven's own. To

---

[66] Once again we recall Adorno's joke that: "It is conceivable that Beethoven actually wanted to go deaf—because he had already had a taste of the sensuous side of music as it is blared from loudspeakers today." Adorno, *Beethoven*, 31.

[67] See Beethoven himself here in his notes from his studies with Albrechtsberger, as we may read these and as Nietzsche would have known them, in Henry Hugo Pierson, ed., *Ludwig van Beethovens Studien im Generalbass, Contrapunkt und in der Compositionslehre aus dessen Handschriftlichen Nachlass gesammelt und herausgegeben von Ignaz Xaver von Seyfried* [1832] (Leipzig/Hamburg/New York: Schuberth & Comp, 1853), throughout but especially 130. Available in English as *Studies in Thorough-bass, Counterpoint and the Art of Scientific Composition. Collected from the Autograph Posthumous Manuscripts of the Great Composer and first published together with Biographical Notices Ignatius von Seyfried, Translated and Edited by Henry Hugh Pierson (Edgar Mannsfeldt), with Beethoven's Portrait, and Other Illustrative Plates* (Leipzig/Hamburg/New York: Schuberth and Comp, 1853). Cf. Johann Georg Albrechtsberger's *Gründliche Anweisung zur Composition mit deutlichen und ausführlichen Exempeln, zum Selbstunterrichte, erläutert; und mit einem Anhange: Von der Beschaffenheit und Anwendung aller jetzt üblichen musikalischen Instrumente* (Leipzig: Breitkopf, 1790). It should be said, of course, that in the interim we have gone to not reading Seyfried at all, as decreed by Gustav Nottebohm, *Beethoveniana: Aufsätze und Mittheilungen* (Leipzig: Rieter Biedermann, 1872), 175ff. Nottebohm's specific complaints are that Seyfried is incomplete, in places inaccurate, and that he transcribes some of Beethoven's studies along with Albrechtsberger and Fux and others, without indicating which is which. Indeed, as Nottebohm concludes, using an argument not unlike the argument used to exclude the material in Nietzsche's

be sure, Beethoven's various (and variously generic) reflections on "dissonance" bear upon Nietzsche's own writings on dissonance as such.[68] However, what makes this connection relevant here is just that Nietzsche also cultivated the ambition of composer. It is for this reason that this reference to Seyfried's edition of Beethoven's *Harmonienlehre* would matter for Nietzsche's own reflections on harmony, as is evident in what Nietzsche writes, especially with respect to his comparison of Wagner and Beethoven, if this connection is to be understood less as an issue with Wagner, as I argue in the present context, than with regard to the differences between Greek musical forms and lyric convention, and thus, for Nietzsche, this also includes a reference to E.T.A. Hoffmann, with the *relationship* between music and words.[69]

What is intriguing in this connection thus takes us back to the citation at the beginning of this chapter, contrasting Beethoven and Mozart. Here the point that Nietzsche sought to emphasize with his focus on the Greeks is that the same Beethoven who composes music about music also, and this is the key, treats words in terms of their musical values, that is to say, explicitly, *as tones*. This point was central for Nietzsche and it recurs again and again: a very musical return of the same.

We began by noting the contrast that Nietzsche himself makes between Beethoven, listening to music everywhere, in the streets, taverns, festival celebrations, and Mozart, who looks at life at its richest, effulgent in the south. But we can be led astray by our agonistic conventionalities of pro and con. Thus we recalled above that commentators tell us that Nietzsche was a Wagnerian no matter what or that Nietzsche favored Bizet over Wagner, just as Mozart here would appear to be praised above Beethoven.

This for and against (like most such) calls for some reflection. And in a passage entitled *Belief in Inspiration*, Nietzsche offers us another consideration that must be taken into account:

---

similarly invented *Will to Power*, "Es ist also, als Ganzes genommen, falsch." Nottebohm, *Beethoveniana*, 203. In the impatient scuttlebutt of modern history, this has meant that one does not read Seyfried and Nottebohm's criticisms have absolute standing. I cannot but leave this to one side, however the facts may stand or fall (and my point here is that this is unquestioned), because the Nietzsche of *The Birth of Tragedy* would only have had reference to Seyfried in any case.

[68]   I discuss Nietzsche's notion here; by contrast, Gregory Polakoff's 2011 dissertation, *"The Centre is Everywhere": Nietzsche's Overcoming of Modernity Through Musical Dissonance* (University of British Columbia), makes the case that Nietzsche anticipates the great liberation or emancipation of twentieth-century dissonance, an idea that has a good deal to recommend it, given the great interest in modern music both for us today and for Adorno.

[69]   As Seyfried's Beethoven formulaically explains: "*Keine Dissonanz soll eher resolvieren, als bis der Sinn der Worte völlig geendet ist—Wo man sich verweilet: lange Noten; wo man wegeilet: kurze Noten.*" *Ludwig van Beethovens Studien im Generalbass, Contrapunkt und in der Compositionslehre aus dessen Handschriftlichen Nachlass gesammelt und herausgegeben von Ignaz Xaver von Seyfried*, 316.

Artists have an interest in having others believe in sudden ideas, so-called inspirations; as if the idea of a work of art, of poetry, the fundamental thought of a philosophy shines down like a merciful light from heaven. In truth, the good artist's or thinker's imagination is continually producing things good, mediocre, and bad, but his power of judgment, highly sharpened and practiced, rejects, selects, joins together; thus we now see from Beethoven's notebooks that he gradually assembled the most glorious melodies and, to a degree, selected them out of disparate beginnings. The artist who separates less rigorously, liking to rely on his imitative memory, can in some circumstances become a great improviser; but artistic improvisation stands low in relation to artistic thoughts earnestly and laboriously chosen. All great men were great workers, tireless not only in invention but also in discarding, sifting, transforming, arranging.[70]

Such "arranging" was, as noted at the start of this chapter, what Nietzsche also called Beethoven's "honeybee gathering," and this collecting and assembling was part of the way Beethoven worked. To this same extent, Beethoven is his standard here, as Nietzsche will also elsewhere invoke Goethe as instantiations of "great men."

As Max Weber begins his discussion of the basics of the harmonic chord system in the West, where he later takes care to emphasize that "musical notation" as such is a "precondition" for "the development of harmonic homophonic music"[71] in his *The Rational and Social Foundations of Music*: "All rationalized music rests upon the octave (vibration ratio of 1:2) and its division into the fifth (2:3) and fourth (3:4) and the successive 12 subdivisions in terms of the formula (n+1) for all intervals smaller than the fifth."[72] As Weber goes on to explain:

The intervals contained in harmonic triads or their inversions are (either perfect or imperfect) consonances. All other intervals are dissonances. Dissonance is the basic dynamic element of chordal music, motivating the progression from chord to chord. Seventh chords are the typical and simplest dissonances of pure chord music, demanding resolution into triads. In order to relax its inherent tension, the dissonant chord demands resolution into a new chord representing the harmonic base in consonant form.[73]

---

[70]   Nietzsche, HH I, 155.

[71]   Max Weber, *The Rational and Social Foundations of Music*, trans. Don Marindale, Johannes Riedel, and Gertrude Neuwirth (Carbondale: Southern Illinois University Press, 1958), 82.

[72]   Ibid., 3.

[73]   Ibid., 6. See, for a contemporaneous discussion, August Halm, *Harmonielehre* (Berlin: Göschen, 1900), and again Lee Allen Rothfarb, *August Halm: A Critical and Creative Life in Music* (Rochester: University of Rochester Press, 2009). Adorno mentions Halm as conspicuously undervalued in *Beethoven*, 47.

I mention Weber here because this account of dissonance may be poised against Schoenberg and because it is related to the tradition from which Nietzsche would have drawn. Dissonance, fundamentally an unresolved chord, as Weber notes, is also inherently always on the way to resolution—Seyfried's Beethoven also emphasizes *resolutio dissonantiarum* as his studies could only detail the varieties of the same. The deferred resolution is also a matter of time, and the longer this takes, that is, the more irresolution, the more discord, that is, the more pain. As Adorno reflects in an allusion recalling Nietzsche's language in *The Birth of Tragedy* of "*playing* with the thorn of dissonance": "Time—as something no longer mastered but depicted—becomes a solace for the suffering. Only the older Beethoven discovered this secret of time in music."[74]

E.T.A. Hoffmann had already highlighted the dissonance and tensions of Beethoven's Fifth, and we have also seen from the start of this chapter that Hoffmann's observations were as influential for Nietzsche as they were for anyone else in his era. Here we also do well to note the classical context of rhythmic analyses of Beethoven, as discussed above.[75]

Today, scholars take gender analyses like McClary's musicological assessment in their stride, even given the disturbingly graphic articulation of dissonance, whether via Weber or Schoenberg, as she deploys this very expression: "the carefully prepared cadence is frustrated, damming up energy which finally explodes in the throttling, murderous rage of a rapist incapable of attaining release."[76] And we have noted that musicologists are able to incorporate this gendered reading by agreeing with her insights, as Robert Fink does, and amplifying the details, as Fink points out, with the support of one with no fewer feminist laurels than the poet Adrienne Rich; the first line of her influential poem, as cited above, also articulates the seemingly irresolute dynamic of

---

[74]   Adorno, *Beethoven*, 93.

[75]   Rudolf Westfall and B. Sokolowsky, "Klangfuss, Klangvers, mit besonderer Beziehung auf Beethovens Sonaten," *Musikalisches Wochenblatt* XVI/28 (Leipzig: Fritzsch, 2 July 1885): 341–3. See the continuation: "Über den Rhythmus in Beethovens Klaviersonaten und das Versmaß der Ode 'An die Freude,' auch im Hinblick auf Matthesons Musiktheorie," *Musikalisches Wochenblatt* 31 (23 July 1885), 377–9. See, too, in connection with Riemann, Justus Hermann Wetzel, "Die ästhetische Vorherrschaft des auftaktigen Rhythmus," *Musikalisches Wochenblatt* 40 (1909): 249–51 and 269–73.

[76]   Originally in Susan McClary, "Getting Down Off the Beanstalk," *Minnesota Composers Forum Newsletter* (January 1987), and again in her *Feminine Endings: Music, Gender, and Sexuality* (Minneapolis: University of Minnesota Press, 1991/2002). This analysis has caused no end of pain for standard readings. See, for the original fussing tear about daring to use such language with respect to Beethoven, Pieter C. van den Toorn, "Politics, Feminism, and Contemporary Music Theory," *The Journal of Musicology* IX (1991): 275–99. See, prior to Fink's defense, as cited above, Ruth A. Solie, "What Do Feminists Want? A Reply to Pieter van den Toorn," *The Journal of Musicology* IX/4 (Fall 1991): 399–410.

Beethoven's dissonance—"A man in terror of impotence, or infertility ..."—such that Beethoven does not explode at all.[77]

Dissonances are always and only heard as such relative to a particular or given context. The point, as Nottebohm's Beethoven also stresses in his own studies of composition, concerns that context and the manner of that resolution.[78] For Schoenberg, as a result of what he describes as the "emancipation of dissonance," dissonance:

> came to be placed on an equal footing as the sounds regarded as consonances (in my *Harmonienlehre* the explanation for this lies in the insight that consonance and dissonance differ not as opposites do but only in point of degree; that consonances are the sounds closer to the fundamental, dissonances those further away; that their comprehensibility is graduated accordingly, since the nearer ones are easier to comprehend than those further off.)[79]

It is not as an anticipation of Schoenberg, uncannily suggestive as that idea would be, much rather it is because what had interested Nietzsche throughout his life turned upon discordances and accordance in the relationship between music and words in ancient Greek, that Nietzsche alludes to Beethoven. But what is to be underscored here is that Nietzsche does not read the text of ancient Greek tragedy as a kind of libretto, where, as some scholars assume, we are simply missing the musical score. But as Nietzsche explicitly argues, the claim already misconceives the relationship between music and words in antiquity as this is not dependent upon the technique of a separate musical notation, quite simply because written Greek is (literally) its own notation. In other words, the addition of musical notation to the text, like the Hebrew vowels to which Illich refers (drawing as he does on the scholarly exploration of the tradition of orality and literality),[80] is a much later supplement, only *needed* subsequent to the death (or suicide) of tragedy, as Nietzsche traces this death.[81] Like davening (Yiddish וענוואַד *davnen*)—that is to

---

[77] See, again, Fink, "Beethoven AntiHero." For a recent discussion of Rich's poem, see Michael Broyles, *Beethoven in America* (Bloomington: Indiana University Press, 2011), 140ff.

[78] "Von der Auflösung der Dissonanzen: *De Dissonanziarum Resolutione*. Eine Gebundene Note ist nichts anderes als ein Verzögerung der folgenden Not." Nottebohm, *Beethoveniana*, 179.

[79] Arnold Schoenberg, "Theory and Composition" [1950], in *Style and Idea*, ed. Leonard Stein (New York: St. Martin's Press, 1975), 260–61.

[80] Ivan Illich and Barry Sanders, *ABC: The Alphabetization of the Popular Mind* (San Francisco: North Point Press, 1988), 13. See Jousse in note 24, in addition to Walter Ong, S.J., *Orality and Literacy: The Technologizing of the Word* (London: Methuen, 1982). As Illich reflects in his *In the Vineyard of the Text*, "the alphabet is a technology" for nothing less than the "recording" of speech (93). See, too, Anne Carson on the liminality of consonants and breath in her *Eros, The Bittersweet* [1986] (Normal, IL: Dalkey Archive Press, 1998).

[81] Nietzsche, BT, §11.

say, like the rhythmic bodily bowing of praying in Hebrew—the physical tradition preserves sound apart from any visual aide memoire.

After the death of tragedy, "committing suicide at its own hand" and by way of the works of Euripides and Platonico-Socratic rationality, Nietzsche argues that Beethoven's "playing" with dissonance can give us insight into the paradox of tragedy as Beethoven plays discord, playing with "the thorn of the unpleasing" [*Stachel des Unlusts*] in the fourth movement of the Ninth Symphony. This fourth movement is Nietzsche's reference point in *The Birth of Tragedy*. At the same time, of course, such dissonance is also to be found throughout the nineteenth century as well, and also indeed in Chopin and Wagner, although of course it is predominantly associated with Schoenberg's twentieth century today.[82] Indeed if one means dissonance apart from harmony, thus apart from its relation to consonance and its resolution—this is the language of sexual tension and rapprochement, as Hölderlin speaks of the conflict of lovers and the promise of happiness that is at least its occasional reconciliation in his *Hyperion*, as this same dynamic also structures the entirety of *The Birth of Tragedy* which similarly begins (and ends) with the reference to the lover's strife between male and female, between masculine and feminine elements in music and art—one has then proceeded well beyond the historic sensibilities of Nietzsche's nineteenth century and well into the realm of what Schoenberg called the "emancipation of dissonance."[83] But the language of emancipation here does not correspond to the liberation of Prometheus, as Nietzsche used this motif from Beethoven to illustrate his book on tragedy. Schoenberg is far more radical, far more recondite, and ultimately irreconcilably modern, and thus, and this Adorno saw, with Schoenberg the musical landscape changes.

As Ethan Haimo observes:

> When the dissonance cannot be identified, its resolution cannot be directed. And when that happens, the emancipation of the dissonance is at hand—not as the result of theoretical speculation about the more remote overtones of the

---

[82] As Adorno puts it, tracing a line between Wagner, Beethoven, and Schoenberg with language that is as Nietzschean as it is Heideggerian: "The manner in which Wagner treats motifs whose aspect inherently contradicts the procedure of variation casts the die of Schoenberg's procedure. It leads to the definitive technical antagonism of post-Beethoven music that between a predetermined tonality—and the substantial detail. Whereas Beethoven developed the musical entity out of nothingness in order to be able to determine it entirely as what becomes, the late Schoenberg demolishes it as what already became." Theodor Adorno, *Philosophy of New Music*, trans. Robert Hullot-Kentor (Minneapolis: University of Minnesota Press, 2006), 61. See, too, Stephen Hinton, "The Emancipation of Dissonance: Schoenberg's Two Practices of Composition," *Music and Letters* 91/4 (2010): 568–79.

[83] See Arnold Schoenberg, "Composition with Twelve Tones," in *Style and Idea*, ed. Leonard Stein (Berkeley: University of California Press, 1975), 216–44.

harmonic series but as a consequence of the extension of the methods of chordal formation to include multiple altered and elaborative tones.[84]

What is called into question is harmony itself, and at issue is the impossibility of discriminating dissonance and consonance; Schoenberg himself makes this point:

> The term *emancipation of the dissonance* refers to its comprehensibility, which is considered equivalent to the consonance's comprehensibility. A style based on this premise treats dissonances like consonances and renounces a tonal center. By avoiding the establishment of a key, modulation is excluded, since modulation means leaving an established tonality and establishing *another* tonality.[85]

In this way, as Haimo also observes, "the lack of directed harmonic progressions" in Schoenberg's compositional schema "throws the existence of a tonic into doubt; the lack of hierarchy abolishes the diatonic scale as a referential collection; the inability to identify the dissonance erases the distinction between consonance and dissonance."[86]

One might argue—though I will not be the one to undertake this here, even given Schoenberg's observation that "Wagner's harmony had promoted a change in the logic and constructive power of harmony"[87]—that Wagner's Tristan chord is to be counted as an inspiration for David's chord. Some of the authors who write on Cohen, as we have cited, seem to go in this direction, although it is a characteristic of more casual pop musicology to avoid such references. What is certainly arguable, although this is not my own argument here, is that the Tristan chord did indeed engender its very own "Tristan-effect" for another—and in many cases (Bayreuth anyone?) still ongoing—generation, including those who point, taking Schoenberg and Adorno with them, to the importance of Wagner for Schoenberg's revolution.[88]

---

[84] Ethan Haimo, "Schoenberg and the Origins of Atonality," in *Constructive Dissonance: Arnold Schoenberg and the Transformations of Twentieth Century Culture*, ed. Juliane Brand and Christopher Hailey (Berkeley: University of California Press, 1997), 71–86, here 81.

[85] Schoenberg, "Composition with Twelve Tones," 216. And he goes on to note that, as a result of the "emancipation of dissonance," it "came to be placed on an equal footing as the sounds regarded as consonances (in my *Harmonienlehre* the explanation for this lies in the insight that consonance and dissonance differ not as opposites do but only in point of degree; that consonances are the sounds closer to the fundamental, dissonances those further away; that their comprehensibility is graduated accordingly, since the nearer ones are easier to comprehend than those further off.)" Schoenberg, "Theory and Composition," 260–61.

[86] Haimo, "Schoenberg and the Origins of Atonality," 82.

[87] Schoenberg, "Composition with Twelve Tones," 216.

[88] See, among others, Norton Dudeque, *Music Theory and Analysis in the Writings of Arnold Schoenberg (1874–1951)* (Aldershot: Ashgate, 2006), 127ff.

For Leonard Cohen's part, to use his own words, what I have been calling the Hallelujah effect grows out of what he calls "the broken" Hallelujah. This broken chord is what Weber emphasizes, apart from the current theme, and other scholars take this up as well with respect to Cohen, while Barbara Barry discusses this in more general cultural terms with respect to Adorno, using the examples as she does of both Beethoven and Mahler.[89]

Inasmuch as Nietzsche emphasized the wondrous meaning (*wunderbaren Bedeutung*) of a musical dissonance,[90] some have been tempted to see Nietzsche as preternaturally modern, ahead of his time.[91] But ahead of time or of his times, what is certain is that Nietzsche poses the question of musical dissonance as a question. We have already seen that this is—along with the question of rhythm, as we have seen that von Bülow foregrounds it, along with Riemann—arguably the question of the nineteenth century. And it is in terms of dissonance that Schopenhauer offers his solution or resolution to Kant's metaphysical prohibition of any kind of access to the heart, or as Hegel would say, to the "inside" of things, as Nietzsche himself also speaks of Goethe's "mothers" of being, via music.[92]

In addition, there is also the musical context of the role of dissonance in composition, the same point that Beethoven emphasized and the point of the same compositional structure on which von Bülow, perhaps unkindly, probably not unfairly, undertook to instruct Nietzsche.[93]

---

[89]   See, for example, on Adorno and the notion of the broken, Barbara R. Barry's review essay, "In Adorno's Broken Mirror: *Towards a Theory of Musical Reproduction*," *International Review of the Aesthetics and Sociology of Music* 40/1 (June 2009): 81–98.

[90]   For a general discussion of what the author calls the "symphonic monument that towered over the nineteenth century," see Daniel K.L. Chua, *Absolute Music and the Construction of Meaning* (Cambridge: Cambridge University Press, 1999), 235f.

[91]   Nietzsche, BT, §25.

[92]   See Lüdger Lüttkehaus, who understands rather more of Hegel than Nietzsche—a handicap in reading Schopenhauer—and emphasizes this point in "The World as Will and Music: Arthur Schopenhauer's Philosophy of Music," in *Sound Figures of Modernity: German Music and Philosophy*, ed. Jost Hermand and Gerhard Richter (Madison: University of Wisconsin Press, 2006), 92–105, here 101, cf. 100.

[93]   Von Bülow was a student of Franz Liszt, Cosima Wagner's father, and would go on to become her teacher and then her husband, before her affair with and eventual marriage to Wagner. Nietzsche sent von Bülow one of his own compositions on 20 July 1872, describing it in his own words as abominable ("entsetzlich"). KSB 4, 27. Von Bülow replied with utter frankness but in a fashion that would have affected Nietzsche deeply, invoking as his explanation for his honesty his esteem for Nietzsche as a genuine scholar, based on his reading of Nietzsche's book on tragedy and as contrasted with the usual "civilized banality" that was customarily expected. Von Bülow pointed to compositional principles and Nietzsche's evident ignorance of the same, wondering if Nietzsche had deliberately and without exception "put every rule of tonality [*Tonverbindung*] to scorn, from the higher syntax to the most ordinary conventions of correct composition". But von Bülow, who already meant to hit a resonant chord by mentioning apollonian principles (and the lack

Indeed, Nietzsche's deferential recognition of von Bülow's critique (not only does Nietzsche reply in a conciliatory mode but their correspondence continues until age makes it impossible for von Bülow himself to reply further, to Nietzsche's distress) makes it plain, as Nietzsche himself underscored in his response, that he recognized the instructive elements of von Bülow's critique, a recognition which would also go back to Nietzsche's theoretical readings in music, including Seyfried's edition of Beethoven's *Harmonienlehre*.

We note that Nietzsche emphasized a similar precision at the heart of poetry in a religious if demystifying context in his own writings: thus he reminds us in *The Gay Science* and elsewhere, including his first book, that rhythm and rhyme are used to influence the deity. In this context, rather than Wagner, as is usually emphasized, and rather than, as others argue, the alternative influences of or preferences for Bizet or Rossini, Beethoven seems to have played the most significant role in Nietzsche's thinking on music.[94]

Although it is Schopenhauer who has more to say about the aesthetics of music, metaphysically speaking, it is Nietzsche who is most commonly associated with music among philosophers, or at the very least, just to vary Lydia Goehr's already cited comment on Adorno, Nietzsche likewise will turn out to be "the most interesting"[95] philosopher with respect to music. This is the point of Nietzsche's perhaps most famous declaration as he writes to Köselitz: "Life without music is simply a mistake, an agony, an exile."[96] In addition to Nietzsche's interest in being a composer—and we have already noted that he was duly chided by Cosima Wagner's first husband, the conductor and music

---

thereof) in Nietzsche's work, also could not but appeal to the exigent sensibilities of the young philologist by concluding: "If you really have a passionate drive to express yourself in the language of tones [*Tonsprache*], it is essential that you acquire the first elements of that language." See, for Nietzsche's letter in English, Christopher Middleton, ed. and trans., *Selected Letters of Nietzsche* (Chicago: University of Chicago Press, 1969), 106–7.

[94]   This is not the same as personally, and Wagner remains important personally, both positively and negatively.

[95]   Thus it is important to place Nietzsche in his own context, not just as someone whose life was enfolded, encircled by music, as the music theorist Curt Paul Janz articulates. See Janz, "Die Musik im Leben Friedrich Nietzsches," *Nietzsche-Studien* 26 (1997): 72–86. Janz also develops this emphasis throughout his three-volume biography of Nietzsche's life, and it is relevant here that Janz has also edited a volume of Nietzsche's own musical work in addition to contributing an essay in the first issue of *Nietzsche-Studien*. See Janz, "Die Kompositionen Friedrich Nietzsches," *Nietzsche-Studien* 1 (1972): 173–84, and Friedrich Nietzsche, *Der musikalische Nachlass*, ed. Curt Paul Janz (Basel: Bärenreiter-Verlag, 1976).

[96]   Once again, Nietzsche's maxim from his *Twilight of the Idols*, "*Ohne Musik wäre mir das Leben ein Irrthum*," is repeated as "Das Leben ohne Musik ist einfach ein Irrthum, eine Strapatze, ein Exil." 15 January 1888, in a letter sent from Nice to Köselitz in Venice: KSB 8, 232.

theorist Hans von Bülow, for this ambition[97]—Nietzsche also lived his music. As a pianist, once again, Nietzsche played at a connoisseur's level of ability— his improvisations impressing his peers, impressing even Wagner who would quip, not without some ambiguity, that a professor had no right to play that well. But what is crucial, as argued above, is that Nietzsche would make the theme of "music and words" his own in his own profession of classical philology, beginning with his writings on rhythm and meter in ancient Greek poetry, speaking again and again of the relation between music and drama in antiquity, thematizing the relation of opera and ancient tragedy, above all and most importantly, on *The Birth of Tragedy out of the Spirit of Music*, here and as I have been doing throughout, to give his first work its initial subtitle.

Nietzsche would reissue *The Birth of Tragedy* with a new subtitle, *Hellenism and Pessimism*, just because he was sensitive (as authors are) to the book's general lack of reception and to its even more limited reception when it came to the question of comprehension among those of his contemporaries who *did* read it. I have argued that it is for this reason that Nietzsche both composed his intriguing "Attempt at a Self-Critique" when he reissued his first book and designed the first four books of *The Gay Science*—which itself is an attempt to reprise many of the points of *The Birth of Tragedy* using the illustration not of the work of ancient Greek musical drama, but the medieval song culture of the knight poets, or troubadours—together with its companion piece, the work that Nietzsche was inspired to call his symphony: the first three books (and the only published books, which would make it an unfinished symphony,) of *Thus Spoke Zarathustra*.[98]

With the declaration that the "great dithyramb is the ancient symphony,"[99] Nietzsche would argue that we fail to understand the Greeks just because we do not raise the question of the origination of tragedy as it should be framed on the basis of or *out of the spirit of music*. Nietzsche underscores this same question in his "self-critique," which was, of course, also a critique of the book's initial readers, particularly those readers who did more than fail to read it, but made of it instead the object of a calumniating misprision.[100] Nietzsche thus denigrates those

---

[97]   See, again, Janz's very musical and musicalogically informed Nietzsche biography. The translator and Nietzsche scholar Reg Hollingdale told me that he had completed a translation of this, but that it had had to be abridged (Janz's biography runs to more than 2000 pages in German) for the sake of the publisher. The Janz family refused to approve its translation, to the detriment of Anglophone scholarship.

[98]   In a letter to Köselitz, Nietzsche contends that his Zarathustra may be ranged under the "rubric" of a "symphony." 4 February 1883, KSB 6, 353. See, for an extended discussion, Curt Paul Janz, "Ist der Zarathustra eine 'Symphonie'?" in Janz, *Friedrich Nietzsche Biographie* (Munich: Hanser, 1993), vol. 2, 211–21.

[99]   Nietzsche, KSA 7, 9 [57], 296.

[100]   This begins with Wilamowitz. It is worth reflecting that, to this day, philologists take Wilamowitz to have settled the affair on the issue of Nietzsche's first book and simply skip any reading of Nietzsche at all, even when their own themes concern his areas of

who represent Aeschylus, Sophocles, and Euripides as literary authors, as literary and cultural theorists do to the present day, for the simple reason that we only know such musical poets through their texts, texts indeed that we can no longer sight-read. We are missing not the music to the text, but the very music of the words themselves as sounded.

Nietzsche's point is that, when it comes to the medium of the text, it makes no difference whether one happens to be trained as a classical philologist or not. Said otherwise, it does not matter whether one reads Aeschylus, Sophocles, and Euripides in the original Greek or in translation, as in either case what one assumes is that one is reading words and not music: just a text, just a book.

Here Nietzsche emphasizes: "I want to talk about these men not as librettists but as composers of opera," adding, still more critically: "I shall be satisfied if by the end you have been convinced that our operas are mere caricatures in comparison to ancient musical drama."[101] This is a crucial point and it bears remarking that Nietzsche's explicitly belittling reference to operas (and he points out that it is obvious that few will concede any such description) as "mere caricatures" by no means excludes Wagner (a point that most scholars today will dispute). Thus Nietzsche continues to write:

> Opera came into being without any foundation in the senses, in accordance with an abstract theory and the conscious intention to achieve the effects of the ancient drama by these means. It is therefore an artificial homunculus, indeed the malicious goblin of our musical development. Here we have a warning example of the damage the direct aping of antiquity can do.[102]

By contrast, Nietzsche argues:

> Among the Greeks, the beginnings of [music] drama go back to the unfathomable expressions of folk impulses: in the orgiastic celebrations of Dionysus people were driven outside themselves—'εκστασις—to such an extent that they acted and felt like transfigured and bewitched beings.[103]

Comparing the musical art form of antiquity, given its folk origins, with the ecstatic Dionysian dynamics of European modalities of folk intoxications and

---

specialization. Even Glenn Most and James Porter do not depart in the main from this view. And those who write on ancient tragedy conspicuously neglect Nietzsche.

[101] Nietzsche, KSA 7, 1 [1], 9.

[102] Ibid.

[103] Ibid., 10; cf. 2 [25], 54–5. See, on this transfiguring effect, Strong, *Nietzsche and the Politics of Transfiguration*, and see, too, Tracy B. Strong, "Philosophy of the Morning: Nietzsche, Politics and Transfiguration," *Journal of Nietzsche Studies* 39/1 (Spring 2009): 51–65. Strong's essay was initially presented as a lecture—to acclaim—at a conference in Leiden.

frenzies (Nietzsche mentions here, as he does elsewhere, the St John's—think of the midsummer leaps over the bonfires of southern France in their festival ceremonies—and St Vitus's dancers), Nietzsche emphasizes that the "ancient musical drama blossomed out of such an epidemic,"[104] all the while contending that the same intoxication turns out to be foreign from the then current cultural institution of the arts. Our art forms have, so Horkheimer and Adorno argue, hardly changed in the interim.

For Nietzsche, what is essential to note is the original identity between music and drama. Thus he reflects that "Absolute music and everyday drama" correspond at the original level to "the two parts of musical drama torn apart."[105]

As is well known, the argument of *The Birth of Tragedy* is an account less of the origination of the tragic art than its decay and ultimately its death. To underscore this, Nietzsche notes that what begins "as a preliminary stage of absolute music" only works as such because it is "one form within the total process"[106]—everything, everyone is involved. And to this same extent, everyone is an artist.

Importantly then, "[t]he Greek artist addresses his work not to the individual," and this also means not to the popular taste, not to the masses, but much rather to "the state and the education of the state, in its turn, was nothing but the education of all to enjoy the work of art."[107] Thus Nietzsche observes, making a point that Georgiades would later reprise in his studies of music and the mass:[108] "today the musical drama of antiquity has only a pale analogue in the union of the arts within the rite of the Catholic church."[109] But if one calls such a drama "a great work of music," it is at the same time utterly crucial to underline, as Nietzsche painstakingly does at the start of his notebook from Winter 1869, that:

> the music was never enjoyed as something absolute but always in connection with divine service, architecture, sculpture, and poetry. In short it was occasional music and the connecting dialogue served only to create occasions for the musical pieces each of which retained its distinctly occasional character.[110]

---

104   Nietzsche, KSA 7, 1 [1], 10.

105   Nietzsche, KSA 7, 1 [27], 17.

106   Nietzsche, KSA 7, 1 [49], 24.

107   Nietzsche, KSA 7, 7 [121], 168–9. Cf. Nicole Loraux, *The Mourning Voice: An Essay on Greek Tragedy*, trans. Elizabeth Trapnell Rawlings (Ithaca: Cornell University Press, 2002).

108   See, again, Thrasybulos Georgiades, *Music and Language: The Rise of Western Music as Exemplified in the Settings* [1974], trans. Marie Louise Göllner (Cambridge: Cambridge University Press, 1982), as well as Eduard Hanslick's 1861 review of "Beethoven's *Missa Solemnis*," in his *Music Criticisms: 1846–1899* (Baltimore: Penguin, 1950), 72–7.

109   Nietzsche, KSA 7, 3 [1], 57; cf. 1 [41], 22.

110   Nietzsche, KSA 7, 3 [1], 57.

Thus we may be tempted to imagine that the Greeks attended their tragic festivals, if not on the model of modern music concerts or summer festivals, then perhaps on the model of a country retreat and for pleasure, at least as medieval festivals, like the German mystery and morality plays, as Nietzsche himself makes just this comparison, and not unlike contemporary recreations of medieval fares. But he argues that such comparisons cannot hold, as he himself outlines for us: where the latter is, in the case of the German folk fest:

> more worldly, despite their subject matter. People came and went, there was no question of a beginning and an end, nobody wanted and nobody offered a whole. Conversely, when the Greeks watched they did so in a religious frame of mind: it was high mass, with the glorification of the god at the end which had to be waited for.[111]

And to the extent that the poet universalizes, so Nietzsche argues, the poet also takes a step towards absolute music. But what is different here is that it remains tied to a certain incontrovertible real—that is, as Nietzsche remarks, "the state in which a human being *sings* was taken as a yardstick."[112] But while what had been, up until Euripides, kept strictly side by side, "so that the world of the eye disappeared when that of the ear began and vice versa," the outcome following Euripides (and Socrates), via "the introduction of dialectics, the tone of the law court," effectively "dismembered ancient musical drama," with the result that "absolute music and family drama came into being."[113] Thus Nietzsche argues in the fall of 1869 that there is a good deal of complexity involved in the totality of the ancient work of musical art, precisely from the point of view of the whole, the ancient *Gesammtkunstwerk*. The point is important enough to cite at length:

> The pure succession is not what one wanted to *overlook*: e.g., a musical piece: it is a mistake to speak here of an architectonic of the entirety; and similarly in the case of drama. Where are the rules of succession? E.g., in the colors that reciprocally challenge one another, in the dissonance that requires resolution, in the wake of emotional currents.

> Seeming units, e.g., many symphonies. There are four parts, the basic character of which stamps out a template unity. One calls for a fiery allegro following a tender or sublime adagio, perhaps after a humoresque, and finally after a Bacchanal. Similarly, the contrasts are already to be had in the Nomos Pythios of the Sakadas.[114]

---

[111]   Ibid., 58.

[112]   Ibid.

[113]   Ibid.

[114]   This point and its comparison would not have been lost on McClain who is similarly interested in what he calls the "harmonical science" of the Bible, Babylonian tuning

> The will is expressed in the sequence, the simultaneous rests in contemplation, the juxtaposition of being ascribed to beholding.
>
> From whence the factual effort of the Greek dramatist toward unity? Especially as philosophy has as yet not made any demands for this?
>
> Wonderful era in which the arts have developed without the artist being confronted with ready-made theories of art![115]

Where, so Nietzsche tells us, Oedipus has quite mythically and precisely—as the product of incest—extraordinary and veritably *heroic*, quasi-divine characteristics, the key is that no qualities compensate, no circumstance allows one to sidestep destiny, even as Oedipus pits himself and himself alone contra the gods, destiny, *moira*. The same impossible conflict haunts the libation bearers, and what Agamemnon does brings doom upon himself, dying wrapped in a sheet in a bath, as Iphigenia was sacrificed similarly veiled in the face of the sea that her father meant to cross for his brother's sake. For the sake of her daughter, Clytemnestra cannot but make common cause with Aegisthus against her husband. And for the sake of his father, Orestes must take vengeance—on whom? On his mother, and he does, and only miraculous intervention stops the engine of destruction. The Greek seeks to collect himself, and thus Nietzsche argues that what resounds in tragedy is the "language of dissonance"—as we hear it from "the parents," that is Apollo and Dionysus, "echoing in the children ..."[116]

From Dionysus and Apollo to Nietzsche and Beethoven

Those who write on Nietzsche and tragedy as on music have tended, understandably enough, to privilege Dionysus. While there is no doubt that such readers suppose themselves to be drawing out Nietzsche's own preferences, Nietzsche himself took care to remind us that for us, precisely as moderns—here we should remember Nietzsche's fondness for Hölderlin, precisely as we find ourselves in an utterly foreign land vis-à-vis the Greeks—the challenge is not understanding Dionysus, which as a conceptual challenge happens not to be particularly difficult in any

---

systems, and what he calls Davidic musicology. See Ernest McClain, "A Priestly View of Bible Arithmetic: Deity's Regulative Aesthetic Activity within Davidic Musicology," in *Hermeneutic Philosophy of Science, Van Gogh's Eyes, and God*, ed. Babette Babich (Dordrecht: Kluwer Academic Publishers, 2002), 429–43; and also his *Meditations on the Quran* (York Beach, ME: Nicolas Hays, 1981).

[115]   Nietzsche, KSA 7, 1 [53], 25.
[116]   Nietzsche, HH I, §379.

Figure 10.3   Nicolas Poussin (1594–1665), *Midas and Bacchus*, 1629–30.
Munich, Bayerische Staatsgemäldesammlungen. Photo: bpk,
Berlin/Art Resource, NY.

event; much rather, the problem will be to understand Apollo himself in all his
alien complexities.[117]

Rather than foregrounding the distinctive juncture of the Dionysian, as if he
were an advocate of Euripides rather than his opponent (Nietzsche set Euripides
together with Socrates, and claims that tragedy meets its death, which is what makes
it a suicide, at Euripides's hand, meaning of course in his works), Nietzsche argues
instead—and it is this emphasis to which Loraux also calls attention, pointing as
she does to the precise significance, as I also have noted elsewhere, that Nietzsche
speaks not of originations, nor indeed even of development or genesis, but rather

---

[117]   On this theme there is a good deal more to be said, but for a start see, in a musical
context, the Wagnerian Martin Vogel, *Apollinisch und Dionysisch* (Regensburg: Gustav
Bosse Verlag, 1966). A further and more philological reference, if not specifically articulated
with respect to Nietzsche, may be found in Marcel Detienne, particularly his *Dionysos mis
à mort* (Paris: Gallimard, 1977), available in English as *Dionysos Slain*, and his *Dionysos
à ciel ouvert* (Paris: Hatchette, 2008). Most significant, however, and importantly bearing
out Nietzsche's emphasis here, see Detienne's *Apollon le couteau à la main. Une approche
expérimentale du polythéisme grec* [1998] (Paris: Gallimard, 2009).

Figure 10.4   Buonaventura Genelli (1798–1868), *Bacchus unter den Musen*,
1868. Dresden: Staatliche Kunstsammlungen, Kupferstich-Kabinett
C 1908-189. Photo: Roland Handrick, April 1962. Dresden: SLUB/
Deutsche Fotothek.

and very specifically of "birth"[118]—that tragedy is born from the seventh-century τραγικοὶ χοροί, the goat choruses and older traditions.

Thus, speaking of the oldest song festivals, "with the potent coming of spring that penetrates all nature,"[119] Nietzsche emphasizes that, "beneath" what he calls here "the charm of the Dionysian," there is not only a communal connection, reaffirming "the union between human being and human being," but a re-union with nature as well. And we recall both Hölderlin and Schiller as well as Goethe when Nietzsche writes: "Freely the earth proffers her gifts, and peacefully the beasts of prey of the rocks and the desert approach."[120] The Arcadian image in question is one of the most celebrated (with all its overtones of union in difference) in depictions of art (Fig. 10.3).

In addition to its manifestations in Schiller, this is also the central theme of Hölderlin's poetry, and we note that Poussin paints Bacchus and Pan as well as Midas, where what is crucial is the calm of the animals in the case of Midas, and Nietzsche found a common theme for discussion when he visited Tribschen,

---

[118]   Loraux, *The Mourning Voice*, 54.
[119]   Nietzsche, BT, §1.
[120]   Ibid.

Figure 10.5   Nicolas Poussin (1594–1665), *A Bacchanalian Revel before a Term*, 1632–33. Photo: © National Gallery, London/Art Resource, NY.

where Wagner displayed a Genelli tapestry (Fig. 10.4) of the same kind of oneness and communion.[121]

Much of what I am saying here points to a *reciprocity* of influence or affinity between Nietzsche and Wagner, whatever it was that first made them friends, a sense of which reciprocity is overlooked in our modern passion for proving intellectual priority, championing either Nietzsche or Wagner, as if shared ideas and their genial exchange were a matter of somehow unique "originality" or demonstrable "copyright."

For Nietzsche—especially as he will go on to emphasize the central importance in these collective festivals of "extravagant sexual licentiousness, whose waves overwhelmed all family life and its venerable traditions" (cf. Fig. 10.5), indeed and not less as he adds, "even that horrible mixture of sensuality and cruelty which has

---

[121]   See Siegfried Mandel, "Genelli and Wagner: Midwives to Nietzsche's The Birth of Tragedy," *Nietzsche-Studien* 19 (1990): 212–25, as well as, for a specific discussion, Dieter Jähnig, "Emancipating the Knowledge of Art from Metaphysics in the Birth of Tragedy," trans. Babette Babich and Holger Schmid, *New Nietzsche Studies* 4/1 & 2 (Summer/Fall 2000): 77–121, and, more generally, Peter Durno Murray, *Nietzsche's Affirmative Morality: A Revaluation Based in the Dionysian World* (Berlin: de Gruyter, 1999), 9.

Figure 10.6   Dionysiac procession, British Museum, about 100 CE, Rome,
Roman Empire. Photo: ArtResource.

always seemed to me to be the real 'witches brew,'"[122]—what ultimately matters
as he highlights this sensual cruelty—in a *musical* move that we have already
observed would not have surprised Ernest McClain, given his own decidedly
more esoteric researches in musical notation—reflects "the Dionysian orgies of
the Greeks, as compared with the Babylonian Sacaea with their reversion of man
to the tiger and the ape, of the significance of festivals of world redemption and
days of transfiguration."[123]

Continuing this classically dark reference with his central claim beginning from
such festivals of world redemption, Nietzsche underlines that it is only with such
festivals "that nature for the first time attains her artistic jubilee; it is with them
that the destruction of the *principium individuationis* for the first time becomes an
artistic phenomenon."[124] Here, the ultimate festive and transfiguring illustration
is Beethoven's musical transposition of Schiller's "Ode to Joy," a setting that, as
Nietzsche earlier declared, first truly gave voice in musical resonance to what the
poet had only provisionally expressed.

---

[122]   Nietzsche, BT, §2.

[123]   Ibid. Of course this is also the central theme of Strong's *Nietzsche and the Politics
of Transfiguration.*

[124]   Nietzsche, BT, §2.

Schiller's *Hymn to Joy* first attains in this way its deeper, genuinely artistic background. We see how the poet attempts to explicate the Germanic depths of this profoundly Dionysian excitement: which he however, as a modern human being, can only stammer with great difficulty. If Beethoven now presents before us the true Schillerian depths, what we thus have is the infinitely higher and more perfect.[125]

This point recurs in Nietzsche's published remark:

> ... Beethoven is the intermediary between an old mellow soul that is constantly crumbling and a future over-young soul that is constantly *arriving*; upon his music there lies that twilight of eternal loss and eternal extravagant hope—the same light in which Europe lay bathed when it dreamed with Rousseau, when it danced around the Revolution's Tree of Liberty and finally almost worshipped before Napoleon. But how quickly *this* feeling is now fading away, how hard it is today even to *know* of this feeling—how strange to our ears sounds the language of Rousseau, Schiller, Shelley, Byron, in whom *together* the same European destiny that in Beethoven knew how to sing found its way into words![126]

Note that there is no question here, for Nietzsche, of Beethoven's ode functioning as an ode to freedom, not if this destiny is to find its way into song. This is not because Nietzsche had some antipathy to the ideal of liberty; hardly so: this is the French Revolution (and its particular Tree of Liberty), together with the Hegelian allusion to the majesty of the world spirit in the person of Napoleon.[127]

Much rather the point here is that a specific word is needed because a specific tone is needed, that is the Hölderlinian effort to speak out the essence of joy, *das freudigste, freudigst zu sagen*, clearly heard in tragedy. And what is key here is that the needed word is *Freude*. The contrast here with Schopenhauer brings to aesthetics what Nietzsche would already find in an ethical mode in Anaximander in his *Philosophy in the Tragic Age of the Greeks*. And indeed he goes on to replicate this contrast between aesthetics or feeling or pathos and ethos in his own words, once again with reference to Beethoven, and echoing here at the start the point that Hoffmann makes in contrast to the means hithertofore at music's disposal in opera with Beethoven. For Nietzsche too:

---

[125] "We see how the poet, seeking to interpret his deep Germanic Dionysian impulse in images that as a modern man he only barely knows how to stammer. If Beethoven now represents what is actually Schiller's underground, we thus have the infinitely-higher and more perfect." Nietzsche's posthumous notes, ca. 1871.

[126] Nietzsche, BGE, §245.

[127] See here, for a broader context, and also with reference to Adorno on this theme, Rose Rosengard Subotnik, "The Historical Structure: Adorno's 'French' Model for the Criticism of Nineteenth-Century Music," *19th Century Music* 2 (July 1978): 36–60.

> Beethoven was the first to allow music to speak a new language, the formerly
> forbidden language of passion ... Thus it almost seemed as if Beethoven had
> set for himself the contradictory task of allowing pathos to be expressed via the
> means of ethos.[128]

And Nietzsche makes the contrast with Wagner explicit by way of an allusion to
Wagner, as indeed to Schopenhauer's own very musical aesthetics:

> Entirely withdrawing into himself from this world the musician is thus, as
> Wagner has described it with reference to Beethoven, very nearly in the sphere
> of holiness: the incomparable purity, emotional lustre of childlike immediacy,
> utterly lacking pretense, the absence of conventionality all belongs to music,
> not the other arts, which stand precisely too close to the phenomenal world as
> images.[129]

This echoes Hoffmann's declaration of the absolute in music in his famous review,
arguing that, as the magic power of music grows stronger, it cannot but shatter—
here there is an allusion to what Nietzsche calls for with regard to Lessing as to
the new Laocoon—every bond to the other arts.[130] For Nietzsche too, arguing as
was his wont that this discovery was already to be found in Wagner in light of
their common reference to Schopenhauer (where the contradiction between what
Nietzsche says here and what Wagner does is fairly plain, a plainness Nietzsche
will later make explicit in his *Nietzsche contra Wagner*):

> Herewith, it would seem that the juxtaposition of music now with the phenomenal
> world must simply be a monstrosity that would be their very incompatibility.
> Here Wagner made his second discovery, once again this was the problem of
> drama. The human being who has taken the soul of music into himself and on
> the basis of this fullness regards the general nature and the fate of humanity
> at all times, not with disgust and hatred: but as Beethoven saw the nature
> of the *Pastorale*: with love, with all understanding compassion. In the great
> representations of human will, he sees the nature of his own volition, only with

---

[128]   See Nietzsche, KSA 1, "Schopenhauer as Educator," §9 vii.

[129]   Ibid.

[130]   To put this in context, as it includes a specific reference to opera, it is worth citing
E.T.A. Hoffmann here: "In dem Gesange, wo die Poesie bestimmte Affekte durch Worte
andeutet, wirkt die magische Kraft der Musik wie das wunderbare Elixier der Weisen, von
dem etliche Tropfen jeden Trank köstlicher und herrlicher machen. Jede Leidenschaft—
Liebe—Haß—Zorn—Verzweiflung etc., wie die Oper sie uns gibt, kleidet die Musik in den
Purpurschimmer der Romantik, und selbst das im Leben Empfundene führt uns hinaus aus
dem Leben in das Reich des Unendlichen. So stark ist der Zauber der Musik, und, immer
mächtiger werdend, mußte er jede Fessel einer andern Kunst zerreißen." From Hoffmann,
"Beethovens Instrumentalmusik."

delusions and false targets before him so that he can anticipate the tragic end of the individual will.[131]

We may profitably read this with reference to Schopenhauer, as Nietzsche's reference to the will also makes plain:

> ... It is the most awful antidote against unusual people, driving them deep into themselves such that their recovery emerges each time as a volcanic eruption. But there is occasionally a demi-god, who can bear to live under such terrible conditions, to live in victory, and if you wish to hear his lonely songs, you will be listening to Beethoven's music.[132]

Here Nietzsche also traces what can seem to be his sharpest musical critique of Wagner on behalf of and by way of Beethoven:

> For Wagner the mistake in the artistic genre of opera is that a *means of expression*, the music, qua end, the purpose of the expression, was made into a means.
>
> Thus music counted for him as a means of expression—very characteristic of the actor. Now one would be asked in a symphony: if the music is a *means of expression* here, what would be the purpose? It cannot lie in the music, as what is essentially a means of expression, now requires something it must express. For Wagner, this is the drama. Without this, music alone would be for him an absurdity: it raises the question "why all this noise?" Consequently he regarded Beethoven's 9th Symphony as Beethoven's actual achievement, because by the inclusion of the word here Beethoven gave music its meaning, as means of expression. Means and ends—music and drama—older teaching. *General* and *Example*—music and drama—newer teaching.[133]

So far, Nietzsche on Wagner. Here we are ready to return to Nietzsche's first book, indeed in the very first section of this first book, given these previous reflections and the context provided, as they offer us a vision of what can otherwise seem to be an impossible fantasy of such a union of all with all:

> Transform Beethoven's song of joy into a painting; let your imagination conceive the multitudes bowing to the dust, awestruck—then you will approach the Dionysian. Now the slave is a free human being; now all the rigid, hostile, barriers that necessity, caprice, or "crude convention" ["*Freche Mode*"] have fixed between human and human are shattered. Now, with the gospel of universal

---

[131] Nietzsche, KSA 8, 12 [24], 263.
[132] Nietzsche, KSA 1, "Schopenhauer as Educator," §3, 355.
[133] Nietzsche, KSA 7, 32 [52], 770.

harmony, each one feels himself not only united, reconciled, and joined with his neighbor but as one with him ...[134]

This is Nietzsche at the start of *The Birth of Tragedy*, and what he then expresses at the end of *The Birth of Tragedy*, as what we have now constantly been citing as the "becoming-human of dissonance,"[135] turns out to have already been anticipated from the first section of his text with a clear reference to Beethoven, as this first section concludes by citing Schiller's poem in a Plotinian modality, as Nietzsche always emphasizes that this is Beethoven's musical transposition of Schiller's words, in this moment of utter transfiguration:

> The noblest clay, the costliest marble, the human being, is here kneaded and hewn, and to the sounds of the chisel strokes of the Dionysian world artist rings out the cry of the Eleusinian mysteries, "Do you prostrate yourselves, millions? Do you sense your maker, world?"[136]

The point for Nietzsche is that the music cannot but go missing for us today, but the achievement that he thinks he has uncovered in the ancient tragic musical artwork is what he names the "Dionysian content of music,"[137] all for the sake of getting "some notion of the way in which the strophic folk song originates, and the whole linguistic activity is excited by this new principle of the imitation of music."[138]

Writing in an ecstatic mode that also corresponds to the Schopenhauerian insight into the nature of the will, Nietzsche reflects that for Schopenhauer, as for the Greeks, "Pain, contradiction is true being, pleasure, harmony is appearance"[139]

In this dissonant way, as Nietzsche emphasizes and as we already noted above, much rather than the Dionysian, *what cannot but* be "hard for us to understand is the Apollonian ..."[140] What is key, and this may be heard in the previous emphasis upon Cohen's "cold and broken Hallelujah," it is also for Nietzsche "the *suffering that resounds*, as opposed to the acting of the epic: the 'picture' of Apollonian culture

---

[134]   Nietzsche, BT, §1.

[135]   Ibid., §24.

[136]   Ibid., §1.

[137]   Ibid., §6.

[138]   Ibid. And here, again, I refer to Robert Fink's above cited email to me concerning the dynamic of Leonard Cohen's *Hallelujah* precisely as such a "strophic song," as well as his *Repeating Ourselves*. Indeed, the earlier discussions of other performances or covers of Cohen's songs also illustrate the way in which musical styling renders strophic song as such. And to be sure, George Plasketes, *Play It Again: Cover Songs in Popular Music* (Farnham: Ashgate, 2010) refers to Cohen in his own direct invocation of Fink's "culture of the copy" in this context (see here 142). Although Plasketes's reading is in line with Bennett's recording consciousness, he does not cite Bennett.

[139]   Nietzsche, KSA 7, 9 [10], 275.

[140]   Ibid.

is presented by the human via enchantment."[141] What "we call 'tragic' is precisely the Apollonian clarification [*Verdeutlichung*] of the Dionysian."[142] The point Nietzsche makes here is an expressly, explicitly compositional and musical one; in this way he can continue to reflect on "dissonance and consonance in music— we may say that a chord *suffers* through a false note."[143] The key is dissonance: "The *pain*, the *contradiction* is the *true being* [*wahrhafte Sein*]. The *pleasure*, the *harmony* is the illusion."[144] In his *Aesthetic Theory*, here manifestly indebted to Nietzsche, Adorno writes that "dissonance, the seal of everything modern, gives access to the alluringly sensuous by transfiguring it into its antithesis, pain."[145]

The tragic artwork illustrates or adumbrates this for those who participated in the cult of which Nietzsche writes in his book on tragedy. Tragedy or music drama for the Greeks was exactly not a night at the theater (or opera). Much rather, the work of ancient musical *techné* was a cultic occasion or happening, as distant as can possibly be envisioned from the notion of *l'art pour l'art*, which cultural preoccupation (with the artist, the genius, the actor, today we add the popstar) Nietzsche never tired of regarding as utter decadence. Thus the tragic work of art dramatized nothing other than the "earthly resolution of tragic dissonance."[146] This is an important but difficult point—for by arguing on behalf of a musical resolution, Nietzsche is precisely not arguing on behalf of an "earthly" resolution, nor indeed for that matter (and whatever that might mean), a "heavenly" one.

Nietzsche argued that ancient Greek musical drama is impossible for us to comprehend to the degree to which we have distinct spheres, because we have culture as such, because we educate ourselves to the possibility of acquiring a certain cultivation, cultivating ourselves as cultured beings. By contrast, Nietzsche writes, as we cite once again: "The Greek artist did not direct himself to the individual public with his artwork but to the state; and conversely the education of the state was nothing but the education of everyone for the enjoyment of the work of art."[147]

Thus Nietzsche, who always writes, as Heidegger writes (but also as Kant and Schopenhauer and Hume had written), against the Roman conventional simplicity of any *adequatio intellectus et rei*, challenges the Grecophiles of his age who praised the notion of an ideal "harmony," that is to say, without recognizing the compulsion that stood behind this harmonic drive for the ancients, without acknowledging the indispensability of "a background illumination of terror."[148]

---

[141] Ibid.

[142] Nietzsche, KSA 7, 7 [128], 192.

[143] Nietzsche, KSA 7 [165], 202.

[144] Ibid., 203.

[145] Theodor Adorno, *Aesthetic Theory*, ed. Gretel Adorno and Rolf Tiedemann, trans. Robert Hullot-Kentor (Minneapolis: University of Minnesota Press, 1997), 15.

[146] Nietzsche, BT, §17.

[147] Nietzsche, KSA 7, 7 [90], 159.

[148] Ibid.

In this sense, when Nietzsche writes as he does about dance for the ancients, he writes about a kind of dance, this he will later speak of as "dancing in chains," here expressed as Apollonian: as betrayed by the lithe sensuousity of the "dance where great power is only potential … thus Greek [tragedies] are externally a beautiful dance. In this sense, they are a triumph of nature that has here come to beauty."[149]

Nietzsche's main question when it came to his first book, as he writes with regard to the "birth" of the tragic art form, bearing as it does on the meaning and role of the lyric poet, on the meaning and role of the chorus, on the relation between Apollo and Dionysus, as we have already implied that this is a far from simple question between Apollo and Dionysus and the very broad question that he named "the science of aesthetics" as such,[150] concerned tragedy per se. And in the same way he raises the question of the concrescence of harmony, of consonance as such: *"Wodurch entsteht ein schoner Akkord?"*[151]

If it is true that Nietzsche means this question quite practically, that is, in terms of his own musical ambitions, this hardly precludes his more theoretical reflections on just this question. Here we note his aesthetic observation that there is, at least in nature, and here he quite conventionally follows Kant, "No such thing as natural beauty, there is much rather the disturbingly ugly and a point of indifference. Think about the reality of dissonance as opposed to the ideality of consonance."[152]

In this sense he argues that "beauty has no share whatever in the domain of music," a point he can make purely formally and purely in terms of his discovery of the musical character of the articulation of ancient Greek: "Rhythm and harmony are the main parts, the melody is only an abbreviation of the harmony,"[153] and this is the coincidence of pathos and music. Like the dissonant chord in music, "it is pain that is productive," that is, it is pain "which as a related counter-color engenders the beautiful," always—and note the musical allusion here—"from an indifferent point."[154]

Hence, for Nietzsche, and we can keep Seyfried's Beethoven's own compositional notes in mind here, the "direction of art is thus towards overcoming dissonance. The drive internal to the world of the beautiful is born of an indifferent point."[155] In this way, referring to an indifferent point, that can, like science, like art, go either way, Nietzsche can identify "dissonance," tracing it as it is drawn into the work of art. And to vary Adorno's question/suggestion, "what can one

---

[149]   Nietzsche, KSA 7, 7 [94], 159.

[150]   Nietzsche, BT, §1.

[151]   Nietzsche, KSA 7, 7 [46], 149.

[152]   Nietzsche, KSA 7, 7 [116], 164.

[153]   Nietzsche, KSA 7, 3 [54], 75.

[154]   Ibid. Thus as we have seen, Adorno writes that: "There is more joy in dissonance than in consonance: This metes out justice, eye for eye, to hedonism." *Aesthetic Theory*, 40.

[155]   Nietzsche, KSA 7, 3 [54], 75.

learn from Schönberg about Beethoven?"[156] as Schoenberg for his own part will later speak of him;[157] for Nietzsche, "the gradual enjoyment of the minor tone and dissonance means the representation of madness, beyond representation on the grounds that a painless contemplation of things is brought forth."[158]

"Music," as Nietzsche also argues, here like Adorno and like Schopenhauer, is what shows or proves or "demonstrates to us that the entire world, in its multiplicity, is no longer felt as *dissonance*."[159] Here and throughout, my point has been that in all this, Nietzsche's example in *The Birth of Tragedy* is Beethoven. If in his unpublished notes Nietzsche focuses on the issue of individuation, reflecting that individuation is the "*result* of suffering, not its cause,"[160] he makes a similar claim in his published *The Birth of Tragedy*, focusing as he does on Beethoven's choral ode in the Ninth Symphony.

As Nietzsche goes on to reflect, with this specific example in mind, "After these premises, imagine what an unnatural, indeed impossible enterprise it must be to compose music *for* a poem."[161] Thus Wagner also wrote his own lyrics. Thus regarded, Beethoven's achievement would be the composer's achievement of setting, transposing, and revising Schiller's poem to music in his Ninth Symphony. In this way, Beethoven was able to use Schiller's words *as music*, precisely as Nietzsche argues. The challenge of such a project, as Nietzsche puts it, is "like that of a son trying to beget his father,"[162] and we note that exactly such a genesis will be a personal project, or at least a recommendation, for Nietzsche in his own later writings. Here, however, what is crucial is that Nietzsche's example, a not incidentally Kantian counter-example (that is to say, whatever is actual is also possible), corresponds to the very actuality of Beethoven: reminding us that Beethoven's images "are no more than sheerly allegorical representations."[163]

What opera wants, as Nietzsche suggests here at this early stage, may be compared to the Münchhausenesque image of a "ridiculous man who tries to lift himself into the air by his own arms"[164]—if opera has ambitions to "press music into the service of a number of images as concepts, using it as a means to an end,"[165] then for Nietzsche this can only be a similarly Münchhausenesque project. "Music," Nietzsche writes, "can never become a means to an end."[166]

---

[156] Adorno, *Towards a Theory of Musical Reproduction*, 91.

[157] See Arnold Schoenberg, *Theory of Harmony 100th Anniversary Edition*, trans. Roy E. Carter (Berkeley: University of California Press, 2010).

[158] Nietzsche, KSA 7, 7 [117], 166.

[159] Ibid.

[160] Ibid.

[161] Nietzsche, KSA 7, 7 [127], 185. Emphasis added.

[162] Ibid., 363. This is an Aristotelian allusion.

[163] Ibid.

[164] Ibid.

[165] Ibid.

[166] Ibid.

Thus "at its best," and perhaps at times, one can be forgiven for supposing, in spite of itself, that opera "is indeed good music and only music."[167] At the very least, as we now see, and as Wagnerians will not be surprised to discover, Nietzsche here expresses a certain ambivalence toward opera—just as Wagner himself distinguished his own work from others, but also arguably and even at this point contra Wagner.

Nietzsche observes in a note on the relation between language and music and "mime and music"[168] that there is more going on in that intrinsically impossible undertaking, as he writes when "a musician composes a song based on a poem"[169] and that that "more" (or what some literary commentators once called a supplement) corresponds to a specifically *musical* impulse, here to be heard in Nietzsche's case in a Greek sense, as Georgiades uses the term *mousiké*, as we have seen above, and one that thus "chooses the text of that song as an expression of itself."[170]

Thus Nietzsche argues that "Beethoven's last quartets, for example, entirely put to shame any intuitive perception and indeed the whole realm of empirical reality."[171] But the real argument, as Nietzsche continues to develop it, is all about what Beethoven achieves in the Ninth Symphony, writing as Nietzsche does in his best courtly mode:

> We hope it will not be taken amiss if ... we include in our reflections the tremendous and inexplicably magical last movement of Beethoven's Ninth Symphony ... That Schiller's poem 'To Joy' is totally incongruent with this music's dithyrambic jubilation over the redemption of the world and is drowned like pale moonlight by that ocean of flames—who would want to rob me of this most certain feeling?[172]

If part of what Nietzsche says here sounds a little like McClary herself on Beethoven, and if another part of what Nietzsche says, not all that remarkably, also echoes Adorno's beer hall reflections on Schiller,[173] the point of Nietzsche's

---

[167]   Ibid.

[168]   Nietzsche, KSA 7, 12 [1], 359.

[169]   Ibid.

[170]   Ibid.

[171]   Ibid.

[172]   Ibid., 366; cf. Nietzsche, BT, §1.

[173]   Theodor Adorno, *Minima Moralia: Reflections From Damaged Life* [1947], trans. E.F. Jephcott (London: Verso, 1996), §53, 88. I have already cited many of those who read Beethoven and Adorno, be it against Adorno or through him; see, for a recent discussion engaging the theoretical concerns of both Adorno and Horkheimer and the "totalitarian" undercurrents in Schiller, Nicholas Vaszonyi, "Hegemony through Harmony: German Identity, Music, and Enlightenment Around 1800," in *Sound Matters: Essays on the Acoustics of German Culture*, ed. Nora M. Alter (Oxford: Berghahn, 2004), 33–48, here esp. 40ff.

argument is not so much to emphasize the ecstatico-erotic violence of "this music's dithyrambic jubilation," or indeed to discuss the contrasts of the contours of this sound with his favored metaphor of light ("like pale moonlight," "oceans of flame"),[174] but much rather to contend in the spirit of his first book that when Beethoven includes the human voice among the instruments that he deploys for his symphony, he does so by treating the voice as a musical instrument among others. Hence, as Nietzsche reflects in an extended note on "the relation of language to music,"[175] and including what he calls "the pure language of tones [*Sprache der Töne*],"[176] the musician and the poet operate in different spheres apart from this same language. The point here has to do with sound and meaning as exemplified in "the last movement of Beethoven's Ninth Symphony."[177] It is precisely where, as Nietzsche says, the "dithyrambic world-redeeming jubilation of this music is utterly incongruent with Schiller's poem 'To Joy'"[178] that it is manifest that Beethoven has transposed the poet's words into nothing other than that same "language of tones" with which Nietzsche began his reflections. Thus he is able to make the claim that "the only reason why this feeling upon listening to that music fails to cry out when we listen to it is precisely that we have been dispossessed for image and word by the music and already *hear absolutely nothing of Schiller's poem at all*?"[179]

By means of this claim, Nietzsche recollects the substance of his earlier theoretical, classicist's reflections on the relation between music and word, and that is here the pitch, or in this case the tone, as "Beethoven himself says to us as he introduces the chorale through a recitative 'O friends, not these tones! Let us raise our voices in more pleasing and more joyful sounds!'"[180] Nietzsche's purpose here is to emphasize that the tones are what counts as "More pleasing and more joyful!"[181] Thus the point is that what is needed is another instrument, another *sound*, another tone, in this case voice, and in this case the sound of joy, namely *Freude*. In this sense, we may add here, despite his independence, that is in spite of his exceptional genius as such, that Beethoven never outgrew this one lesson from Haydn. Thus Beethoven, whom we have already cited as a listener to music in all its forms as Nietzsche puts it, already had at his disposal what was required when what was needed was the "innocent air of the folk song. The sublime master, in his longing for the most soulful collective sonority of his orchestra, reached not

---

[174] Nietzsche, KSA 7, 12 [1]. See again, for my discussion of Nietzsche's use of synaesthetic metaphor, Babette Babich, "Between Hölderlin and Heidegger: Nietzsche's Transfiguration of Philosophy," *Nietzsche-Studien* 29 (2000): 267–301.

[175] Nietzsche, KSA 7, 12 [1], 366.

[176] Ibid.

[177] Ibid.

[178] Ibid.

[179] Ibid.

[180] Ibid., 367.

[181] Ibid.

for the word but for the 'more pleasing' sound, not for the concept but for the most intimately joyful tone."[182]

In this way, Nietzsche is able to argue that it is Beethoven indeed who brings us—as I have been arguing in a different way that listening to k.d. lang can also take us some way in the same direction, if, to be sure, to a different end—*closer* to an understanding of the ancient tragic musical work of art. Hence, for Nietzsche:

> What we observed in the last movement of the Ninth, that is, on the highest peaks of modern musical development—that the verbal content is drowned unheard in the universal ocean of sound—is nothing unique or strange. But the universal and eternally valid norm of the vocal music of all ages, which alone corresponds to the origin of lyrical song. Neither the man in a state of Dionysian arousal nor the orgiastic crowd require a listener to whom they have something to communicate.[183]

There is, in this important sense, no audience per se in this Greek antiquity.

The same Nietzsche who writes "there is no outside" when he speaks of the will that finds its immediate expression in Schopenhauer (and thus no mediation, no distinction from any representative art "before"—as Nietzsche highlights this contrast—"witnesses") also means this perfectly literally. There is no "spectator" as such in the case of Greek art, which is also the reason that Nietzsche continually emphasizes what he calls the cult status of tragedy in *The Birth of Tragedy*, highlighting their rare periodic quality, with, as he says, protracted intervals between festival events, and the "entirety in harmony and resonance with the folk religion, with the priesthood,"[184] and pointing out—perhaps the sharpest contrast with modern musical theatre, especially Wagner's opera—that "no monetary advantage was expected for the poet,"[185] as one can also argue that the Greeks even lacked a word for art per se.[186] Nietzsche's further remark that "decent women were excluded" from ancient Greek theater also reflects Nietzsche's important distinction between what he calls a "masculine" and a "feminine" aesthetics (unfortunate as this terminology may be, as

---

[182]   Ibid.

[183]   Ibid.

[184]   KSA 7, 1 [76], 34.

[185]   Ibid.

[186]   Thus Ernst Hans Gombrich emphasizes the dangers of historical "presentism," echoing Nietzsche and Heidegger, and here specifically the classical historian H.D.F. Kitto as he does so, that it is "always risky to assume that the ancient Greeks operated with the same concepts of religion, science and art as we do. They had no word for art ..." Gombrich, *The Image and the Eye: Further Studies in the Psychology of Pictorial Representation* (London: Phaidon, 1982), 218. Again, Gombrich observes (like Heidegger), in his encyclopedia article "Kunstliteratur," *Atlantisbuch der Kunst: eine Enzyklopädie der bildenden Künste* (Zurich: Atlantis Verlag, 1952), 665–79, "the concept of art was alien to antiquity and both the Greek *techne* and the Latin *ars* referred to 'any form of skill.'" Here 667.

only the former is a creator's or subject's aesthetics, where the latter is an aesthetics, as it were, before witnesses). It is thus, as I have argued, no accident that Nietzsche examines the problem of the artist, and we have already seen that this is Nietzsche's word for Wagner, in terms of the histrionic, that is to say, in terms of the problem of the actor, the woman, the Jew.[187]

For Nietzsche, regarded from the perspective of the creative artist, "art" has a melancholy aspect, as we already noted Matthew Arnold's *Dover Beach*, reflecting on the musical pathos of the Aegean, "Sophocles heard it long ago," and as Nietzsche writes in *Human, All-too-Human*, in the section entitled *The Souls of Artists and Writers*:

> *Art makes the thinker's heart heavy*—How strong the metaphysical need is and how hard nature makes it to bid it a final farewell, can be seen from the fact that even when the free spirit has divested itself of everything metaphysical the highest effects of art can easily set the metaphysical strings, which have long been silent or indeed snapped apart, vibrating in sympathy; so it can happen, for example, that a passage in Beethoven's Ninth Symphony will make him feel he is hovering above the earth in a dome of stars with the dream of *immortality* in his heart; all the stars seem to glitter around him and the earth seems to sink farther and farther away.[188]

For Nietzsche, and this is perhaps why his elitism remains insuperable, "the ecstatic servant of Dionysus is … understood only by his own kind."[189] Hence, as Heidegger writes of the lark, as Angelus Silesius, the Cherubinic Wanderer, gives us the rose to which Nietzsche also refers, the "lyric poet" here "sings 'as the bird sings,' alone, out of an innermost need and would fall silent if the listener confronts him with any demands …"[190]

The demand in question is the demand for comprehensibility and Nietzsche identifies this as the very specific "spirit of science," as this is the force of his argument against Euripides's fatal impulse and achievement, which he characterizes as articulating a "*Socratic aesthetics*," as expressed in the formula "Everything must be understandable in order to be beautiful."[191] This can seem a mere metaphor, but in this context Nietzsche takes some pains to make it clear that he means it literally, and later in his first book, he offers the following analogy:

> To the listener who desires to hear the word clearly under the singing, corresponds the singer who speaks more than sings and intensifies the expressions of pathos

---

[187]   See here Babich, "Nietzsche's Erotic Artist as Actor/Jew/Woman," in *Words in Blood, Like Flowers*, 147ff.

[188]   Nietzsche, HH, I, §153.

[189]   Ibid.

[190]   Ibid.

[191]   Nietzsche, BT, §12.

in this half-singing. By this intensification of pathos he renders the words easier to understand and overpowers that part of the music which remains. Yet the real danger that threatens here is that at any inopportune moment the major emphasis may be given to the music, such that the pathos in the speech and clarity of the words necessarily vanish immediately.[192]

Herewith we also find a different understanding of Nietzsche's reflections on Aristotle as he offers these critical reservations in *The Birth of Tragedy*, as indeed his reflections on the "role" of the chorus, and we also gain for the first time a new perspective on Nietzsche's citations from Schiller or, better said, from Beethoven's transposition: *Seid umschlungen*, he writes, *erkennst du deinen Schöpfer, Welt?* Above all, Nietzsche also foregrounds the significance of an entire community in harmony, as a harmony in every conventional sense, describing the "Greek chorus" in a serial fashion: "Once as living sounding board, thence as the sounding pipe through which the actor's sentiments were colossally conveyed to the viewers, thirdly, the coming to voice of the lyrically pitched passionately singing spectator."[193] The reference is to Schlegel's notion of the chorus as ideal spectator, as Nietzsche describes the various theoretical functions of the chorus. Here, Nietzsche seems to highlight the resonant acoustics of the chorus, however interpreted. The focus in Nietzsche's later reflections, *Diesen Kuss der ganzen Welt!* in Beethoven's phrasing of Schiller's line, also permits us to recall that Nietzsche had earlier deployed the same resonance or phrasing in his gloss of Empedocles, the philosopher and rhetorician, "'Liebe und Kuss den ganzen Welt'."[194]

If some have heard in Nietzsche's criticisms a strong parallel to the famous tale of Schumann repeating a piece he had played as a response to a request to explain its meaning, in the eternally told tale of musical ineffability, what is at issue for Nietzsche is not ineffability. As he argues:

> No one should ask himself whether, with the poems of the great ancient lyric poets in hand, these poets could have had any idea of making their images and thoughts clearer to the listening crowd around them: and one should answer this serious question with Pindar and the Aeschylean choral songs in mind.

---

[192]   Nietzsche, BT, §19.

[193]   Nietzsche, KSA 7, 1 [40], 20. Cf. Nietzsche's lecture, "The Greek Music Drama," for a description of the heavily padded actor and the immense mask through which the actor had "to speak and sing in the strongest tones in order to be understood by a mass of spectators of more than 20,000 human beings." *Das griechische Musikdrama*, KGW III/2, 10.

[194]   Nietzsche, KGW III/4, 21 [22], 122. I discuss this in Babette Babich, "Nietzsche's Zarathustra, Nietzsche's Empedocles: The Time of Kings," in *Becoming Loyal to the Earth: Nietzsche's Teaching as a Therapy for Political Culture*, ed. Eli Friedlander and Horst Hutter (London: Continuum, 2013). See, too, Babette Babich, "The Philosopher and the Volcano," *Philosophy Today* 36 (Summer 2011), 213–31.

These boldest and darkest knots of thought, this swirl of images tempestuously born and reborn, this oracular tone of the whole, which we are so often unable to penetrate, even with the most concentrated attention and without being distracted by music and dance—should this whole world of miracles have been as transparent as glass to the Greek mass, an interpretation of music in fact, by way of images and concepts? And with such mysteries of thought as are found in Pindar, would this wondrous poet have wanted to make music, so powerfully clear in itself, yet clearer?[195]

Nietzsche invites us to reflect on our lived or felt experience of music. But this call to reflect on our own experience is not an invocation of the listener's or the spectator's rational comprehension, nor is it even a matter of the literal understanding of the words as such, just to the extent that, as it turns out, it is not about the listener at all.

For this reason, what is at issue is not a matter of communication, in part because the audience already knows what is said, but also because what is at issue is all about speaking and singing well, in face of "a public that obdurately penalized every excess in pitch, every incorrect accent."[196] Nietzsche's example here, in the vision he gives us of ancient Greece, of the lyric poet singing his hymn, the masked actor engaging the audience attuned to the tonality of his every word, suggests, here not unlike the high mass of his earlier reference, that what is at stake is nothing other than "the people singing the folk song, for themselves," and here we can and should think of Beethoven's Ninth Symphony and its "Chorale," as Nietzsche also invokes this in his Fragment, *Music and Word*,[197] for the sake of the people who are singing, "as the lyricist sings his hymn" (and this parallel is at the heart of his continued reference to folksong). The people singing the folksong sing as they do "out of an inner urge, *without caring whether the words are intelligible to anyone* who does not join in the singing."[198]

In this way, Nietzsche's argument is that, like the ancient Greek experience of the lyric poet, of tragic musical drama, we ourselves have our own experience, and here indeed, arguably, his reference includes a classical reference to *Hallelujah*; and here, as I read the cadence of the examples he gives, this would likely be nothing other than Handel's *Hallelujah Chorus*. For Nietzsche's point is that if:

We think of our experience with music of the higher artistic kind: how much would we understand of the text of a mass by Palestrina, of a cantata by Bach,

---

[195]   Nietzsche, KGW III/3, 387.

[196]   Nietzsche, *Das griechische Musikdrama*, KGW III/2, 10.

[197]   Nietzsche, KGW III/3, 386–7.

[198]   Ibid., 387. See, further, Tracy B. Strong's extraordinary discussion of Rousseau and music, indeed folk music as the literally community-building music of the people, in this case the people of Geneva, in Strong, *Jean-Jacques Rousseau: The Politics of the Ordinary* (Lanham, MA: Rowman & Littlefield, 2002), xxvii, 4–8.

of an oratorio by Handel, if we ourselves did not sing them? Only for those who
join in the singing, is there a lyric, is there vocal music …[199]

The (polemical) point for Nietzsche is that singing such a song, the point of such
a singing, entails that the music that the singer sings is different from the music
that the listener hears, who is by contrast offered the prospect of nothing less than
"absolute music."[200]

It is all a matter of joining in the song—and it *really* doesn't matter which,
no matter whether it is Handel's *Hallelujah* or Beethoven's *Freude!*, or Leonard
Cohen's or John Cale's or k.d. lang's *Hallelujah*—any song that brings us, draws
us to song (and we may be reminded again, as cited above, of the poet Hölderlin
who recalled for us that singular, beautiful day when every art of song might be
heard, in order to recall to mind for the length of time that we human, all-too-
human, beings have been what we are, namely the same "conversation" that we
are and that Gadamer for his part always emphasized, contra Heidegger, as the
essence of language).

The Becoming-Human of Dissonance

As noted from the start, Nietzsche refers to Beethoven throughout *The Birth of
Tragedy*, especially foregrounding a dissonance made human, as Beethoven was
associated with such a humanization, as this "secular humanism," despite its
contemporary currency, must be set in historical context, as the musicologist Ruth
A. Solie has taken some pains to show.[201] Prefacing her own essay on Beethoven
with a marvelous, nearly Nietzschean epigraph from Edward Dannreuther—"The
spirit of Beethoven is as humanising as the spirit of Sophocles"—it is plain
that the terms we have been examining in this chapter have had a more than
ordinarily complex share in a history of mythologizing (and often concomitant
demythologizing), but with Nietzsche's concerns here, together with our earlier
reflections on Adorno's Beethoven, it is worth repeating Solie's quotation of
Dannreuther's claim that Beethoven is the "first to become conscious of the
struggles and aims of mankind en masse, and he is the first musician, if not the

---

[199]   Nietzsche, KGW III/3.

[200]   Ibid.

[201]   See Ruth A. Solie, "Beethoven as Secular Humanist: Ideology and the Ninth
Century in Nineteenth Century Criticism," in *Explorations in Music, the Arts, and Ideas:
Essays in Honor of Leonard Meyer*, ed. Eugene Narmour and Ruth Solie (New York:
Pendragon, 1988), 1–42; also included as the first chapter in Ruth A. Solie, *Music in Other
Words: Victorian Conversations* (Berkeley: University of California Press, 2004). As
Solie points out, drawing instructively on Barthes, the terms "Titan" and "Prometheus"
are widely associated with Beethoven (3–4), and of course, to be sure, these terms run
throughout Nietzsche's first book. Solie's studies are invaluable for this context.

first poet, who consciously offers himself as the singer of humanity."[202] Like the Wagnerian, Franz Brendel, writing in 1854, Graf Laurencin writes in 1861 with respect to Beethoven's *Missa Solemnis* as a becoming human (*Menschwerdung*). This "becoming human" is the same terminology that Nietzsche uses, as Nietzsche himself also uses Wagner's favorite convention, which Brendel glosses as the "becoming-human of music,"[203] where Nietzsche sets dissonance in the place of music, much as Wagner himself also varies the notion of a *deus ex machina* with the "becoming-human of mechanism." Point for point, Nietzsche engages Wagner and, as Solie already suggests, and as my reading here confirms, there would already be, fairly early in Nietzsche's works, a turn contra Wagner[204]—a turn that I argue as having been, already and from the start, a return to Beethoven.

Here it is worth recalling, as Nietzsche also did and also from the start, that beginning with Hölderlin's *Sophocles*, the heart of tragedy is "joy": that is, to quote Hölderlin again, *das freudigste, freudig zu sagen* [the most joyful, joyously to say].[205] Thus Nietzsche notes that "The transition of the spirit of music in poetry, that is tragedy, the tragic."[206] And at the end of his first book, Nietzsche undertook to illustrate what he called "the music" of the tragic art form in terms of what he there describes as "playing" with dissonance, playing with the "thorn" of suffering, as already quoted above.[207] For his part, Adorno takes care to highlight the connection of dissonance with joy, writing in a complex connection of art's redemptive power that "Art indicts superfluous poverty by voluntarily undergoing its own."[208] For this reason, as already noted, he observes: "There is more joy in dissonance than in consonance."[209] The metaphor, as we have seen, is a musically

---

[202] Edward Dannreuther, *Beethoven and his Works: A Study*, here as cited in Solie, "Beethoven as Secular Humanist," 14. Solie cites Nietzsche's invocation, word and tone, the very point (16), but she does not comment further as it serves only to set off Wagner's crowning/contestation of Beethoven.

[203] Franz Brendel, *Die Musik der Gegenwart und die Gesammtkunst der Zukunft* (Leipzig: Bruno Hinze, 1854), 173. Here Brendel also cites, as Solie does, Wagner's "Denn die Musik ist ein Weib." And see Ferdinand Laurencin, "Beethovens Missa Solemnis und deren Stellung zur Gegenwart und Vergangenheit," *Neue Zeitschrift für Musik* (5 July 1861): 10–12, here 10. See Solie for a discussion of these and further references.

[204] See, for a related argument concerning Nietzsche and Wagner, Tracy B. Strong, "In Defence of Rhetoric: Or How It Is Hard to Take a Writer Seriously. The Case of Nietzsche," *Political Theory* 41/4 (August 2013), and his "Friedrich Nietzsche and the Case of the 'Advance Scout,'" *New Nietzsche Studies* 10/1 & 2 (2014).

[205] Beethoven and Hölderlin were both born in 1770 and, as the Germanist Günter Miethe observes, the influence of Schiller's Ode to Joy, "An die Freude," is to be seen in Hölderlin's representation of Bacchus as "Freudengott," in Miethe, *Friedrich Hölderlin: Zeit und Schicksal* (Würzburg: Königshausen & Neumann, 2007), 113.

[206] Nietzsche, KSA 7, 9 [29], 281.

[207] Nietzsche, BT, §25.

[208] Adorno, *Aesthetic Theory*, 40.

[209] Ibid.

technical one. Hence Adorno writes in this technical sense that "Dissonance is the truth about harmony."[210] And with the additional reference to Beethoven's, we are well underway to what Schoenberg called the "emancipation of dissonance" and indeed to the inauguration of the modern age. This emancipation is the heart of the break that makes modern music and indeed aesthetic modernity altogether.[211]

Here I have been emphasizing that it will matter to know why it is that dissonance, or discord, with all its mythic Titanic associations, might have had to be liberated or unbound or emancipated in the first place, and something about an understanding of what counts as dissonance (and note that this is a fundamentally hermeneutic question, although few musicologists emphasize the value of hermeneutics, though it is patently relevant, Ian Bent being an important exception to this rule).[212]

---

[210]   Ibid., 110.

[211]   See Thomas Harrison, *1910: The Emancipation of Dissonance* (Berkeley: University of California Press, 1996). As a sign of the influential force of Harrison's text, see Gregory Polakoff's dissertation, *"The Centre is Everywhere"*, testifying to the allure of Harrison's argument, which for its own part only echoes arguments also available elsewhere.

[212]   See Ian Bent, "Plato-Beethoven: A Hermeneutics for Nineteenth-Century Music?" *Indiana Theory Review* 16 (1995): 1–33. A former student of Gadamer (like the present author herself), Bent offers an insightful discussion of the working of hermeneutics in classical philology, as well as classical musicology, in both senses of "classical." Andrew Bowie's valuable "Adorno, Heidegger and the Meaning of Music," *Thesis Eleven* 56 (February 1999): 1–23 somehow makes less of an hermeneutic contribution, perhaps because handicapped by the supposition, characteristic of rather a lot of Anglophone philosophy, that philosophical discussions lack credibility unless coordinated with mainstream names in mainstream philosophy (such as Roger Scruton or Charles Taylor). Thus if Bowie's reading falls short of Heidegger, it broadens (and I believe that may be Bowie's goal in any event) traditionally analytic conceptions of Wittgenstein. But when philosophy is adjudged on analytic terms, with analytic categories, what is incommensurable is inevitably excluded— not ultimately but from the start. What is excluded is a great deal of Adorno, Heidegger and, of course, all of Nietzsche. This does not mean that there is not a great deal in this essay, as in Bowie's studies in general, but it is lessened by the need to touch base with Scruton (or Taylor) as if either might be counted as informed on either Heidegger or Adorno. Note that I am not saying that one ought not bring in the concerns of analytic philosophy, especially regarding the linguistic signification of music. What I am saying is that one cannot get to the continental by remaining fixed on the mainstream. This plea for hermeneutic sensitivity is essential where Adorno's own concerns have everything to do with the "becoming quotation" of music, that is also its culinary commodification. Subotnik offers a useful discussion of the relevance of syllogism, antecedent and consequent, in music, in her essay, "The Historical Structure," also bringing in temporality and the relevance of the temporal in music as this works out in musical practice, as Subotnik here argues (see esp. 45). There is no doubt that the notion of necessity as Subotnik invokes it owes more to Kant than Hegel, here conjoining Kant with the "Beethovenische muss." Thus Subotnik may be read as going a good way toward answering Bowie's reflective point of departure regarding the challenge of Adorno's aesthetic analysis of the music itself.

In an 1822 Ersch-Gruber Encyclopedia (today known as the Brockhaus), dissonance is listed under the rubric of "binding,"[213] and the terminology of such a bond can be helpful in understanding dissonance, both in terms of the preparation needed for the ear to hear it as such and also as requiring or on the way to resolution. The terminology of the "emancipation of dissonance" is usually attributed to Arnold Schoenberg's famous invocation.[214] Here I have sought to emphasize a certain historical contextualization for discussing dissonance by noting that a reflection on rhythm permeates the nineteenth century.[215] We have

---

[213]   Johann Samuel Ersch, Johann Gottfried Gruber, et al., eds, *Allgemeine Encyclopädie der Wissenschaften und Künste* (Leipzig: F.A. Brockhaus, 1822), 202. Gottfried Weber was the author of the entry, as well as of *Theory of Musical Composition: Treated with a View to a Naturally Consecutive Arrangement of Topics*, trans. John F. Warner (London: Robert Cocks and Co., 1851), volume 1, including a section exploring traditional definitions of dissonance. The first mentioned encyclopedia entry is drawn in part from the larger book, in the section on tied or slurred or bound dissonances, in his chapter on preparation (234ff). James Tenney's nuanced *A History of "Consonance" and "Dissonance"* (London: Routledge, 1988) begins where it is best to begin—with harmony, a beginning which also has the consequence of losing dissonance as discord from the start. Thus Tenney's first footnote underlines nothing other than "the currently equivocal status of *dissonance* and *consonance*" (32).

[214]   As noted, Schoenberg uses it in his 1926 essay, "Gesinnung oder Erkenntnis?" [1926], in Schönberg, *Stil und Gedanke. Aufsätze zur Musik*, ed. Ivan Vojtěch (Frankfurt am Main: Fischer, 1976), vol. 1, 211. But for a discussion of the origination of Schoenberg's "Emanzipation der Dissonanz," see August Halm, *Harmonielehre* (Berlin: Göschen, 1900) analyzed as "Befreiung der Dissonanz." See too, again, Rafael Köhler, *Natur und Geist. Energetische Form in der Musiktheorie* (Stuttgart: Franz Steiner Verlag, 1996).

[215]   Auguste Helmholtz analyzes consonance and dissonance in these terms, speaking of pulses or beats, in his *On the Sensations of Tone* [1862] (New York: Dover, 1954). Using the language of wave interference and the terminology of entanglement that may be familiar to readers of popular science authors on quantum mechanics, the nineteenth-century physicist and student of physiological psychology defines consonance in his "Retrospect" as "*a continuous, dissonance an intermittent sensation of tone. Two consonant tones flow on quietly side by side in an undisturbed stream; dissonant tones cut one another up into separate pulses of tone*" (352). The beauty of this definition is that is allows a mathematical model, but the point of the distinction is already expressed for Helmholtz in Euclid, whom he cites: "Consonance is the blending of a higher with a lower tone. Dissonance is incapacity to mix, when two tones cannot blend, but appear rough to the ear." See, on this, Robert Fink's discussion of Helmholtz in his *The Origin of Music: A Theory of the Universal Development of Music* (Saskatoon: The Greenwich-Meridian Co., 1981), 132ff., in addition to the brilliant historian of science H. Floris Cohen's discussion, in his *Quantifying Music: The Science of Music at the First Stage of Scientific Revolution 1580–1650* (Frankfurt am Main: Springer, 1984), foregrounding a beautiful discussion of Zarlino and Kepler on distinguishing consonance and dissonance. Today's scientistically minded cognitive philosophy makes much of this, and recent research feeds this interest. See, for example, Karen Johanne Pallesen, Elvira Brattico, et al., "Emotion Processing of Major, Minor, and Dissonant Chords: A Functional Magnetic Resonance Imaging Study," *Annals*

also explored the progression of David's chord, explicitly citing the consonant fourth and fifth (while seventh, for example, would be considered dissonant, although it is important to remember that one usually speaks of a dissonant note or tone rather than a chord, for a range of complex reasons).[216]

This is Nietzsche's context when he uses the term to conclude his reflections on *The Birth of Tragedy* and speaks of the "becoming-human of dissonance." Thus it is important that Nietzsche himself uses a visual metaphor for this "emancipation," one referring directly to Beethoven in Nietzsche's self-commissioned woodcut illustrating the liberation of Prometheus in the frontispiece for his first book. The liberation of the Titanic, the Ur-Chthonic, is also the liberation of a certain, creative dissonance. The reference is to Beethoven's *Die Geschöpfe des Prometheus*, Op. 43, and section nine of Nietzsche's *The Birth of Tragedy* alludes to Aeschylus's Prometheus in a creative mode, as Goethe expresses in his *Prometheus*: "Here sit I, fashioning humanity in my own image."[217] The passage is crucial for Nietzsche and he uses it to distinguish between active and passive transgression (Greek and Judeao-Christian), but also between active/masculine and passive/feminine creativity. The "titanic figures" of Prometheus and Oedipus are characterized as "masks" of the primordial tragic hero, Dionysus.

Of course the claims in this regard go even further back in the nineteenth century—we have already cited E.T.A. Hoffmann on music's magical power to break its bonds with the other arts, a circumstance to be expected given the dynamic between consonance and dissonance, the same tension as Seyfried's Beethoven discusses.[218]

---

of the New York Academy of Sciences. The Neurosciences and Music II: From Perception to Performance 1060 (December 2005): 450–53. I would note here, without pursuing it further, that Pallesen et al. tilt their results, despite the impressive epistemological appeal of their mathematical models, to the extent that they begin with hermeneutically expert subjects, namely musicians.

[216] The fourth is also sometimes named dissonant. Tenney, in his chapter on dissonance from Rameau to Rousseau and Riemann, cites Riemann's distinction at some length (which is also tied to Rameau). I reproduce only a portion of that citation here: "*Musically* speaking, *there are not really dissonant intervals, but only dissonant notes* [Tenney's emphasis]. Which note is dissonant in an interval physically (acoustically) dissonant, depends on the clang to which that interval has to be referred ... By thus distinguishing dissonant ... notes in place of the old system of intervals and chords, a much clearer view of chords is obtained. *Every note is dissonant which is not a fundamental note* (unchanged), *neither third or fifth of the major or minor chord forming the essential elements of a clang* [Riemann's emphasis]." Tenney, *A History of "Consonance" and "Dissonance"*, 73.

[217] "Hier sitz' ich, forme Menschen / Nach meinem Bilde, / Ein Geschlecht, das mir gleich sei, / Zu leiden, weinen, / Genießen und zu freuen sich, / Und dein nicht zu achten, / Wie ich." Goethe, Prometheus, in J.W. Goethe, *Goethe's Werke: Vollständige Ausgabe letzter Hand*, vol. II [1773] (Stuttgart: J. Cotta'sche Buchhandlung, 1827), 76–8.

[218] See here, more generally, and among her other essays, Barbara R. Barry, *The Philosopher's Stone: Essays in the Transformation of Musical Structure* (New York:

Figure 10.7   Woodcut, frontispiece to Nietzsche's 1872 *Geburt der Tragödie.*
Public domain.

As the reader will have seen, there is reason to contend that, of all of Nietzsche's books, his first continues to be the least read and the least understood, and of course this circumstance began during his own lifetime where it is worth noting that Nietzsche, with all his writerly talent and all his powers of expression, lacked the ability to change this. The reason for this is not due to some scotosis or opacity in the receptive powers of his readers—that is, apart from the ordinary sort that characterizes scholarship in any age and in any discipline.

Something else gets in the way. And while an explication of the reception history of *The Birth of Tragedy* is beyond my capacity and certainly beyond the current thematic, we can say that part of what is at issue concerns the misunderstanding of Nietzsche's project as having to do with music in general and with Greek tragedy in particular.[219]

Pendragon Press, 2000).

[219]   See, on Nietzsche on tragedy, some of the sources I cite in Babich, "Musik und Wort in der Antiken Tragödie," particularly always M.S. Silk and J.P. Stern, *Nietzsche*

Nietzsche typically tends to be read again and again, both in his own times and in ours, as if he were speaking to the general need for a cultural revival such that Wagner might thrive.[220] The result of this interpretation left Nietzsche from the start not only a failed or loser philologist but also a none-too-distinctive Wagnerian. If Nietzsche answered by contesting *both* judgments, posterity made its own judgment by ignoring his protests.[221]

Nietzsche's own musical understanding of dissonance was arguably drawn from contemporary accounts, including the focus on Beethoven as exemplar of the same, a focus that Wagner would repeat for his own part. I note, however, that to the extent that we focus on Wagner, we do tend to miss the overall context and thus ascribe to Nietzsche an all-or-nothing kind of dependency on Wagner. This can be especially dangerous when it comes to Nietzsche's understanding of music in general, as well as when it comes to his notoriously poorly understood first book on tragedy.

Nietzsche was influenced by Wagner's music as well as his theoretical writings, and I am not arguing against that; and because the literature abounds in arguments of this kind, I have not felt the need to repeat them here. Rather, I have been arguing that Nietzsche, like Wagner himself, was influenced by Beethoven's music and particularly by the notes on counterpoint that he thought he could rightly take from Beethoven, but which, as we noted above, Seyfried fails to underscore as they also drew on other teaching notes which could also have resonated with Nietzsche in this way. Thus I also argue that Nietzsche was influenced by yet another nominal relative of Wagner, starting with the first sentence of his first book on tragedy.

---

on Tragedy (Cambridge: Cambridge University Press, 1981), as well as Rudolf Fietz, *Medienphilosophie: Musik, Sprache und Schrift bei Friedrich Nietzsche* (Würzburg: Königshausen & Neumann, 1997) who, for his part, refers to both Robert Rethy's insightful discussion of Nietzsche and tragedy and indeed Alphonso Lingis, but who focuses in the end, as a good deal of contemporary scholarship persists in doing, on the body and at the expense of a discussion of the Greeks. Likewise, Erik Oger, writing on the art of language and the "language" of art is led or "tempted" (as he suggests) to understand language in Aristotelian terms, but precisely not in terms of music. See Oger, *Die Kunst der Sprache und die Sprache der Kunst* (Würzburg: Königshausen & Neumann, 1994). The task of our own era is to discover the culture of music as Nietzsche understood it—and only in this sense did he call for a rebirth of the Hellenic artworld. Aldo Venturelli, in *Kunst, Wissenschaft und Geschichte bei Nietzsche Quellenkritische* (Berlin: de Gruyter, 2003), does see this very patent musical connection, even if he does so in unremittingly Wagnerian terms, and to this extent overlooks some of the issues I am seeking to raise here, both with respect to antiquity and to Nietzsche's musical breadth.

[220] Today, of course—this need hardly be said—the focus on Wagner has been transposed into whatever art form one might favor, from rock and roll to jazz to the blues and so on.

[221] Despite, of course, the efforts in the past by William Arrowsmith, Hugh Lloyd-Jones and others, as already noted.

This *other* Wagner, Johann Jakob Wagner's *Aesthetik*, thus frames Nietzsche's first line in his first book, illuminating what Nietzsche here calls "the science of aesthetics."[222] Indeed, this same connection is also repeated in Nietzsche's notes from this period where he writes:

> The fact that nature linked the origin of tragedy to those two fundamental drives, the Apollonian and the Dionysian, may be considered as much an abyss of reason as that same nature's device of attaching procreation to the duplicity of the sexes, which always appeared astonishing to the great Kant.[223]

In a Greek as in a musical context, this otherwise perplexing point should now make sense, given our above discussion of the creatures of Prometheus and Nietzsche's notion of an active and a passive aesthetics, and thus quite apart from corresponding to the parochial force of nineteenth-century sexism to which Nietzsche was as subject as Wagner and indeed anyone else (one could argue that we are still feeling the effects of this sexism to the present day).

I have sought above to emphasize that Nietzsche's resolution of the question of tragedy was musical,[224] referring to the sound, the music of very words themselves, that is, to Greek as it was intoned or spoken and sung.[225] But where our reflections return to k.d. lang, singing of desire *and* its indigence, its failures, as in Jane

---

[222] Nietzsche, BT, §1. In fact, the reference to the battle between the sexes makes sense both generically and specifically if we add in the importance of this aesthetics of music. "Prime ist der Ton der ganzen Saite, Oktave der der halben Saite, und umgekehrt in der Bewegung: Prime ist der Ton der einfachen, Oktave der der doppelten Bewegung. Prime und Oktave verhalten sich in Masse und Bewegung wie 1 zu 2. Ist die Oktave in der Schwingung doppelt so schnell und hat die Prime nur die Hälfte ihrer Schwingung, so ist bei jener nur die Hälfte der Masse von der Prime. Prime und Oktave sind identisch, weil beide doppelt und beide halb sind. Das ist das reine Consonanzverhältniß. Eine Consonanz ist, wenn der eine Ton gerade so viel Bewegung mehr hat, als der andere Masse. Ist das Verhältniß nicht so, so entsteht eine Dissonanz. Das Verhältniß von Prime und Oktave ist ein Weltverhältniß, denn das Reale hat gerade soviel Masse mehr, als das Geistige Bewegung mehr hat. Im Geschlechtsverhältniß heißt die Consonanz Ehe. Der Mann hat die Ganzheit von Geist und Halbheit von Gemüth, das Weib die Ganzheit von Gemüth und Halbheit von Geist,—Die Prime steigt zur Oktave hinauf durch Terze und Quinte und die Oktave steigt durch sie zur Prime herab. Terze und Quinte sind Mittelstufen und drücken das Erlöschen der Prime und Hervortreten der Oktave aus. Sie sind im magnetischen Stabe die Pole. In der Mitte liegt der Indifferenzpunkt; rechts und links davon, wo der Plus- und Minus-Pol anfängt sichtbar zu werden, sind die von dem Entdecker ungeschickt sogenannten Gulminationspunkte." Johann Jakob Wagner, *Aesthetik*, ed. Philip Ludwig Adam (Ulm: Adams Verlag, 1855), 83. In addition, Johann Jakob Wagner also discusses the chorus and the nature of dissonance, consonance, accord, and so on.

[223] Nietzsche, KSA 7, 7 [123], 179.

[224] Nietzsche, BT, §22.

[225] I discuss this, as noted, in Babich, "Musik und Wort in der Antiken Tragödie."

Siberry's *love forgot to make me too blind to see*—as we recall Cohen's lover's counterturn: *love is not a victory march*—referring to the paradoxical question that illuminates the problem of pleasure *and* pain in the ancient Greek tragedy play, speaking of the very phenomenon of "musical dissonance,"[226] we are returned to k.d. lang as she sings and the physicality of her singing: repeating Cohen's *Hallelujahs* and including the gut pain of loss and disappointment in oneself; both defiantly and, as she crouches into this, drawing her singing out of the depths: *Hallelujah* in the face of pain, hence and thus they embody, *incarnate*, Nietzsche's description of the "becoming-human"[227] of dissonance.

For Ernest McClain, as we have seen, this is the strength, not the weakness, of popular music and this is why, if we follow his argument, so many artists are drawn to "cover" Cohen's *Hallelujah*:

> The appended Hallelujahs sung here are freely varied by the singer to please herself (and NOT what is printed). They are an equivalent to your expected Greek choral response, and Lang makes them her own as a "reaction" to the memory of the verse she has just sung, a counterpoise of nostalgia and disappointment shared universally—in which the audience is invited to participate sympathetically and does; people are partly applauding themselves along with her professionalism.[228]

Subsequently, McClain softened the force of his assertion; indeed, if k.d. lang does anything, it is to sing the notes as written, indeed, and then some. But there is an extent to which McClain is correct—and the differences between lang's individual performances make this plain enough, be it a matter of shortening a phrase or catching up with a lyric, bringing the *Hallelujah* down to a full resonant throat, or cutting it short; and what she cuts short is less Cohen's *Hallelujah* than her own fuller interpretations (and lang's recordings vary, as YouTube video length indicators helpfully inform us, all too quantitatively, by a significant degree).

McClain's point also remains where it is part of the movement towards the emancipation of dissonance (where, at its extension, its modern explosion or protention, all dissonances remain unresolved, impossible in context, of course, which is why we no longer hear Schoenberg to the extent that one hears him at all today, in the way his original audiences did, so too, and so too, *ceteris paribus*, may we say the same of Berg and Stravinsky, and likewise, as we sought to make this point, and as Adorno also argues for the same reasons, in the case of Beethoven for Hoffmann and others).

I would suggest that it might follow from k.d. lang's own characterization of the difference that it makes for her to sing with a symphonic back-up, as it were, rather than as she sang at the start of her career and as she is currently doing with

---

[226] Nietzsche, BT, §24.

[227] Ibid., §25.

[228] Ernest McClain, email to the author.

a new band brought together for that express purpose. In passing, I have been keen to emphasize from the start that the language of "cover" is a music industry term: all about copyright and royalties.

Here this pecuniary issue should take us to the heart of the "problem of the artist," as Nietzsche posed it, although it should be noted that Nietzsche only raises the question as he does because of his concern for what he also called the "genius of the heart," that quality, whatever it would take, that would be able to break everything, as Nietzsche says, "self-satisfied" about us. But the rule of cupidity rules: to emphasize once again, it cost the author—as SONY charges such fees to the individual author, not to the publisher—nearly a thousand dollars for the privilege of citing Cohen's *Hallelujah* in this very academic book, just in order to write about it here. The very same cupidity, the same reduction of everything to the level of the chargeable, the costable, remains, if the point of profit, and this is what I seek to emphasize in this context, is always *someone else's* profit or advantage, usually the same "culture industry" that Adorno was talking about in his writings, and is never for the individual author's sake and never or almost never for the artist's sake. This may be the new venality—industrial, corporate venality—and we, users in our role as so-called content providers on YouTube and Facebook, play along, create content for the same industry to sell and we pay for the privilege of doing so, as Günther Anders, already in 1956, emphasized as part of the idea of the investment in and the deployment and development of radio and TV; and we can add the so-called internet, including social networking, and we can add music videos and YouTube, all as commercial enterprises for the sake of commercial enterprises, including self-fabricated projects; as YouTube says: "Broadcast yourself." And we remain consummate masters at what Adorno called "self-satisfaction" in just this self-enclosure, self-absorption, even as our world goes, as it were, to hell in a handbasket—animals, life of all kinds, destroyed at a pace like no other, human beings along with every other being, and the earth with it.[229]

This genius of the heart might expose us, where being so exposed is the first condition for reflection, compassion, for what Heidegger called thinking.

Here we note the reality of dissonance in tension with the ideality of consonance—dissonance is again for Adorno "the truth about harmony."[230] And it is for this reason that in his notes Nietzsche gives us his reflections on *pain* as generative, that is to say, it is here that Ernest McClain's usually esoteric analyses of pain in musical metaphorics can be useful to us,[231] related as counter-color and as *generating* the beautiful, to use the language of generation as (Johann Jakob) Wagner and also McClain illustrate it musically.

---

[229] See my discussion of this in connection with Adorno and Nietzsche (among others), in Babette Babich, "Adorno on Science and Nihilism, Animals, and Jews," *Symposium: Canadian Journal of Continental Philosophy/Revue canadienne de philosophie continentale* 14/1 (2011): 1–36.

[230] Adorno, *Aesthetic Theory*, 110.

[231] See McClain, "A Priestly View of Bible Arithmetic," 429–43.

The indifference, the equanimity in the face of either pleasure or pain that is an allusion to Schopenhauer in Nietzsche, is also the same that alludes to the dreamer's insight into, or through, the veil of Maja. It is we ourselves who are the figures in the dream of a god—figures, as Nietzsche reflects upon Schopenhauer's initially Buddhist point, who have figured out *how* that god dreams.

Beyond Nietzsche's published work on the work of art, on the artist, on consonance, dissonance, harmony in *The Birth of Tragedy*, and including discussions of both tragedy and music in *Human, All-too-Human*, one has in the notes numerous discussions of these themes, but in each case it makes all the difference to note the relevance of Nietzsche's inquiry into what he titles in his notes the "Origin and Goal of Tragedy." As Nietzsche here explains: "What is the feeling for harmony? On the one side, a subtraction [*wegnehmen*] of the with-sounding *mitklingenden* overtones, on the other side, a not-individual-hearing of the same."[232]

To explore what we might here call Nietzsche's *Harmonienlehre* further would require a hermeneutic of influence and reference which would of course also require a book of its own. Here, it may be sufficient to recall that *any* reference to dissonance is also part of a discourse of tonality and one that inevitably includes references to consonance, and some are fond of taking this to be Apollo, where, like chaos, dissonance refers to Dionysus. What is certain, as we learn from Nietzsche's conjugal yoke between the two—this is nothing but the currently popular cultural theme of gay marriage, here a marriage between two gods—is that both refer to harmony. In this context, it is worth noting that in the same locus we read of Nietzsche's critical accord with Schopenhauer, invoking nothing less "modern," as it might seem to us, than the notion of a "false tone"[233] included together with pain—and we may think of Cohen's "cold and broken Hallelujah," as we also recall what I once called "Nietzsche's impossibly calm ideal,"[234] in order to characterize his elusive image of a "cold angel," just short of the calm that is the extraordinary breath that is the end of k.d. lang's 2005 Juno *Hallelujah*.

The question of the artist, the question of the performer, of the dynamic actuality of the singer, invokes the working power of the work of the composer, as it is this that was also for Nietzsche the very political question of musical culture. There is for the Greek *no term for art*, there is for the Greek *no cult of the artist*, but rather a contest between artists, in a democratic culture of contests that involved the entire polis. It is thus that I understand Nietzsche's musing: "*es muß viele Übermenschen geben.*"[235] As Aristotle also emphasized, good, meaning

---

[232]   Nietzsche, KSA 7, 164.

[233]   Ibid., 202.

[234]   Babette Babich, "Nietzsche's Critical Theory: The Culture of Science as Art," in *Nietzsche, Theories of Knowledge, Critical Theory: Nietzsche and the Sciences II*, ed. Babich, in consultation with R.S. Cohen (Dordrecht: Kluwer, 1999), 1–24, here 13.

[235]   Nietzsche, KSA 35 [72], 541.

excellent and outstanding things, can *only* develop among like and similarly good or exemplary and outstanding things.

But this makes the exemplar, the excellent, that which is outstanding, problematic. With this, we are back to the rhetorical question of queering, speaking of the queer, the freak, the ambiguous. As artistic devices and as marketing devices, such distinctions function positively, as the working of a kind of literal or anticipatory dissonance. It is relevant to Adorno's analysis that he could already trace just the appeal to the unique and the rare in the case of the general individual as an appeal to a "standardized ubiquity," as we cited from the start in his writings on the *Current of Music*; and the same reference he repeats in his writings on the "Culture Industry," which we encounter again, with the same references to the stereo no less, in Herbert Marcuse's reflections on what he—perfectly accurately but all-too-complicatedly for his commentators, all of whom to this day prefer the relative simplicity of McLuhan—named "repressive desublimation" and its consummate political efficacy, especially but not only in the United States.[236]

Thus everything that Adorno and others write about the culture industry continues very politically, on every possible real level, to block culture today. This does not mean that we do not have culture, one last pacifying word for the anti-Adorno theorists all around. What it means is that we are still suffering, as Adorno also understood it, under the age of capitalism and the price it exacts for the "capital" of the heart and the head, to use Nietzsche's terminology and as Nietzsche understood this same economico-political era. To this extent, we still offer "reflections of a damaged life."

Nietzsche guessed at this damaged life—as Adorno speaks of it—in advance of the century that would bring it home, writing as he did at the end of the nineteenth century, at once inspired and disappointed by Wagner's own collusion with the comparable forces of the same cultural industry in his own day. Thus Nietzsche sought to raise the critical question of critique itself, expressed as the question of science with respect to art and coordinating both reflections in the light of life, which was the only thing that mattered for him and indeed for the supposed pessimist, Schopenhauer, the only philosopher who matched him, word for word, insight for insight, on music. For Nietzsche, the scientist or theorist or scholar is an artist, but an artist of the kind who not only fails to know this artistry about him- or herself, but who also denies it, dissembling whenever an inkling of this truth comes to light, be it for him- or herself but above all for society—inasmuch as here, too, one finds (as everywhere) will to power, and insofar as it is science today, rather than religion, that is the very best means for the advancement of both our slavish capacities and our slavish morality, where for Nietzsche, of course, there is no other kind of morality than slave morality.

Unlike the self-denying artistry of the scholar or the scientist, the artist knows that what he or she does is art, that is to say, illusion. And k.d. lang, so I have

---

[236]   Herbert Marcuse, *One Dimensional Man: Studies in the Ideology of Advanced Industrial Society* (Boston: Beacon Press, 1964).

Figure 10.8   Krumme Lanke, Berlin, 1 May 2011. Photo: © Babette Babich.

argued above, would seem to know all this—and more—about the artist. And thus Nietzsche privileges the artist above the scientist, but he only privileges the artist as he does, for the sake of life.

As k.d. lang sings what Leonard Cohen would say—Hallelujah.

Bibliography

Adam, John. *Hallelujah Junction: Composing an American Life*. New York: Picador, 2009.

Adorno, Theodor. "The Radio Symphony: An Experiment in Theory." In *Radio Research*, edited by Paul Lazarsfeld and Frank N. Stanton. New York: Duell, Sloan, and Pearce, 1941.

————— "A Social Critique of Radio Music." *Kenyon Review* 7 (1945): 211–13.

————— *Zur Metakritik der Erkenntnistheorie. Studien über Husserl und die phänomenologischen Antinomien*. Stuttgart: Kohlhammer, 1956.

————— *Introduction to the Sociology of Music*. Translated by E.B. Ashton. New York: Seabury Press, 1976.

————— *Against Epistemology: A Metacritique*. Translated by Willis Domingo. Cambridge, MA: MIT Press, 1983.

————— *Zum Anbruch: Exposé, Gesammelte Schriften 19*, edited by Rolf Tiedemann and Klaus Schulz, 601–2. Frankfurt: Suhrkamp, 1984.

————— *Beethoven: The Philosophy of Music*. Translated by Edmund Jephcott. Stanford: Stanford University Press, 1988.

————— with the assistance of George Simpson. "On Popular Music" [1941]. In *On Record: Rock, Pop, and the Written Word*, edited by Simon Frith and Andrew Goodwin, 256–67. New York: Pantheon, 1990. Also in *Introduction to the Sociology of Music*, 21–38, and (with supplementary materials) in *Current of Music*, 411–76.

————— "On the Fetish Character of Music and the Regression of Listening." In Adorno, *The Culture Industry*, edited by J.M. Bernstein, 29–60. New York: Routledge, 1991.

————— *The Culture Industry: Selected Essays on Mass Culture*. London: Routledge, 1991.

————— *Quasi Una Fantasia: Essays on Modern Music* [1963]. Translated by Rodney Livingstone. London: Verso, 1992.

————— *Minima Moralia: Reflections From Damaged Life* [1947]. Translated by E.F. Jephcott. London: Verso, 1996.

————— *Aesthetic Theory*. Edited by Gretel Adorno and Rolf Tiedemann. Translated by Robert Hullot-Kentor. Minneapolis: University of Minnesota Press, 1997.

————— *Current of Music: Elements of a Radio Theory*, edited by Robert Hullot-Kentor. Frankfurt am Main: Suhrkamp, 2006.

————— "Chapter V. Time Radio and Phonograph." In *Current of Music*, 120–28.

————— "Radio Physiognomics." In *Current of Music*, 73–200.

———— *Philosophy of New Music*. Translated by Robert Hullot-Kentnor. Minneapolis: University of Minnesota Press, 2006.

———— *Towards a Theory of Musical Reproduction: Notes, a Draft, and Two Schemata*. Translated by Wieland Hoban. London: Polity, 2006.

———— "On Jazz." In *Night Music: Essays on Music 1928–1962*. Translated by Wieland Hoban. Chicago: Seagull Books, 2009.

———— and Max Horkheimer. "Kulturindustrie: Aufklärung als Massenbetrug" [1944]. In *Dialektik der Aufklärung. Philosophische Fragmente*, 128–76. Frankfurt am Main: Suhrkamp, 1969.

———— and Max Horkheimer. *The Dialectic of Enlightenment*. New York: Continuum, 1993.

———— et al. "'Optimistisch zu denken ist kriminell'. Eine Fernsehdiskussion über Samuel Beckett." In *Frankfurter Adorno Blätter*, vol. III, *Theodor W. Adorno Archiv*, 78–122. Munich: edition text + kritik, 1994.

Alberti. *De re aedificatoria libri decem IX/5*. 1962, 815.

Albrechtsberger, Johann Georg. *Gründliche Anweisung zur Composition mit deutlichen und ausführlichen Exempeln, zum Selbstunterrichte, erläutert; und mit einem Anhange: Von der Beschaffenheit und Anwendung aller jetzt üblichen musikalischen Instrumente*. Leipzig: Breitkopf, 1790.

Allan, Blaine. "Music Television." In *Television: Critical Methods and Applications*, edited by Jeremy G. Butler, 287–324. Mahwah, NJ: Erlbaum, 2007.

Allen, Louise. *The Lesbian Idol: Martina, kd and the Consumption of Lesbian Masculinity*. London: Cassell, 1997.

Allison, David B. *Reading the New Nietzsche*. Lexington: Rowman and Littlefield, 2001.

Anders, Günther [Günther Stern]. "Spuk und Radio." *Anbruch* 12/2 (February 1930): 65–6.

———— *Die Antiquiertheit des Menschen, Bd. 1: Über die Seele im Zeitalter der zweiten industriellen Revolution* [1956]. Munich: Beck, 1987.

———— "Die Welt als Phantom und Matrize. Philosophische Betrachtungen über Rundfunk und Fernsehen" ["The World as Phantom and Matrix: Philosophical Observations on Radio and Television"]. In *Die Antiquiertheit des Menschen*, 97ff.

———— *Die Kirschenschlacht, Günther Anders und Hannah Arendt—eine Beziehungsskizze*. Munich: Beck, 2011.

Anderson, Warren D. *Music and Musicians in Ancient Greece*. Ithaca: Cornell University Press, 1994.

Appleyard, Bryan. "Hallelujah! On Leonard Cohen's Ubersong." *The Sunday Times*, 9 June 2005.

Archilochus. *Elegies*. In Martin L. West, *Iambi et Elegi Graeci*. Oxford: Oxford University Press, 1955.

Arnheim, Rudolf. "Form and the Consumer." In *Toward a Psychology of Art: Collected Essays*. Berkeley: University of California Press, 1966.

Arnold, Matthew. *Dover Beach*.

Ashby, Arved. *Absolute Music: Mechanical Reproduction*. Berkeley: University of California Press, 2010.

Aufderheide, Patricia. "Music Videos: The Look of the Sound." *Journal of Communication* 36/1 (1986): 57–8.

———— *The Daily Planet: A Critic on the Capitalist Culture Beat*. Minneapolis, MN: University of Minnesota Press, 2000.

————, Peter Jaszi, and Renee Hobbs. "Media Literacy Educators Need Clarity About Copyright and Fair Use." *The Journal of Media Literacy* 54/2–3 (Winter 2008): 41–4.

Austerlitz, Saul. "I Want My MTV." In *Money for Nothing: A History of the Music Video from the Beatles to the White Stripes*. London: Continuum, 2006.

Babich, Babette. "On Nietzsche's Concinnity: An Analysis of Style." *Nietzsche-Studien* 19 (1990): 59–80.

———— *Nietzsche's Philosophy of Science: Reflecting Science on the Ground of Art and Life*. Albany: State University of New York Press, 1994.

———— "The Logic of Woman in Nietzsche: The Dogmatist's Story." *New Political Science: A Journal of Politics and Culture* 36 (1996): 7–17.

———— "Nietzsche and Music: A Partial Bibliography." *New Nietzsche Studies* 1/1–2 (1996): 64–78.

———— "On the Order of the Real: Nietzsche and Lacan." In *Disseminating Lacan*, edited by David Pettigrew and François Raffoul, 48–63. Albany: State University of New York Press. 1996.

———— "Physics vs. *Social Text*: The Anatomy of a Hoax." *Telos* 107 (Spring 1996): 45–61.

———— "The Hermeneutics of a Hoax: On the Mismatch of Physics and Cultural Criticism." *Common Knowledge* 6/2 (September 1997): 23–33.

———— "Nietzsche's Critical Theory: The Culture of Science as Art." In *Nietzsche, Theories of Knowledge, Critical Theory: Nietzsche and the Sciences II*, edited by Babich, in consultation with R.S. Cohen, 1–24. Dordrecht: Kluwer, 1999.

———— "Between Hölderlin and Heidegger: Nietzsche's Transfiguration of Philosophy." *Nietzsche-Studien* 29 (2000): 267–301.

———— "Nietzsche and Eros Between the Devil and God's Deep Blue Sea: The Erotic Valence of Art and the Artist as Actor—Jew—Woman." *Continental Philosophy Review* 33 (2000): 159–88.

———— "Postmodern Musicology." In *Routledge Encyclopedia of Postmodernism* [1999], edited by Victor E. Taylor and Charles Winquist, 153–9. London: Routledge, 2001. 2nd edn.

———— "On the Analytic-Continental Divide in Philosophy: Nietzsche's Lying Truth, Heidegger's Speaking Language, and Philosophy." In *A House Divided: Comparing Analytic and Continental Philosophy*, edited by C.G. Prado, 63–103. Amherst, NY: Prometheus, 2003.

———— "Nietzsche's *göttliche Eidechse*: 'Divine Lizards,' 'Greene Lyons' and Music." In *Nietzsche's Bestiary*, edited by Ralph and Christa Acampora, 264–83. Lanham: Rowman & Littlefield. 2004.

———— "The Science of Words or Philology: Music in *The Birth of Tragedy* and The Alchemy of Love in *The Gay Science*." In *Revista di estetica*, n.s. 28, XLV, edited by Tiziana Andina, 47–78. Turin: Rosenberg & Sellier, 2005.

———— *Words in Blood, Like Flowers: Philosophy and Poetry, Music and Eros in Hölderlin, Nietzsche, and Heidegger.* Albany: State University of New York Press, 2006.

———— "Nietzsche's Erotic Artist as Actor/Jew/Woman." In *Words in Blood, Like Flowers*, 147f.

———— "Nietzsche's 'Gay Science': Poetry and Love, Science and Music." In *Words in Blood, Like Flowers*, 55f.

———— "The Birth of Tragedy: Lyric Poetry and the Music of Words." In *Words in Blood, Like Flowers*, 37ff.

———— "The Genealogy of Morals and Right Reading: On the Nietzschean Aphorism and the Art of the Polemic." In *Nietzsche's On the Genealogy of Morals*, edited by Christa Davis Acampora, 171–90. Lanham: Rowman & Littlefield, 2006.

————"Musik und Wort in der Antiken Tragödie und *La Gaya Scienza*: Nietzsche's 'Fröhliche' Wissenschaft." *Nietzsche-Studien* 37 (2007): 230–57.

———— "Nietzsche und Wagner: Sexualität." Translated by Martin Suhr. In *Wagner und Nietzsche. Kultur—Werk—Wirkung. Ein Handbuch*, edited by H.J. Brix, N. Knoepffler, and S.L. Sorgner, 323–41. Reinbek b. Hamburg: Rowohlt, 2008.

———— "Reflections on Greek Bronze and the Statue of Humanity: Heidegger's Aesthetic Phenomenology, Nietzsche's Agonistic Politics." *Existentia* XVII 5/6 (2008): 243–471.

———— "Become the One You Are: On Commandments and Praise—Among Friends." In *Nietzsche, Culture, and Education*, edited by Thomas Hart, 13–38. London: Ashgate, 2009.

———— "Nietzsche's Philology and Nietzsche's Science: On the 'Problem of Science' and '*fröhliche Wissenschaft*'." In *Metaphilology: Histories and Languages of Philology*, edited by Pascale Hummel, 155–201. Paris: Philologicum, 2009.

———— "Can't You Smile? Women and Status in Philosophy." *Radical Philosophy* 160 (March/April 2010): 36–8.

———— "Early Continental Philosophy of Science." In *The New Century Volume Three: Bergsonism, Phenomenology and Responses to Modern Science: History of Continental Philosophy*, edited by Keith Ansell-Pearson and Alan Schrift, 263–86. Chesham: Acumen, 2010.

———— "*Ex aliquo nihil*: Nietzsche on Science and Modern Nihilism." *American Catholic Philosophical Quarterly* 84/2 (Spring 2010): 231–56.

———— "Great Men, Little Black Dresses, and the Virtues of Keeping One's Feet on the Ground." *MP: An Online Feminist Journal* 3/1 (August 2010): 57–78.

———— "Le Zarathoustra de Nietzsche et le style parodique. A propos de l'hyperanthropos de Lucien et du surhomme de Nietzsche." *Diogène. Revue internationale des sciences humaines* 232 (October 2010): 70–93.

———— "Towards a Critical Philosophy of Science: Continental Beginnings and Bugbears, Whigs and Waterbears." *International Journal of the Philosophy of Science* 24/4 (December 2010): 343–91.

———— "Adorno on Science and Nihilism, Animals, and Jews." *Symposium: Canadian Journal of Continental Philosophy/Revue canadienne de philosophie continentale* 14/1 (2011): 1–36.

———— "An Impoverishment of Philosophy." Interview. *Purlieu* 1/3, special edition: *Philosophy and the University*, edited by Dennis Erwin and Matt Story (2011): 37–71.

———— "Artisten Metaphysik und Welt-Spiel in Fink and Nietzsche." In *Welt denken. Annäherung an die Kosmologie Eugen Finks*, edited by Cathrin Nielsen and Hans Rainer Sepp, 57–88. Freiburg im Briesgau: Alber, 2011.

———— Review of "Daniel Maier-Katkin, *Stranger from Abroad: Hannah Arendt, Martin Heidegger, Friendship and Forgiveness*. NY: Norton, 2010." *Shofar: An Interdisciplinary Journal of Jewish Studies* 29/4 (Summer 2011): 189–91.

———— "Nietzsche, Lou, Art and Eros: The 'Exquisite Dream' of Sacro Monte." In *Lou Andreas-Salomé, muse et apôtre*, edited by Pascale Hummel, 174–230. Paris: Philologicum, 2011.

———— "Reading Lou's Triangles." *New Nietzsche Studies* 8/3 & 4 (2011/2012): 82–114.

———— "Skulpturen und Plastiken bei Nietzsche." In *Grenzen der Rationalität: Teilband 2: Vorträge 2006–2009*, edited by Beatrix Vogel and Nikolaus Gerdes, 391–421. Munich: Allitera Verlag, 2011.

———— "The Birth of kd lang's *Hallelujah* out of the 'Spirit of Music': Performing Desire and 'Recording Consciousness' on Facebook and YouTube." <http://www.furious.com/perfect/kdlang.html>. *Perfect Sound Forever online music magazine* (October/November 2011).

———— "The Philosopher and the Volcano." *Philosophy Today* 36 (Summer 2011): 213–31.

———— "On Nietzsche's Judgment of Style and Hume's Quixotic Taste: On the Science of Aesthetics and 'Playing' the Satyr." *The Journal of Nietzsche Studies* 43/2 (2012): 240-259.

———— "Philosophische Figuren, Frauen und Liebe: Zu Nietzsche und Lou." In *Nietzsche–Forschung*, edited by Renate Reschke, 113–39. Berlin: Akademie Verlag, 2012.

———— "The Aesthetics of the Between: Space and Beauty." In *Jeff Koons: The Painter and The Sculptor*, edited by Vinzenz Brinkmann, Matthias Ulrich, and Joachim Pissarro, 58–69. Frankfurt: Schirn Kunsthalle Frankfurt, 2012.

———— "Nietzsche's Phenomenology: Musical Constitution and Performance Practice." In *Nietzsche and Phenomenology: Power, Life, Subjectivity*, edited by Élodie Boubil and Christine Daigle. Bloomington: Indiana University Press, 2013.

———— "Nietzsche's Zarathustra, Nietzsche's Empedocles: The Time of Kings." In *Becoming Loyal to the Earth: Nietzsche's Teaching as a Therapy for Political Culture*, edited by Eli Friedlander and Horst Hutter. London: Continuum, 2013.

Bargh, John A. "The Most Powerful Manipulative Messages Are Hiding in Plain Sight." *Chronicle of Higher Education* 45/21 (1999): B6.

———— "Losing Consciousness: Automatic Influences on Consumer Judgement, Behaviour, and Motivation." *Journal of Consumer Research* 29 (2002): 280–85.

———— "What Have We Been Priming All These Years? On the Development, Mechanisms, and Ecology of Nonconscious Social Behavior." *European Journal of Social Psychology* 36 (2006): 147–68.

Barry, Barbara R. *The Philosopher's Stone: Essays in the Transformation of Musical Structure*. New York: Pendragon Press, 2000.

———— "In Adorno's Broken Mirror: *Towards a Theory of Musical Reproduction*." *International Review of the Aesthetics and Sociology of Music* 40/1 (June 2009): 81–98.

Barthel, Michael. "'It Doesn't Matter Which You Heard': The Curious Cultural Journey of Leonard Cohen's 'Hallelujah'." <http://www.scribd.com/doc/37784045/It-Doesn-t-Matter-Which-You-Heard-The-Curious-Cultural-Journey-of-Leonard-Cohen-s-Hallelujah>.

Baudrillard, Jean. *The Intelligence of Evil or The Lucidity Pact*. Translated by C. Turner. Oxford: Berg, 2005.

Beauvoir, Simone de. *The Second Sex*. Translated by H.M. Parshley. New York: Vintage, 1989; London: David Campbell [Everyman's Library], 1993.

Bekker, Paul. *Die Sinfonie von Beethoven bis Mahler*. Berlin: Schuster & Loeffler, 1918.

Benne, Christian. "Good Cop, Bad Cop: Von der Wissenschaft des Rhythmus zum Rhythmus der Wissenschaft." In *Nietzsches Wissenschaftsphilosophie. Hintergründe, Wirkungen und Aktualität*, edited by Günter Abel and Helmut Heit, 189–212. Berlin: de Gruyter, 2011.

Bennett, H. Stith. *On Becoming a Rock Musician*. Amherst: University of Massachusetts Press, 1980.

———— "Realities of Practice." In *On Becoming a Rock Musician*. Reprinted in Frith and Goodwin, eds, *On Record*, 185f.

———— "Notation and Identity in Contemporary Popular Music." *Popular Music* 3 (1983): 215–34.

Bennett, M.R., and P.M.S. Hacker. *Philosophical Foundations of Neuroscience*. Oxford: Wiley-Blackwell, 2003.

———— *History of Cognitive Neuroscience*. Oxford: Wiley-Blackwell, 2008.

Bent, Ian. "Plato-Beethoven: A Hermeneutics for Nineteenth-Century Music?" *Indiana Theory Review* 16 (1995): 1–33.

Bergoffen, Deborah. *The Philosophy of Simone de Beauvoir: Gendered Phenomenologies, Erotic Generosities*. Albany: State University of New York Press, 1996.

Berman, Russell A. "Sounds Familiar? Nina Simone's Performances of Brecht/ Weill Songs." In *Sound Matters: Essays on the Acoustics of German Culture*, edited by Nora M. Alter, 171–82. Oxford: Berghahn, 2004.

Bernays, Edward. *Crystallizing Public Opinion* [1923]. New York: Liveright, 1961.

————— *Propaganda*. New York: Liveright, 1928.

————— *The Engineering of Consent*. Norman, OK: University of Oklahoma Press, 1955.

Bertolotti, David S. "The Atomic Bombing of Hiroshima." In Bertolotti, *Culture and Technology*, 81–112. Bowling Green: Bowling Green State University Popular Press, 1984.

Bertram, Ernst. *Nietzsche: Attempt at a Mythology*. Translated by Robert E. Norton. Champaign, IL: University of Illinois Press, 2009.

Beyer, Robert T. *Sounds of Our Times: Two Hundred Years of Acoustics*. Dordrecht: Kluwer, 1999.

Binion, Rudolph. *Frau Lou: Nietzsche's Wayward Disciple*. Princeton: Princeton University Press, 1968.

Björnberg, Alf. "Learning to Listen to Perfect Sound: Hi-Fi Culture and Changes in Modes of Listening, 1950–1980." In *The Ashgate Research Companion to Popular Musicology*, edited by Derek B. Scott, 105–30. Farnham: Ashgate, 2009.

Blasius, Leslie David. "Nietzsche, Riemann, Wagner: When Music Lies." In *Music Theory and Natural Order: From the Renaissance to the Early Twentieth Century*, edited by Suzannah Clark and Alexander Rehding, 93–107. Cambridge: Cambridge University Press, 2001.

Boehme, Rudolf. "Deux points de vue: Husserl et Nietzsche." *Archivo di Filosofia* 3 (1962): 167–81.

————— "Husserl und Nietzsche." In *Vom Gesichtspunkt der Phänomenologie*, 217–37. The Hague: Nijhoff, 1968.

Boelderl, Artur R. *Alchimie, Postmoderne und der arme Hölderlin. Dreis Studien zur philosophischen Hermetik*. Vienna: Passagen Verlag, 1995.

Bornmann, Fritz. "Nietzsches metrische Studien." *Nietzsche-Studien* 18 (1989): 472–89.

Bosco, Lorella. *"Das furchtbar-schöne Gorgonenhaupt des Klassischen". Deutsche Antikebilder (1755–1875)*. Wüzrburg: Königshausen & Neumann, 2004.

Botstein, Leon. "Sound and Structure in Beethoven's Orchestral Music." In *The Cambridge Companion to Beethoven*, edited by Glenn Stanley, 165–85. Cambridge: Cambridge University Press, 2000.

Böttcher, Martin. "Wir sind die Roboter. Wie in der Popmusik mit der Stimme experimentiert wird." *Tagesspiegel* (22 May 2012): 21.

Boubil, Élodie, and Christine Daigle, eds. *Nietzsche and Phenomenology: Power, Life, Subjectivity*. Bloomington: Indiana University Press, 2012.

Boucly, Etienne. "La mimique hébraïque et la rythmo-pédagogie vivante." *Cahiers juifs* N 15 (May–June 1935): 99–210.

Bourdieu, Pierre. *Distinction: A Social Critique of the Judgement of Taste*. Cambridge: Harvard University Press, 1984.

Bowie, Andrew. "Adorno, Heidegger, and the Meaning of Music." *Thesis Eleven* 56 (February 1999): 1–23.

Boyle, James. *The Public Domain: Enclosing the Commons of the Mind*. New Haven: Yale University Press, 2008.

Brambaugh, Robert. *Plato's Mathematical Imagination*. Bloomington: Indiana University Press, 1954.

Braun, Hans-Joachim. *Music and Technology in the Twentieth Century*. Baltimore: Johns Hopkins University Press, 2000.

Bremer, John. *On Plato's Polity*. Houston: Institute of Philosophy, 1984.

——— "Some Arithmetical Patterns in Plato's *Republic*." *Hermanathena* 169 (Winter 2000): 69–97.

——— "Plato, Pythagoras, and Stichometry." *Stichting Pythagoras. Pythagoras Foundation Newsletter* 15 (December 2010). <http://www.stichting-pythagoras.nl/>.

Brendel, Franz. *Die Musik der Gegenwart und die Gesammtkunst der Zukunft*. Leipzig: Bruno Hinze, 1854.

Brett, Philip, Elizabeth Wood, and Gary C. Thomas, eds. *Queering the Pitch: The New Gay and Lesbian Musicology* [1994]. London: Routledge, 2006.

Brillat-Savarin, Jean Anthelme. *Physiologie du goût ou Méditations de gastronomie transcendante. Ouvrage théorique, historique, et à l'ordre du jour, dédié aux gastronomes parisiens*. Paris: Charpentier, 1825.

——— *The Handbook of Dining; or Corpulency and Leanness Scientifically Considered*. Translated by L.F. Simpson. New York: D. Appleton and Company, 1865.

Brower, Harriette. *Piano Mastery: The Harriet Brower Interviews. Talks with Paderewski, Hofmann, Bauer, Godowsky, Grainger 1915–1926*, edited by Jeffrey Johnson. New York: Dover, 2003.

Broyles, Michael. *Beethoven in America*. Bloomington: Indiana University Press, 2011.

Bruzzi, Stella. "Mannish Girl: k.d. lang from Cowpunk to Androgyny." In *Sexing the Groove: Popular Music and Gender*, edited by Sheila Whiteley, 191–206. London: Routledge, 1997.

Buck-Morss, Susan. "The Flâneur, the Sandwichman and the Whore: The Politics of Loitering." *New German Critique* 39, *Second Special Issue on Walter Benjamin* (Autumn 1986): 99–140.

Burns, Lori. "'Joanie' Get Angry: k.d. lang's Feminist Revisions." In *Understanding Rock: Essays in Musical Analysis*, edited by John Covach and Graeme M. Boone. New York: Oxford University Press, 1997.

————— "Genre, Gender, and Convention Revisited: k.d. lang's cover of Cole Porter's 'So in Love'." *Repercussions* (Spring/Fall 1999/2000): 299–325.

————— "Vocal Authority and Listener Engagement: Musical and Narrative Expressive Strategies in Alternative Female Rock Artists (1993–95)." In *Sounding Out Rock*, edited by John Covach and Mark Spicer. Ann Arbor: University of Michigan Press, 2010.

Bush, Vannevar. "As We May Think." *Atlantic Monthly* (July 1945): 101–8.

Capuzzo, Guy. "Neo-Riemannian Theory and the Analysis of Pop-Rock Music." *Music Theory Spectrum* 26/2 (2004): 177–99.

Carson, Anne. *Eros the Bittersweet* [1986]. Normal, IL: Dalkey Archive Press, 1998.

Certeau, Michel de. *L'Invention du Quotidien. Vol. 1, Arts de Faire*. Paris: Union générale d'éditions 10-18, 1980. [English edition: *The Practice of Everyday Life*. Translated by Steven Rendall. Berkeley: University of California Press, 1984.]

Chanan, Michael. *Musica Practica: The Social Conventions of Western Music from Gregorian Chant to Postmodernism*. London: Verso, 1994.

————— *Repeated Takes: A Short History of Recording and its Effects on Music*. London: Verso, 1995.

————— *From Handel to Hendrix: The Composer in the Public Sphere*. London: Verso, 1999.

Chua, Daniel K.L. *Absolute Music and the Construction of Meaning*. Cambridge: Cambridge University Press, 1999.

Cicero. *Orator*.

Cohen, H. Floris. *Quantifying Music: The Science of Music at the First Stage of Scientific Revolution 1580–1650*. Frankfurt am Main: Springer, 1984.

Cohen, Leonard. *Beautiful Losers* [1966]. New York: Vintage, 1994.

————— *Stranger Music: Selected Poems and Songs*. Toronto: McClelland and Stewart, 1994.

Comotti, Giovanni. *Music in Greek and Roman Culture*. Translated by Rosaria V. Munson. Baltimore: The Johns Hopkins University Press, 1977.

Cook, Nicholas. *Music: A Very Short Introduction*. Oxford: Oxford University Press, 1998.

Corbier, Christophe. "*Alogia* et Eurythmie chez Nietzsche." *Nietzsche-Studien* 38 (2009): 1–38.

Daffner, Hugo von. *Friedrich Nietzsches Randglossen zu Bizets Carmen*. Regensburg: Gustave Bosse, 1912.

Dahlhaus, Carl. *Between Romanticism and Modernism: Four Studies in the Music of the Later Nineteenth Century* [1974]. Translated by Mary Whittall. Berkeley: University of California Press, 1980.

Dale, Amy M. *The Lyric Metres of Greek Drama* [1948]. Cambridge: Cambridge University Press, 1968.

————— "Words, Music and Dance." In Dale, *Collected Papers*, 156–69. Cambridge: Cambridge University Press, 1969.

Dallmayr, Fred. "Review of Hermann Mörchen's *Adorno und Heidegger: Untersuchung Einer Philosophischen Kommunikationsverweigerung.*" *Diacritics*: Heidegger: Art and Politics 19/3–4 (Autumn–Winter 1989): 82–100.

Damschen, Gregor. "Das lateinische Akrostichon. Neue Funde bei Ovid sowie Vergil, Grattius, Manilius und Silius Italicus." *Philologus* 148 (2004): 88–115.

Dannreuther, Edward. *Beethoven and his Works: A Study*. London: Macmillan, 1876.

Davidson, James. *Courtesans and Fishcakes: The Consuming Passions of Classical Athens* [1997]. New York: Harper, 1999.

——— "Dover, Foucault and Greek Homosexuality: Penetration and the Truth of Sex." *Past and Present* 170 (2001): 3–51.

——— *The Greeks and Greek Love: A Radical Reappraisal of Homosexuality in Ancient Greece*. London: Weidenfeld and Nicolson, 2007.

Derrida, Jacques. *Edmund Husserl's "Origin of Geometry": An Introduction*. Translated by John P. Leavey Jr. Lincoln: University of Nebraska Press, 1989.

Detienne, Marcel. *Dionysos mis à mort*. Paris: Gallimard, 1977. [In English translation by Mireille and Leonard Muellener as *Dionysos Slain*, 1979.]

——— *Dionysos à ciel ouvert*. Paris: Hatchette, 2008.

——— *Apollon le couteau à la main. Une approche expérimentale du polythéisme grec* [1998]. Paris: Gallimard, 2009.

Deutscher, Penelope. *The Philosophy of Simone de Beauvoir: Ambiguity, Conversion, Resistance*. Cambridge: Cambridge University Press, 2008.

Dichter, Ernst. *The Strategy of Desire*. New York: Doubleday, 1960.

Dijksterhuis, Ap, Henk Aarts, and Pamela K. Smith. "The Power of the Subliminal: On Subliminal Persuasion and Other Potential Applications." In *The New Unconscious*, ed. Ran R. Hassin, James S. Uleman, and John A. Bargh, 77–106. Oxford: Oxford University Press, 2005.

Dorlin, Elsa. *L'Évidence de l'égalité des sexes. Une philosophie oubliée du XVIIe*. Paris: L'Harmattan, 2001.

Dosse, François. *Michel de Certeau: Le marcheur blessé*. Paris: La Découverte, 2002.

Dover, Kenneth. *Greek Homosexuality*. Cambridge, MA: Harvard University Press, 1978.

Dudeque, Norton. *Music Theory and Analysis in the Writings of Arnold Schoenberg (1874–1951)*. Aldershot: Ashgate, 2006.

Dufour, Eric. "La physiologie de la musique chez Nietzsche." *Nietzsche-Studien* 30 (2001): 222–45.

——— *L'esthétique musicale de Nietzsche*. Lille: Presses Universitaires du Septentrion, 2005.

Dyson, Frances. "When Is the Ear Pierced?" In *Immersed in Technology*, edited by Mary Anne Moser and Douglas MacLeod, 73–101. Bloomington: Indiana University Press, 1999.

Ehrhardt, Damien. "Aspects de la phraséologie riemannienne." *Musurgia* 4/1 (1997): 68–83.

Ellensohn, Reinhard. *Der andere Anders: Gunther Anders als Musikphilosoph*. Bern: Peter Lang, 2008.

Ellul, Jacques. *The Technological Society*. Translated by John Wilkinson. New York: Vintage Books, 1965.

———— *Propaganda: The Formation of Men's Attitudes*. Translated by Konrad Kellen and Jean Lerner. New York: Knopf, 1973.

Erlmann, Veit. *Reason and Resonance: A History of Modern Aurality*. Cambridge, MA: Zone Books, 2010.

Ersch, Johann Samuel, Johann Gottfried Gruber, et al., eds. *Allgemeine Encyclopädie der Wissenschaften und Künste*. Leipzig: F.A. Brockhaus, 1822.

Famhy, Shahira, and Wayne Wanta. "Testing Priming Effects: Differences Between Print and Broadcast Messages." *Studies in Media & Information Literacy Education* 2 (May 2005): 1–12.

Feher, Ferenc. "Weber and the Rationalization of Music." *International Journal of Politics and Society* 1/2 (Winter 1987): 147–62.

Fein, Ellen, and Sherrie Schneider. *The Rules*. New York: Grand Central Publishing, 1995.

———— *The Rules for Online Dating*. New York: Gallery Books, 2002.

Feuerbach, Anselm. *Der vatikanische Apoll. Eine Reihe archäologisch-ästhetischer Betrachtungen* [1833]. 2nd edn. Stuttgart, Augsburg: Cotta, 1855.

Fietz, Rudolf. *Medienphilosophie: Musik, Sprache und Schrift bei Friedrich Nietzsche*. Würzburg: Königshausen & Neumann, 1997.

Fink, Robert. *The Origin of Music: A Theory of the Universal Development of Music*. Saskatoon: The Greenwich-Meridian Co., 1981.

———— "Beethoven Antihero: Sex, Violence, and the Aesthetics of Failure, or Listening to the Ninth Symphony as Postmodern Sublime." In *Beyond Structural Listening: Postmodern Modes of Hearing*, edited by Andrew Dell'Antonio, 109–53. Berkeley: University of California Press, 2003.

———— *Repeating Ourselves: American Minimal Music as Cultural Practice*. Berkeley: University of California Press, 2005.

Finn, Geraldine. *Why Althusser Killed his Wife*. Amherst, NY: Humanity Books, 1996.

Flichy, Patrice. *The Internet Imaginaire*. Cambridge, MA: MIT Press, 2007.

Footman, Tim. *Leonard Cohen, Hallelujah: A New Biography*. New Malden, Surrey: Chrome Dreams, 2009.

Foucault, Michel. *The Use of Pleasure*. New York: Pantheon Books, 1985.

Frith, Simon. *Sound Effects*. London: Constable, 1983.

———— and Howard Horne. *Art into Pop*. New York: Methuen, 1987.

———— and Andrew Goodwin, eds. *On Record: Rock, Pop, and the Written Word*. New York: Pantheon, 1990.

Frye, Northrop. "Review of Leonard Cohen." *University of Toronto Quarterly* (April 1957).

Gadamer, Hans-Georg. *The Relevance of the Beautiful and Other Essays*, trans. Nicholas Walker. Cambridge: Cambridge University Press, 1986, p. 7.

Gentili, Carlo. "Die radikale Hermeneutik Friedrich Nietzsches." *Nietzscheforschung* 8, 333–6. Berlin: Akademie Verlag, 2001.

George, Stefan. *Song.*

Georgiades, Thrasybulos. *Musik und Rhythmus bei den Griechen. Zum Ursprung der abendländischen Musik.* Hamburg: Rowohlt, 1958.

—— *Music and Language: The Rise of Western Music as Exemplified in the Settings* [1974]. Translated by Marie Louise Göllner. Cambridge: Cambridge University Press, 1982.

Gilman, Sander L. "Nietzsche, Bizet, and Wagner: Illness, Health, and Race in the Nineteenth Century." *The Opera Quarterly* 23/2–3 (Spring–Summer 2007): 247–64.

Goehr, Lydia. *The Imaginary Museum of Musical Works: An Essay in the Philosophy of Music.* Oxford: Oxford University Press, 1992.

—— *Elective Affinities: Musical Essays on the History of Aesthetic Theory.* New York: Columbia University Press, 2008.

—— "On Broken Strings." Unpublished.

Goerlich, Katharina Sophia, Jurriaan Witteman, Niels O. Schiller, Vincent J. Van Heuven, André Aleman, and Sander Martens. "The Nature of Affective Priming in Music and Speech." *Journal of Cognitive Neuroscience.* MIT. Posted online 23 February 2012.

Goethe, J.W. *Goethe's Werke: Vollständige Ausgabe letzter Hand.* Vol. II [1773]. Stuttgart: J. Cotta'sche Buchhandlung, 1827.

Goetz, Benoît. "Nietzsche aimait-il vraiment Bizet?" *La Portique* 8 (2001).

Gombrich, Ernst Hans. "Kunstliteratur." In *Atlantisbuch der Kunst: eine Enzyklopädie der bildenden Künste,* 665–79. Zurich: Atlantis Verlag, 1952.

—— *The Image and the Eye: Further Studies in the Psychology of Pictorial Representation.* London: Phaidon, 1982.

Goodman, Steve. *Sonic Warfare: Sound, Affect, and the Ecology of Fear.* Cambridge, MA: MIT Press, 2010.

Goodwin, Andrew. "Sample and Hold: Pop Music in the Age of Digital Reproduction." In *On Record: Rock, Pop, and the Written Word,* edited by Simon Frith and Andrew Goodwin, 220–34. New York: Pantheon, 1990.

—— *Dancing in the Distraction Factory: Music Television and Popular Culture.* Minneapolis: University of Minnesota Press, 1992.

Guck, Marion A. "Two Types of Metaphoric Transfer." In *Metaphor: A Musical Dimension,* edited by Jamie C. Kassler, 1–12. Sydney: Currency Press, 1991.

Günther, Friederike Felicitas. *Rhythmus beim frühen Nietzsche.* Berlin: Walter de Gruyter, 2008.

—— "Am Leitfaden des Rhythmus. Kritische Wissenschaft und Wissenschaftskritik in Nietzsches Frühwerk." In *Der Tod Gottes und die Wissenschaft. Zur Wissenschaftskritik Nietzsches,* edited by Carlo Gentili and Cathrin Nielsen, 107–22. Berlin: de Gruyter, 2010.

Hacker, P.M.S. "Hacker's Challenge." Interview with James Garvey. *TPM, The Philosopher's Magazine* 51. 25 October 2010.

Hailey, Christopher. "The Paul Bekker Collection in the Yale University Music Library." *Notes*, 2nd series 51/1 (September 1994): 13–21.

Haimo, Ethan. "Schoenberg and the Origins of Atonality." In *Constructive Dissonance: Arnold Schoenberg and the Transformations of Twentieth Century Culture*, edited by Juliane Brand and Christopher Hailey, 71–86. Berkeley: University of California Press, 1997.

Hakim, Catherine. *Erotic Capital: The Power of Attraction in the Boardroom and the Bedroom*. New York: Basic Books, 2011.

Halberstam, Judith. *Female Masculinity*. Durham, NC: Duke University Press, 1998.

Halm, August. *Harmonielehre*. Berlin: Göschen, 1900.

Hanslick, Eduard. "Beethoven's *Missa Solemnis*" [1861]. In Hanslick, *Music Criticisms: 1846–1899*. Baltimore: Penguin, 1950.

Harrison, Thomas. *1910: The Emancipation of Dissonance*. Berkeley: University of California Press, 1996.

Haslanger, Sally. "Changing the Ideology and Culture of Philosophy: Not by Reason (Alone)." *Hypatia* 23/2 (2008): 210–23.

Hathorn, Richmond Y. *Greek Mythology*. Lebanon: American University of Beirut, 1977.

Havelock, Eric A. *The Muse Learns to Write: Reflections on Orality and Literacy from Antiquity to the Present*. New Haven: Yale University Press, 1988.

Heidegger, Martin. *Being and Time* [1927]. Translated by John Macquarrie and Edward Robinson. New York: Harper & Row, 1962.

——— *On the Way to Language*. Translated by Peter D. Hertz. New York: Harper & Row, 1971.

Heilman, Anja. *Boethius' Musiktheorie und das Quadrivium*. Göttingen: Vandenhoeck & Ruprecht, 2007.

Helmholtz, Auguste. *On the Sensations of Tone* [1862]. New York: Dover, 1954.

Herrick, Robert. *Upon Julia's Clothes*.

Higgins, Kathleen Marie. "Musical Idiosyncrasy and Perspectival Listening." In *Music and Meaning*, edited by Jenefer Robinson, 83–102. Ithaca: Cornell University Press, 1997.

Himmelfarb, Gertrude. *On Looking Into the Abyss*. New York: Knopf, 1994.

Hines, Thomas Jensen. *The Later Poetry of Wallace Stevens: Phenomenological Parallels With Husserl and Heidegger*. Cranbury, NJ: Associated University Presses, 1975.

Hinrichsen, Hans-Joachim. *Musikalische Interpretation. Hans von Bülow*. Stuttgart: Franz Steiner Verlag, 1999.

——— "Musikalische Rythmustheorien um 1900." In *Rhythmus: Spuren eines Wechselspiels in Künsten und Wissenschaften*, edited by Barbara Naumann, 141–56. Würzburg: Königshausen und Neumann, 2005.

Hinton, Stephen. "Not *Which* Tones? The Crux of Beethoven's Ninth." *Nineteenth Century Music* XXII/1 (Summer 1998): 61–77.

———— "The Emancipation of Dissonance: Schoenberg's Two Practices of Composition." *Music and Letters* 91/4 (2010): 568–79.

Hodge, Joanna. "Poietic Epistemology: Reading Husserl Through Adorno and Heidegger." In A*dorno and Heidegger: Philosophical Questions*, edited by Iain Macdonald and Krzysztof Ziarek, 64f. Stanford: Stanford University Press, 2007.

Hödl, Hans Gerald. "Rezension: Babich, *Nietzsche's Philosophy of Science.*" *Nietzsche-Studien* 26 (1997): 583–8.

Hoffmann, E.T.A. "Beethovens Instrumentalmusik." *Allgemeine musikalische Zeitung*. Leipzig: Breitkopf & Härtel, 1810.

Hölderlin, Friedrich. *Bread and Wine* [*Brot und Wein*].

———— *Friedensfeier*.

———— *Poems and Fragments*. Translated by Michael Hamburger. Ann Arbor: University of Michigan Press, 1966.

———— *Sophokles*.

Holland, Samantha. *Pole Dancing, Empowerment and Embodiment*. New York: Palgrave Macmillan, 2010.

Horkheimer, Max, and Theodor W. Adorno. "Kulturindustrie: Aufklärung als Massenbetrug." In Horkheimer and Adorno, *Dialektik der Aufklärung. Philosophische Fragmente*, 128–76. Frankfurt am Main: Suhrkamp, 1969.

———— *Dialectic of Enlightenment: Philosophical Fragments*. Translated by Gunzelin Schmid Noerr. Stanford: Stanford University Press, 2002.

Huhtamo, Erkki, and Jussi Parikka, eds. *Media Archaeology: Approaches, Applications, and Implications*. Berkeley: University of California Press, 2011.

Hullot-Kentor, Robert. *Things Beyond Resemblance: Collected Essays on Theodor W. Adorno*. New York: Columbia University Press, 2006.

———— "Second Salvage: Prolegomenon to a Reconstruction of Current of Music." In Hullot-Kentor, *Things Beyond Resemblance: Collected Essays on Theodor W. Adorno*, 94–124. New York: Columbia University Press, 2006.

———— "Vorwort des Herausgebers." In Theodor W. Adorno, *Current of Music: Elements of a Radio Theory*, 7–69. Frankfurt am Main: Suhrkamp, 2006.

Husserl, Edmund, *L'origine de la géométrie*. Translated by Jacques Derrida. Paris: PUF, 1962.

Hutcheon, Linda. *A Theory of Parody: The Teachings of Twentieth-Century Art Forms*. Champaign, IL: University of Illinois Press, 2000.

Illich, Ivan. *Deschooling Society*. New York: Harper & Row, 1971.

———— *In the Vineyard of the Text: A Commentary to Hugh's Didascalicon*. Chicago: University of Chicago Press, 1996.

———— and Barry Sanders, *ABC: The Alphabetization of the Popular Mind*. San Francisco: North Point Press, 1988.

Ingarden, Roman. *The Work of Music and the Problem of Its Identity*. Translated by Adam Czerniawski. Berkeley: University of California Press, 1986.

———— "The Musical Work and Its Score." In *The Work of Music and the Problem of Its Identity*, 34–40.

An Intermediate Greek–English Lexicon, Founded Upon the Seventh Edition of Liddell and Scott's Greek–English Lexicon. Oxford: Clarendon Press, 1889.

Irigaray, Luce. "The Question of the Other." Translated by Noah Guyum. *Yale French Studies* 87 (1995): 7–19.

Jäger, Lorenz. *Adorno: A Political Biography.* New Haven: Yale University Press, 2004.

Jahn, Otto. *W.A. Mozart, Zweiter Theil* [1856]. Leipzig: Breitkopf & Hartel, 1867.

Jähnig, Dieter. "Emancipating the Knowledge of Art from Metaphysics in *The Birth of Tragedy.*" Translated by Babette Babich and Holger Schmid. *New Nietzsche Studies* 4/1 & 2 (Summer/Fall 2000): 77–121.

Janich, Peter. "Augustins Zeitparadox und seine Frage nach einen Standard der Zeitmessung." *Archiv für Geschichte der Philosophie* 54 (1972): 169–86.

Janz, Curt Paul. "Die Kompositionen Friedrich Nietzsches." *Nietzsche-Studien* 1 (1972): 173–84.

——— "Nietzsche Verhältnis zur Musik seiner Zeit." *Nietzsche-Studien* 7 (1978): 308–26.

——— *Friedrich Nietzsche Biographie.* Munich: Hanser, 1993. Three volumes.

——— "Ist der Zarathustra eine 'Symphonie'?" In *Friedrich Nietzsche Biographie.* Vol. 2, 211–21.

Jenemann, David. *Adorno in America.* Minneapolis: University of Minnesota Press, 2007.

Jousse, Marcel. *Les Récitatifs rythmiques*: *I, Genre de la maxime, Etudes sur la psychologie du geste.* Paris: Ed. Spes, 1930.

——— *L'anthropologie du geste*, II: *La Manducation de la parole.* Paris: Gallimard, 1975.

——— *The Oral Style.* Translated by Edgard Richard Sienaert and Richard Whitaker. [Albert Bates Lord Studies in Oral Tradition.] New York: Garland, 1990.

Kane, Brian. "L'Objet Sonore Maintenant: Pierre Schaeffer, Sound Objects and the Phenomenological Reduction." *Organised Sound* 12/1 (2007): 15–24.

Karim, Karim Haiderali. "Cyber Utopia and the Myth of Paradise: Using Jacques Ellul's Work on Propaganda to Analyse Information Society Rhetoric." *Information, Communication & Society* 4/1 (2001): 113–34.

Katz, Mark. *Capturing Sound: How Technology Has Changed Music* [2004]. Revised. Berkeley: University of California Press, 2010.

Kennedy, Jay B. "Plato's Forms, Pythagorean Mathematics, and Stichometry." *Apeiron* 43/1 (2010): 1–31.

Kerman, Joseph. *Musicology.* London: Fontana, 1985.

Kinder, Marsha. "Music Video and the Spectator: Television, Ideology and Dream." *Film Quarterly* 38/1 (1984): 2–15.

Kingsley, Peter. *In the Dark Places of Wisdom.* Inverness: Golden Sufi Press, 1999.

Klein, John W. "Nietzsche and Bizet." *The Musical Quarterly* 11/4 (October 1925): 482–505.

Köhler, Rafael. *Natur und Geist. Energetische Form in der Musiktheorie*. Stuttgart: Franz Steiner Verlag, 1996.

Kot, Greg. "Turn it Up: Why Leonard Cohen's Hallelujah Endures." *Chicago Tribune*, 30 April 2009.

Kremer-Marietti, Angèle. *Nietzsche et la rhétorique*. Paris: PUF, 1992.

——— "Rhétorique et Rythmique chez Nietzsche." In *Rythmes et philosophie*, edited by Pierre Sauvanet and Jean-Jacques Wunenburger, 181–95. Paris: Kimé, 1996.

Kreuzer, Franz, Gerd Prechtl, and Christoph Steiner. *A Tiger in the Tank: Ernest Dichter: An Austrian Advertising Guru* [2002]. Translated by Lars Hennig. Riverside: Ariadne, 2007.

Krims, Adam. "What Does it Mean to Analyse Popular Music." *Music Analysis* 22/i and ii (2003): 181–209.

Kugelmass, Joseph. "Why I am Leaving Facebook." *Kugelmass Episodes*. <http://kugelmass.wordpress.com/2012/04/08/why-i-am-leaving-facebook/>.

lang, k.d. Interview with Fiona Sturges. *The Independent*, Friday 17 June 2011.

——— "Interview." *Word* (January 2005).

——— Television Interview with Peter Gzowski. *Our Stories*. Canadian Biography Channel (1986).

Lanier, Jaron. *You Are Not a Gadget: A Manifesto*. New York: Vintage, 2011.

La Rue, Jan. *Guidelines for Style Analysis*. Michigan: Harmonie Park Press, 1992, 1997.

Laurencin, Ferdinand. "Beethovens Missa Solemnis und deren Stellung zur Gegenwart und Vergangenheit." *Neue Zeitschrift für Musik* (5 July 1861): 10–12.

Lee, M. Owen. *Athena Sings: Wagner and the Greeks*. Toronto: University of Toronto Press, Scholarly Publishing Division, 2003.

Leiner, George. "To Overcome One's Self: Nietzsche, Bizet and Wagner." *Journal of Nietzsche Studies* 9/10 (Spring/Autumn 1995): 132–47.

Levarie, Siegmund. "Noise." *Critical Inquiry* 4/1 (Autumn 1977): 21–31.

——— *Fundamentals of Harmony*. Westport, CT: Greenwood Publishing Group, 1984.

——— and Ernst Levy. *Tone: A Study in Musical Acoustics*. Kent, OH: Kent State University Press, 1968.

——— *Musical Morphology: A Discourse and a Dictionary*. Kent, OH: Kent State University Press, 1983.

——— *A Theory of Harmony*. Albany: State University of New York Press, 1985.

Levin, Thomas Y. "For the Record: Adorno on Music in the Age of Its Technological Reproducibility." *October* 55 (Winter 1990): 23–47.

——— "Tones From Out of Nowhere." *Grey Room* 12 (Summer 2003): 33–79.

——— with Michael von der Linn. "Elements of a Radio Theory: Adorno and the Princeton Radio Research Project." *The Musical Quarterly* 78/2 (1994): 316–24.

Light, Alan. *The Holy or the Broken: Leonard Cohen, Jeff Buckley, and the Unlikely Ascent of "Hallelujah"*. New York: Atria Books, 2012.

Lippman, Edward A. "The Phenomenology of Music." In *A History of Western Musical* Aesthetics, 437–69. Lincoln: University of Nebraska Press, 1992.

———— *The Philosophy & Aesthetics of Music*. Omaha: University of Nebraska Press, 1999.

Lloyd-Jones, Hugh. "Nietzsche and the Study of the Ancient World." In *Studies in Nietzsche and the Classical Tradition*, edited by James C. O'Flaherty, Timothy F. Sellner, and Robert M. Helm, 1–15. Chapel Hill, NC: University of North Carolina Press, 1976.

Loraux, Nicole. *The Mourning Voice: An Essay on Greek Tragedy*. Translated by Elizabeth Trapnell Rawlings. Ithaca: Cornell University Press, 2002.

Lord, Albert B. *The Singer of Tales*. Cambridge, MA: Harvard University Press, 1960.

Love, Frederick. *Nietzsche's Saint Peter: Genesis and Cultivation of an Illusion*. Berlin: de Gruyter, 1991.

Lovink, Geert. *Uncanny Networks: Dialogues with the Virtual Intelligentsia*. Cambridge, MA: MIT Press, 2002.

Lüttkehaus, Lüdger. "The World as Will and Music: Arthur Schopenhauer's Philosophy of Music." In *Sound Figures of Modernity: German Music and Philosophy*, edited by Jost Hermand and Gerhard Richter, 92–105. Madison: University of Wisconsin Press, 2006.

Macdonald, Iain, and Krzysztof Ziarek, eds. *Adorno and Heidegger: Philosophical Questions*. Stanford: Stanford University Press, 2007.

MacDougald, Duncan. "The Popular Music Industry." In *Radio Research 1941*, ed. Paul Lazarsfeld and Frank Stanton, 65–109. New York: Duell, Sloane and Pearce, 1941.

Maconie, Robin. *The Concept of Music*. Oxford: Clarendon, 1990.

Mandel, Siegfried. "Genelli and Wagner: Midwives to Nietzsche's The Birth of Tragedy." *Nietzsche-Studien* 19 (1990): 212–25.

Mander, Jerry. *Four Arguments for the Elimination of Television*. New York: William Morrow, 1978.

Marcuse, Herbert. *One-Dimensional Man: Studies in the Ideology of Advanced Industrial Society*. Boston: Beacon Press, 1964.

Markus, György. "Adorno and Mass Culture: Autonomous Art Against the Culture Industry." *Thesis Eleven* 86 (August 2006): 67–89.

Marx, Eduardo. *Heidegger und der Ort der Musik*. Würzburg: Königshausen & Neumann, 1998.

McCay, John, and Alexander Rehding. "The Structure of Plato's Dialogues and Greek Music Theory: A Response to J.B. Kennedy." *Apeiron* 44/1 (2011): 359–75.

McClain, Ernest. *The Myth of Invariance: The Origin of the Gods, Mathematics and Music from the Rg Veda to Plato*. York Beach, ME: Nicolas Hays, 1976.

————— *The Pythagorean Plato: Prelude to the Song Itself.* York Beach, ME: Nicolas Hays, 1978.

————— *Meditations on the Quran.* York Beach, ME: Nicolas Hays, 1981.

————— "A Priestly View of Bible Arithmetic: Deity's Regulative Aesthetic Activity within Davidic Musicology." In *Hermeneutic Philosophy of Science, Van Gogh's Eyes, and God,* edited by Babette Babich, 429–43. Dordrecht: Kluwer Academic Publishers, 2002.

McClary, Susan. "Getting Down Off the Beanstalk." *Minnesota Composers Forum Newsletter* (January 1987).

————— *Feminine Endings: Music, Gender, and Sexuality.* Minneapolis: University of Minnesota Press, 1991/2002.

————— "Living to Tell: Madonna's Resurrection of the Fleshly." In McClary, *Feminine Endings,* 148–66.

————— "This is not a Story My People Tell: Musical Time and Space According to Laurie Anderson." In McClary, *Feminine Endings,* 132–47.

————— and Robert Walser. "Start Making Sense! Musicology Wrestles with Rock." In *On Record: Rock, Pop and the Written Word,* edited by Simon Frith and Andrew Goodwin, 277–92. London: Routledge, 1990.

McLeod, Kembrew. "Making the Video: Constructing an Effective Counter-Hegemonic Message in Only Forty-Nine Minutes." *Journal of Popular Music Studies* 14 (2002): 79–88.

Meijer, P.A. *Parmenides Beyond the Gates.* Leiden: Brill, 1997.

Mertin, Josef, and Siegmund Levarie, *Early Music: Approaches to Performance Practice.* New York: Da Capo Press, 1986.

Meyer, Donald C. "Review." *American Music* 16/4 (Winter 1998): 487–91.

Middleton, Christopher. "Nietzsche on Music and Metre." *Arion* 6/1 (Spring 1967): 58–65.

————— ed. and trans. *Selected Letters of Nietzsche.* Chicago: University of Chicago Press, 1969.

Miethe, Günther. *Friedrich Hölderlin: Zeit und Schicksal.* Würzburg: Königshausen & Neumann, 2007.

Milner, Greg. *Perfecting Sound Forever: An Aural History of Recorded Music.* New York: Faber and Faber, 2009.

Minasi, Mark. *The Software Conspiracy: Why Companies Put Out Faulty Software, How They Can Hurt You and What You Can Do About It.* New York: McGraw Hill, 1999.

Mitchell, Tim. *Sedition and Alchemy: A Biography of John Cale.* London: Peter Owen Publishers, 2003.

Mockus, Martha. "Queer Thoughts on Country Music and k.d. lang." In *Queering the Pitch: The New Gay and Lesbian Musicology,* edited by Philip Brett and Elizabeth Wood. New York: Routledge, 2006.

Monroea, Kristen, Saba Ozyurta, Ted Wrigley, and Amy Alexander. "Gender Equality in Academia: Bad News from the Trenches, and Some Possible Solutions." *Perspectives on Politics* 6 (2008): 215–33.

Moore, Allan F. "U2 and the Myth of Authenticity in Rock." *Popular Musicology* 3 (1998): 4–24.

———— "Analizzare il rock: strumenti e finalità." *Musica realtà* 62 (July 2000): 95–118.

———— *Rock: The Primary Text*. Aldershot: Ashgate, 2001.

———— "Authenticity as Authentication." *Popular Music* 21/2 (May 2002): 209–23.

———— *Song Means: Analysing and Interpreting Recorded Song*. Aldershot: Ashgate, 2012.

Morley, Louise. *Quality and Power in Higher Education*. Maidenhead: Society for Research into Higher Education and McGraw Hill, 2003.

Morozov, Evgeny. *The Net Delusion: The Dark Side of Internet Freedom*. Jackson, TN: Public Affairs, 2011.

Morrison, David E. "*Kultur* and Culture: The Case of Theodor W. Adorno and Paul Lazarsfeld." *Social Research* 44 (1978): 331–55.

Moulaison, Heather L. "The Minitel and France's Legacy of Democratic Information Access." *Government Information Quarterly* 21 (2004): 99–107.

Mowitt, John. *Radio: Essays in Bad Reception*. Berkeley: University of California Press, 2011.

Murray, Peter Durno. *Nietzsche's Affirmative Morality: A Revaluation Based in the Dionysian World*. Berlin: de Gruyter, 1999.

Nagle, Jill, ed. *Whores and Other Feminists*. New York: Routledge, 1997.

Naredi-Rainer, Paul von. *Architektur & Harmonie, Zahl, Maß und Proportion in der abendländischen Baukunst*. Cologne: Dumont, 1982.

Negus, Keith. *Popular Music in Theory: An Introduction*. Cambridge: Polity Press, 1996.

Nehamas, Alexander. *Only a Promise of Happiness: The Place of Beauty in a World of Art*. Princeton: Princeton University Press, 2007.

———— "Plato's Pop Culture Problem and Ours." *New York Times*, 29 August 2010.

Nicholson, Graeme. *Illustrations of Being*. Atlantic Highlands: Humanities Press, 1992.

Nicolàs, Antonio de. *Avatara: The Humanization of Philosophy Through the Bhagavad Gita*. York Beach, ME: Nicolas Hays: 1976.

Nielsen, Nanette. "*Sein oder Schein*?: Paul Bekker's 'Mirror Image' and the Ethical Voice of Humane Opera." *The Opera Quarterly* 23/2–3 (Spring–Summer 2007): 295–310.

Nietzsche, Friedrich. *Der musikalische Nachlass*, edited by Curt Paul Janz. Basel: Bärenreiter-Verlag, 1976.

———— *Die Geburt der Tragödie. Kritische Studienausgabe*, edited by Mazzino Montinari and Giorgio Colli. Vol. 1. *The Birth of Tragedy out of the Spirit of Music*. Berlin: de Grutyer, 1980.

———— "Music and Word." Translated by Walter Kaufmann. In Dahlhaus, *Between Romanticism and Modernism*, 103–19.

————— *Twilight of the Idols*. Translated by Richard Polt. Indianapolis: Hackett, 1997.

————— *Samtliche Briefe. Kritische Studienausgabe. In 8 Banden*, edited by Giorgio Colli and Mazzino Montinari. Berlin: de Gruyter, 2003.

————— *Griechische Lyriker, Kritische Gesamtausgabe*, edited by Mazzino Montinari and Giorgio Colli. Vol. II/2. 375-395. Berlin: de Gruyter, 1993.

————— *Griechische Rhythmik*, KGW II/3. 101-201. Berlin: de Gruyter, 1993.

————— "Homer und die klassische Philologie." KGW II/1, 247–69. Berlin: de Gruyter, 1982.

————— *Das griechische Musikdrama*. KGW III/2, 5–22. Berlin: de Gruyter, 1973.

————— *Human, All-too-Human, The Wanderer and his Shadow*. In *Kritische Studienausgabe*. Vol. 2.

————— *The Gay Science*. KSA. Vol. 3.

————— *Thus Spoke Zarathustra*. KSA. Vol. 4.

————— *Beyond Good and Evil*. KSA. Vol. 5.

————— *On the Genealogy of Morals*. KSA. Vol. 5.

————— *Ecce Homo*. KSA. Vol. 6.

Nørretranders, Tor. *The User Illusion: Cutting Consciousness Down to Size*. New York: Viking, 1998.

Nottebohm, Gustav. *Beethoveniana: Aufsätze und Mittheilungen*. Leipzig: Rieter Biedermann, 1872.

Oger, Erik. *Die Kunst der Sprache und die Sprache der Kunst*. Würzburg: Königshausen & Neumann, 1994.

Ong, Walter, S.J., *Orality and Literacy: The Technologizing of the Word*. London: Methuen, 1982; New York: Routledge, 2002.

Otto, Detlef. "Die Version der Metapher zwischen Musik und Begriff." In *Centauren-Geburten: Wissenschaft, Kunst und Philosophie beim Jungen Nietzsche*, edited by Tilman Borsche, Federico Gerratana, and Aldo Venturelli, 167–90. Berlin: de Gruyter, 1984.

————— *Wendungen der Metapher: zur Übertragung in poetologischer, rhetorischer und erkenntnistheoretischer Hinsicht bei Aristoteles und Nietzsche*. Munich: Fink, 1998.

Packard, Vance. *The Hidden Persuaders* [1956]. New York: Pocket/Simon & Schuster, 2007.

Paley, Nina. Interview with Cameron Parkins on the CreativeCommons blog, 3 June 2009. <http://creativecommons.org/weblog/entry/14760>.

Pallesen, Karen Johanne, Elvira Brattico, et al. "Emotion Processing of Major, Minor, and Dissonant Chords: A Functional Magnetic Resonance Imaging Study." *Annals of the New York Academy of Sciences. The Neurosciences and Music II: From Perception to Performance* 1060 (December 2005): 450–53.

Parikka, Jussi. *What is Media Archaeology*. Cambridge: Polity, 2012.

Parikka, Jussi, and Tony D. Sampson, eds. *The Spam Book: On Viruses, Porn, and Other Anomalies from the Dark Side of Digital Culture*. Cresskill: Hampton Press, 2009.

Pariser, Eli. *The Filter Bubble*. Hassocks: Penguin Press, 2011.

Pater, Walter. "The School of Georgione." In *The Renaissance*. Oxford: Oxford University Press, 1986.

Percy, William. *Pederasty and Pedagogy in Archaic Greece*. Champaign/Urbana: University of Illinois Press, 1996.

Pichler, Axel. *Nietzsche, die Orchestikologie und das dissipative Denken*. Wien: Passagen Verlag, 2010.

Pierson, Henry Hugo, ed. *Ludwig van Beethovens Studien im Generalbass, Contrapunkt und in der Compositionslehre aus dessen Handschriftlichen Nachlass gesammelt und herausgegeben von Ignaz Xaver von Seyfried* [1832]. Leipzig/Hamburg/New York: Schuberth & Comp, 1853.

——— *Studies in Thorough-bass, Counterpoint and the Art of Scientific Composition. Collected from the Autograph Posthumous Manuscripts of the Great Composer and first published together with Biographical Notices Ignatius von Seyfried, Translated and Edited by Henry Hugh Pierson (Edgar Mannsfeldt), with Beethoven's Portrait, and Other Illustrative Plates*. Leipzig/Hamburg/New York: Schuberth and Comp, 1853.

Plasketes, George. *Play It Again: Cover Songs in Popular Music*. Farnham: Ashgate, 2010.

Plato. *Euthydemus*.

——— *Phaedo*.

——— *Republic* [*Politeia*].

Pöhlmann, Egbert. *Denkmaler altgriechischer Musik. Sammlung, Ubertragung und Erlauterung aller Fragmente und Fälschungen*. Nurnberg: Verlag Hans Carl, 1970.

——— and Martin L. West. *Documents of Ancient Greek Music: The Extant Melodies and Fragments Edited and Transcribed with Commentary*. Oxford: Clarendon Press, 2001.

Polakoff, Gregory. *"The Centre is Everywhere": Nietzsche's Overcoming of Modernity Through Musical Dissonance*. Dissertation. University of British Columbia, 2011.

Pont, Graham. "Analogy in Music: Origins, Uses, Limitations." In *Metaphor: A Musical Dimension*, edited by Jaimie C. Kassler. Basel: Gordon and Beacon, 1994.

Porter, James. *Nietzsche and the Philology of the Future*. Stanford: Stanford University Press, 2000.

——— "'Rare Impressions.' Nietzsche's Philologica: A Review of the Colli-Montinari Critical Edition *Nietzsches Werke: Kritische Gesamtausgabe* ['KGW'] by Giorgio Colli; Mazzino Montinari." *International Journal of the Classical Tradition* 6/3 (Winter 2000): 409–31.

Poschl, Viktor. "Nietzsche und die klassische Philologie." In *Philologie und Hermeneutik im 19 Jahrhundert. Zur Geschichte und Methodologie der Geisteswissenschaften*, edited by Hellmut Flaschar, Karlfried Gründer, and Axel E.A. Horstmann, 141–55, 368–70. Göttingen: Vandenhoeck und Ruprecht, 1979.

Poulain de la Barre, François. *Three Cartesian Feminist Treatises*. Translated by Vivien Bosley. Chicago: University of Chicago Press, 2002.

Pound, Ezra. *Near Perigord*.

Pseudo-Dionysius. *Pseudo-Dionysii Areopagitae de Caelesti Hierarchia in Usum Studiosae Iuventutis* (Textus Minores, vol. XXV), edited by Petrus Hendrix. Leiden: Brill, 1959.

Rehding, Alexander. *Hugo Riemann and the Birth of Modern Musical Thought*. Cambridge: Cambridge University Press, 2003.

Reznor, Trent (Nine Inch Nails). Interview with Thursday's Geoff Rickly. *AP Altpress* 194 (September 2004).

Rich, Adrienne. *The Ninth Symphony of Beethoven Understood At Last As a Sexual Message*. In *Diving into the Wreck*. New York: W.W. Norton, 1994, 43.

Rilke, Rainer Maria. *Duineser Elegien. Die Sonneten an Orpheus*. Stuttgart: Reclam, 1997.

Rosen, Charles. "The New Musicology." In Rosen, *Critical Entertainments: Music Old and New*, 255–72. Cambridge: Harvard University Press, 2000.

Rothfarb, Lee Allen. *August Halm: A Critical and Creative Life in Music*. Rochester: University of Rochester Press, 2009.

Rowell, Lewis. *Thinking About Music: An Introduction to the Philosophy of Music*. Amherst: University of Massachusetts Press, 1983.

Rowling, Joanne Kathleen. *Harry Potter and the Philosopher's Stone*. London: Bloomsbury, 1997.

Sachs, Curt. *The Rise of Music in the Ancient World: East and West*. New York: W.W. Norton, 1943.

Said, Edward W. *Musical Elaborations*. New York: Columbia University Press, 1991.

Sauvanet, Pierre. "Nietzsche, philosophe-musicien de l'éternel retour." *Archives de Philosophie* 64 (2001): 343–60.

Schaeffer, Pierre. *Traité des objets musicaux*. Paris: Éditions du Seuil, 1966.

——— *La musique concrète*. Paris: Presses Universitaires de France, 1967.

Schmid, Holger. *Kunst des Hörens*. Cologne: Böhlau, 1999.

Schmid, Walter. *Frühschriften Sallusts im Horizont des Gesammtwerks*. Neustadt/ Aisch: P.Ch.W. Schmidt, 1993.

Schoenberg, Arnold. "Composition with Twelve Tones." In *Style and Idea*, edited by Leonard Stein, 216–44. Berkeley: University of California Press, 1975.

——— "Theory and Composition." In *Style and Idea* [1950], edited by Leonard Stein, 260–61. New York: St. Martin's Press, 1975.

——— "Gesinnung oder Erkenntnis?" [1926]. In Schönberg, *Stil und Gedanke. Aufsätze zur Musik*, edited by Ivan Vojtěch, vol. 1, 211. Frankfurt am Main: Fischer, 1976.

——— *Theory of Harmony 100th Anniversary Edition*. Translated by Roy E. Carter. Berkeley: University of California Press, 2010.

Schürmann, Reiner. *Broken Hegemonies*. Translated by Reginald Lilly. Bloomington: Indiana University Press, 2003.

Schwartz, Hillel. *The Culture of the Copy: Striking Likenesses, Unreasonable Facsimilies*. Cambridge, MA: MIT Press, 1996.

Schwartz, Michael. "'Er redet leicht, schreibt schwer'. Theodor W. Adorno am Mikrophon." *Zeithistorische Forschungen* 8/2 (2011): 286–94.

Schwarzkopf, Stefan, and Rainer Gries, eds. *Ernest Dichter and Motivation Research: New Perspectives on the Making of Post-war Consumer Culture*. London: Palgrave Macmillan, 2010.

Shakespeare, William. *Richard II*.

———— *Troilus and Cressida*.

Sherman, David. *Sartre and Adorno: The Dialectics of Subjectivity*. Albany: State University of New York Press, 2007.

Siegel, Lee. *Against the Machine: How the Web Is Reshaping Culture and Commerce—and Why It Matters*. New York: Spiegel & Grau, 1996.

———— *Against the Machine: Being Human in the Age of the Electronic Mob*. New York: Spiegel & Grau, 2006.

Sienaert, Edgard Richard. "Marcel Jousse: The Oral Style and the Anthropology of Gesture." *Oral Tradition* 5/1 (1990): 91–106.

Silk, M.S., and J.P. Stern. *Nietzsche on Tragedy*. Cambridge: Cambridge University Press, 1981.

Simone, Nina, with Stephen Cleary. *I Put a Spell On You: The Autobiography of Nina Simone*. New York: da capo, 1993.

Simons, Peg, ed. *The Philosophy of Simone de Beauvoir: Critical Essays*. Bloomington: Indiana University Press, 2006.

Sloop, John M. *Disciplining Gender: Rhetorics of Sex Identity in Contemporary US Culture*. Amherst: University of Massachusetts Press, 2005.

Smith, F. Joseph. *The Experiencing of Musical Sound: Prelude to a Phenomenology of Music*. New York: Gordon and Breach, 1979.

Solie, Ruth A. "Beethoven as Secular Humanist: Ideology and the Ninth Century in Nineteenth Century Criticism." In *Explorations in Music, the Arts, and Ideas: Essays in Honor of Leonard Meyer*, edited by Eugene Narmour and Ruth Solie, 1–42. New York: Pendragon, 1988.

———— "What Do Feminists Want? A Reply to Pieter van den Toorn." *The Journal of Musicology* IX/4 (Fall 1991): 399–410.

———— *Music in Other Words: Victorian Conversations*. Berkeley: University of California Press, 2004.

Solomon, Miriam, and John Clarke. "The CSW Jobs for Philosophers Employment Study." *APA Newsletter: Feminism and Philosophy* 8/2 (Spring 2009): 3–6.

Solomos, Makis. *Schaeffer phénoménologue*. In *Ouïr, entendre, écouter, comprendre après Schaeffer*, edited by F. Delalande, 53–67. Paris: Buchet/Chastel, 1999.

Stanley, Glenn. "Introduction." In Stanley, ed., *Cambridge Companion to Beethoven*, 14–31. Cambridge: Cambridge University Press, 2000.

Starr, Victoria. *K.D. Lang: All You Get Is Me*. New York: St. Martin's Press, 1994.

Stauth, Georg, and Bryan S. Turner. *Nietzsche's Dance: Resentment, Reciprocity and Resistance in Social Life*. Oxford: Blackwell, 1988.

Steinskog, Erik. "Queering Cohen: Cover Versions as Subversions of Identity." In *Play It Again: Cover Songs in Popular Music*, edited by George Plasketes, 139–52. Farnham, Surrey: Ashgate, 2010.

Sterne, Jonathan. *The Audible Past: Cultural Origins of Sound Reproduction*. Durham, NC: Duke University Press, 2003.

——— "The Death and Life of Digital Audio." *Interdisciplinary Science Reviews* 31/4 (2006): 338–48.

Stevens, Wallace. *Notes Toward a Supreme Fiction*.

——— *Peter Quince at the Clavier.*

——— *The Blue Guitar*.

Stillwell, Robynn J. "Hysterical Beethoven." *Beethoven Forum* 10/2 (2003): 162–82.

Strong, Tracy B. "Introduction." In Nietzsche, *Twilight of the Idols*, vii–xxx. Translated by Richard Polt. Indianapolis: Hackett, 1997.

——— *Nietzsche and the Politics of Transfiguration* [1974]. Berkeley: University of California Press, 2000.

——— *Jean-Jacques Rousseau: The Politics of the Ordinary*. Lanham, MA: Rowman & Littlefield, 2002.

——— "Philosophy and the Politics of Cultural Revolution." *Philosophical Topics* 33/2 (Fall 2005): 227–47.

——— "Philosophy of the Morning: Nietzsche, Politics and Transfiguration." *Journal of Nietzsche Studies* 39/1 (Spring 2009): 51–65.

——— *Politics Without Vision*. Chicago: University of Chicago Press, 2012.

——— "In Defence of Rhetoric: Or How It Is Hard to Take a Writer Seriously. The Case of Nietzsche." *Political Theory* 41/4 (August 2013), forthcoming.

——— "Friedrich Nietzsche and the Case of the 'Advance Scout.'" *New Nietzsche Studies* 10/1 & 2 (2014), forthcoming.

Stuurman, Siep. *François Poulain de la Barre and the Invention of Modern Equality*. Cambridge: Harvard University Press, 2004.

Subotnik, Rose Rosengard. "The Historical Structure: Adorno's 'French' Model for the Criticism of Nineteenth-Century Music." *19th Century Music* 2 (July 1978): 36–60.

——— *Developing Variations: Style and Ideology in Western Music*. Minneapolis: University of Minnesota Press, 1991.

——— *Deconstructive Variations: Music and Reason in Western Society*. Minneapolis: University of Minnesota Press, 1996.

Supa, Dustin W. "The Origins of Empirical Versus Critical Epistemology in American Communication." *American Communication Journal* 11/3 (Fall 2009).

Sweeney, Eileen. *Logic, Theology, and Poetry in Boethius, Abelard, and Alan of Lille: Words in the Absence of Things*. London: Palgrave Macmillan, 2006.

———— *Anselm of Canterbury and the Desire for the Word*. Washington, DC: Catholic University of America Press, 2012.

Szabó, Árpád. *The Beginnings of Greek Mathematics*. Dordrecht and Boston: Reidel, 1978.

Tagg, Philip. "Analysing Popular Music: Theory, Method and Practice." *Popular Music* 2 (1982): 37–69.

———— *Fernando the Flute* [1991]. New York: Mass Media Music Scholars' Press, 2000.

Taylor, Deems. "The Scorned Ingredients." In Taylor, *Of Men and Music*. New York: Simon and Schuster, 1937.

Taylor, Timothy D. *The Sounds of Capitalism: Advertising, Music, and the Conquest of Culture*. Chicago: University of Chicago Press, 2012.

The Economist. "Sex and Advertising: Retail Therapy. How Ernest Dichter, An Acolyte of Sigmund Freud, Revolutionised Marketing." [No author listed.] *The Economist*, 17 December 2011.

Tenney, James. *A History of "Consonance" and "Dissonance"*. London: Routledge, 1988.

Theon, *Mathematica*, I.

Thurmond, James Morgan. *Note Grouping: A Method for Achieving Expression and Style in Musical Performance* [1982]. Galesville, MD: Meredith Music Publications, 1991.

Tomlinson, Gary. "Modes and Planetary Song: The Musical Alliance of Ethics and Cosmology." In *Music in Renaissance Magic: Toward a Historiography of Others*. Chicago: University of Chicago Press, 1993.

Toorn, Pieter C. van den. "Politics, Feminism, and Contemporary Music Theory." *The Journal of Musicology* IX (1991): 275–99.

Treitler, Leo. *With Voice and Pen: Coming to Know Medieval Song and How It Was Made*. Oxford: Oxford University Press, 2003.

Trimpi, Wesley. *Muses of One Mind: The Literary Analysis of Experience and Its Continuity*. Princeton: Princeton University Press, 1983.

Troemel-Ploetz, Senta. "Selling the Apolitical." *Discourse Society* 2/4 (1991): 489–502.

Turkle, Sherry. *Life on the Screen: Identity in the Age of the Internet*. New York: Simon and Schuster, 1995.

———— *Simulation and Its Discontents*. Cambridge, MA: MIT Press, 2009.

———— *Alone Together: Why We Expect More from Technology and Less from Each Other*. New York: Basic Books, 2011.

Tymoczko, Dmitri. "The Sublime Beethoven: Did the Composer Share an Aesthetic Principle with Immanuel Kant?" *Boston Review: A Political and Literary Forum* (2000).

Vagnetti, Luigi. "Concinnitas, riflessioni sul significato di un termine albertiano." *Studi e documenti di architetura* 2 (1973): 139–61.

Valentine, Gill. "Creating Transgressive Space: The Music of k.d. lang." *Transactions of the Institute of British Geographers* ns. 20/4 (1995): 474–85.

Valian, Virginia. *Why So Slow? The Advancement of Women*. Cambridge, MA: MIT Press, 1998.

Van Camp, Julie. "Tenured/Tenure-Track Faculty Women at 98 US Doctoral Programs in Philosophy." <http://www.csulb.edu/~jvancamp/doctoral_2004.html>. Updated 14 April 2008.

Vaszonyi Nicholas. "Hegemony through Harmony: German Identity, Music, and Enlightenment Around 1800." In *Sound Matters: Essays on the Acoustics of German Culture*, edited by Nora M. Alter, 33–48. Oxford: Berghahn, 2004.

Venturelli, Aldo. *Kunst, Wissenschaft und Geschichte bei Nietzsche Quellenkritische*. Berlin: de Gruyter, 2003.

Vernallis, Carol. *Experiencing Music Video: Aesthetics and Cultural Context*. New York: Columbia University Press, 2004.

Vogel, Martin. *Apollinisch und Dionysisch. Geschichte eines genialen Irrtums*. Regensburg: Gustav Bosse Verlag, 1966.

Wagner, Johann Jakob. *Aesthetik*, edited by Philip Ludwig Adam. Ulm: Adams Verlag, 1855.

Wagner, Richard. *Beethoven*. Leipzig: E.W. Fritzsch, 1870.

Weber, Gottfried. *Theory of Musical Composition: Treated with a View to a Naturally Consecutive Arrangement of Topics*. Volume 1. Translated by John F. Warner. London: Robert Cocks and Co., 1851.

Weber, Max. *The Rational and Social Foundations of Music*. Translated by Don Marindale, Johannes Riedel, and Gertrude Neuwirth. Carbondale: Southern Illinois University Press, 1958.

West, Martin L. *Iambi et Elegi Graeci*. Oxford: Oxford University Press, 1955.

——— *Ancient Greek Music*. Oxford: Clarendon, 1992.

——— *Greek Lyric Poetry*. Oxford: Oxford University Press, 1994.

Westfall, Rudolf, and B. Sokolowsky, "Klangfuss, Klangvers, mit besonderer Beziehung auf Beethovens Sonaten." *Musikalisches Wochenblatt* XVI/28 (Leipzig: Fritzsch, 2 July 1885): 341–43.

——— "Über den Rhythmus in Beethovens Klaviersonaten und das Versmaß der Ode 'An die Freude,' auch im Hinblick auf Matthesons Musiktheorie." *Musikalisches Wochenblatt* 31 (23 July 1885): 377–9.

Wetzel, Justus Hermann. "Die ästhetische Vorherrschaft des auftaktigen Rhythmus." *Musikalisches Wochenblatt* 40 (1909): 249–51, 269–73.

Whitely, Sheila. "Popular Music and the Dynamics of Desire." In *Queering the Popular Pitch*, edited by Sheila Whitely and Jennifer Rycenga, 249–62. New York: Routledge, 2006.

——— "Who Are You: Research Strategies of the Unruly Feminine." In *The Ashgate Research Companion to Popular Musicology*, edited by Derek B. Scott, 205–20. Farnham, Surrey: Ashgate, 2009.

Whitford, Margaret. *An Irigaray Reader*. Oxford: Blackwell, 1991.

Wicke, Peter. "The Art of Phonography: Sound, Technology, and Music." In *The Ashgate Research Companion to Popular Musicology*, edited by Derek B. Scott, 147–68. Farnham: Ashgate, 2009.

Wilson, Elizabeth. "The Invisible Flâneur." *New Left Review* I/191 (January–February 1992): 90–110.

Wilson, Steven Lloyd. "The Minor Fall, The Major Lift." <http://www.pajiba.com/miscellaneous/the-minor-fall-the-major-lift.php>.

Wittkower, Rudolf. *Architectural Principles in the Age of Humanism*. New York: Norton, 1971.

Wolff, Janet. "The Invisible Flâneuse: Women and the Literature of Modernity." *Theory Culture and Society, The Fate of Modernity* 2/3 (1985): 37–46.

Žižek, Slavoj. *Looking Awry: An Introduction to Jacques Lacan through Popular Culture*. Cambridge, MA: MIT Press, 1991.

——— *Enjoy Your Symptom! Jacques Lacan in Hollywood and Out*. London: Routledge, 1992.

——— *Flash Art* Interview with Josefina Ayerza (1992). <http://www.lacan.com/perfume/zizek.htm>.

Index